Authentic Connection

SERIES EDITOR
JUNE BOYCE-TILLMAN

PETER LANG
Oxford · Bern · Berlin · Bruxelles · New York · Wien

Authentic Connection

Music, Spirituality, and Wellbeing

Karin S. Hendricks and
June Boyce-Tillman (eds)

PETER LANG

Oxford · Bern · Berlin · Bruxelles · New York · Wien

Bibliographic information published by Die Deutsche Nationalbibliothek.
Die Deutsche Nationalbibliothek lists this publication in the Deutsche National-
bibliografie; detailed bibliographic data is available on the Internet at http://dnb.d-nb.de.

A catalogue record for this book is available from the British Library.

Library of Congress Cataloging-in-Publication Data

Names: Boyce-Tillman, June, 1943- editor. | Hendricks, Karin S., 1971-editor.
Title: Authentic connection : music, spirituality, and wellbeing / [edited by] June Boyce-
    Tillman, Karin S. Hendricks.
Description: Oxford ; New York : Peter Lang, 2021. | Series: Music and spirituality,
    2296-164X ; vol 13 | Includes bibliographical references and index.
Identifiers: LCCN 2021027543 (print) | LCCN 2021027544 (ebook) |
    ISBN 9781800791596 (paperback) | ISBN 9781800791602 (ebook) |
    ISBN 9781800791619 (epub) | ISBN 9781800791626 (mobi)
Subjects: LCSH: Music--Social aspects. | Music--Psychological aspects. | Music therapy. |
    Spirituality.
Classification: LCC ML3916 .A96 2021 (print) | LCC ML3916 (ebook) |
    DDC 306.4/842--dc23
LC record available at https://lccn.loc.gov/2021027543
LC ebook record available at https://lccn.loc.gov/2021027544

Cover design by Peter Lang Ltd.

ISSN 2296-164X
ISBN 978-1-80079-159-6 (print) • ISBN 978-1-80079-160-2 (ePDF)
ISBN 978-1-80079-161-9 (ePub) • ISBN 978-1-80079-162-6 (mobi)

© Peter Lang Group AG 2021

Published by Peter Lang Ltd, International Academic Publishers,
52 St Giles, Oxford, OX1 3LU, United Kingdom
oxford@peterlang.com, www.peterlang.com

This publication has been peer reviewed.

Contents

List of Figures   ix

List of Tables   xi

Acknowledgments   xiii

PART I: Music and Authenticity in the Contemporary
Context: Individualism, Community, and
Negotiations of Diversity   1

KARIN S. HENDRICKS AND JUNE BOYCE-TILLMAN
1:   Music, Connection, and Authenticity   3

STEPHEN B. ROBERTS
2:   Music and Spirituality in a Polyphonic Public Sphere   17

BRUCE ELLIS BENSON
3:   Improvisation as Spiritual Exercise: The Improvisational
Virtues of Empathy, Humility, and Trust   33

AMIRA EHRLICH
4:   Popular Music for Religious Authenticity in Israeli Jewish
Religious Education   47

ESTELLE R. JORGENSEN

5: On Values and Life's Journey through Music: Reflections on
   the Eriksons' Life Stages and Music Education   67

PART II: Authentic Connection and Wellbeing   81

DEBORAH J. SAIDEL

6: A Pathway to Wellbeing: Transcending a Compensatory
   History of Women in Music   83

JUNGMIN GRACE HAN

Interlude 1: The Sacred Space Within: Towards Mind-Body
             Unity through Musical Performance   97

MARIA GIULIA MARINI

Interlude 2: Music: To Each Their Own When Illness Comes
             but Rhythm Is Universal   103

KEITH D. THOMASSON

7: *Creative Spirit*: Conversations that Accompany Creativity in
   the Lives of Young People Who Are at Risk of Homelessness   111

LIESL VAN DER MERWE, JANELIZE MORELLI, AND CATRIEN WENTINK

8: Exploring Lived Experiences of Relationality during
   Participatory Performances of Sacred Musics at a Care Home
   for the Elderly   129

GARETH DYLAN SMITH

9: *Mud Drums* and Magic: Spirituality and Collaborative
   Improvised Drumming   141

ANNE T. JONES

Interlude 3: A Counselor's Search to Understand How Her
Post-Traumatic Growth and Recovery Were
Facilitated by Music   157

PART III: Therapy, Education, and Caring   165

GIORGOS TSIRIS

10: Tracing Spirituality in Everyday Music Therapy Contexts:
Methodological Reflections   167

JILLIAN SCHOFIELD

Interlude 4: Healing with Shamanic Drums   183

JUNE BOYCE-TILLMAN

11: Music, Meditation, and Mandalas: Re-Enchanting the Care
Home   189

LAURA BENJAMINS

12: Facilitating Relational Spaces of Musicking: A Music
Educator's Practice of Care   219

KARIN S. HENDRICKS

13: Authentic Connection in Music Education: A Chiastic Essay   237

FABIAN LOCHNER AND MICHELE KEIM

14: "Only When I Think the Light...": Teaching Religion
Inclusively in a Camphill SEND Setting   255

FAITH HALVERSON-RAMOS

15: Gerotranscendence and Music Therapy: Supporting a
Transpersonal Dimension to Aging   275

PART IV: Ecology   291

DAVE CAMLIN

16: Recovering Our Humanity: What's Love (and Music) Got
to Do with It?   293

JENNIFER KERSHAW

Interlude 5:   This Holy Adventure: A Meditation in
                Loving Memory of Paul Robertson   313

CHRIS ROBERTS

17: Re-Imagining Ritual, Creating Communitas   319

TAWNYA D. SMITH

18: Spiraling to Life: Listening and Sounding toward a Life-
Sustaining Society   335

Notes on Contributors   353

Index   363

Figures

Figure 4.1.   The Star of David as a working model for
              religious authenticity through pop music   56

Figure I.1.   The word cloud of the participants' responses   105

Figure 9.1.   Boyce-Tillman's model of spirituality (2020, p. 74)   143

Figure 11.1. A socio-ecological model of factors involved
              when music is played in a health care setting
              (adapted from Preti & McFerran, 2015)   196

Figure 11.2. The Labyrinth design in Chartres cathedral   201

Figure 11.3. A Christian Celtic cross   202

Figure 11.4. Basic mandala shape   203

Figure 11.5. Example of a plain and colored mandala   204

Figure 11.6. Mandala shapes used in the project   208

Figure 12.1. Conceptual framework   229

Figure 13.1. Essay themes in chiastic form   239

Figure 17.1. Post-preliminary crossfade   328

Tables

Table 15.1. Addressing the Three Dimensions of
            Gerotranscendence through Music   286

Table 17.1. Overlapping Ritual Processes   325

Table 17.2. Concert Model   331

Acknowledgments

This volume reflects the minds, hearts, and hands of many scholars and music practitioners around the world who share an interest in music, spirituality, wellbeing, and human connection. It offers a large array of perspectives and approaches, while sharing a broad vision of hope and healing through music. I offer sincere gratitude to the chapter and interlude authors, who have offered us much to contemplate and envision. I also thank the international collective of abstract and manuscript reviewers for their invaluable insights: Bruce Benson, Terry Biddington, Ian Bradley, Liora Bresler, Maria Busen-Smith, Amira Ehrlich, Jane Erricker, Christopher Findlay, Anne-Marie Forbes, John Habron, Graham Harvey, Frank Heuser, Gavin Hopps, Ruth Illman, Brian Inglis, Marian Liebmann, Christo Lombaard, George Lotter, Koji Matsunobu, John Moxon, Hetta Potgieter, Noah Potvin, Susan Quindag, Stephen Roberts, Gareth Dylan Smith, Tawnya Smith, Giorgos Tsiris, Liesl Van der Merwe, Etienne Viviers, and Katherine Zeserson.

I offer heartfelt thanks to research assistants Cheryl Freeze and Delaney Finn for their thoughtful and thorough editing of every manuscript in this volume. Their dedication, time, and attention to detail have been truly remarkable, and their work has made the timely publication of this volume possible. I would like to thank June for inviting her to collaborate on this project, and for sharing generously of her wisdom, energy, and friendship. I am grateful as always to Tawnya for her unfailing patience and support, and for many dear friends and colleagues who have provided much-needed humor. I also acknowledge the unexpected musical gifts of encouragement and direction that were offered by my former student Sarah Huppi, and former choir director Robert Nakea, who – quite serendipitously – each sent me heartfelt videos of themselves playing music within the very hours that I finished this project. Clearly there are angels on earth.

– Karin S. Hendricks, Associate Professor and Chair, Music Education, Boston University

I am very grateful for a group of people around me during the pandemic who have encouraged me and supported me to keep going including Sue Lawes, David McDonald, the Very Rev James Atwell (now sadly deceased), the Rev David Page, Henry Morgan, Penny Toller, Dr. Carol Boulter, Diane Berry MBE, Hannah Stanislaus, Jana Richvalska, Della Edwards, the community of All Saints Church Tooting, the Rev Elizabeth Baxter from Holy Rood House, and Althea de Carteret. Some of these papers came from the last conference of the Tavener Centre and the Centre for the Arts and Wellbeing at the University of Winchester who supported me in my academic life, including especially Professor Simon Jobson, Dean of the Faculty of Health and Wellbeing, Professor Joy Carter, the Vice Chancellor, Dr. Terry Biddington, The Dean of Spiritual Life, Professor Inga Bryden Head of Research in the Arts Faculty, Dr. David Walters Convenor of the Centre and Holly Pye, the administrator. The steering group of Music Spirituality and Wellbeing, some of whom are represented in this volume, keep the energy of this series going: The Rev Dr. Stephen Roberts, Dr. Brian Inglis, Dr. Amira Ehrlich, Dr. Giorgos Tsiris, Maria Soriano, Professor Tawnya Smith, my three colleagues from North-West University, Potchefstroom, South Africa, Professor Chris van Rhyn, Professor Liesl Van der Merwe and Professor Hetta Potgieter, and finally Professor Karin Hendricks, my co-editor, with whom it is wonderful to cooperate. Professional colleagues who have encouraged the idea include Neil Valentine, Dr. Vicky Feldwick, Dr. Olu Taiwo, and Meta Killick. I am also grateful to Petra Griffiths of the Living Spirituality Network and the forming of the group interested in the Spirituality of Music within that organization. The Rev Jonathan Evens from HeartEdge at St. Martins in the Fields has also been very encouraging. Without Lucy Melville at Peter Lang this series would never have happened. Alongside me through the pandemic have been my two sons, Matthew and Richard, and my beautiful granddaughter Scarlett. Without all these people to continue my creative work would have been impossible. I am profoundly grateful.

— The Rev Professor June Boyce-Tillman, Professor Emerita of Applied Music University of Winchester; Extraordinary Professor at North-West University, South Africa; Associate of the Institute for Theology, Imagination and the Arts, St. Andrews University, Scotland

Music and Authenticity in the Contemporary Context: Individualism, Community, and Negotiations of Diversity

KARIN S. HENDRICKS AND JUNE BOYCE-TILLMAN

1 Music, Connection, and Authenticity

By the end of March 2020, the world's citizens were fully engaged in a global quarantine to minimize the spread of the respiratory virus COVID-19. Unlike the pandemic of 1918, the COVID-19 "social distancing" exercise was accompanied by technological tools that allowed us to connect virtually, beyond our individual places of shelter and into the living rooms of others anywhere else across the world. Introverts breathed a sigh of relief at the opportunity to stay at and work from home, while extroverts looked for ways to use various technologies to fill their energy repositories through human connection.

At this unprecedented time of virtual connection, two activities in particular began to fill social media networks: storytelling and music, both of which have been mechanisms for human connection since primal times (Boyce-Tillman, 2000; Hendricks, under review; Solórzano & Yosso, 2002). Well-known performers such as Josh Gad, Betty White, Lupita Nyong'o, and Jimmy Fallon read children's stories to youth – and simultaneously reminded many adults of the need for the children in all of us to be soothed at times of crisis (Cadden, 2020). Meanwhile, countless videos of musicians began to emerge with musical messages of hope, encouragement and humor (Tennessee Performing Arts Center, 2020), and even admonitions to wash our hands regularly and stay at home (Frishberg, 2020). Global virtual music events such as Lady Gaga's *Together at Home* fundraiser, which raised over $128 million for the World Health Organization, provided musical artists and fans across the world a space to collectively process the grief and shock of the pandemic, create global solidarity, and honor frontline workers (Watercutter, 2020). Such acts of sharing stories and music remotely helped people continue to connect emotionally and spiritually despite physical separation.

The difference between authentic versus virtual connection became more apparent than ever during the 2020 pandemic, as sheltered-in-place individuals who had an abundance of technologies for human interaction nevertheless demonstrated an overwhelming need to connect emotionally and spiritually with others – turning en masse to the mechanisms of music to do so. It seems fitting in this unprecedented era of *virtual* connection to more fully articulate the qualities of *authentic* connection, and to demonstrate the ways in which music is uniquely poised to facilitate the latter even in some of the most challenging and physically isolating times.

The Essence of Authentic Connection

The essence of authentic connection has been described in the context of compassionate music teaching (Hendricks, 2018a) as a spiritual experience that might occur between co-musickers who have fostered a collective space of trust, empathy, inclusion, and community. It is also present in instances of musical entrainment, where individuals in a group coordinate movement through synchronous musical activity (Boyce-Tillman, 2016; Clayton, 2012; Clayton et al., 2005). Although we acknowledge that rhythmic entrainment has the possibility to lead to either positive or negative group outcomes,[1] this volume focuses on the ways in which mutual musical engagement can lead to healthful, life-giving experiences of emotional effervescence (see Collins, 2004; Durkheim, 1912/1995; Emdin, 2016), communitas (Turner, 2012), and eudaimonia (Boyce-Tillman, 2020; Smith & Silverman, 2020).

Furthermore, although it is possible to engage in electrifying musical rituals that connect people in myriad forms of spiritual experience, in this volume we focus specifically on those experiences that also invoke a sense of authenticity. Here, the notion of authentic connection extends beyond connection to others, to include connection within oneself (Boyce-Tillman,

---

1   We might contrast, for example, the ways in which music has been used in Nazi and neo-Nazi rallies with the World Health Organization fundraiser mentioned previously.

2016), as an experience of heart/mind coherence (see Childre & Martin, 1999). The authors consider ways in which musickers might look inward and outward with self- and other-awareness, demonstrating a willingness to be vulnerable as their authentic selves are exposed – and challenged – through activities of musical and emotional risk-taking.

Chapters and interludes address topics such as relationship building, community, wellbeing, therapy, education, and ecology, each describing various ways in which individuals connect authentically with themselves, others, the music they make, and the physical and spiritual world around them. Broader concepts that inform this work include:

- Attunement (Kossack, 2009)
- Authenticity and integrity (Hendricks, 2018a; Palmer, 2017)
- Caring and compassion (Hendricks, 2018a; Noddings, 1984, 2012; Silverman, 2012, 2013)
- Communicative musicality (Malloch & Trevarthen, 2009)
- Communitas (Turner, 2012)
- Community and hospitality (Boyce-Tillman, 2000, 2016; Higgins, 2007, 2008; Higgins & Campbell, 2010)
- Diversity, equity, and inclusion (Emdin, 2016; Hendricks, 2018a, 2018b, in press; Smith & Hendricks, 2021; Spellers, 2006)
- Ecology and ecophilosophy (Boyce-Tillman, 2016, 2020; Macy & Brown, 2014)
- Empathy (Eisenberg & Strayer, 1990; Hendricks, 2018a)
- Entrainment (Boyce-Tillman, 2000, 2016; Leonard, 1978; McCraty et al., 1996)
- Eudaimonia (Boyce-Tillman, 2020; Smith & Silverman, 2020)
- Emotional effervescence (Collins, 2004; Durkheim, 1912/1995; Emdin, 2016; Williams, 2021)
- Mindfulness (Boyce-Tillman, 2016; Chödron, 2004, 2007)
- Musicking (Small, 1998)
- Pentecostal Pedagogy (Emdin, 2016)
- Relationality (Buber, 1970)
- Trust (Hendricks, 2018a; Hoy & Tschannen-Moran, 1999; Tschannen-Moran & Hoy, 2000)
- Vulnerability and risk-taking (Boyce-Tillman, 2016; Hendricks, 2018a; Higgins & Campbell, 2010; Palmer, 2017)

Chapters and interludes provide nuanced views of the ways in which musicking and authentic connection stimulate and reinforce one another.

Music and Authenticity in the Contemporary Context: Individualism, Community, and Negotiations of Diversity

In our current global world, the polarity of individualism/community (Boyce-Tillman, 2000) regularly appears at the forefront of lived experience. Technological connections bring individuals together in community from all parts of the world, including as we make music together in new and innovative ways (Boyce-Tillman, in press). The COVID-19 pandemic offered a distinctive opportunity for individual and collective self-reflection:

> [It] was a unique global situation in which every human being was forced to take pause – for safety and health – because much of the world was on lockdown. We were all forced to share a new reality, one that created a new global community. (Williams, 2021, p. 121)

This new global community has brought a novel set of challenges, however, as we have had to rely on the actions of strangers to keep us healthy and safe – yet as opinions about how to accomplish this are as diverse as is the global population. Pandemic life is illustrated poignantly by the experience of virtual choirs and instrumental ensembles, where a viewer (separated in time and space from the performance) watches numerous boxes of individuals with varied backdrops, each striving to do their part with a hope to not only survive, but thrive through virtual music-making. These act of vicarious musicking – while critical for maintaining a sense of community – nevertheless act as a painful reminder of our present physical isolation.

Not only is separation particularly tangible at this time, but also our awareness of our diversity as humans (Smith & Hendricks, 2021; Spellers,

2016). Several authors in this volume address simultaneous global crises of racism, nationalism, environmental injustice, and associated climate catastrophes. Although we share a natural drive toward human connection, efforts toward inclusion in a pluralistic world cannot happen without a fair amount of negotiation (Spellers, 2016). In this volume, Stephen Roberts addresses the negotiation of difference in "Music and Spirituality in a Polyphonic Public Sphere," using religious diversity and music as a starting point to envision creative interactions that might forge new and authentic understandings. Bruce Benson's chapter "Improvisation as Spiritual Exercise" further deepens the discourse surrounding negotiation, by articulating how attunement in musical improvisation requires empathy, which in turn requires humility and trust.

In "Popular Music for Religious Authenticity in Israeli Jewish Religious Education," Amira Ehrlich describes her own negotiations with diversity as she and her colleagues came to embrace popular, rock, and jazz music as a way to support students in their authentic expressions of identity. Combining three myths of rock/pop music (authenticity, rebellion, youth culture) with three aspects of Jewish identity (spirituality, exploration, deliberation), Ehrlich proposes a Star of David model to demonstrate how *yeshiva* music majors engaged in popular music genres as a means of constructing their religious and musical identity. She concludes her chapter by embracing negotiation and dialogue, stating, "how else, if not through deliberation and argument, can we keep moving?" Estelle R. Jorgensen reminds us in her chapter "On Values and Life's Journey through Music" that authentic expressions of self, particularly as one engages with music learning, are not fixed, but change in tandem with differing values as one moves through various stages of adulthood.

Authentic Connection and Wellbeing

Just as the polarities of individualism and community live in dynamic relationship with music to promote wellbeing (Boyce-Tillman, 2000), so does a balanced relationship between one's internal and external worlds: "Making genuine connections with others – whether [with] students, colleagues, or musical audiences – requires a certain level of personal authenticity" (Hendricks, 2018a, p. 147). Yet in many instances throughout modern history, musical experience has been severed artificially from personal experience, particularly as music has been objectified as an aesthetic art, impervious to context or personhood.

As Deborah J. Saidel argues in "A Pathway to Wellbeing," spirit injury can take place when musical experience is extracted from its life-giving, embodied dimensions. She describes her journey toward spiritual and musical healing as she departed from androcentric and Eurocentric musicology to study – on her own terms – the ways in which music functioned in the everyday lives of women. She expresses her own empowerment in coming to understand how women "drew strength, inspiration, and direction from their everyday embodied experiences and channeled their individual energy effectively within the most ancient and widespread system of mind-body healing known to humanity" – and suggests that other women might similarly become attuned to their individual power and agency through music. Jungmin Grace Han describes the essence of musical embodiment and spiritual empowerment in her interlude "The Sacred Space Within."

The contrast between wellbeing and illness is illustrated by epidemiologist Maria Giulia Marini, whose interlude "Music, To Each Their Own When Illness Comes" offers a compelling portrait of the soul-crushing silence in intensive care units during the height of the COVID-19 pandemic in Italy. She describes the various ways in which people turned to music to lift their spirits during a time of intense physical and emotional distress. In "Creative Spirit" Keith Thomasson offers additional insights into the ways that art can foster wellbeing. He explains the work of the Alabare Christian Care and Support program, which pairs at-risk youth with a caring adult in shared creative activities (e.g., art, gardening, baking, and songwriting) where conversations and mutual trust can develop in ways that facilitate healing.

Liesl Van der Merwe, Janelize Morelli, and Catrien Wentink explore wellbeing and relationality through a narrative inquiry of eight older adults' lived experiences when singing sacred songs together during weekly musicking sessions. The authors define relationality as connection to self, others, the environment, and a transcendent or divine Other, and view music (in an intentionally anthropomorphic way) as a kind of mediator to restore and maintain these relationships.

In his chapter "*Mud Drums* and Magic," Gareth Dylan Smith further explores spirituality in relationship, describing connections forged while engaging in collaborative improvisation with his friend Martin. He frames his conversations with Martin within Boyce-Tillman's (2020) model of spirituality and human flourishing, to consider the spiritual dimensions of the autotelic experiences they shared while drumming together. In her interlude "A Counselor's Search to Understand," Anne T. Jones adds her witness to the power of music in forging authentic connections with others, writing: "Our authentic presence builds connections to others and encourages others to risk being vulnerable too."

Therapy, Education, and Caring

Music therapists and educators hold a unique opportunity – and responsibility – to act as midwives of authentic connections. This sacred work requires a delicate dance between structure and agency, as carers foster the safe spaces that the cared-for need to heal, while also challenging them to enter new places where they are vulnerable enough to grow. In these liminal spaces, authentic connections may be forged in unexpected and exciting ways as therapist/educator and client/student interact with, and learn from, one another (see Hendricks, 2018a, 2018b).

In his chapter "Tracing Spirituality in Everyday Music Therapy Contexts: Methodological Reflections," Giorgos Tsiris advocates for such a "fluid, context-responsive, and emergent notion of spirituality" – not only in music therapy practice, but also in research about spirituality and music therapy. In the interlude "Healing with Shamanic Drums," Jillian Schofield offers a fitting analogy for such an emergent nature of spirituality (such as authentic connections forged in therapy and education) when describing the relationship between shamanic drum and drummer: "The drum connects to the energy of the journey and plays itself." Liminal spaces are further explored in the context of music, visual art, and mindfulness in June Boyce-Tillman's chapter "Music, Meditation, and Mandalas: Re-Enchanting the Care Home."

Two chapters in this volume draw upon the writings of Noddings (1984, 2012) and Silverman (2012, 2013) to provide insights into how caring relationships in music education might foster authentic connections. First, Laura Benjamins addresses an ethic of care in her chapter "Facilitating Relational Spaces of Musicking." Benjamins emphasizes music educators' responsibility to engage with students through modeling, dialogue, practice, and confirmation, so that "students may be better positioned to enter into relational spaces of music-making and learn to encounter the world in a new and different way." In "Authentic Connection and Music Education," Karin Hendricks uses a quasi-chiastic essay form to outline parallels and/ or opposites on either side of a disconnection/connection spectrum, first as they relate to society at large, and then in music teaching and learning specifically. Hendricks considers Silverman's (2013) notion of musical meaningfulness to propose that caring *with* – in addition to Noddings's (1984) notions of caring *for* and *about* – might facilitate authenticity and equity in musical relationships.

Conversations of equity and inclusion continue in "'Only When I Think the Light...': Teaching Religion Inclusively in a Camphill SEND Setting," a chapter written by Fabian Lochner and Michele Keim. The authors describe their arts-based approach to teaching religion to students with a range of needs and abilities, including students with autism, Down syndrome, fragile-X, cerebral palsy, and others. Finally, the therapeutic needs of elders are considered in the chapter "Gerotranscendence and Music Therapy." Here, Faith Halverson-Ramos argues that music offers an effective, accessible, and culturally responsive mechanism for supporting Baby Boomers as they develop toward gerotranscendence, or the final stage of maturation. Music, she suggests, can aid in accessing a transpersonal dimension where "we can recognize a deep interconnectedness that exists between ourselves and others, as well as between ourselves and the planet."

Ecology

Authentic connections with self, others, and the planet are explored further in the final section of this volume. Here, authors invite us to deepen our awareness both inward and outward, and to broaden our gaze beyond our individual worlds and music-making settings to consider how what we do – and to what we attune – might play a role within the greater universal ecology. In "What's Love (and Music) Got to Do with It?" Dave Camlin uses music (including artful section headings referencing popular songs) as a means of transporting the reader through the past, present, and future, to consider how our musical predispositions might "be sympathetically entangled" with our innate need for human connection. He urges us to consider how music might not only serve as a means of coping through difficult times, but to play a critical role in re-humanizing us as a global community as we navigate the effects of late capitalism, climate emergency, and the COVID-19 pandemic. The interlude "This Holy Adventure" by Jennifer Kershaw continues the conversation of connection to self, others, the environment, and transcendent others through a meditation upon the death of her dear friend and mentor Paul Robertson.

Ecology is considered in terms of mutual musical vulnerability and spiritual/emotional bonding in Chris Robert's chapter "Re-Imagining Ritual, Creating Communitas." Here, Roberts explains his quest to transform participatory care home concerts from what Buber (1970) termed an "I-It" relationship to one of "I-Thou" – where mutual engagement bridged the divide between performers and audience. This leveling of hierarchies is reminiscent of the essence of compassion that Hendricks (2018a) suggests is requisite for authentic connection. In this volume's final chapter, "Spiraling to Life," Tawnya Smith offers a benediction on the collection that serves simultaneously as an invocation for beginning the work of musicking for connection – to self, to others, and to the greater planetary ecology. Drawing upon ecophilosophers Macy and Brown's (2014) *Coming Back to Life*, Smith models for her readers a spiraling progression of meditations as she processes her grief about environmental degradation and considers ways that music-making might help us work toward a life-sustaining society.

Conclusion

Although the volume ends here, the work toward authentic connection continues – enlivened by hope and kindled through the courage to be vulnerable, to take risks, and to better understand ourselves and one another. Yet as several authors in this book suggest, the process of authentic connection is not easy in a world that values competition (Hendricks, 2018a) and normalizes individualism (Boyce-Tillman, 2016). There is a particular loneliness in the individualistic journey:

> The male hero narrative … tells of one who asserts his individuality and "finds himself" through the undertaking of a journey. This usually occurs without a permanent companion […] Autonomy and independence are valued over intimacy and closeness. (Boyce-Tillman, 2016, p. 241)

On the other hand, music-making evokes connection:

> Community building is not a heroic journey. It is the story of women in many cultures and of the poor in most cultures with whom the community musicking traditions often reside; it is often devalued and has few financial returns. […] It is accompanying that is required for community music making. The process of coming together to sing, drum, and move to music somehow can make us psychologically, spiritually and physically more like each other. (Boyce-Tillman, 2016, p. 241)

Community building is the journey of humanity – of radical inclusion (Spellers, 2006). And just as beliefs in superiority or entitlement can be literally suffocating to all of us (Hendricks, this volume), so can authentic understandings of our ecological connections bring new life. As the authors of this volume attest, music is a unique and auspicious art form for creating such understandings – and a balanced practice of improvisation and trust, coupled with a sense of wonder and curiosity, might propel us forward into unknown territory where new possibilities for humanity await us.

Bibliography

Boyce-Tillman, J. (in press). Musicking the cosmos. In J. Boyce-Tillman & K. S. Hendricks (Eds.), *Living song: Singing, spirituality, and wellbeing* (in press). Peter Lang.

Boyce-Tillman, J. (2000). *Constructing musical healing: The wounds that sing.* Jessica Kingsley.

Boyce-Tillman, J. (2016). *Experiencing music–restoring the spiritual: Music as wellbeing.* Peter Lang.

Boyce-Tillman, J. (2020). An ecology of eudaimonia and its implications for music education. In G. D. Smith & M. Silverman (Eds.), *Eudaimonia: Perspectives for music learning* (pp. 71–89). Routledge.

Buber, M. (1970). *I and Thou* (W. Kaufmann, Trans.). Simon & Schuster. (Original work published 1937).

Cadden, M. (2020, March 23). *Jimmy Fallon, Betty White and more celebs read books to kids with online story time.* USA Today, <https://www.usatoday.com/story/entertainment/books/2020/03/23/coronavirus-online-storytime-celebrities-betty-white-jimmy-fallon/2886194001/>

Childre, D., & Martin, H. (1999). *The HeartMath Solution.* HarperCollins.

Chödrön, P. (2004). *Start where you are: A guide to compassionate living.* Shambhala Publications.

Chödrön, P. (2007). *The places that scare you: A guide to fearlessness in difficult times.* Shambhala Publications.

Clayton, M. (2012). What is entrainment? Definition and applications in musical research. *Empirical Musicology Review, 7*(1–2), 49–56. <https://doi.org/10.18061/1811/52979>

Clayton, M., Sager, R., & Will, U. (2005). In time with the music: The concept of entrainment and its significance for ethnomusicology. *European Meetings in Ethnomusicology, 11*, 1–82. <https://dro.dur.ac.uk/8713/1/8713.pdf>

Collins, R. (2004). *Interaction ritual chains.* Princeton University Press.

Durkheim, E. (1995). *The elementary forms of religious life* (K. T. Fields, Trans.). Free Press. (Original work published 1912)

Eisenberg, N., & Strayer, J. (Eds.). (1990). *Empathy and its development*. Cambridge University Press.

Emdin, C. (2016). *For white folks who teach in the hood … and the rest of y'all too: Reality pedagogy and urban education*. Beacon Press.

Frishberg, H. (2020, March 23). *Neil Diamond posts 'Sweet Caroline' coronavirus remake: 'Hands – washing hands.'* New York Post. <https://nypost.com/2020/03/23/neil-diamond-posts-sweet-caroline-coronavirus-remake-hands-washing-hands/>

Hendricks, K. S. (2018a). *Compassionate music teaching: A framework for motivation and engagement in the 21st century*. Rowman & Littlefield.

Hendricks, K. S. (2018b). Gaga spirituality. In K. S. Hendricks & J. Boyce-Tillman (Eds.), *Queering freedom: Music, identity and spirituality* (pp. 243–260). Peter Lang.

Hendricks, K. S. (in press). Counternarratives: Troubling majoritarian certainty. *Action, Criticism, and Theory for Music Education*.

Higgins, L. (2007). The impossible future. *Action, Criticism, and Theory for Music Education, 6*(3). <http://act.maydaygroup.org/articles/Higgins6_3.pdf>

Higgins, L. (2008). The creative music workshop: Event, facilitation, gift. *International Journal of Music Education, 26*(4), 326–338. <https://doi.org/10.1177/0255761408096074>

Higgins, L., & Campbell, P. S. (2010). *Free to be musical: Group improvisation in music*. Rowman & Littlefield.

Hoy, W. K., & Tschannen-Moran, M. (1999). Five faces of trust: An empirical confirmation in urban elementary schools. *Journal of School Leadership, 9*(3), 184–208. <https://doi.org/10.1177/105268469900900301>

Kossak, M. S. (2009). Therapeutic attunement: A transpersonal view of expressive arts therapy. *The Arts in Psychotherapy, 36*(1), 13–18. <https://doi.org/10.1016/j.aip.2008.09.003>

Leonard, G. (1978). *The silent pulse*. E. P. Dutton.

Macy, J., & Brown, M. Y. (2014). *Coming back to life: The updated guide to the work that reconnects*. New Society Publishers.

Malloch, S., & Trevarthen, C. (Eds.). (2009). *Communicative musicality: Exploring the basis of human companionship*. Oxford University Press.

McCraty, R., Tiller, W. A., & Atkinson, M. (1996). *Head-heart entrainment: A preliminary survey*. Paper presentation at the Key West Brain-Mind, Applied Neurophysiology, EEG Biofeedback 4th Annual Advanced Colloquium.

Noddings, N. (1984). *Caring: A feminine approach to ethics and moral education*. University of California Press.

Noddings, N. (2012). The caring relation in teaching. *Oxford Review of Education, 38*(6), 771–781.

Palmer, P. (2017). *The courage to teach: Exploring the inner landscape of a teacher's life* (3rd ed.). John Wiley & Sons.

Silverman, M. (2012). Virtue ethics, care ethics, and "The good life of teaching". *Action, Criticism, and Theory for Music Education, 11*(2), 96–122. <http://act.maydaygroup.org/articles/Silverman11_2.pdf>

Silverman, M. (2013). A conception of "meaningfulness" in/for life and music education. *Action, Criticism, and Theory for Music Education, 12*(2), 20–40. <http://act.maydaygroup.org/articles/Silverman12_2.pdf>

Small, C. (1998). *Musicking: The meanings of performing and listening.* Wesleyan University Press.

Smith, G. D., & Silverman, M. (Eds.). (2020). *Eudaimonia: Perspectives for music learning.* Routledge.

Smith, T. D., & Hendricks, K. S. (2021). Diversity, inclusion, and empowerment. In G. E. McPherson (Ed.), *The Oxford handbook of musical performance* (in press). Oxford University Press.

Solórzano, D. G., & Yosso, T. J. (2002). Critical race methodology: Counter-storytelling as an analytical framework for education research. *Qualitative Inquiry, 8*(1), 23–44. <https://doi.org/10.1177/107780040200800103>

Spellers, S. (2006). *Radical welcome: Embracing God, the other, and the spirit of transformation.* Church Publishing, Inc.

Spellers, S. (2006). *Radical welcome.* Church Publishing.

Tennessee Performing Arts Center (2020, March 19). *#SocialDistancing: When you can't go to the arts, the arts come to you.* <https://www.tpac.org/news-center/socialdistancing-when-you-cant-go-to-the-arts-the-arts-come-to-you/>

Tschannen-Moran, M., & Hoy, W. K. (2000). A multidisciplinary analysis of the nature, meaning, and measurement of trust. *Review of Educational Research, 70*(4), 547–593.

Turner, E. (2012). *Communitas: The anthropology of collective joy.* Springer.

Watercutter, A. (2020, March 20). *Lady Gaga's together at home raised $128 million for Covid-19 relief.* WIRED Entertainment News. <https://www.wired.com/story/lady-gaga-covid-19-coronavirus-relief/>

Williams, R. (2021). *Full participation in parochial chorus* [Unpublished doctoral dissertation, Boston University].

STEPHEN B. ROBERTS

2 Music and Spirituality in a Polyphonic Public Sphere

In a world marked by diversity on a global, national, and local level, how can music help us live with difference? That is the question at the heart of this chapter. Differences we negotiate daily to some degree include race, ethnicity, class, gender, sexuality, faith, spirituality, and various forms of non-belief. As a Christian theologian, it is religious diversity that most exercises me. There is a well-established theological debate about how best to understand the pluralism of religions, with approaches ranging from the narrowly exclusive to the radically open and inclusive (D'Costa, 2009; Knitter, 2002). Elsewhere I have investigated a distinctive musical contribution to that debate by analyzing John Tavener's theology of religions as articulated in *The Veil of the Temple* (Roberts, 2020). There, Tavener explicitly addresses theological questions about religious diversity through composition. The focus here is different: I am stepping back from these theological questions to pursue the question of how musicians engage with difference through their work. I am interested not so much in what musicians *think* about religious diversity as reflected in their music, but how they *negotiate* religious diversity in practice. And while the primary focus is on the pluralism of religious traditions, this is set in the context of wider questions about negotiating difference more generally.

The first part of the chapter outlines my approach to the relationship between music and theology, focusing on public theology. This is followed by a discussion of approaches to thinking about music and diversity. The main body of the chapter consists of three case studies: Jordi Savall, D'Angelo, and Nitin Sawhney. Between them they raise different issues while reflecting different musical styles and diverse religious traditions.

Theology Listening to Music

This study informs a larger project exploring the relationship between music and public theology, with a focus on the question of living well with diversity. The larger project engages music as dialogue partner in developing an interdisciplinary approach to public theology, working on an understanding of public theology I have already articulated in relation to music (Roberts, 2017). There are different ways of conceiving public theology, but at its core is a concern with questions that resonate beyond the churches. So, for example, theologians wrestling with questions relating to immigration and the refugee crisis are doing public theology, whereas those seeking to develop more adequate formulations of the doctrine of the Trinity, generally speaking, are not.

My approach to public theology draws on thinking about the public sphere as theorized by Jürgen Habermas (1962/1989, 1992/1996) and Nancy Fraser (1992). The public sphere is a significant space within democratic societies in which public opinion is formed and shared, ultimately influencing political debate and policy. I am interested in that space as a plural space, made up of many publics, and how a diverse range of voices – including the religious – is brought into conversation (Roberts, 2017, pp. 181–186). Because of the way diverse publics form what Habermas calls a " 'wild' complex" (1992/1996, p. 307) ultimately contributing to the wider political process, I use "polyphony" as a metaphor for the way in which multiple voices contribute to a larger democratic whole.

But what has music got to do with it apart from supplying a metaphor? Public theology, often with roots in practical theology, is an inherently interdisciplinary approach to theology drawing, for example, on social science, critical theory, and philosophy. I am exploring what public theology might gain from dialogue with music and those who study it – music as interdisciplinary dialogue partner in the work of public theology. I aim to develop a distinctive approach to public theology while exploring new avenues in the relationship between theology and music.

My question, then, is how music can help shape a theological contribution to thinking about how we negotiate (religious) difference in a polyphonic public sphere. There is a specific rationale for using music to explore questions about religious diversity, which is the close relationship between music and religion in many different historical and contemporary cultural contexts. An implication of this recognition is to support the turn in religious studies, and some areas of theology, toward an understanding of religion as a matter of performative practice rather than intellectual assent.

Musicians Negotiating Difference

Music is a valuable resource for thinking about diversity. Sometimes intentionally, but often implicitly, musicians negotiate diversity through composition, performance, collaboration, improvisation, curation, and therapeutic practice. Much can be learned from investigating their work, as has been done from a variety of perspectives (Born & Hesmondhalgh, 2000; Lipsitz, 1994). In the existing literature, however, the ways in which musicians negotiate religious diversity has received less attention (although see Illman 2010, 2014) and that is the focus of this study.

Musicians contribute to our experience of difference in numerous ways. Music provides, for example, a means of giving voice to different cultures in the public sphere, with varying degrees of integrity and authenticity. This might include the use of popular, non-art music to enrich the compositional practice of composers such as Poulenc, Milhaud, Copland and Gershwin with Jazz, and Bartok, Kodaly, Stravinsky and Vaughan Williams with folk traditions (Born & Hesmondhalgh, 2000, p. 13). Or it might include the different ways in which so-called "world musics" find their way to Western ears and dancing feet: from Paul Simon's celebrated but controversial *Graceland* (1986; Lipsitz, 1994, pp. 56–60), to Afro Celt Sound System mixing traditional Irish and West African traditions with electronic dance music (e.g., 2018). Such examples face critical questions about the commodification of musical styles and traditions and associated questions about who profits most from such ventures. A detailed discussion is beyond the scope of this study, but raising the question in this context opens new ways of approaching questions of religious diversity, because questions about the economic aspects of dialogue and the potential for cultural appropriation in hybrid forms of religious identity are rarely considered.

George Lipsitz, while alert to such questions regarding music, makes a strong case for there being potential as well as danger:

> The interconnectedness of cultures displayed by world music is not without utopian possibilities, but the ravages of unimpeded capital accumulation create grave dangers as well. These crossroads are dangerous for all of us; how well we negotiate them may determine what kind of future we will face – or whether we will face any future at all. Dangers await at the crossroads, but never with more peril than when we refuse to face them. (1994, pp. 19–20)

In his study, Lipsitz works at the intersection between different local cultures rooted in place, and the hyper-mobility of global capital, investigating the potential of the former in face of the latter. The book's title, *Dangerous Crossroads* (1994), translates "Kalfou Danjere," a song by Haitian group Boukman Eksperyans (1992), which was banned by the military dictatorship it opposes. The song draws on the spiritual resources of Afro-Haitian religion – including "God" (the supreme deity) and the "lwa" (ancestral spirits and deities) – in attacking the oppressive regime. Elsewhere on the album other religious traditions – Christianity, Hinduism, and Buddhism – are enlisted in the revolutionary cause, the dangerous political crossroads thus being a meeting point for religious difference. Significantly for the understanding of public theology outlined above, Lipsitz sees popular musicians as contributing to "the emergence of a new public sphere" (1994, p. 12). Despite the ambiguities of the commercial culture within which they work the hip-hop artists and others he discusses can still "serve as exemplars of post-colonial culture with direct relevance to the rise of new social movements emerging in response to the imperatives of global capital and its attendant austerity and oppression" (1994, p. 27).

Thus far I have outlined the significance of music for public theology and illustrated some ways in which musicians negotiate difference in the public sphere. To investigate further the potential of music for thinking theologically about religious diversity I turn now to the case studies.

Jordi Savall

In 2007 Jordi Savall set out to negotiate difference musically in a work set in one of the most dangerous crossroads of all, Jerusalem. Savall is an example of a musician intentionally negotiating religious difference through music, although, unlike Tavener, he does not explore theological themes directly in his work.

Jerusalem: The City of the Two Peaces (2008) was commissioned by La Cité de la Musique in Paris, where it was first performed in April 2008. Lasting some two and a half hours, it is a musical reflection on the rich yet fraught history of Jerusalem and its relationship with the three Abrahamic religions. The work begins with a fanfare of shofars precipitating the destruction of the walls of Jericho – music and religion associated with violence. It ends with another fanfare of shofars, also calling for a tearing down of walls; but this time it is the "barriers of the spirit," the internal, spiritual walls of fear that divide and that Savall seeks to break down through his music. Between these fanfares is music and text from Judaism, Christianity, and Islam, drawing on Savall's early music expertise and reflecting a diversity within and across the traditions. The Syballine Oracles are Greek text, drawing on Jewish sources and set to Aramaic music; there are Qur'anic recitations reflecting Sufi sources; medieval Crusader songs mark the period of the Christian city; there are Palestinian and Armenian laments, pleas for peace in several languages, and a hymn to the victims of Auschwitz. The historical and religio-cultural breadth of the material conveys a sense of the difference and diversity that has both divided and made the city of Jerusalem what it is. The whole rich musical tapestry culminates, before the final fanfare, in a "Dialogue of Songs" featuring singers and instruments from different traditions associated with Jerusalem, and a final ensemble where all join together.

Reflecting on her experience of a performance of *Jerusalem*, Ruth Illman (2014) makes bold claims for the music: "The experience of taking part in the concert is deeply moving. At least these musicians will not go out and kill each other, I think as I leave the concert hall. The world really is changed" (p. 74). I too find the music to be profoundly moving. And

I can easily be persuaded that the world is changed in some sense by the performance. But is it changed in a way that finally and definitively prevents the musicians involved being caught up in a genocidal conflict that leads to them being at least complicit in killing one another? The danger of such a claim is in encouraging complacency about ever-present possibilities of violence against the other where constant vigilance is required. But if this aspect of Illman's claim is a claim too far, then in what ways might the world be changed because of an encounter with Savall's *Jerusalem*? Or, to consider this question from a different angle, what sort of relationship to religious and cultural difference is contained in Savall's work? How does it invite us to negotiate these differences?

As an exponent of early music, a distinctive contribution Savall makes to our thinking about music and difference is his concern with the integrity of musical traditions. As someone whose work involves the appreciation of distinct musical styles in particular historical periods, he understands not only major, but subtle difference. Savall sees both the necessity and creative potential of such difference. Musical dialogue should give space for conflict as well as similarity; and Savall aims for "sharing but not mixing" (Illman, 2014, p. 78), preserving distinctiveness. Illman (2014) observes, "In the concert *Jerusalem*, this principle is innovatively put into practice by the musicians who remain firmly within the frames of their own traditions but still manage to perform together in a meaningful way" (p. 78).

Music, for Savall, allows dialogue to move beyond intellectual concern with the problem of truth into a creative space of being together with difference and allowing different voices to sound together, contributing to a larger whole without losing their distinct identity. Illman captures this well:

> It is not about competing or begrudging, not about musical mishmash, nor is it about a forced cooperation with superficial combinations [...] It is not about unbridgeable differences, but about respectful openness and sensitive integrity, a community solid and large enough to contain even the most irreconcilable variations and the unique expression of each musician as an individual and a bearer of a tradition at the same time. (Illman, 2014, p. 85)

But what is it about music that allows this to happen? In her work exploring religious diversity through music, June Boyce-Tillman uses the language of "framing" to describe how music can provide a space for different faiths to meet. She describes her vocation as creating "artistic frames where the differences and similarities between the faiths can be shared, expressed and experienced" (Boyce-Tillman, 2018, p. 130). This way of describing the musical space created for the meeting of religions seems apt for Savall's work also: The traditions remain distinct, but they speak to one another and as they speak to one another they also speak together.

Savall's is a very deliberate approach to negotiating difference musically. There are other musical spaces where something more organic is taking place, more concerned with blurring than preserving boundaries between religious, cultural, and musical traditions.

D'Angelo

It is just such blurring that we encounter in the second case study. D'Angelo is sometimes described as a "neo-soul" singer, although he considers this too restrictive to capture his musical project. He is particularly interesting as an example of the negotiation of religious and spiritual diversity because of the way he gives voice to what Anthony Pinn (2017) has called *The Varieties of African American Religious Experience*. And he does so while negotiating the socio-political difference of racism. Faith Pennick highlights the challenge in African American experience of "living fully present in the body you have, while shielding it from threats" (2020, p. 41), and the musical and religious themes serve the twin foci of this celebration of Black life and resistance to racial injustice.

Like Savall, D'Angelo draws on diverse musical traditions, though in this case it is different strands of Black music he is fusing – the metaphor of "weaving" no longer works because in this creative process there is less concern for the distinctive strands. Instead, they are part of an ongoing stream of African American music which he continues. Responding to a question about his sound, D'Angelo said, "I make black music" (Fulton, 2015, p. 8). Drawing out the significance of this statement, Fulton sees it as revealing "the crux of D'Angelo's creative process," in which there is a "compounding of black music genres, reclaiming and reconciling styles and eras toward evoking a historically unified African American music" (Fulton, 2015, p. 8).

Alongside his integration of different strands of Black music is something similar regarding religion. He has emphasized the importance of the inspiration of (the) S/spirit(s) – the terminology varies – and this was reflected in his second album:

> I named the album Voodoo because I really was trying to give a notion to how powerful music is and how we as artists [...] need to respect the power of music. Voodoo is ancient African tradition. We use "voodoo" in the drums or whatever, the cadences and call-out to our ancestors and that in itself will invoke spirits. And music has the power to do that, to evoke emotions, evoke spirit. That's something I learned in the church when I was very young and that's what I wanted to get across. (Jet Magazine, 2000, p. 62)

As well as voodoo, then, the church is a major influence, and both are reflected aurally. Sounds of voodoo ritual are heard at the beginning of "Playa Playa" (D'Angelo, 2000), and he regularly incorporates stylistic references to the music of the Black church, such as "Higher" on *Brown Sugar* (1995). On the surface this track is a love song, but one in which eroticism and spirituality are closely entwined; and musically it sounds like a straightforward Gospel song. Here, then, he negotiates sacred / secular difference while evoking an influential form of Black music. This is even more prominent in *Voodoo* (2000) which, as Pennick observes, is "a marriage of all of D'Angelo's inspirations, equal church hall and dance hall" (2020, p. 26).

The third album brings further religious themes to the fore, again in the very title of the album: *Black Messiah* (2014). The second track samples a sermon about the Black Jesus, thus referencing Black Christian theology, but here mediated through Khalid Muhammad, then of the Nation of Islam, adding to the interreligious complexity and illustrating the diversity of Black religion (Pinn, 2017). Again, religious and musical diversity coalesce, the opening track being "an aural statement – a tapestry of genres of African American music" (Fulton, 2015, p. 11). And it is the musical evocation of s/Spirit(s) that unites both. Some have noted a mumbling quality to the vocals on this album, which D'Angelo says is "all about capturing the spirit" in the first take: "The first time, cut that mic on and the spirit is there and what comes on the mic, even if I'm mumbling, I like to keep a lot of that initial thing. […] Cause that's the spirit" (D'Angelo, cited in Fulton, 2015, p. 11). Because D'Angelo finds this openness to being a channel for (the) S/spirit(s) particularly in the church, he used a number of church musicians on *Black Messiah* (Fulton, 2015, p. 12).

We see in D'Angelo, then, a musician negotiating musical diversity within the context of African American culture, reflecting the breadth of musical traditions within that culture. Like Jordi Savall, he seeks to give contemporary voice to historic sounds and traditions, in this case of Black music; but rather than providing a frame for them to sound distinctly, he synthesizes them into a whole new distinctive sound.

We have seen the centrality of (the) S/spirit(s) for his musical process, and so alongside the musical diversity we find a musician negotiating the religious diversity of that same culture, and doing so in a way that fuses different streams of religious and spiritual experience into a whole. Is this syncretism? Is it hybridity? Or are both of those terms linked to discourses that don't quite fit this context? While having roots in the Black church, both musically and spiritually, he exemplifies Pinn's call for a Black theology that moves beyond a narrow a focus on the Black church (Pinn, 2017, p. xxii). There is a comparative Black theology implicit – and sometimes explicit – in his music.

Nitin Sawhney

For the third case study we turn to Britain, and another musician who fuses different traditions of music into new hybrid forms. Nitin Sawhney is a prolific musician, a British Asian brought up in Kent by Punjabi immigrant parents. Much of his early music, in the late 1990s, was a creative means of negotiating the different cultures that shaped his identity. In a 1997 interview with ethnomusicologist Martin Clayton, he spoke of music as a language with which he could explore his experience as a British Asian (Clayton, 1998).

Clayton analyzes the title track of Sawhney's second album, *Migration*, in the light of a fourfold process of migration described in the sleeve notes: departure, arrival, adaptation, and fusion. The 10' track begins with sounds from an Indian forest, continues with Indian musical sounds – tabla drums, the double-reed shehnai, and voice – initially over an electronic drone, then over drum kit. The latter becomes more prominent and a full-blown jazz-funk groove takes over at 4'18", with electric bass and Fender Rhodes keyboard sound. At 6'02" the Indian music returns until 6'43" when the jazz-funk groove returns, but this time with Indian vocals and increasingly prominent tabla. The rest of the track has shifting instrumentation and styles reflecting processes of adaptation and fusion. It is still possible to hear the distinctive sounds of Indian music and British jazz funk (Sawhney played for a period in the James Taylor Quartet), but these are now part of a new fusion.

Reflecting on Sawhney's work in the wider context of Asian contributions to the British music scene opens further dimensions in thinking about music and difference in the polyphonic public sphere. Against the background of debates about multiculturalism, such fusions can be subject to critique in terms of their cultural consumption by wider non-Asian publics. Koushik Banerjea is critical of what he saw as an "uncritical appetite for multiculture and its richly syncretic produce" (Banerjea, 2000, p. 65). He is writing here about *Soundz of the Asian Underground* (Singh, 1997), an album of music from Talvin Singh's Anokha club night, and is strident in highlighting the problem: "Marked by the ready appropriation of *bindis*, *saris*, incense and the more narcoleptic aspects of Ravi Shankar, these are spaces which offer a primarily middle-class constituency a sanitized encounter with an imagined Asian 'other'" (Banerjea, 2000, p. 65).

Whether or not this is justified, it at least raises a critical question. Yet, uncompromising as Banerjea's judgment here might be, he does not deny the possibility of "liminal spaces for cultural refabulation. Spaces thrown up for instance by the messy contingencies of popular musical cultures" (Banerjea, 2000, p. 66). Sawhney exemplifies such possibilities, his own experience providing the liminal space for exploring multicultural life.

While Banerjea rightly warns of dangers lurking at the musical crossroads of multiculturalism, there is so much in Sawhney's work – particularly these early albums (1995, 1996, 1999) – that offers insightful reflection on the negotiation of difference.

Arguably Sawhney's most celebrated album remains *Beyond Skin* (1999), continuing the theme of *Migration* (1995) by exploring what it means to be British and Indian, expressing the view he articulates on the sleeve notes: "I believe in Hindu philosophy. I am not religious. I am a pacifist. I am a British Asian. My identity and my history are defined only by myself – beyond politics, beyond nationality, beyond religion and Beyond Skin" (Sawhney, 1999).

The album between *Migration* and *Beyond Skin* explored the place of religion in British Asian identity. *Displacing the Priest* (1996) continues the fusion of *Migration* as discussed above, with similar movements between Indian sounds, funky grooves, and house beats that are ultimately fused in a distinctive sound world and style that also incorporates Brazilian ("Saudades") and flamenco ("Herecica Latino") influences. In the sleeve notes, Linton Chiswick sees the whole album as "a personal reflection upon spirituality and organized religion, and the gulf that can sometimes exist between the two" (Sawhney, 1996). But it is in the opening track, "Oceans and Rain," and the title track, "Displacing the Priest," that this reflection is most pronounced as part of negotiating a multicultural identity.

"Oceans and Rain" begins with Hindu chanting recorded in an Indian temple, continues with sounds of rain combined with ambient electronics before a beat takes over and Jayanta Bose's vocalizing dominates the rest of the track until it concludes, recapitulating sounds of rain and chanting. The poem accompanying the track on the sleeve notes and Chiswick's commentary suggest an interpretation which celebrates a more ephemeral spirituality derived from but no longer dependent on traditional religion. The same theme emerges in "Displacing the Priest" through Charles Oleghe's rap in which the resources of religion are turned against its official guardians in favor of the individual spiritual quest. As several musical styles and influences serve the creative negotiation of identity in a multicultural context, so it is with religion. Negotiating multicultural identity, personal spirituality draws on deeply rooted religious traditions while rejecting their authority. Here again, different forms of religion and spirituality are voiced with different musical styles in the polyphonic public sphere as a multicultural society seeks social wellbeing through negotiating difference.

Conclusion

How can music contribute to social wellbeing by helping in the negotiation of difference, particularly in the realm of religion and spirituality? To address this question, I have examined three examples of musicians doing this, contributing in different ways to a vibrant, polyphonic public sphere. Many avenues for further research arise from this study. Numerous other musical examples could be investigated. There is scope for moving beyond the literature and recording-based approach, using qualitative methodologies to explore how those involved in musicking difference are influenced by the music. What difference has music made to Jordi Savall, D'Angelo, Nitin Sawhney, and the musicians with whom they worked? What difference has it made to those who listen to their music? Answering these questions would require empirical studies to further our understanding of the place music plays in shaping approaches to difference in the public sphere. At least I hope to have demonstrated the potential significance of music in this regard.

But what, finally, of my concern with public theology? Three insights from this study inform theological explorations of religious difference:

1. The music considered revealed examples both of preserving distinct traditions within a wider musical frame (Savall) and of fusing different traditions into a new musical style, either based on an underlying cultural unity (D'Angelo), or creating a hybrid (Sawhney). Theologians in debates about pluralism are often nervous of hybridity, fearing compromise. If, analogously to music, religious and spiritual traditions can be conceived less in terms of

doctrinal belief and more in terms of culture and practice, then hybrid forms that synthesize different traditions into something new can be valued alongside approaches that, like Savall in music, seek rather to preserve the integrity of traditions (Roberts, 2018).

2. Approaching religion and spirituality differently, the three artists discussed each demonstrate the value of creativity in exploring difference and diversity. With greater openness to new fusions and hybrid forms, theologians might give more space to creativity in their own approach to these questions alongside the value of preserving and working within distinct traditions. Something of this is already underway in comparative theology (e.g., Barnes, 2012; Clooney, 2010), which is closer to Savall's musical approach, and in practices of dual belonging, which is closer to Sawhney's (Drew, 2011).

3. Responding to the critical focus on the economic, social, and political framing of musical dialogues and hybridities – questions relating to cultural appropriation and multicultural commodification – might suggest that theologians take an equally critical stance when it comes to interreligious encounter. They might ask more questions about the power differentials in interfaith relations, about who benefits and in what ways, and about what attitudes to deeply rooted religious traditions are formed by interreligious fusions.

The generativity of this dialogue between music and theology in exploring how we negotiate difference suggests it is a conversation worth continuing. What I have described as the "polyphony" of the public sphere includes multiple musical and religious voices, with many examples of creative interaction, between musics, between religions, and between music and religion. While such interactions are open to critical evaluation, there are certainly creative crossings and authentic connections among them. I have shown that public theology may be enriched by attending to them.

Bibliography

Afro Celt Sound System. (2018). *Flight* [Album]. ECC Records.

Banerjea, K. (2000). Sounds of whose underground? The fine tuning of diaspora in an age of mechanical reproduction. *Theory, Culture & Society, 17*(3), 64–79. <https://doi.org/10.1177/02632760022051220>

Barnes, M. (2012). *Interreligious learning: Dialogue, spirituality and the Christian imagination.* Cambridge University Press.

Born, G., & Hesmondhalgh, D. (Eds.). (2000). *Western music and its others.* University of California Press.

Boukman Eksperyans. (1992). *Kalfou danjere: Dangerous crossroads* [Album]. Mango Records.

Boyce-Tillman, J. (2018). *Freedom song: Faith, abuse, music and spirituality – A lived experience of celebration.* Peter Lang.

Clayton, M. (1998). "You can't fuse yourself": Contemporary British-Asian music and the musical expression of identity. *East European Meetings in Ethnomusicology, 5,* 73–87.

Clooney, F. X. (2010). *Comparative theology: Deep learning across religious borders.* Wiley-Blackwell.

D'Angelo. (1995). *Brown sugar* [Album]. EMI.

D'Angelo. (2000). *Voodoo* [Album]. Virgin Records.

D'Angelo. (2014). *Black messiah* [Album]. RCA.

D'Costa, G. (2009). *Christianity and world religions: Disputed questions in the theology of religions.* Wiley-Blackwell.

Drew, R. (2011). *Buddhist and Christian? An exploration of dual belonging.* Routledge.

Fraser, N. (1992). Rethinking the public sphere: A contribution to the critique of actually existing democracy. In C. Calhoun (Ed.), *Habermas and the public sphere* (pp. 109–142). The MIT Press.

Fulton, W. (2015). The performer as historian: *Black Messiah, To Pimp a Butterfly,* and the matter of albums. *American Music Review, 44*(2), 8–17.

Habermas, J. (1989). *The structural transformation of the public sphere: An inquiry into a category of bourgeois society* (T. Burger, Trans.). Polity Press. (Original work published 1962)

Habermas, J. (1996). *Between facts and norms: Contributions to a discourse theory of law and democracy* (W. Rehg, Trans.). Polity Press. (Original work published 1992)

Illman, R. (2010). Plurality and peace: Inter-religious dialogue in a creative perspective. *International Journal of Public Theology, 4*, 175–193. <https://doi.org/10.1163/156973210X491886>

Illman, R. (2014). *Art and belief: Artists engaged in interreligious dialogue*. Routledge.

Jet Magazine. (2000, July 3). Hot singer: D'Angelo. *Jet Magazine*, 98(4), 58–62. <https://books.google.co.uk/books?id=17QDAAAAMBAJ&pg=PA58>

Knitter, P. F. (2002). *Introducing theologies of religions*. Orbis Books.

Lipsitz, G. (1994). *Dangerous crossroads: Popular music, postmodernism, and the poetics of place*. Verso.

Pennick, F. A. (2020). *Voodoo*. Bloomsbury Academic.

Pinn, A. B. (2017). *Varieties of African American religious experience: Toward a comparative black theology* (20th anniversary ed.). Fortress Press.

Roberts, S. B. (2017). Beyond the classic: Lady Gaga and theology in the wild public sphere. *International Journal of Public Theology, 11*(2), 163–187. <https://doi.org/10.1163/15697320-12341481>

Roberts, S. B. (2018). Is the Pope Catholic? A question of identity in Pope Francis's practical theology of interreligious dialogue. In H. Kasimow & A. Race (Eds.), *Pope Francis and interreligious dialogue: Religious thinkers engage with recent papal initiatives* (pp. 129–144). Palgrave Macmillan.

Roberts, S. B. (2020). John Tavener's musical theology of religions. In J. Boyce-Tillman & A.-M. Forbes (Eds.), *Heart's ease: Spirituality in the music of John Tavener*. Peter Lang.

Savall, Jordi. (2008). *Jérusalem – La Ville des deux paix: La paix celeste et la paix terrestre* [Album and accompanying book]. Alia Vox.

Sawhney, N. (1995). *Migration* [Album]. Outcaste Records.

Sawhney, N. (1996). *Displacing the priest* [Album]. Outcaste Records.

Sawhney, N. (1999). *Beyond skin* [Album]. Outcaste Records.

Simon, P. (1986). *Graceland* [Album]. Warner Bros. Records.

Singh, T. (1997). *Soundz of the Asian underground* [Album]. Mango Records.

3   Improvisation as Spiritual Exercise

The Improvisational Virtues of Empathy, Humility, and Trust

Introduction: Getting in Tune

Consider the English lyrics set to the Antonio Carlos Jobim tune "Desafinado" by Jon Hendricks. Here's a version by the New York Voices:

> Love is like a never ending melody,
> Poets have compared it to a symphony,
> A symphony conducted by the lighting of the moon,
> But our song of love is slightly out of tune ….
> Once your kisses raised me to a fever pitch,
> Now the orchestration doesn't seem so rich,
> Seems to me you've changed the tune we used to sing,
> Like the bossa nova love should swing ….
> We used to harmonize two souls in perfect time,
> Now the song is different and the words don't even rhyme,
> 'Cause you forgot the melody our hearts would always croon,
> What good's a heart that's slightly out of tune?
> Tune your heart with mine the way it used to be,
> Join with me in harmony and sing a song of love,
> We're bound to get in tune again before too long,
> There'll be no Desafinado when your heart belongs to me completely
> Then you won't be slightly out of tune, you'll sing along with me!

Those last two lines tell us pretty much everything we need to know about how to end "*desafinado*," a Portuguese term that means "out of tune." Once your heart belongs to *me*, then we'll be singing in tune *because you will be singing exactly what I'm singing*.

We might be inclined to dismiss these lyrics as an aberration, something unusual in the realm of popular song. Yet that would be too hasty.
Nietzsche reminds us that "sexual love … reveals itself as a craving for new
property," since "the lover wants unconditional and sole possession of the
longed-for person." What seems to be "the opposite of egoism" may actually turn out be "the most candid expression of egoism" (Nietzsche, 2001,
§14).[2] A quick look at love songs and poetry confirms that Nietzsche is
often right, so we shouldn't be surprised that we have the language of "when
your heart belongs to me completely." My personal favorite in this genre of
love-as-possession songs is titled "You are My Personal Possession," which
rhymes the lines "I own you exclusively" and "Darling, you belong to me."

But let's pass over that point for now. The whole idea behind the tune
is a lack of attunement. However, the difficulty is how to re-establish that
attunement. In the English lyrics of "Desafinado" written by Hendricks,
we begin with melody, move to symphony and orchestration, and then to
harmony. Two hearts are out of tune, but the remedy is that "you tune your
heart with mine." Although Hendricks was an African American, he was
also male. Alas, it is a typical male move of expecting the woman to submit
to his tune. In such a case, attunement happens by way of coercion. Before
going any further, though, I want to note that the original Portuguese lyrics
written by Newton Mendonca are *remarkably* different in how they depict
this lack of attunement and how it would be resolved. That difference is
evident in the translation by Gene Lees, which goes (in part) like this:

> When I try to sing you say I'm off key
> Why can't you see how much this hurts me
> With your perfect beauty and your perfect pitch
> You're a perfect terror
>
> When I come around must you always put me down
> You will hurt my feelings don't you see my love
> I wish I had an ear like yours
> A voice that would behave
> But all I have is feelings and the voice God gave

2   I think Nietzsche's case for this claim of "desiring territory" is actually quite strong,
     as I demonstrate in Benson (2009).

These lyrics give us the *reverse* of the Hendricks's lyrics. The singer (we'll say "he") admits to being incapable of singing in tune. *He's* the one who's causing the problem. Even more important, rather than suggesting that the other person submit to his will, he closes by singing:

> That even though I may be out of tune
> When I attempt to say how much I love you
> All that matters is the message that I bring
> Which is my dear one I love you.

Of course, it isn't hard to see that these two sets of lyrics illustrate mirror-like and problematic responses to a lack of attunement. In the first case, the male demands something which we might call "obedience": You will do what I say and we'll be back in tune. Attunement by way of coercion. In the second case, the male expresses something like emasculation: He is terrified of the perfection of his partner and humbly requests that his lover overlook his *desafinado*. Neither of these ways of responding to being out of tune is likely to lead to anything like a healthy attunement. If being in tune is simply a matter of coercion, then it is like a holiday picture in which, for one brief moment in the midst of scabbling, the family smiles pretending that all is well. To be sure, probably many holiday photographs have been taken under such conditions.

However, of these two responses, the second is clearly *better*: It starts with admitting a weakness and asks for compassion. The goal of *these lyrics* is the communication of humility and a willingness to compromise. In this chapter, I wish to show that improvisation is best accomplished when attunement takes place by all of the voices being attuned to one another. In *that* sense, it is a spiritual exercise that requires empathy for those with whom one is improvising. Further, empathy requires both humility and trust. The point of humility is that, apart from opening oneself up to the other, I can only remain in tune with *myself*. Yet, opening oneself up to the other requires a kind of trust that others with whom I'm improvising are willing to listen to *one another*. Such listening is crucial for improvisation and proves to be a valuable spiritual exercise.

Still, this version by the New York Voices, two women and two men, makes the lyrics by Jon Hendricks sound rather different, and provides a way of thinking improvisational attunement in a different way. They are *all* singing "tune your heart with mine." The effect (which I have no reason to think that they *intend*) is to invert the lyrics, subverting its hostile-takeover message: for the goal is now one of tuning one's heart with the other three. But what does it mean to be attuned not merely to *one* other but *three*? How does that happen?

Improvising Music Together

In his suggestive essay "Making Music Together" (Schutz, 1964, p. 167) speaks of the "web of social relationships called musical culture." Schutz is (as were most of his contemporaries) mired in what I have come to call the "divine composer command theory" of musical performance, a view that I have deconstructed in my book *The Improvisation of Musical Dialogue* (Benson, 2003) and attempted to replace in my book *Liturgy as a Way of Life* (2013). The view Schutz employs sees the performer as an "intermediary" between composer and listener, whose job is to "obey" the "commands" of the composer (Schutz, 1964, pp. 159, 163). It is hard not to see such a move as a form of coercion. However, despite beginning with this basic musical paradigm, we can read Schutz as taking steps that, in effect, help undermine that paradigm and help us move to a different relationship. What Schutz does bring to light what he calls "the mutual tuning-in relationship, the experience of the 'We', which is at the foundation of all possible communication" (Schutz, 1964, p. 173). That We has a particular context. It is first and foremost the sharing of humanity, but that in turn has to do with culture, language, formation, our various intersectional communities, and certainly music itself. Schutz puts this as follows:

> The player approaching a so-called unknown piece of music does so from a historic-ally – in one's own case, autobiographically – determined situation, determined by his stock of musical experiences at hand in so far as they are typically relevant to the anticipated novel experience before him. This stock of experiences refers indirectly

to all his past and present fellow men whose acts or thoughts have contributed to the building up of his knowledge. (Schutz, 1964, p. 168)

What constitutes the "mutual tuning-in relationship"? Elsewhere I have characterized this relationship as a kind of dialogue. If that description is apt (and I have also defended it in Benson, 2010), then Gadamer's observation about the structure of genuine dialogue may be helpful here: He claims that a genuine dialogue has the *"logical structure of openness"* (Gadamer, 1989, pp. 362–363). Without there being some "loose-play" or uncertainty, genuine conversation (as opposed, say, to parallel monologues) is impossible. I think Gadamer is right, but what does this mean in practice? My relation to someone with whom I am making music naturally requires that I be open to that person. Empathy is an ability to understand another person, however limited and inexact such understanding may be. Humility is the realization that the other person has something to contribute and the corresponding willingness to learn. Put in the strongest possible terms: Humility before another person comes about from the recognition that the other has something to teach me. Trust, as a primal aspect of being human, is the dependency we all have upon others epistemically, to be sure, but also in many other ways. Trust in the musical other is a fundamental given for music-making.

The tuning required is that of a "mutual tuning-in," which means that we are tuned in to something beyond ourselves. We are tuned into the business at hand – playing music. Of course, the way in which we tuned into that business is going to differ depending upon what sort of music we are tuning into. In jazz, that tuning is much less focused on the strict parameters of the music at hand and more on the somewhat elusive goal of creating something loosely based on a particular tune or pattern. Yet, while making music with the other requires being attuned to something outside of us, it also requires being tuned to one another. One cannot create music *with* the other without a focused listening *to* the other. We could describe this relation to the other in terms of openness: For us to work together, we must be open to the other. But, as a musician, I am not *simply* open to the other, in the sense that I make a conscious choice to do so. More accurately, I feel a kind of pull from the other, a pull which keeps me from going my own way and playing whatever I happen to feel at the moment. This pull is going to be different, again, depending upon the kind of music we are playing. In classical music, I am listening to the other to make sure that our pitches, tempi, intonation, and such blend together. In jazz, the need for listening to the other is raised to an entirely different pitch: not only are we listening for these elements but we are listening for much more. If I stop listening to the other – even for a few seconds of daydreaming – the result can prove catastrophic. The other(s) may be changing various chords or even providing alternate ways of playing the piece and I had better be aware of what is happening.

However, this tension must be felt on all sides: there needs to be a *mutual* tuning-in. It is not enough for me to be open to the other, to listen and respond to the other; the other must be likewise open and listening and responding to me. In an interview, Sam Rivers (who plays free jazz) says "there's nothing I can do wrong, nothing." But we have to take this with a significant grain of salt. Most likely, Rivers is talking here of making a *musical* mistake. But, if he is playing with other musicians, there are various *ethical* mistakes that one could make, such as playing over someone else or not respecting what others in the group are doing. Note how closely mistakes of an ethical and musical nature are intertwined. To be sure, playing over someone is probably going to lead to bad music-making. But it is even more serious as an ethical violation. At stake here are not simply rules of etiquette (though they are certainly present, as in all human activity). Thus, Howard Becker rightly admits that, even though he uses the term, "etiquette might not even be the right word to describe the kind of attentiveness, care, and willingness to give ground and take direction from each other involved" in the improvising process (Becker, 2000).

To be attentive to the other is precisely what ethics is about. Emmanuel Levinas makes the important point that our responsibility is first and foremost *to other people*, not to abstract rules or ethical generalities. He insists (rightly, I believe) that moral responsibility stems from the other simply *being there*. Thus, Levinas says that "to approach the Other is to put into question my freedom, my spontaneity" (Levinas, 1979, p. 303). Levinas here is criticizing the elevation of autonomy by Kant. In formulating the categorical imperative, Kant emphasizes that one needs to be truly autonomous in making moral decisions, rather than looking to someone else's judgment for approval or guidance. In stark contrast, Levinas reminds us that my autonomy often comes at the expense of someone else's autonomy. To counter Kant's privileging of autonomy, Levinas (1993) instead privileges "heteronomy," by which he (and Kant) means that my actions take into account the existence of other people. Another reason, then, why improvisation is not purely spontaneous is that (at least in playing with and for others), my freedom is checked simply by their being there. In improvisation, I am responsible to those whose music I play, those with whom I am improvising, and those who are in the audience. It is entirely appropriate, then, that Marcel Corbussen and Nanette Nielsen's book *Music and Ethics* (2012) opens with a chapter on listening. Music-making, in its most basic sense, is a social activity that requires being tuned in to other people (including other music makers and the audience). As such, it is an example of what Alasdair MacIntyre (1984) calls a "practice," which "involves standards of excellence and obedience to rules as well as the achievement of goods. To enter into a practice is to accept the authority of those standards" (p. 190). Yet it is also to enter into a kind of ethical contract with others, one that involves a deep sense of responsibility to them. Jeff Warren (2014) provides a helpful (and amusing) anecdote of an improvisation that starts to go so right musically that the players actually have to pull back dynamically when they remember that their gig is that of playing background music for a corporate gathering. As Aristotle reminds us, getting all of these responsibilities to various parties right is difficult.

There must be empathy, humility, and trust in return. The music-making relationship can degenerate into a dictatorship. Depending upon the kind of group under consideration, there may indeed be a designated leader, someone to whom everyone in the group must be attuned. But music-making requires a *reciprocal* sort of relationship: for what would it mean to make music *together* if I could not expect the other to be likewise attentive to me? Indeed, one great danger of seeing relationships – of any kind – merely in terms of a one-sided openness is that, while the call for openness on my part (or your part) can have the positive effect of making me responsive to the other, the call of openness can just as easily be the occasion for oppression and domination. I can oppress you precisely because you are supposed to be open, and many dysfunctional relationships probably are best characterized as stemming from a one-sided openness. Again, we are back at the problem of coercion.

So, the relationship of making music requires a mutual sort of tension. Attunement is the result of the correct degree and kind of tension. It is not as if, in some sort of ideal relationship, that we would want this tension to be gone; rather that tension is precisely what makes the relationship possible. But then something important happens: I am *not* free to do whatever I want precisely because I want to make music *with* you. My own take is that the most creative jazz groups are those in which you can almost feel the tension of interplay taking place between them. It is not a paralyzing tension, on the one hand, nor a static sort of openness, on the other. It is something in between. True, relationships which have too much tension or tension of the wrong sort are going to be dysfunctional. What this means is that, while part of my relation to the other in making music is characterized by listening, just as important is the part which is characterized by questioning. In line with what we noted earlier, the relationship is perhaps best characterized not by "opposition" but "apposition." We do not simply "bend" to the other's will, for that would mean that the relationship would not be a mutual one. That may mean that other challenges me or sets a counterexample. In any case, the best jazz players clearly play off of one another. What the other says is celebrated but, in turn, provides the context for further improvisation.

Yet I am not always going to be attuned to the other. The tension constituting attunement and makes harmony possible is not a steady state but a continually changing reality. The ideal may be that I am constantly attuned to the other, but even in the most ideal of relationships that attunement at best happens only some of the time. The truth is that I am constantly going in and out of tune with the other. My attunement to others is always increasing and decreasing, as well as changing it focus. I may be attentive – at least for a moment – to the rhythmic pattern played by the bass player and be less unaware of everything else. But then suddenly I realize that I have been neglecting others and need to widen my attention. Moreover, I can be more or less attuned to the other: One moment my attention is almost purely focused on the other, whereas the next moment that level of attention drops down to a kind of peripheral or horizontal awareness.

I have a vague sensation of what the other is doing, but I do not have a direct apprehension or not a thematized one. Indeed, often the way one improvises with the other is by an almost intuitive awareness of the other, one which is not necessarily immediate or even fully conscious. And often this is simply because there is too much on which to concentrate.

There is a further and wider aspect of this changing attunement. Music-making communities – like all other communities – are not static entities: they are always in the process of rearranging and reforming themselves. That improvisational change may take place very gradually over a long period of time or very quickly over a short period of time. On what we might call the micro level, one aspect of this which can be seen in jazz improvisation is the ever-changing relationship between leader and those led: if I am playing in a jazz duo, at one moment I may be leading and in the next moment I may be led. There is a constant interplay of musical ideas, meaning that the balance between listening and leading is constantly changing. But one thing is clear: No community survives – if it survives at all – except by continuous tuning, whether on a grand scale or almost imperceptibly. In making music together, we are not worried about trying to create some ideal blend but making this one work – right now, in the middle of this song. Communal tuning, then, is directed toward making things work as best they can, given the circumstances, given the members of the community, given all factors positive and negative.

In his book *Black Music Matters: Jazz and the Transformation of Music Studies*, Ed Sarath (2018) shows us how jazz "exemplifies the interplay of individual and ensemble that runs deep in black music" (p. xii). He quotes from George Lewis, who writes: "Pursuit of individualism within an egalitarian frame has been central to not only to the jazz moment, but also to African American music before and since that movement" (Lewis, 2008, p. xii). Yet Lewis prefaces that quotation with one from anthropologist John Szwed, who writes:

> The esthetics of jazz demand that a musician play with complete originality, with an assertion of his own musical individuality … At the same time jazz requires that musicians be able to merge their unique voices in the totalizing, collective improvisations of polyphony and heterophony. The implications of this esthetic are profound and more than vaguely threatening, for no political system has yet been devised with

> social principles which reward maximal individualism within the framework of spon-
> taneous egalitarian interaction. Thus when Europeans and white Americans embrace
> the music, they also commit a political act of far more radical dimensions than that
> of simply espousing a new political ideology. (Szwed, 1980, p. 588)

Improvisation in jazz is about joining a political community that allows
for – *requires* – that one both asserts one's own individuality and
recognizes the individuality of those with whom one is improvising in
such a way that a community is formed.

How Might Musical Improvisation Be a *Spiritual* Exercise?

As Socrates lay dying, he says: "In the course of life I have often had the
same dream … 'Socrates, practice and cultivate the arts.' In the past I used
to think that it was impelling and exhorting me to do what I was actually
doing … practicing the arts, because philosophy is the greatest of the arts,
and I was practicing it. But ever since my trial … I have felt that perhaps it
might be this popular form of art that the dream intended me to practice"
(Plato). The word Socrates uses here is the Greek "*mousikê*," which does
include actually composing or playing music (as we mean it today), but it
can also be "a philosophical quest for the cultivation of the soul" (Goehr,
1998, p. 1). Music, then, is not some other *thing* than "reason" (even
though it is something *more* than reason defined as logic or dialectic).
Second, *mousikê* is defined even more broadly than that, for in ancient
Greece "people described as *mousikoi*," *musici,* are often not musicians but
students of musical theory and philosophy" (Hornblower et al., 1996, s.v.
"Music"). Indeed, any sort of endeavor in which one depended upon the
muses – originally poets, but later artists in general, philosophers, and
intellectuals (Ibid, s.v. "Muses") – would have counted as *mousikê*. So,
while a *principal* definition of the *mousikos* would be of a person "*skilled
in music*," a *secondary* definition would be "*man of letters and accomplishments, scholar*" (Liddell & Scott, 1996, s.v. "*Mousikos*"). Socrates' confusion should now be clear: He thinks he *is* practicing *mousikê*. For Socrates,

practicing music (whether literal music or philosophy) is something that touches the deepest realm of the soul. Put otherwise: It could *not* be anything else other than a spiritual exercise.

My reading here is quite dependent upon Nietzsche (Benson, 2008). Oddly enough, Nietzsche has been my best spiritual director. But my concern here is with the status of music, which can be defined "as a general metaphor symbolizing a repository for all that was unknowable by ordinary cognitive or logical means" (Goehr, 1998, p. 18). This broader sense of "music" leads us to see that "practicing music" would have been broad enough to include any art that required skill and practice. We should think of practicing the very kinds of skills that are part of *living life*. It's not hard to see how this can be connected with the idea of *askêsis*. Given that someone who is accomplished and skilled is a *"mousikos"* – and given that "practicing music" is likewise synonymous with cultivating the soul – then practicing music in this broad sense necessarily is engaging in an *askêsis* (a spiritual exercise).

Pierre Hadot has helped remind us that, for ancient philosophers, philosophy always meant *living a certain kind of way*. It was about practicing spiritual disciplines, or *askêsis* [the ancient Greek term for spiritual exercises], which is designed so that we *"let* ourselves be changed, in our point of view, attitudes, and convictions. This means that we must dialogue with ourselves and hence do battle with ourselves." It's not hard to see that *askêsis* is a thoroughgoing process that involves our very being in the deepest possible sense. Hadot describes the result of *askêsis* as "a conversion which turns our entire life upside down, changing the life of the person who goes through it" (Hadot, 1995, pp. 91, 83). The Christian word for "conversion" is *metanoia*, which literally means a change of mind but indicates a complete change of life. It carries with it the idea of a 180-degree turn – an utter reversal of the direction of one's life. While Christians tend to think that "spiritual disciplines" are something unique to Christianity, the reality is that such disciplines long predated the advent of Christianity.

The "spiritual" in spiritual disciplines does *not* mean that such exercises are either mental or *simply* pertain to the soul; instead, they involve the whole person – body and soul. What the Stoics called *"prosokhê"* [attention] "supposes that, at each instant, we renew our choice of life ... and that we

keep constantly present in our minds the rules of life which express that
choice" (Hadot, 2004, p. 193). We must constantly be aware of ourselves,
of our motives and actions, and this is what attention is designed to do. Yet
musical improvisation – the mutual "tuning-in" relationship – takes the
self-centeredness of attention and breaks it open. When I improvise with
others (and, actually, even when I improvise with myself), my attention
moves away from me to the others with whom I'm improvising. I feel the
tension of the mutual tuning-in and I am lifted beyond myself, out of my
own little world. The *askêsis* of improvisation upends the very notion of
"self-mastery" – but in a good way. What the others have given me is the
release from myself. Whereas Kant thinks that acting according to one's
own personal rational lights is what frees us, Levinas realizes that there
is a *different* kind of freedom, one in which I find my freedom through
being attuned to the needs of others. Levinas terms this "heteronomy,"
though one could likewise speak of "heterophony," the kind of allowing
for a differing voice to be heard and to change the conversation. Through
becoming attuned to the other, we are converted from the mistaken belief
that any one of us "owns" the musical dialogue.

Bibliography

Becker, H. S. (2000). The etiquette of improvisation. *Mind, Culture, and Activity*,
    7(3), 171–176. <https://doi.org/10.1207/S15327884MCA0703_03>
Benson, B. E. (2003). *The improvisation of musical dialogue: A phenomenology of
    music.* Cambridge University Press.
Benson, B. E. (2008). *Pious Nietzsche: Decadence and Dionysian faith.* Indiana
    University Press.
Benson, B. E. (2009). Appropriating Westphal appropriating Nietzsche: Merold
    Westphal as a theological resource. In B. K. Putt (Ed.), *Gazing through a
    prism darkly: Reflections on Merold Westphal's hermeneutical epistemology*
    (pp. 61–73). Fordham University Press. <https://doi.org/10.5422/fso/
    9780823230457.003.0005>

Benson, B. E. (2010). Gibt es 'musikalischen Dialog'? *Journal Phänomenologie*, *33*, 27–41.

Benson, B. E. (2013). *Liturgy as a way of life: Embodying the arts in Christian worship*. Baker Academic.

Corbussen, M., & Nielsen, N. (2012). *Music and ethics*. Ashgate.

Gadamer, H.-G. (1989). *Truth and method* (J. Weinsheimer & D. G. Marshall, Trans.; 2nd ed.). Crossroad.

Goehr, L. (1998). *The quest for voice: On music, politics, and the limits of philosophy*. University of California Press.

Hadot, P. (1995). *Philosophy as a way of life: Spiritual exercises from Socrates to Foucault* (A. I. Davidson, Ed.; M. Chase, Trans.). Blackwell.

Hadot, P. (2004). *What is ancient philosophy?* (M. Chase, Trans.). Harvard University Press.

Hornblower, S., Spawforth, A., & Eidinow, E. (Eds.). (1996). *The Oxford classical dictionary* (3rd ed.). Oxford University Press.

Levinas, E. (1979). *Totality and infinity: An essay on exteriority* (A. Lingis, Trans.). Martinus Nijhoff.

Levinas, E. (1993). Philosophy and the idea of the infinite. In A. Peperzak (Ed.), *To the other: An introduction to the philosophy of Emmanuel Levinas* (pp. 88–119). Purdue University Press.

Lewis, G. E. (2008). *A power stronger than itself: The AACM and American experimental music*. University of Chicago Press.

Liddell, H. G., & Scott, R. (1996). *Greek-English lexicon* (9th ed.). Clarendon Press.

MacIntyre, A. (1984). *After virtue* (2nd ed.). University of Notre Dame Press.

National Public Radio. (1998, March 28). *Modern jazz pioneer Sam Rivers profiled* [Radio]. NPR Weekend Edition.

Nietzsche, F. (2001). *The gay science* (J. Nauckhoff, Trans.). Cambridge University Press.

Plato. (1961). *The collected dialogues*. Princeton University Press.

Sarath, E. (2018). *Black music matters: Jazz and the transformation of music studies*. Rowman & Littlefield.

Schutz, A. (1964). Making music together: A study in social relationship. In A. Schutz & A. Brodersen (Eds.), *Collected papers II, studies in social theory* (pp. 159–178). Martinus Nijhoff.

Szwed, J. (1980). Josef Skvorecky and the tradition of jazz literature. *World Literature Today*, *54*(4), 586–590. <https://doi.org/10.2307/40135327>

Warren, J. R. (2014). *Music and ethical responsibility*. Cambridge University Press.

AMIRA EHRLICH

4 Popular Music for Religious Authenticity in Israeli Jewish Religious Education

The current study documents a unique educational approach developed in a Jewish Orthodox *yeshiva* high school for boys in Israel. The school, founded in 1998, aims to create an innovative opportunity for religiously observant boys to enjoy the benefits of a strict religious education while allowing them to major in music, a major that such religious institutions previously rarely offered. Between 2004 and 2010, the school conducted an action-research-based program to explore the educational and religious frameworks related to the combination of and interactions between the types of Jewish and musical education. The dominance of popular music, as a repertoire and a core pedagogical approach, emerged as a surprise to the research team and became conceptualized as a strategic gateway leading the students to newfound religious authenticity. In 2019–2020, reconsideration of these past research findings in light of new discourse on popular music education lead to the construction of a conceptual working model, linking notions of authenticity and identity construction attributed to youth culture – especially to popular music genres – to the cultivation of an authentic religious identity.

Judaism: A Rockstar Religion

Jewish tradition is a tradition of deliberation with God. Noah, Abraham, Moses, and Jonah are just a few of the most famous Jewish spiritual leaders who argued with God. Jewish and non-Jewish scholars often frame Judaism as a religion of rebellion and deliberation (e.g., Janowski, 2013; Lane, 1986; Laytner, 1990). In this chapter, I take this notion one step further by suggesting that Judaism is a kind of "rockstar" religion, musically speaking. By demonstrating parallels between mythic characteristics of pop and rock music traditions and Jewish spirituality, I propose the educational relevance of this music to the cultivation of a Jewish religious authenticity, which I suggest is most applicable to adolescents. I present a working conceptual model in this chapter to show how this can work, and highlight some evidence to ground this model in a pilot study that I led between 2004 and 2010.

In structuring a parallel between religious and musical authenticity – between Judaism and rock and popular music – I rely on three main myths of popular music: that of authenticity, that of rebellion, and that of youth culture (e.g., Bennett, 2000). It is way beyond the scope of the current chapter to analyze the historic and sociological discourses of these three myths. My choice to focus on these three attributes was greatly influenced by the Israeli sociologist, Moti Regev's early contributions to Israeli academic discourse on popular music (e.g., Regev, 1990; 1995; 2007).

In terms of music education, the existence of these three myths were – for a long time – quite instrumental in keeping rock and popular music outside the classroom. Hebert and Campbell (2000), for example, summarized common objections to the incorporation of rock music in American music education, noting a tendency to believe that this music is not only aesthetically inferior, but that it can actually encourage rebelliousness and antieducational behavior.

Recent discourse on popular music in education has, however, been breaking down the barriers and exploring educational applications of popular music repertoires and popular music pedagogies (e.g., Dunbar-Hall & Wemyss, 2000; Green, 2001; Rodriguez, 2004). Powell et al. (2019) cited a recent abundance of publications, including the *Routledge Research Companion to Popular Music Education*, the *Bloomsbury Handbook of Popular Music Education*, and regular issues of the new *Journal of Popular Music Education* (p. 23). Also worthy of mention are the establishments of the International Society of Music Education's (ISME) Popular Music

Education special interest group, the Association of Popular Music Education (APME), and the American National Association for Music Education's (NAfME) special research interest group for popular music education.

In light of the conceptual and practical shift in the music education field, I now find it much easier to claim that popular music – as a repertoire and as a pedagogy – is not only an important and potent aspect of music education, but is also a wonderful laboratory for the cultivation of religious authenticity in Jewish adolescents. The working model I present below became possible only in retrospect of fieldwork done a decade ago, thanks to conceptual work done in many of the publications mentioned above in the popular music education field.

The First and Only Musical High School *Yeshiva* in the World

I first developed the ideas presented in this chapter during a six-year pilot study facilitated and funded by the Israel Ministry of Education's Department of Innovation. I acted as Principal Investigator between 2004 and 2010, leading an in-school teacher research team in a Jewish religious high school for music in central Israel. Our study was structured as a teacher-lead action research model, aimed at developing an innovative educational model that would integrate music education into the Israeli Jewish religious high school's concept of education, known as a high school *yeshiva*.

A description of some basic structures of Israeli public education is necessary to understand this setting's framework and the educational challenge at hand. The Israel Ministry of Education exists as a top governmental organization, which oversees four main steams of public education: (a) Jewish secular education, (b) Jewish religious (Orthodox) education, (c) Jewish Ultraorthodox education, and (d) Arab and non-Jewish education. Sociologically speaking, the geopolitical and socioreligious segregation of these four categories characterize many infrastructures of Israeli society (Carter, 2007; Semyonov & Tyree, 1981). The current chapter relates to the second category, the Jewish religious (Orthodox) education, and focuses on a case study of a boys' high school.

In Israeli Jewish religious public education, it is common, but not obligatory, for boys and girls to study in separate institutions. Furthermore, traditions of Jewish religious education often allocate different social roles to men as opposed to women, with important impact on the design of respective educational institutions. Gender and socioreligious affiliation play an instrumental role in this study. The most salient traditional model of Jewish male secondary education is that of the *yeshiva*, the institution for holy study.

The Israeli religious stream of education invented the *yeshiva* high school in the 1950s, which describes an innovative model aimed at encouraging both holy study and secular studies for young religiously observant boys, which they summarized as a balance of *"torah and avoda"*: scriptures and work; the sacred and the mundane (Bar Lev, 1982; Stahl, 1992). Most of these institutions developed as boarding schools where students lived and studied. Mornings were dedicated to holy *Talmud* and *Torah* studies, and afternoons and evenings were dedicated to secular subjects like math, English, and science. Until the late 2000s, arts and music as school subjects were scarce in these institutions.

The current chapter describes my experiences as a female music teacher in a high school *yeshiva* for boys, and leading an in-school teacher research team. This particular *yeshiva* – the first ever musical high school *yeshiva* in the world – was established with an innovative goal of integrating music education as a core subject and spiritual outlet. The Israeli music high school matriculation exam and its curriculum were the initial foundations of this effort. All students accepted to the school had to commit to private instrumental and/or vocal training alongside four years of theory, ear training, music history, and ensemble class work. Rather than solely teaching music as an additional school subject, our aim was to discover and develop intricate connections between the religious and musical aspects of student development.

Spirituality, Religion, and Authenticity

Some religions conceptualize a divide between the religious (i.e., practical, dogma, authority, action) from the spiritual (i.e., transcendental, interpretative, personal, meaning; Ammerman, 2013; Boyce-Tillman, 2016; van Niekerk, 2018). Many forms of Judaism, however, promote a collapse between the religious and the spiritual. Enactments of Jewish religion often require, for example, both action and intention (Kepnes, 2011). Imhoff (2006) described Jewish religious tradition as unique in its insistence on inherent "bonds between body and soul; action and spirituality" (p. 66).

In his studies of Jewish Israeli male religious adolescents, Fisherman (2002, 2004, 2008, 2016) presented a model of healthy religious identity development. Fisherman explained healthy development as a shift from empty ritualistic and behavioral adherence to religion toward what he called a "personal spiritual identity" (2002, p. 69). Fisherman characterized this spiritual identity as entailing ongoing acts of deliberation, and as embracing doubt as an integral element of faith.

Describing the dangers of unhealthy religious identity development, Fisherman (2002) explains:

> This discrepancy between religious behavior and belief impairs the sense of sincerity and authenticity and threatens the adolescent's consolidation of ego identity. To diminish this gap, he chooses to separate these two aspects of his religiosity. He gives up on consolidating his faith and devotes himself to "religious" behavior stemming from behavior rooted in folklore or superstition. This separation allows him to avoid dealing with his own religiosity; he feels exempt from defining and consolidating his religious identity. (p. 74)

Fisherman (2002) seeks to encourage an authentic, personal, and spiritual form of Judaism that emerges through a process of exploration and deliberation. Fisherman notes the importance of what he calls "roundabout methods" (p. 75) in his educational recommendations that allow a safe space for exploration that can begin in third-person story contemplation, works of art, and other forms of fiction, before moving on to the intensity of first-person expressions.

Rock Music as a Laboratory for Spiritual Exploration

As a music educator, I took interest in applying Fisherman's notion of "roundabout methods" and began to explore popular music – as a repertoire and a pedagogy – as a wonderful laboratory for the cultivation of religious authenticity in Jewish adolescents. I had the privilege of exploring this claim between 2004 and 2010 when I led a pilot study in a Jewish religiously observant musical high school *yeshiva* for boys. Following Fisherman's theories of Jewish religious identity construction, I began experimenting with the use of popular music as a field of religious exploration.

At the start of the pilot study in the early 2000s, popular music was not an integral part of my music teaching curriculum.[3] Nevertheless, my attempts at engaging the *yeshiva* students in music history classes included an open invitation for students to share music of their choice in class. I admit that through these acts of sharing I gained more knowledge of Anglo-British-American popular music than I had ever been exposed to throughout my teacher training.

While I was already incorporating some of the bands I grew up on as a child (e.g., The Beatles, the Rolling Stones, Eric Clapton, Simon and Garfunkel), my initial use of such works was as elaborations on Western classical notions I wanted to explore further in symphonies and concertos. Only once I began to explore new repertoires brought in by students did I begin to further contemplate pedagogical and educational possibilities. I will never forget, for example, how embarrassed I was to admit I had never heard of the iconic band, Weather Report, until a young bass student

3   For a critical description and discussion of the Israeli high school music curriculum in English, see: Ehrlich, 2016.

brought an album of theirs to class. Since then, they have become one of my favorite bands. In class I began preparing musical discussions of such works as independently worthy of our attention, alongside the official curriculum's Western classical canon.

While my own knowledge was expanding, colleagues of mine at the *yeshiva* who were teaching music theory, private instrumental lessons, and ensembles, were way ahead of me. As I was slowly opening up to the educational potentials of new musical worlds, much of the work of my colleagues was grounded in rock, pop, and jazz repertoires and pedagogies. Lead sheets were more common in those classes than proper scores; the ability to pull together a group performance of a rock, pop, or jazz standard was a central skill being taught, alongside on-the-spot arrangements, and group and individual improvisation.

The musical heroes inspiring campus discussion, listening, and performance included David Gilmore, David Bowie, George Harrison, Genesis, the Rolling Stones, Queen, and many others; alongside local Israeli bands including Berry Sakharof, Algir, Kaveret, and Arik Einstein. Some teachers on our staff were then young emergent stars-to-be of Jewish Israeli popular music: Aaron and Yonatan Razel, Naor Carmi, and Daniel Zamir; alongside musical heroes like Andre Hajdu, and even the legendary Arnie Lawrence who taught in our school for a few months.

The peak of this educational turn emerged when students began to become more and more engaged in group and personal singing-songwriting practices. This became so pertinent during the 2007–2008 school year that, as a team, we decided to shift some of our funds from teacher-lead ensembles to independent student-run groups. We even hired a young alumnus as a freelance mentor to coach and respond to these independent groups. The impact of this shift became evident in the increasing number of original arrangements and original musical numbers performed at the yearly school concert. As an in-school teacher research team, we began to question the prominence of popular music, wondering how this emergent reality was related not only to the students' ages and genders, but to our spiritual enterprise as well.

International Youth Culture and the New Israeli Jewish Rock

The first way we explained the prominence of popular music genres in our school was through the lens of popular music as an international youth culture (e.g., Bennett, 2000). Attributing this stylistic dominance to youth culture, however, raised troubling questions of appropriateness and moral implications that such repertoires might entail.[4] As an educational team, we began to wonder if we were giving in to musical tendencies that were working against our spiritual-educational goals or if there was something else at play.

The tipping point of our group contemplation emerged as a focus on the attribute of authenticity. Our discussion was, no doubt, impacted by the personas of the many music teachers who were, in their own lives, quite inclined toward popular music genres. Nevertheless, the debate between those teachers and myself – classically trained music appreciation and history teachers – and between the music staff and Rabbis who were teaching holy study – most of whom had no musical training themselves – reached an interesting consensus when debating the notion of authenticity.

What was so invigorating about the musical performances and debates in our *yeshiva* that convinced us something new was emerging? A vast amount of spiritual energy was becoming infectious around campus. Teachers of sacred and secular subjects felt it; students discussed it; parents and community members testified to it; and our Ministry of Education research mentors spoke of our school as a phenomenon, invited student ensembles to perform at all of their important gatherings, and encouraged us to try and give this emergent singularity a name.

Historically speaking, our work on this emergent model occurred during the formative years of two important developments: the development of popular music discourse in music education, and the second development of the so-called "New" Jewish music – a new style of popular

4   For examples of such questioning, see: Badarne and Ehrlich, 2019.

Jewish music that shifted from a tradition of simplistic musical settings of scripture toward original lyrics set to new musical styles ranging from jazz, to pop, rock, heavy metal, and hip-hop. The emergence of this new form of Jewish pop music coincided with our educational pilot and had a somewhat zeitgeist-feeling impact, but we also made our own impact on the music industry in Israel as our educational project developed. To date, many of the musical high school *yeshiva* alumni can be found interacting with the most key figures of the New Jewish Israeli popular music industry as instrumentalists, singer-songwriters, and producers. Some of these alumni have even become local stars.

The Star of David as a Working Model for Religious Authenticity through Pop Music

Reflecting on the 2004–2010 pilot study almost ten years later, in 2019, the developments in popular music education, alongside the sea of change through which Israeli popular music has become dominated by young religious male (and female[5]) artists, new insights allowed me to summarize our work in the form of a conceptual working model. I embedded the three myths of rock/pop music: authenticity, rebellion, and youth culture built on Fisherman's model of Jewish religious identity constructed of spirituality, exploration, and deliberation (see Figure 4.1). The result is a working model of musical exploration through which high school *yeshiva* music majors engaged in listening, performing, and creating popular music genres as a central aspect of their religious identity construction processes.

---

5   In 2010, the musical high school *yeshiva* opened a campus for girls based on the same educational principles, incorporating many of the existing teachers. Research, however, was not yet conducted on the girls' campus.

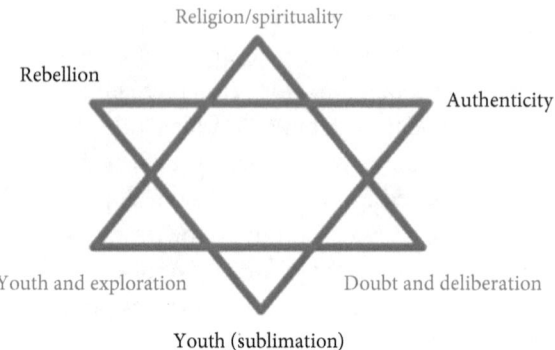

Figure 4.1. The Star of David as a working model for religious authenticity through pop music

Gender and Sexuality as Spiritual Outlets

The current design of this star of David (SoD) model places religion/ spirituality on the central horizontal axis facing youth (sublimation), or what can also be called sexuality or sexual energy. This point is much easier to address in retrospect than it was in the course of the study. At the time, I was immersed in the experience of being one of several female teachers in an all-boys high school. I pride myself on the feedback often expressed by parents who are pleased their sons are learning from women and not only from men. Nevertheless, being a female music teacher on this campus was challenging at times.

Having attended an all-girls religious high school in my youth, and coming from a family of mostly girls, it took me a while to understand – and even longer to articulate – the impacts of sexual energies embodied in some of the music we prioritized. Male adolescent sexuality was not something I had encountered or been exposed to, or had to negotiate in my own youth, and I admit I was less aware of this aspect during the early years of the study. I recall a major "a-ha" moment, when students performing onstage aroused enthusiastic dancing of their fellow students who then bombarded the stage. This spontaneous outburst of dance felt like quite a natural response to the jazz-rock fusion arrangement of a Chassidic melody being played. So natural, that it took the staff a while to decipher the sense of discomfort felt by some teachers who wanted to rush up and ask the students to go back to their seats.

Debates that followed this incident focused on the balance between the natural response of dance, and the atmosphere and movements students chose. The school synagogue always smiled upon dance and enthusiasm, and we began to wonder about the differences between dances in the synagogue and in the concert hall. As a research team and school staff, we never openly discussed sexuality in large meetings. But smaller discussions and personal reflections led me to conclude that even if we were unsure of our exact educational take on it, sexual energies were clearly channeled toward spiritual expression and sublimation.

This conclusion sits well with the mystical Jewish traditions often taught by the school Rabbis. Mcginn (1993) described this approach of Judaism as follows:

> In the related monotheistic religions of Judaism and Islam, for instance, sexual practice, as well as sexual images, could and often did play an integral role in the mystical itinerary to God. This is especially true in Judaism, where the commandment to procreate was the culmination of the way in which many mystics, particularly of the major schools of Kabbalah. (p. 48)

While the word "sexuality" may not have been uttered in educational gatherings, the notions of music and dance as outlets for youth energies, and of the incorporation of the body in the worship of God, was very often explicitly expressed. In retrospect, I deem this approach as central to the educational model, and perhaps the most important axis of the star to negotiate.

Exploration, Doubt, Deliberation, Rebellion, and Authenticity

The remaining four points of the SoD model can and perhaps should be in constant rotation, so that the model should perhaps be designed as a fluctuant animated GIF rather than a static diagram. If forced to pin it down, I would offer the following equation: *Exploration [Doubt + Deliberation + Rebellion] = Authenticity*. It is not by chance that Fisherman's model is the result of his academic fascination with young Jewish Israeli youth who have so-called "left the fold." In many ways, Fisherman's work is dedicated to the pursuit of educational strategies and tactics aimed at minimizing the abandonment of religious faith, identity, and practice of Israeli youth.

Aligning with this approach, I propose that the engagement of male adolescents with music that emanates personal expressions of doubt, deliberation, and rebellion can be a wonderful safe space for processes of exploration. Creating, sharing, and discussing musical expressions of doubt and rebellion, and responding to them in performance, dance, and discussion, is perhaps less dangerous to religious structures than nonaesthetic actions along the same lines. Fisherman's work convinced me that such work is not only less dangerous, but actually positively constructive to the cultivation of an authentic Jewish spiritual identity.

When Sabbath Ends: Original Compositions of Alumni

I complied a final research report during the 2008–2009 school year, as our pilot study was ending and as I was taking my first steps into higher education and getting ready to leave this school. I submitted this report to the Department of Innovation in Israel Ministry of Education. It was approved but never published.[6] Seeking to endow the final report with the spirit of the study, I designed the presentation as a CD complied of original music composed by the musical high school *yeshiva* alumni.

One way to summarize Fisherman's model is to seek and develop ways for adolescents to experience a live, personal, and ongoing dialogue with

6   Ehrlich, 2011.

God. While working on my final research report, I used this formulation as a key question in an online survey that I sent to the school's alumni, which was followed by six narrative interviews. Rather than ask them if, sociologically speaking, they still considered themselves "religiously observant" or "Jewish Orthodox," I was more interested in their testimony of a relationship with God. The six alumni chosen for interviews each represented one cohort and were chosen for their willingness to share an originally composed recording of their music they had composed during their high school years.

Of the six original compositions, two were based on traditional Jewish texts: a piano-vocal soft rock rendition of *Psalms 23* "The Lord of my shepherd, I shall not want" and a progressive rock ensemble arrangement of texts from *Ecclesiastes*. Two other works were based on original texts and music in the singer-songwriter tradition; and the last two pieces were instrumental, close to the jazz-rock fusion style. Common to all the compositions was the notion of questions of faith, falling, and longing.

The themes explored in all six compositions became epitomized in one of the instrumental works entitled, *Motzei Shabbat*, or – in English – *When Shabbath Ends*. The composer of this rhapsody fusion style piece for electric guitar, soprano saxophone, electric bass, and drums, described his music as "an attempt to describe the spiritual fall that one experiences at the end of the holy day." The wailing guitar solo at the center of the work aimed to depict a soul struggling to hold on to sacred vibes as the special presence of God begins to diminish.

The composer of the *Ecclesiastes* texts described his music as an attempt to deliberate with notions of emptiness and futility that challenge faith. Interestingly, the intensity of doubt and deliberation experienced through this piece when performed at an end-of-year concert led a Ministry of Education official (from the Department of Jewish Religious Education) to question our educational choice to showcase this work. This response only strengthened our pride in the composition and its composer, as all the school staff, including teachers, music teachers, and Rabbis, fully agreed that this was exactly the kind of exploration we had hoped to inspire in students.

Negotiating the Sacred and the Secular

Whether setting traditional texts to new music, or writing original texts, all the composers described the act of composition as aspiring to create a personal expression of their inner dilemmas and feelings. One alumnus described having felt "an expectation embedded in the school atmosphere, not only to be musically creative, but to delve deep down and create something from my innermost emotional and spiritual consciousness." The two songs composed to original lyrics ("First Light" and "Pure") deal with the intensity of desire:

> First light raises, shines / From sparks of darkness I see / Light for a split second / My hand cannot reach it. / In prayer / I call for more / The thirst within me is burning. (First Light)

> Answer me, God / I call out to you / Longing for an answer / I kneel down on one knee / Show me the way to serve you in truth / So I can be free of sin, I will make it to the source / My heart will be pure. (Pure)[7]

The recurring themes of longing and desire are the focus of the *Psalms 23* setting and the addition instrumental piece entitled "Chesed Ilie," or "Exalted Grace." All of these works exhibit a negotiation between earthly experiences of longing and spiritual aspirations. God is addressed as a potential partner or companion in addition to being a source of grace and a savior. The intensity of desire echoes with possible undertones of the duality between human love relationships and spiritual communion, much in the spirit of the *Song of Songs'* biblical tone.

All of the alumni composers made at least some explicit reference to traditional Jewish religious texts in one way or another in their works. When asked about these references, one interviewee expressed a habit encouraged by the school's atmosphere "to maintain an open and on-going personal dialogue with traditional texts." The composer of "Pure" confessed that "traditional texts usually arouse in me more questions than answers – but

---

7   For the purpose of this chapter, I translated portions of these song lyrics from Hebrew to English.

that is exactly the point." Another alumnus described "the constant inter-action between external and internal, and never ending negotiation of how to hook-on to the spiritual in the secular world that we live in."

Personal Creativity and "Being Real"

Prominent in all the interviewees' narratives was the combination of their personal development in high school and musical creativity. One alumnus explained: "In order to create you have to mess around. For us this meant messing around with sound. The fact that we had pianos avail-able all the time allowed this to happen." Another composer confessed:

> The mix of emotions during puberty makes it difficult to make a clear statement. But being creative in a way forces you to take a stand. And that in itself kind of forces you to deal – to deal with life, to deal with issues.

There is something about the popular music culture that invites this kind of creativity without too much delay. While Western classical tra-ditions tend to place composition at the end of a long process of initial music education, popular music promotes an ethic of personal creativity in performance and provides spaces for on-the-spot improvisation. One of the interviewees described,

> The way we were engaged with pop rock and jazz was very stimulating – it was easy for us to relate the music to our own adolescence. We were busy growing up in those years, and the music we were engaged with made it explicit and put our own personal development on the table: it pushed us to be real.

Conclusions and Implications

The model presented and exemplified in this chapter is the retrospective summary of an action research field study. The development of the model

proceeded through cycles of observation, contemplation, and analysis
that were then interpreted into action, beginning a new cycle. As a group
teacher-research team, we were looking at what was happening in school
and assessing educational choices in light of our vision of creating a meaningful interaction between music as a school subject and the religious/
spiritual environment of the high school *yeshiva*. When we pinpointed
choices and actions that seemed to bring us closer to our goals, we focused on those choices and actions and found new ways to expand them.
Throughout the years, some things that seemed to happen by chance were
later constructively built into school structures.

The most significant revelation in this process came when we embraced
popular, rock, and jazz music as key factors in our educational enterprise.
This included a major shift from a former somewhat-apologetic approach
that prioritized Western classical aesthetics. Our understanding of values
of authenticity and deliberation, alongside the emergent abundance of
musical creativity these musical styles seemed to encourage, convinced us
to pursue this line of music education more purposefully.

Our pilot study concluded more than ten years ago, and I have since
left my position at that school in favor of higher education and academic
research. Much has changed, but some things remained constant. In addition to the boys' musical *yeshiva*, the school's leadership has opened a new
musical high school for religious girls. I have made efforts to present my
ideas to current teachers and new alumni, most of whom agree that the
basics of the SoD model resonate deeply with their school experiences.
Further research is still necessary to trace similarities and differences in
the girls' school.

It is now much easier to argue for arts and music education in Jewish
religious schools than it was in 2010. Likewise, the relationship between
popular music and Jewish religious authenticity seems to be more mainstream than ever. For two years running the top three popular choice awards
for musicians on Israeli Radio stations have included two Orthodox religiously observant singer-songwriters, whose music is appreciated by religious and secular audiences with no distinction.

In times like these it is perhaps plausible that other educational institutions may want to experiment with the SoD model. I believe many

institutions may already be doing so in their own ways (e.g., Nagan, 2014), and I imagine that a greater impact and deeper contemplation can be attained through an explicit awareness of the model and its components. More research needs to be done through and with this model which will surely challenge some of the assumptions I present, and may result in further enrichment of Jewish Israeli education and culture. I aim to engage educators and musicians who would dispute me – for how else, if not through deliberation and argument, can we keep moving?

Bibliography

Ammerman, N. T. (2013). Spiritual but not religious? Beyond binary choices in the study of religion. *Journal for the Scientific Study of Religion, 52*(2), 258–278. <https://doi.org/10.1111/jssr.12024>

Badarne, B., & Ehrlich, A. (2019). Dancing on the limits: An interreligious dialogue. In A. A. Kallio, P. Alperson, & H. Westerlund (Eds.), *Perspectives on music, education and religion: A critical inquiry* (pp. 262–272). Indiana University Press.

Bar Lev, M. (1982). HaYeshiva ha'tichonit u'meuravuta ba'chinuch ja'mamlachtu dati bi'Israel. [The high school yeshiva and its involvement in the religious state education system in Israel]. In M. Eliav & Y. Rephael (Eds.), *Sefer Ha'Shragai* [*The Shragai book – Chapters in national religious research and the immigration to the land of Israel*] (pp. 206–222). Mosad HaRav Kook.

Bennett, A. (2000). *Popular music and youth culture.* Red Globe Press.

Boyce-Tillman, J. (2016). *Experiencing music: Restoring the spiritual.* Peter Lang.

Carter, G. R. (2007). Learning together, living together. *Educational Leadership, 65*(2), 82–84.

Dunbar-Hall, P., & Wemyss, K. (2000). The effects of the study of popular music on music education. *International Journal of Music Education, 36*, 23–34. <https://doi.org/10.1177/025576140003600104>

Ehrlich, A. (2011). *The role of musical creative processes in spiritual struggles and challenges of National-Religious male adolescents*, Spoken paper, Challenges of Jewish Education Conference, at Bar Ilan University in Tel Aviv, January 2011.

Ehrlich, A. (2016). Dictating "diversity": A case of how language constructs policy in Israeli music education. *Finnish Journal of Music Education, 19*(2), 30–47.

Fisherman, S. (2002). Spiritual identity in Israeli religious male adolescents: Observations and educational implications. *Religious Education*, *97*(1), 61–79. <https://doi.org/10.1080/0034408802753595267>

Fisherman, S. (2004). Ego identity and spiritual identity in religiously observant adolescents in Israel. *Religious Education*, *99*(4), 371–384. <https://doi.org/10.1080/00344080490513090>

Fisherman, S. (2008). Identity and intimacy in religiously observant and non-religiously observant adolescents and young adults in Israel. *Religious Education*, *103*(5), 523–552. <https://doi.org/10.1080/00344080802427192>

Fisherman, S. (2016). Development of religious identity through doubts among religious adolescents in Israel: An empirical perspective and educational ramifications. *Religious Education*, *2*, 119–136. <https://doi.org/10.1080/00344087.2016.1107950>

Green, L. (2001). *How popular musicians learn: A way ahead for music education.* Ashgate.

Hebert, D. G., & Campbell, P. S. (2000). Rock music in American schools: Positions and practices since the 1960s. *International Journal of Music Education*, *36*(1), 14–22. <https://doi.org/10.1177/025576140003600103>

Imhoff, S. (2006). The spirit of the law: Spirituality in American Judaism. In C. H. Lippy (Ed.), *Faith in America: Changes, challenges, new directions* (pp. 63–84). Praeger.

Janoswki, B. (2013). *Arguing with God: A theological anthropology of the psalms.* Westminster John Knox Press.

Kepnes, S. (2011). Holiness: The unique form of Jewish spirituality. *Conversations*, *9*, 30–44.

Lane, B. C. (1986). Hutzpa k'lapei shamaya: A Christian response to the Jewish tradition of arguing with God. *Journal of Ecumenical Studies*, *23*(4), 567–586.

Laytner, A. H. (1990). *Arguing with God: A Jewish tradition.* Rowman & Littlefield.

Mcginn, B. (1993). Mysticism and sexuality. *The Way*, *77*, 46–54. <https://www.theway.org.uk/Back/s077McGinn.pdf>

Nagan, M. (2014). Kodesh vi'rock: Chinuch li'avoda pnimit vi'omek Emunah derech shirim yisreeliyim achshavi'im. [Sacred and rock: Education to internal work and depth of faith through contemporary Israeli songs.] In Y. N. Rimon (Ed.), *Torah vi'Avoda Uma Shebeineihem [Torah and work and what is between them]* (pp. 223–231). Etzion.

Powell, B., Smith, G. D., West, C., & Kratus, J. (2019). Popular music education: A call to action. *Music Educators Journal*, *106*(1), 21–24. <https://doi.org/10.1177/0027432119861528>

Regev, M. (1990). *Bo'ou shel ha'rock: Mashmaut, hitmodidut, u'mivne bi'sde hamusica hapopularit bi'Isreal. [The coming of rock: Meaning, coping, and structure on the field of popular music in Israel*]. [Unpublished doctoral dissertation, Tel Aviv University].

Regev, M. (1995). *Rock musica vi'tarbut [Rock music and culture]*. Dvir.

Regev, M. (2007). Tarbut popularit [Popular culture]. In Y. Yuval, Y. Tzaban, D. Shaham, D. Miron, & H. Hever (Eds.), *New Jewish time: Jewish culture in a secular age* (Vol. 3, pp. 181–185). Keter.

Rodriguez, C. X. (2004). *Bridging the gap: Popular music in music education*. MENC.

Semyonov, M., & Tyree, A. (1981). Community segregation and the costs of ethnic subordination. *Social Forces, 59*(3), 649–666.

Stahl, A. (1992). Who shall be religiously educated? The dilemma of Israeli religious state education. *Religious Education, 87*(1), 5–17.

van Niekerk, B. (2018). Religion and spirituality: What are the fundamental differences? *HTS Teologiese Studies/Theological Studies, 74*(3), Article 4933. <https://doi.org/10.4102/hts.v74i3.4933>

ESTELLE R. JORGENSEN

5 On Values and Life's Journey through Music

Reflections on the Eriksons' Life Stages and Music Education

The premise of this chapter is that the values that guide music educa-tion and the objectives and methods consistent with them should be tailored to people at each phase of life. Thinking of a theme, "Life's journey through music," I sketch different values that should guide music education throughout the adult phases of life proposed in Erik and Joan Erikson's psychosocial stage theory, namely, young adulthood, adulthood, old age, and gerotranscendence, respectively. Practical im-plications of the differing objectives and approaches commensurate with these values are suggested and a critique of the analysis is offered.

Erik and Joan Erikson (Erikson, 1980; Erikson & Erikson, 1982/1997) posit nine stages of life from birth to old age. Five of their stages focus on the early years from infancy to young adulthood that are the focus of music educational systems around the world; four describe the years from young adulthood that lie beyond the school age years. The Eriksons originally for-mulated eight life stages but Joan realized that they needed to describe yet another, gerotranscendence, and expanded their life stages from eight to nine. Their theory was developed in two phases. First, Erikson (1980) links the eight life stages – infancy, early childhood, play age, school age, ado-lescence, young adulthood, adulthood, and old age – to "basic strengths," or what I prefer to think of as values, of hope, will, purpose, competence, fidelity, love, care, and wisdom, respectively. Second, the ninth stage of gerotranscendence, added later by Joan (Erikson & Erikson, 1982/1997, p. 124), features a trio of values of grace, communion, and transcendence – a sense that one is "on holy ground."

My focus in this writing is on the Eriksons' four final stages, namely, young adulthood, adulthood, old age, and gerotranscendence. I sketch possible links between these life phases and the values that suggest differing purposes and approaches for music education throughout this part of life's journey and critique the analysis with reference to its usefulness for music education thought and practice focused on adults rather than children. The term "andragogy" was coined by Malcolm Knowles (Knowles et al., 2015) to focus on adult education in contrast to pedagogy that focused on children and youth. Rather than regarding andragogy and pedagogy as dichotomous, I prefer to think of a continuum stretching from pedagogy centered on the children and youth to andragogy focused on adults. Even then, pedagogy tends to homogenize the experience of infants, children, and youth, as andragogy tends to homogenize the educational experience of young, middle aged, and old adults. This categorical distinction between pedagogy and andragogy can be ameliorated by accounting for the various phases of life through which people pass and the related specific values (with their implicit objectives and approaches) that obtain at each phase of life (see, e.g., Overstreet, 1949; Cohen, 2005).

My own experience of life leaves me uncomfortable with describing life as a series of hard-and-fast, categorical stages, and the Eriksons do not see them this way. Rather, their stages are general and exploratory and dynamic rather than specific and definitive and static. These phases seem to flow from and merge with one another. I see these phases as ideal types in the sense that they offer archetypal characteristics of each phase (Jorgensen, 1997, p. 34). Their interest is not in atypical instances and they describe their phases at a high level of generality. People may arrive at or leave different phases earlier or later than others. They may never arrive at all phases. These phases serve a comparative purpose as general guideposts marking points throughout life and are described in terms of White people in the West. Since their analysis is framed by their White and Western heritage and experience, the examples I cite are consistent with their theory. Accordingly, I draw on typical rather than atypical instances of White, Western, working, and middle-class music education. The Eriksons are relatively silent on issues of culture, race, gender, social class, the differently gendered and abled, and I regard these problematics as lying beyond the focus of their theory. Accordingly, since I seek the common humanity that underlies significant societal differences in the ways in which age affects beliefs, values, and practices in music education, I sketch their theory employing examples consistent with it, and then move to a critique that accounts for complexities with which they do not grapple (Gaita, 2002; Yob & Jorgensen, 2020).

In reflecting on the Eriksons' life stages and music educational values, my focus is not upon those values that characterize professional musicians throughout a working lifetime because it is obvious that values such as artistry, skill, taste, and style will remain important throughout life. Rather, I am concerned in this writing with those music educational values that will be important to the great majority of people who, while they may be active musicians, regard music as an avocation and follow it for the love of it rather than out of the need to create and sustain a musical livelihood. Some of this public will be skilled musicians by the time they reach young adulthood; others may possess some or little skill as music makers. Whatever their level of skill and irrespective of the specific role music plays in their lives, all are likely to participate in music in some ways throughout their lives. Music educators desirous of enriching music's role in people's lives will be necessarily interested in the values that may be important throughout the adult phases of life's journey for this vast proportion of people. Here, I illustrate the various values and the ways in which values in music education may apply differently at each phase. Space prevents the more exhaustive goal of highlighting all the differing purposes and approaches to music education for those who may differ in terms of gender, race, ability, social class, gender identification, ethnicity, and musicality throughout adulthood.

I begin with the Eriksons' association of values with the phases of adulthood. They see four principal values – one corresponding to each phase of adulthood – as of overriding importance. They begin with the value of love in young adulthood as young people find a life partner and determine which passions they will pursue in their life work. In adulthood, they regard the value of care as of crucial importance during the time that people are bringing up their families and pursuing their careers. In old age, they underscore the value of wisdom as people are able to bring to bear the knowledge and experience they have acquired throughout their lives.

In gerotranscendence they value grace in the infirmity of the very old, the sense that things may begin to fall apart, and a growing closeness to their mortality.

In counterpoint with the Eriksons' quartet of values and associated stages, I see a different array of values for music education. For example, corresponding with the Eriksons' emphasis on love in young adulthood, I think of curiosity, imagination, desire, friendship, pleasure, loyalty, community, artistry, style, skill, and taste as among the prominent values in musical education, particularly in schools, colleges, and universities. During adulthood, in counterpoint with the Eriksons' value of care, I see values of happiness, joy, inclusion, community, restraint, dignity, spirituality, community, artistry, and skill that need to be evident in amateur musical organizations. In old age, parallel to the Eriksons' emphasis on the value of wisdom, I consider values of wisdom, spirituality, joy, energy, inclusion, and community in music education. And in gerotranscendence, in counterpoint with Joan Erikson's emphasis on grace, I see music educational values such as consolation, courage, equipoise, inclusion, hope, reverence, and community. With this overview in mind, I reflect on each of the Eriksons' life phases in turn.

Young Adulthood

The Eriksons see this period as a time in which love is a preeminent value in the minds of young people. They are finding mates, beginning in the world of work, finding places and homes in which to live, and in advanced societies, often completing their formal education in colleges, universities, and apprenticeships. Values of love, friendship, pleasure, and desire resonate especially at this phase. Particularly in formal education settings, values of artistry, acquiring a sense of style and taste, and polishing the artistic skills that they have already begun to acquire are important values. Within higher education, artistic and aesthetic values are compelling aspects of a broad liberal education, as they should also be in advanced vocational programs. The emphases on artistry, style, taste, and skill may differ, but artistic values need to be present in every educational setting.

By young adulthood, many have already developed inclinations toward differing art forms, but imaginative programs of study that enable students from a broad array of disciplines and academic, professional, and vocational interests to participate in music and broaden and deepen their interests are vital to a well-rounded education. I think, for example, of innovative musical subjects for study at Harvard University and ways in which this university seeks to ensure that students broadly come to know music in its many traditions and genres (Harvard Alumni Association, 2017). Building on the curiosity, imagination, and acquisition of knowledge at this point in life and making intersections between the fine and performing arts, humanities, and sciences, among other fields, are crucial for music education.

Instead of thinking just of elite and selective music courses and ensembles offered at educational institutions, informal and formal opportunities for participating in music within colleges, religious institutions, commercial enterprises, and families and communities are also important (Jorgensen, 1997). These institutions offer important opportunities for music educators to foster musical and social experiences for young adults. Many young people are particularly interested in the musics of our time, and opportunities to engage these immediate impulses and interests need to be abundant. In a time of globalization, it is also critical that young adults participate in the traditional musics of their places so that these diverse local and regional practices are conserved and thrive. Young adults have choices in the ways they participate musically, therefore, the onus on music educators is to present relevant and attractive opportunities that meet the musical, social, and psychological needs at this point in life.

Adulthood

For the Eriksons, adulthood is a period of procreativity where care constitutes a compelling value. At this point, attention turns to home and family, earning a livelihood, and making one's way in the world. Family members are committed to caring for young and old alike and hopefully seeing their children grow into adulthood. For those without children of their own, there are familial ties to other relatives who also need affection and care. Work also constitutes an important focus during this period, and the claims of work or the want of it impacts one's livelihood and sense of wellbeing, identity, and self-worth. Surviving or thriving is dependent in large measure on being able to successfully navigate work and family life. For much of history, women's activities have been prescribed by the need to care for the home and the family members and raise much of the food for the family. Today, women's participation in the world of paid work may be equally challenging where home work also continues as it did before (e.g., Azcona et al., 2020). In too many places, the absence of work, especially industrial work for men, places even greater strains on families and on the relationship between men and women (e.g., Broman et al., 1996).

At this point in life, music offers places and times to be, at least temporarily, free from care. Values of happiness, joy, inclusion, and a sense of community are particularly compelling in their appeal to adults who seek respite from the sense of care that often weighs upon them. Among the historical examples of amateur musical organizations that seek to be a source of joy and happiness, I think of the Welsh choirs comprised of coal miners, the amateur choral organizations of the English midlands comprised of working people, the working people's singing schools in France and in New England and Appalachia (Keene, 2009; Rainbow & Cox, 2006). Singing is a particularly apt vehicle of musical expression because the human voice provides an opportunity for immediate self-expression. Still, the amateur bands and orchestras established throughout North America, Australasia, and Europe are important alternatives. I mention inclusion and community because adults enjoy the sense of belonging and the opportunity to achieve immediate musical results, especially where work is too often competitive, repetitive, and, especially following the advent of online employment, solitary.

Throughout adulthood, there is a desire for spirituality, artistry, and additional skill. For this reason, the amateur singing movements of the nineteenth and twentieth centuries were populated by adults who sought additional knowledge and skill and were led by musicians with an understanding of how to create a communal artistry that was deeply moving to participants. This is still the case in the twenty-first century, and music educators are needed to foster ensembles and informal learning opportunities that enable individuals to be part of something magical and greater and larger than themselves. These experiences are possible in community, musical, religious, political, and commercial settings.

Old Age

The Eriksons see old age as a phase characterized by the value of wisdom. In the best of worlds, wisdom derives from the capacity to integrate prior life experience into a unity. I see their emphasis on wisdom as profoundly optimistic. In societies that revere the aged, the presumption that people who have lived long lives are in the position to have learned from their experience leads their youngers to value their insights and perspectives. At least, we would hope that they would have acquired wisdom. Maybe this hope makes us disappointed to encounter foolishness in those who are not suffering dementia and should know better. Technology has helped to both lengthen life and increase the possibility of mental decline and dementia in some parts of the world. Still, many people are living in good health and continuing to make contributions to society well into old age. It ought to be the objective of music educators to take advantage of the many opportunities to involve the old in music-making and taking (e.g., Creech et al., 2013). For example, doing so is the objective of the New Horizons International Music Association (2020) and choruses in American retirement centers, and in the music-making opportunities in the civic centers I saw in China with elders playing traditional Chinese instruments and taking group dancing lessons.

Regarding the values that need to obtain at this point in life, my sense is that while optimistic, wisdom is an important value in enabling elders to integrate their life's musical experiences. This is a time for effecting closure and integration in life. By closure, I do not mean closed-mindedness. Rather,

I refer to completing a circle of life that validates one's past musical interests. For those who are fortunate, retirement offers an opportunity to take up musical pursuits that had to be laid aside earlier in life for want of time or opportunity. I have met many in their 60s, 70s, and 80s who have rejoined choirs, taken up instruments they played early in life, pursued new musical interests, taken music classes at their community colleges and universities, and traveled to other countries with music as the focus of their interest. Joy, the energy that is derived from making music, inclusion that invites people into a musical group, and community and the attendant sense of belonging become especially important at times when elders may otherwise be lonely or discouraged. Old age is not for the faint hearted, and with a growing sense of one's mortality, spirituality rather than religiosity is particularly important. Watching choirs of elders whose faces light up as they sing reminds me of the ways in which making music that highlights these values can directly meet the needs of this age group. At this point in life, since there is less of it left than has been lived, using one's time to best advantage is especially important. Musical education for old age should present as an attractive and social opportunity that is thoroughly enjoyable and stimulating.

Gerotranscendence

I have yet to live into this stage, so I have Joan Erikson's ideas in mind as I contemplate the values that seem particularly apropos to this life phase. I also draw on my memory of the many occasions when, as a young musician, I performed in care facilities for the aged, nursing homes, and retirement centers. As Joan puts it, "At ninety the vistas changed; the view ahead became limited and unclear. Death's door, which we always knew was expectable but had taken in stride, now seemed just down the block" (Erikson & Erikson, 1982/1997, p. 4). Things began to fall apart. This is a time when more people need assistance in living their lives and nursing care. One might hope to "live long and die short," and while some might live in excellent health until shortly before death, the last stage of life often requires the help of others. The deaths of spouses, family members, and close friends are distressing, as is the increasing awareness of physical frailty. It is understandable when the very old withdraw into a comfort of smaller and more intimate spaces that seem to be cocoons offering warmth and safety. At this point, death looms closer as does the spiritual world of mind, memory, and possibility. One remains the person one has been only more so. In memory's eye, I see my aunt, in her 100th year, listening raptly to music, happy with her lot at a retirement home, playing the piano for her fellow residents, and being a source of inspiration to family, friends, and the residence staff. Despite strokes and falls, she remains eager for what life offers, and her habitual optimistic attitude sustains her now that her world has shrunken.

Joan Erikson (Erikson & Erikson, 1982/1997) notices the grace and transcendence in the very old. Although bodies and minds may betray them, they somehow rise above their physical limitations to exult and find solace in the memory of times past and people they treasured. I wish to add to Joan's values, those of consolation, courage, equipoise, inclusion, hope, and reverence. Contemplating one's imminent death, as I have known elders to do, requires the consolation of finding joy amidst memory of a life lived, courage to face the existential angst of contemplating "ceasing to be" in this life, equipoise to find a steadiness and balance of mind, soul, and body, inclusion in the accessibility of musical experience to all in this situation, hope in the religious faith or philosophy to which one adheres, reverence in the bittersweetness and preciousness of this present moment, and community in knowing that one is not alone but is valued and understood by others who share one's experience. Music needs to be a vital part of experience at this phase of life. Singing the songs that one knew in the past and evoking individual and shared memories is very important. The texts of songs need to be hopeful, spiritual, and evocative.

Hearing music, even if one is unable to play or sing, positively affects the mind, soul, and body in ways that contribute to wellbeing (e.g., Creech et al., 2013; Lehmberg & Fung, 2010; Tabei et al., 2017). I can never forget a dying woman surrounded by her family and close friends who, in one of her last sentient moments, requested that we sing some well-known songs. Playing the piano for the family who sought to sing while she lay mouthing the words brought tears to our eyes. I was never so grateful for the ability to improvise and play as when I led the singing that day. Music needs to be a part of every hospice and place where people are dying. We should remember its therapeutic value, especially for the very old, and its consolation to the dying and those who are dear to them.

Critique

Notwithstanding the beguiling simplicity and clarity of this four-stage model with its associated music educational values and policy implications at each life phase, things are not this simple. As I have noted, the Eriksons were untroubled by the complexities of cultural distinctions both in terms of how age is viewed and practiced from young adulthood to adulthood, old age, and gerotranscendence and in the differing experiences of women, minorities, the differently abled and gendered, the homeless and dispossessed, the immigrants and strangers at every stage of adulthood. These difficulties are also compounded by the fact that my examples at each stage do not encompass all the differing musical cultures and experiences of music education. This is the case especially in young adulthood where for many young people around the world, this phase is compressed, and they move into the world of work at a very young age. I think of a family of brickmakers in Cambodia beside the Mekong with whom I visited: Every able-bodied child is put to work in the family's operation. For too many young people, apprenticeships and tertiary educational opportunities are worlds apart, they marry at an early age, and their lives are consumed by care from childhood. Since the values I have sketched are parasitic on the Eriksons' life stages, aside from a short period around puberty, young adulthood as the Eriksons see it may be almost non-existent. The same may also be true of experiences of Western music education that cannot pretend to encompass every musical tradition in the West let alone the entire world.

Although my examples may be valid and important when seen through Western and White eyes, it is important to also acknowledge the limits of one's experience and invite different others to describe how, in their cultures and societies, these life phases would be exemplified in music educational values. Although I have seen adults in Asia, Africa, Australia, Europe, and South America experience music education in some of the self-same ways I have described, I have also seen important differences. For this reason, the perspectives from these other musical cultures and societies are needed in conversations about the intersections between values, music education, and the various phases of adulthood. Although I have lived much of my musical life within the classical tradition of the West, I have seen many synergies and consonances between this tradition and other classical and vernacular traditions. Nevertheless, exponents of other musical traditions need to articulate the differing insights they bring to how values, music, and the stages of adulthood should intersect. These conversations can highlight the complexities of intersections between values, life stages, and music education, enable musician-educators around the world to listen to the differing yet authentic experiences of others, and contribute to the richness and variety of adult music education around the world.

The broad and catholic approach I am advocating resonates with what Deanne Bogdan (2020) calls a "situated sensibility." This approach acknowledges that one's perspectives are necessarily framed by specific situations. One may write authentically about one's values, experience, and expertise but there are limits beyond which one should not go in seeking to shape the values that others hold. While there may be broad generalizations on which people may agree, there are also important specific distinctions. Practically speaking, musicians and educators need to be guided by the claims of the specific situations in which they find themselves.

In seeking differences, it is possible to fall into stereotyping people and failing to grasp important nuances. This realization came home to me while on a life-changing trip to China. I had previously thought of the elders in China as being held in high esteem, possibly higher than was the case in the West. The reality was quite shocking when we toured places with concentrations of elders isolated by distance from younger members of their families. After the onset of COVID-19, I began to understand something of how they may have felt this isolation. Like these Chinese elders who felt warehoused in places alien to them, separated from their younger family members, I realized that too many Americans were willing to isolate their elders to get back to the lives they wanted to live. I began to grasp that this sense of isolation may be common to Chinese and American elders – much more so than I thought beforehand. Likewise, realities of high unemployment among young adults and adults around the world may differ significantly from one race and culture to another. Still, the experience of poverty, lack of self-worth, and anger at those with wealth unites those who undergo it. While these life phases and their associated music educational values may be manifested in differing circumstances, nevertheless there are common threads that bind us together as members of the human family. So, it is crucial to think of these phases and values generously, inclusively, and to avoid drawing narrow distinctions on the one hand and overgeneralizing or stereotyping them on the other.

It is also important to carefully examine psychological and educational tendencies to sort human beings and draw distinctions between them in terms of such things as age, gender, social class, intelligence, and musicality. Julia Koza (2021) excavates the historical linkage between White supremacist and eugenicist movements and music education. Such thinking has penetrated music educational ideology in North America and elsewhere to the detriment of an egalitarian and inclusive approach to music education. Importantly, linkages between race and gender privileged white males and devalued women and girls and other minorities. Music education's construal to focus on childhood and young adulthood marginalizes or excludes those not yet of school age or those who are beyond it. Sorting people into age categories turns out to be a blessing and a curse. On the one hand, by highlighting the extent to which music educators have ignored adult music education, it may prompt a redefinition of music education as a "lifelong" enterprise. Expanding the notion of music education to a lifelong enterprise multiplies the challenges for music education and complicates its *raison d'être*. On the other hand, it may be tempting for some to double down on a narrow construal of music education as school music and regard musical education in the rest of life as something else, for example, community music. Intersections of race, class, gender, among the other differences among people, may only exacerbate the privileging of some and the marginalization or exclusion of others.

Notwithstanding these important caveats to the Eriksons' theory and the implications for music educational values and practices that I have sketched, it is worth rescuing the central claims of the Eriksons' view of life as unfolding in phases. By taking account of the differences through adulthood, it is useful to tailor the aims and methods of music education to the compelling interests and values likely to resonate at each phase. Putting this theory to the test by including multiple gendered, racialized, and cultural perspectives can enrich the theory. This comparative approach can forward a broad view of music educational values, beliefs, and practices that is truly lifelong and inclusive.

Life's journey needs to be full of music from beginning to end. Music has an important place from birth to death, on formal and informal occasions, through joy and sadness, in privilege and deprivation, and in war and peace. Expanding our sights as musicians and teachers beyond the school age years to adulthood enables us to take advantage of the rich possibilities of andragogy as well as pedagogy and to grasp music's vital place in the whole of life rather than as a decontextualized object of study in schools. Our role is to preserve, foster, and transform music and its publics and ensure that we attend carefully to every phase of life's journey. In so doing, as we touch and enrich the lives of all with whom we make and take music, we help to create a more humane society. We effect positive social change and leave the world a better place for our being here.

Bibliography

Azcona, G., Bhatt, A., & Love, K. (2020, July 9). *Ipsos survey confirms that COVID-19 is intensifying women's workload at home*. UN Women. <https://data.unwomen.org/features/ipsos-survey-confirms-covid-19-intensifying-womens-workload-home>

Bogdan, D. (2020). Dissociation/reintegration of literary/musical sensibility. In I. M. Yob & E. R. Jorgensen (Eds.), *Humane music education for the common good* (pp. 232–247). Indiana University Press.

Broman, C., Hamilton, V. L., & Hoffman, W. S. (1996, Winter). The impact of un-employment on families. *Michigan Family Review*, *2*(2), 83–91. <http://dx.doi.org/10.3998/mfr.4919087.0002.207>

Cohen, G. D. (2005). *The mature mind: The positive power of the aging brain.* Basic Books.

Creech, A., Hallam, S., McQueen, H., & Varvarigou, M. (2013). The power of music in the lives of older adults. *Research Studies in Music Education*, *35*(1), 87–102. <https://doi.org/10.1177%2F1321103X13478862>

Erikson, E. H. (1980). *Identity and the life cycle.* W. W. Norton.

Erikson. E. H., & Erikson, J. M. (1982/1997). *The life cycle completed (extended version).* W. W. Norton.

Gaita, R. (2002). *A common humanity: Thinking about love and truth and justice* (2nd ed.). Routledge.

Harvard Alumni Association. (2017, September 15–16). *Question + Create: A Harvard alumni gathering on the arts.* Harvard University.

Jorgensen, E. R. (1997). *In search of music education.* University of Illinois Press.

Keene, J. A. (2009). *A history of music education in the United States* (2nd ed.). Glenbridge.

Knowles, M. S., Holton III, E. F., & Swanson, R. A. (2015). *The adult learner: The definitive classic in adult education and human resource development* (8th ed.). Routledge.

Koza, J. E. (2021). *"Destined to fail": Carl Seashore's world of eugenics, psychology, education, and music.* University of Michigan Press.

Lehmberg, L. J., & Fung, C. V. (2010). Benefits of music participation for senior citizens: A review of the literature. *Music Education Research International*, *4*, 19–30. <http://cmer.arts.usf.edu/content/articlefiles/3122-MERI04pp.19-30.pdf>

New Horizons International Music Association. (2020). Concept and philosophy. <https://newhorizonsmusic.org/Concept_and_Philosophy>

Overstreet, H. A. (1949). *The mature mind.* W. W. Norton.

Rainbow, B., & Cox, G. (2006). *Music in educational thought and practice: A survey from 800 BC* (2nd ed.). Boydell Press.

Tabei, K., Satoh, M., Ogawa, J., Tokita, T., Nakaguchi, N., Nakao, K., Kida, H., & Tomimoto, H. (2017, June 7). Physical exercise with music reduced gray and white matter loss in the frontal cortex of elderly people: The Mihama-Kiho scan project. *Frontiers in Aging Neuroscience.* <https://doi.org/10.3389/fnagi.2017.00174>

Yob, I. M., & Jorgensen, E. R. (Eds.) (2020). *Humane music education for the common good.* Indiana University Press.

PART II

Authentic Connection and Wellbeing

DEBORAH J. SAIDEL

6 A Pathway to Wellbeing

Transcending a Compensatory History of Women in Music

I believe that generating descriptions about prehistoric women's sonic experiences and sharing them with others begins to innovatively address the lack of a women-centric music tradition that is situated within deep history: a tradition that provides a spiritually based connectivity across time and place, a tradition that provides a unique pathway to wellbeing. To immediately clarify, the terms "women" or "woman" are to be understood as pragmatic writing tools that do not automatically refer to an abstract universal or one biological sex, but rather, to a spectrum of possibilities. My motivation for engaging with this topic stems from my own years of spirit injury that I experienced throughout most of my professional musical training where I found that many tacit normative customs endure despite their ensuing toxic consequences. I have also witnessed this spirit injury in my young female (and male) university students as well.

In my doctoral thesis, *Women in Music: Letting a Long Story Be Long, Contemplating Women's Sonic, Musical, and Spiritual Experiences in Prehistory*, the wellspring of this chapter, I explore the auditory and spiritual lives of Paleolithic women (Saidel, 2018). I consider their agency in mediating the spiritual power of sound and how doing so contributes to a multifaceted musicality, one that reorients the framework of the narrative of women in music. It makes it possible to rethink how music history is investigated and interpreted, to explore what a more inclusive music history narrative might be, what it might look and sound like. It also makes it possible to integrate notions of spirituality into the entire women-in-music discourse.

Working on my dissertation certainly moved me toward my academic goal of earning a Ph.D. degree, but additionally it was simultaneously an unanticipated pathway to my overall wellbeing. The research that I conducted facilitated a spiritual healing for me, in part, by allowing me to tell the story about the evolution of my spiritual approach to musicianship, along with my growing feminist awareness of the androcentric hierarchy in academic music. I also discovered that by choosing to investigate the discipline of sound studies and consequently to integrate its perspectives into a depiction of likely experiences of prehistoric women, that I had truly entered exciting and uncharted territory. With the passing of time, the lens of hindsight has facilitated deeper insights into the wisdom of my research choices. Because of where my research eventually led me, along with feedback from colleagues and students, I concluded that broadening the parameters of musical experiences (by including sonic experiences) did resonate with others and could stimulate dialogues about alternative approaches to historical narratives regarding women in music, all of which has been personally empowering.

Western scholars have constructed a narrative of historical musicology whose narrow focus is both androcentric and Eurocentric, a focus in which musical participation by women is rarely sufficiently documented or included. I observed that the transfer of existing musicological methodologies onto the experiences of women has not been authentically transformative or empowering for women in music. Moreover, compensatory historical writing is the most common approach to women's history, which could be viewed as a form of making amends for generally leaving women out of the writing of history. I argue that although women have become aware of some of their musical past, it is truly not a musical *heritage* because compensatory scholarship creates an awareness of some of women's musical past but does not necessarily create an awareness of women in music history on their own terms. It usually features biographical material lauding extraordinary women's accomplishments and provides information about women that are chosen because *they had done what men had done.* They then can be added to the existing narrative, a hegemonic narrative that remains preoccupied with the experiences of men.

My interdisciplinary project is broad in scope. Within its theoretical framework I grapple with a gamut of topics, from ways of rethinking the writing of history and reckoning with time, to sound studies and the study of acoustics in ancient sites, to a critical examination through a feminist lens of normative disciplinary scholarship in anthropology and archeology (including rock art), religious studies, and musicology. I explore potential audio-visual-lithic relationships for their implications for deepening an understanding of the spiritual aspects of Paleolithic life. Many experiential aspects overlap and are often enmeshed. Through integrative discussions I was able to describe a plausible matrix of Paleolithic women's sonic, musical, and spiritual experiences by constructing a heterarchical network. In this present chapter, which is about formulating an alternative historical portrayal of women in music as a pathway to wellbeing, the primary connective topical thread consists of theorizing Paleolithic audio-visual-lithic relationships via the discipline of sound studies, and then linking them to a gynocentric notion of ancient spirituality.

What attracted me to thinking about women in prehistory is the fact that prehistory constitutes such an immense span of time of people living on this planet. I marveled at how (for the most part) this vast segment of humanity is shunned by the contemporary world, as if they were not real people, which could be referred to as "temporally othering" them. In contrast, my research negotiated the tension of considering our predecessors in the distant past as complex individuals who were situated in a multitude of relationships as I simultaneously emphasized trends and processes more than particular events and persons. Idealistically, I initially wanted uncluttered discursive space free and clear of the strife of how the patriarchy came about or its consequences for women, free from the complexities of reactions to the patriarchy, and a space within which to challenge the uncritical formulation of simplistic popular narratives about prehistoric people. I learned that rather than homogenizing the cultures and lifestyles of the first human populations, one can expect degrees of variation across time and place and by extension, degrees of variation in women's activities and the meaning they assigned to them.

The Paleolithic world I am referring to is archaeologically based on stone tool cultures. Specifically, the Paleolithic Age falls within the same timeframe as the Pleistocene, which is geologically based on the repeating cycles of glaciation (or Ice Ages) during this time, referring to the epoch spanning from roughly 2.6 million years ago to about 12,000 years ago. The Upper Paleolithic (c. 40,000–c. 10,000 years ago), ending when the Ice Age ended and as agriculture began taking over, is the approximate timeframe under discussion. This chronological framework allows me to direct my focus onto the lifeways of foragers, onto spirituality situated within an animistic cosmology rather than one with formal gendered deities, and I also chose this time period because cave art production increased with an apparent uptick in both quantity and diversity (Conkey, 1985).

Bounteous Sound Studies

According to Nordic music archaeologist Cajsa S. Lund (2008), Homo sapiens have continued to relate to their sound environments in consistently similar ways for 40,000 years (p. 17). In other words, even though the content, context, and culturally mediated meanings that our ancestors constructed may differ from those of today's world, much of the human process of sonically knowing and being in one's world is remarkably similar. Moreover, the notion that sounds of an ancient place may have been part of its purpose and meaning is gaining momentum.

The field of sound studies is a research area which explores the nature of sound and listening, and their role in experience and perception. From a sound studies perspective, music is regarded as but *one sonic phenomenon among many*. Hence, a sound studies perspective can develop an aural connection to earlier generations that includes everyday sounds. Critical aspects of social and cultural life emerge by paying attention to sonic phenomena that could be overlooked in traditional, visually oriented historical writing. Notions of the acoustic environment can provide insight into the aural aesthetics and musicality expressed by people in prehistoric times.

Because of the breadth of the disciplinary roots of sound studies, the research and methodological approaches engaged in by sonically focused scholars vary greatly. Many sound studies scholars' approaches are situated within a cultural anthropological paradigm, whereas others pursue traditional scientific technological studies. Technical advances and new analytical techniques have enabled scholars to effectively apply their findings to both ancient and current societies. Potential discursive trajectories that focus on either what is heard, or how or where it is heard, can become aspects of a more nuanced narrative about the meanings of the auditory lives of people in the distant past, and by implication, about the spiritual or musical lives of these people.

Auditory archeology is a field of sound studies inquiry that considers the potential of everyday, mundane, and unintentional sounds in the past, and how these may have been significant to people. The approaches to the study of sound within auditory archeology have fostered a range of multi-valent interpretations. Psychologist Alfred Bregman (1994 as cited in Mills, 2014) coined "auditory scene analysis," which is a concept that represents or refers to all the sounds a person can hear at a given time or place. It considers how sound is encoded with information about the world. The concept of a "sonic fabric" posits that places have a sonic fabric or texture which can be used to describe their auditory content. This approach creates a way of thinking about how people come to live in ways specific to their surroundings, how they engage with their world, which is helpful in contemplating the lived experiences of people in prehistory.

Music archeology is a field that has emerged from the intersection of the interests of the traditional disciplines of archeology, musicology, and ethnomusicology, homing in on the musicality of ancient societies. Music archeology was greatly impacted by the digital revolution, with digital technology fostering a new set of possibilities, especially by radically changing the field of acoustics. "New approaches to the analysis of sound transformed fieldwork which allowed researchers to carry out experiments that mixed music archaeology with acoustics, resulting in a new field that was dubbed archaeoacoustics" (Eneix, 2014, p. 24).

Archaeoacoustics has been described as the study of past sounds reconstructing past existence. It is an interdisciplinary field that has no uniform or generally accepted theories, methodologies, or data. Archaeoacoustic evidence for the ancient use of sound in sacred monuments and other sites has been documented, revealing that the use of sound was far more widespread than previously estimated. The researchers work from the premise that ancient people must have noticed the sound effects of these places. Portable digital technology has allowed acoustic experiments to more readily enter the field. Acoustic fingerprints can be created using a "sine sweep" that records the response of the space to sounds, and it has been discovered that images in Paleolithic caves correspond to areas with the greatest resonance. This suggests to several researchers that Paleolithic people were coordinating the sonic and visual aspects of the caves (Eneix, 2014).

Connecting Sound to Prehistoric Visual Artifacts

At this juncture I am introducing audio-visual-lithic relationship highlights pertaining to prehistoric art as proposed by three eminent archeoacoustic scholars: Iegor Reznikoff, Paul Devereux, and Steve Waller. They have been selected because each one of them has significantly contributed to both the quantitative and qualitative knowledge base concerning sound in very ancient sites.

Iegor Reznikoff is credited with being one of the founders of the field of Archaeoacoustics and is well known for his 1988 pioneering work in collaboration with Michel Dauvois. The duo studied three caves in the Ariege department at the foot of the Pyrenees where they were able to describe a complex acoustic network by documenting a noticeable correspondence between the points of resonance and the locations of paintings within the caves (Till, as cited in Eneix, 2014). These scholars introduced the practice of looking at the entire lithic structure as a sonic production device.

Specifically within the context of cognitive archeology, Paul Devereux (2001) investigates whether it is possible to actually hear what Stone Age people heard. Drawing from quantitative data, he considers possible correlations between the visual artifacts that are embedded in structural rock surfaces, ritual times, and the acoustics of the environment. Devereux explored

locations in England, Ireland, France, Spain, and Central America that included various rock formations such as: caves, cliffs, megalithic chambered
mounds, chambered barrows, exposed slabs of dolmen situated on a ridge,
Irish stone mounds known as cairns, and recumbent stone circles. He writes
about the spiritual implications of sounds (including infrasound waves or
silent sound) and how they can affect humans. Devereux describes possible ritualized events where sound serves in a complex array of important
functions, illustrating the frequent association of unusual sounds with the
presence of spirits. He suggests that the most basic musical sounds would
have been percussive ones, naturally occurring when rocks and stones were
struck. They are known as "ringing rocks," sounding most closely at times
like either bells or drums, and "evidence of their ancient usage is usually
found in the form of 'chatter marks' or 'cupules', which are small cup-like
depressions created by repeated and carefully aimed striking of the rock's
surface with a hammerstone" (p. 119).

Devereux also writes about ringing rock-research that has been conducted by others such as an investigation of the Preseli Hills in Brittany by
Bernard Fagg in the 1950s, where Fagg found two massive rock-gongs in
one of the villages called Maenclochog (Ringing Rocks). Belgian archeologist Lya Dams (1985) conducted a detailed study of the musical features of
stalactites, which came to be known as lithophones (any of a class of percussion instruments that are made of stone and whose sound is produced
by striking). Devereux posits that the cave lithophones are compelling
evidence of intentionally created sounds by Paleolithic people, and that
the places where sounds issued from were regarded as holy.

Archeologist Steve Waller's direct experience of powerful echoes eman-
ating from a cave in France during the 1980s, in answer to sounds made
outside of it, was the beginning of his research in which he investigates the
relationships between the echoes of rock structures and their images and
mythology. He initially experimented with single percussive sounds and
subjectively judged their characteristics. While doing so "he discovered
that when rocks are struck together in the manner of one making stone
tools, the echoes sound remarkably like the hoof beats of galloping horses"
(Devereux, 2001, p. 113). For Waller, this auditory discovery provided a link
between the context and the content of the art.

Waller (2014) eventually formalized an acoustic theory of rock-art motivation in which he referred to rock art as acoustic images. Depictions in the caves are mostly of animals, and he found that rock-art panels of hoofed animals produced the highest decibel levels of reflected sound, the most intense reverberations, whereas unpainted surfaces tended to be flat. Where there were mirror-image mammoths facing one another or two back-to-back images of bison, Waller found echoes to be stereophonically symmetrical with identical sound reflection in each direction. While standing very close to a painted cave wall, Waller inadvertently discovered that his loud yelling instantly rebounded back with such force that it seemed as if the person depicted in the nearby rock wall painting was actually talking to him. He states:

> Echo myths around the world attest to the belief that sound reflection was perceived as spirits calling out from rocks, an example of animism. Just as virtual images appear deep within a mirror due to light waves bending, virtual acoustic images can seem to emanate sound from deep within a rock wall due to sound waves bouncing ... The rock art is located at locations with the strongest echoes and there are legends associated with rock art describing supernatural portals through the rock from which sound can be heard to emanate. (Waller, as cited in Eneix, p. 100)

Waller argued that it was plausible to consider that perhaps the art was an attempt to depict the spirits and animals responsible for the magical sounds at these acoustic hotspots.

Reznikoff, Devereux, and Waller combined data from the scientific study of sound waves with their personal experiences of interacting with stone structures through sound which provided both quantitative and qualitative evidence for their association of acoustics with rock art. Although some of their work focused on Neolithic sites, their observations and interpretations hold implications for thinking about the experiences of Paleolithic people. I began to envision Paleolithic people seeking magical or spirit-haunted resonant places for paintings as they mapped out complex acoustic networks.

Archaeoacoustics offers a fresh take on the difficult issue of being able to discern intentionality, making it possible for the diverse activities that comprise prehistoric art to be understood not only contextually (in a vast continuum of cultural and historical specifics), but *as context*. They are contexts in which the auditory sense and visual experience of the landscape combine in a vital interplay, becoming transmitters of different kinds of spiritual wisdom. "Whether visual or auditory, the underlying sense seems to have been that rock surfaces were regarded as the interface between the physical and spiritual worlds" (Devereux, 2001, p. 150). When sonic phenomena is integrated into rock art interpretation, another important dimension for thinking about ancient spirituality/cosmologies emerges, and by implication, ancient musicality.

Notions of Paleolithic Spirituality as Sonic Experiences

Christina Puchalski, MD, Director of the George Washington Institute for Spirituality and Health, contends that "spirituality is the aspect of humanity that refers to the way individuals seek and express meaning and purpose and the way they experience their connectedness to the moment, to self, to others, to nature, and to the significant or sacred" (University of Minnesota, 2016, para. 3). Puchalski's description of spirituality is deeply attuned to how I regard spirituality, and therefore, I offer hers as a working definition for the discussion at hand. Since the late-1800s the spiritual practices of Paleolithic people have been theoretically linked by Western researchers to the painted or engraved images found on the walls of caves, cliffs, megaliths, and open-air sanctuaries (parietal art). However, scholarly focus on the acoustic environment or soundscape of such sites is a much more recent endeavor. Indeed, there are a plethora of theoretical orientations to consider when contemplating Paleolithic spiritual practices. In the third chapter of my dissertation, "Paleolithic Spiritual Practices," where I create a conceptual space for contingency, specificity along with broad patterns, and diversity in ancient lifeways, I explore potential audio-visual-lithic relationships. I do this by systematically introducing the previously discussed disciplines of sound studies and archaeoacoustics and their respective contributions in much more depth, then I address the concepts of musicality and ritual, before turning to a discussion of the visual components. However, my intention here is not to rehash my dissertation, but rather to draw from it as a springboard to talk about spiritual aspects of life experiences of Paleolithic women, depictions situated within lifeways that emerge from a synthesis of meticulously researched disciplinary threads.

I think the fundamental centerpiece for women's culturally specific expressive or meaning-making practices in prehistory lies in the functional aspects of their daily activities, which were influenced by their circadian rhythms. Speaking here in broad terms or trends, specific sonic events per se need not to have been highly organized, but rather, sound-production and sound-interpretation were intrinsically and spontaneously part of their world, often crucial to physical survival. Paleolithic women's expressive practices likely consisted of (but were not limited to) vocal and percussive accompaniment to walking, foraging, pre-hunting rituals and hunting, hygiene regimens, making tools, painting and engraving images on rock surfaces, child-directed prosody, selection of sexual partners, rites of passage, preparation of food, and caring for the dead. Objects incorporated into sound-production (which may also be categorized as music-making) could be made from leaves, sticks, vines, stones, tree trunks, reeds, bark, gourds and seeds, shells, stalactites or ice, and bones. Paleolithic women also possibly imitated the sounds they heard in their environments, which could have emanated from animals and insects or sounds such as flowing water or the effects of the wind. They interacted with their soundscapes and used the sounds they heard; their lives were also shaped by them.

Attitudes to sound are culturally and historically specific and David Tame (1984) argues that "the further we go back in history, the more sacred and vital the significance we find to have been attached to the phenomenon of sound itself" (p. 13). Tame's comment is highly relevant when thinking about the spirituality of prehistoric people, to considering what its characteristics might be. Animism, which is an anthropological construct, denotes a worldview in which people do not see themselves as separate from their environment, an environment that is considered to be sustained by an endless circulation of a distinctive spiritual energy or essence with which humans engage. Moreover, every object, place, physical element of landscapes, type of creature, weather system, climate, and, yes, sound, is considered to be spiritually alive. As previously described, many ancient cultures considered the blurred reverberations of percussive sounds within caves to come from supernatural beings and also attributed powerful magic to the very loud natural thunderous sounds in the sky. People in prehistory considered humanly produced sound capable of directly affecting changes in their world, as having authority to influence events and people.

Today's scholars widely accept animism as the ubiquitous ancestral mode of experience, and it is also widely accepted that an enduring thread of humanity's oldest spiritual traditions seems to lie in the animistic-based shamanic paradigm. A shaman is an anthropological term for a person who acts as intermediary between the natural and supernatural worlds and whose primary concern is to heal and maintain the spiritual balance within the community. Thomas DuBois (2009) writes about how music/sound functions as it serves both the practitioner and community within the shamanic paradigm. He points out that music/sound is a key tool employed by shamans in order to enter trance states, and it is a medium of multidirectional communication between the shaman, spirits, and community members.

Shamans often deliver their healing word/sounds through songs and, hence, it is through music/sound that they are able to also actualize other realities for the benefit of the world. Often, the consequences of ritual action extend beyond the ritual itself, inspiring far-reaching actions and transforming mindsets in other areas of life. Max Dashu (2010) and Barbara Tedlock (2005) have convincingly shown that women have a long history as active agents or practitioners within the shamanic paradigm and that women have profoundly influenced the development of their respective communities in previously unacknowledged ways.

A different understanding of Paleolithic spiritual practices is possible when one sees that despite there being relatively little material culture, a contextually specific, animistic spiritual-based knowledge system existed that includes the integration of previously ignored or unknown sonic phenomena. Paleolithic women's musical/sonic performances within shamanic ritualized spaces could have simultaneously functioned as a musical performance or sonic experience *and* as a spiritual role. Moreover, this different understanding recognizes that women were active agents who were essential to the completeness of Paleolithic spiritual practices.

Conclusion

I propose that a more holistic approach to articulating the musicality of prehistoric women is one in which the following are included: a fluctuating coalescence of shamanic musicality co-existing with the everydayness of their auditory worlds, the repetitive sounds of soundscapes, and the music embedded in the functionality of common activities. As Paleolithic women mediated the spiritual power of sound as sound-producers and sound-interpreters, their music-making aligned with the production of culturally specific knowledge-making. Their musicality can be regarded as an enduring form or mode of knowledge in and of itself, as sonic knowledge. Such mediation of sound illustrates a sphere of personal power for Paleolithic women that is also applicable to contemporary women living today. This interpretation (linking sound mediation with spheres of personal power and sonic knowledge) is a connective thread linking generations of women's musical experiences, not in uniformity, but rather in a chain of contextual and culturally specific spiritual expressions. One can also productively rethink what music-making means or signifies, rethink the consequences of extracting it from its context. It is one way to conceptualize a musical heritage for women.

A complexity emerges, leading us to rethink our current accepted knowledge about ancient spiritual practices and in turn, to reconsider what constitutes the modernity of contemporary ones. Recognizing the sonically strategic placement of ancient images of rock art might be of crucial importance, in that it facilitates thinking of the rock art not just as mute representations of primitive superstitions or as cognitive evolutionary milestone markers, nor as decorative – or art for art's sake. But rather, it can influence our spiritual and musical mindset, allowing us to become receptive to the energy or power or principle the images are intended to express.

Music history narratives typically encompass a network of inter-dependent activities and experiences. Somatic, emotional, and intellectual processing of sound creates relationships and meanings that when attached to musical experiences and through consensus of opinion, become traditions. Lawrence Kramer (1990) encourages musicologists to abandon the myth of music's autonomy as a transcendental experience or object, to welcome the complex situatedness of music in webs of extra-musical forces. Women's lived experiences shape their personal aesthetics and they have again and again participated in valuable music-making, which is a form of meaning making. Women's collective musicality can persist in being understood as multidimensional when and if individual women consciously choose to be aware of their personal power or agency in relationship to sound.

Within my augmented timeline, I acknowledge and value innumerable generations of women's participation as spiritual healers within the shamanic paradigm, providing different types of role models, different criteria pertaining to women's experiences of music-making. Knowing that women have dynamically participated in the production of musical culture across time and space, that they drew strength, inspiration, and direction from their everyday embodied experiences and channeled their individual energy effectively within the most ancient and widespread system of mind-body healing known to humanity, is empowering. Women could choose to view themselves as belonging to an endless tradition or lineage of hierophants – being revelations of the sacred, being emotional conduits, being spheres of power. Furthermore, by situating oneself in such an expanded time frame, one can then look at the Eurocentric tradition from a different perspective, far beyond the confines of a few hundred years of a linear narrative, an alternative perspective within which the Eurocentric tradition now has to fit. Ultimately, it is a matter of ownership. There certainly is no grand counter-narrative regarding music history in the making here. Instead, I offer a way to re-conceptualize traces of ancient practices, perhaps to be inspired enough by them to claim them and benefit from one's authentic connections with them.

Bibliography

Conkey, M. W. (1985). Ritual communication, social elaboration, and the variable trajectories of Paleolithic material culture. In T. D. Price & J. A. Brown (Eds.), *Prehistoric Hunters-Gatherers* (pp. 299–323). Academic Press.

Dams, L. (1985). Palaeolithic lithophones: Descriptions and comparisons. *Oxford Journal of Archaeology*, 4(1), 31–46. <https://doi.org/10.1111/j.1468-0092.1985.tb00229.x>

Dashu, M. (Producer & Director). (2010). *Woman shaman: The ancients*. [DVD]. Suppressed History Archives.

Devereux, P. (2001). *Stone Age soundtracks: The acoustic archaeology of ancient sites*. Sterling Publishing Company, Inc.

DuBois, T. A. (2009). *An introduction to shamanism*. Cambridge University Press.

Eneix, L. C. (2014). *Archaeoacoustics. The archaeology of sound. Publication of proceedings from the 2014 conference in Malta*. CreateSpace Independent Publishing Platform.

Kramer, L. (1990). *Music as cultural practice*. Berkeley.

Lund, C. S. (2008). Prehistoric soundscapes in Scandinavia. In F. Mossberg (Ed.), *Sounds of history, publications from Listening Lund* (pp. 12–29). Sound Environment Centre at Lund University.

Mills, S. (2014). *Auditory archaeology: Understanding sound and hearing in the past*. Left Coast Press.

Saidel, D. J. (2018). *Women in music: Letting a long story be long, contemplating women's sonic, musical, and spiritual experiences in prehistory* [Unpublished doctoral dissertation, Virginia Commonwealth University].

Tame, D. (1984). *The secret power of music: Transformation of self and society through musical energy*. Destiny Books.

Tedlock, B. (2005). *The woman in the shaman's body: Reclaiming the feminine in religion and medicine*. Bantam.

Till, R. (2014). Sound archaeology: An interdisciplinary perspective. In L. C. Eneix (Ed.), *Archaeoacoustics: The archaeology of sound: Publication of proceedings from the 2014 conference in Malta* (pp. 23–32). CreateSpace Independent Publishing Platform.

University of Minnesota. (2016). What is spirituality? Taking charge of your health & wellbeing. https://www.takingcharge.csh.umn.edu/what-spirituality

Waller, S. (2014). Auditory illusions in the soundscapes of rock art and Stonehenge. In L. C. Eneix (Ed.), *Archaeoacoustics: The archeology of sound – Publication of proceedings from the 2014 conference in Malta* (pp. 99–106). CreateSpace Independent Publishing Platform.

JUNGMIN GRACE HAN

Interlude 1

The Sacred Space Within

Towards Mind-Body Unity through Musical Performance

> [A] spiritual experience is an experience of aliveness of mind and body as a unity. Moreover, this experience of unity transcends not only the separation of mind and body but also the separation of self and [the] world. The central awareness in these spiritual moments is a profound sense of oneness with all, a sense of belonging to the universe as a whole. (Capra, 2002, p. 68)

Can a performing musician ever get to this sense of spiritual experience? If so, what does this spiritual experience have to do with one's inner capacity for music and self? June Boyce-Tillman (2016) described in her book "the development of spirituality based on [a] process rather than dogmas" (p. 4). As indicated in the title of her book *Experiencing Music – Restoring the Spiritual*, her notion demonstrates that the experiential and the spiritual are, in fact, intrinsically interdependent elements underlying the nature of music. She elaborated as follows: "In making music, we are participating in these vibratory patterns using our creative agency to influence events and be part of musicking the divine … this means that by musicking, we can potentially be part of the evolving creativity of the universe" (2016, p. 9).

Music is the art of managing sound. More than any other musical experience, performing musical arts necessitates delicate skilled movements because the performer is a first-hand creator of living sounds. Despite the profound physical nature of music performance, however, text-based compositional abstraction has long been the dominant way of understanding music. In this abstraction, the performing body has been ignored as if it were a finite object. This issue, I extrapolate at large, is a part of the body–mind dualism rooted in Western culture – where the body has been neglected and the attention is on the mind, with a significant loss of the body's sentient feelings and thoughts (Shusterman, 2004). This yields a "high" musical mind but "low" bodily technique in the tradition of performing musical arts and its pedagogy (Han, 2019).

This paradigm overlooks the significance of the human body as the agent of the musical self – a living creature with a pre-existing logic that can only be fully comprehended and completed by *corporeal* actions and sensibilities. The static, unconsciously habitual performing body consequently represents the fracturing of the body from the mind and self from music, with loss of the potential for lifelong musical transformation and growth. In the context of classical musical performance, in particular, this broken relationship – fundamentally caused by *the ignored body* – results in an inhibited, static musical capacity, as the body (in its relationship with an instrument) plays a significant part in bridging the experiential, spiritual nature of music.

In the past, I experienced this *inhibited, static* realm. Despite relentless daily practice, with the fear of potential mistakes, I could not make myself feel or get any better. My cello playing was plateauing at what seemed to be the best level that humans can reach. On a day when I was practicing the *Bach Cello Suite No. 6* with that continuing fear I coincidentally encountered my old teacher and got a chance to play that piece for her. After the sound of music ended, she had me change my right thumb position on the bow and then said, "Roll your shoulder down and put your armpit weight onto the cello and then try the piece again."

In that brief moment, the sound swiftly flowed through my whole body as if it were transparent breaths of genuine air that could hold and infuse my true musical imagination. My self was no longer imposing itself upon sound. Rather, I felt as if my entire body were an integral part of the sound. Indeed, the profound corporeal involvement in cultivating sounds was the process of *re-forming* my musical self as a musical, artistic whole, restoring the intrinsic connectivity of the body and the mind and, eventually, self and music. At the moment when I merged into the sound, the subject "I" and the object "music" (i.e., "I play music") soon disappeared, and only the sound, the sole presence of music, spoke for itself.

Previously, my left fingers had been trained to articulate each note as pronounced as possible; my bow arm had been taught to react to a robust musical piece with a big motion. Such blind actions of performance – which had been unconsciously accumulated – constantly disrupted the natural physical principle internalized in motor trajectories. To renew my entire musical being, I had to completely deny my old self, which was grounded in my habitual body's deadlocks; this was interestingly intertwined with the egocentric mind, which I discovered later in the process of self-transformation. It required excessively rigorous self-reflexivity to sense the space of my internal body and selfless mind when I play. Through the process, by cultivating internal bodily paths, I came to understand the inherently experiential logic of the performing body and its direct relationship with the sound being crafted.

This restoration of valuing the inherent space or form of the body as a Christian classical cellist led me to the realization that whoever seeks such a principle within self will restore a sense of belonging to a well-ordered universe; the performer-self ceases to exist, surrendered to the presence of music within its very nature. In resonance with Capra's (2002) notion of the mind–body/self-world connectedness, if the "oneness" underlying the embodied self in musical performance exists, it means that across a type of religion and musical genre, every individual contains the inherent capacity to restore the infinite possibilities underlying this pre-existing physical principle. In this sense, the spiritual in musical performance cannot be separated from the restored *bodily* space underlying its natural principle. Hence, spirituality is the manifestation of the utmost knowledge of humaneness in performing music that is palpably experiential and embodied.

Thus, *the sacred space*, in my imaginative term, reflects the restored whole musical self, underlying the intrinsic connection of the body to the mind and of self to music. My experience in restorative corporeal action toward this *sacred space* or the whole musical self as a Christian musician posits evidence of universal musical spirituality with our sentient body–mind in making music. *The loss of self* enables us to have an invisible, yet more intrinsic and permanent power for living, as the Holy Bible emphasizes.[8] Although my idea of *the sacred space* has been born out of this Biblical

---

8   "For whoever would save his life will lose it, but whoever loses his life for my sake will save it" (Luke 9:24).

notion of being selfless, submission of self universally opens the door for the inherent infinite capacity for self within the well-ordered universe of music.[9]

In his book *The Archetype of Initiation: Sacred Space, Ritual Process, and Personal Transformation*, Robert Moore (2001) asserted, "New life cannot begin to germinate until the old has been torned [*sic*] down and cleared away in a process manifesting adequate containment" (p. 31). He distinguished the sacred space from a religious place, considering it as a regenerative space with the capacity for renewal and rebirth. He described entering into the sacred space in his term of initiation:

> Initiation really refers to something that is part and parcel of the universal spiritual journey, the pilgrimage of human life. Initiation is the process of dying and [being] reborn. This archetype is so powerful in human life that it turns up in all parts of human experience, and once you have the eyes to see it, a lot of things that you have wondered about will begin to fall into place. (2001, p. 78)

He described how, in the state of liminality, one is in touch with self – more closely than any time in one's life (the equivalent of "220,000 volts of spiritual and psychological archetypal energy" [2001, p. 80]) – in this process of deconstructing the old self involving humility and submission. He referred to Eliade's concept of initiation:

> In Christian thinking, the Cross is the center of the universe, the *axis mundi,* the world tree. Through the cross of Christ, the nourishment of God passes to the world … For Eliade, the structure of initiation is in the special sacred space and time where you get connected to the divine source. (2001, pp. 91–92)

In correspondence with Moore's (2001) idea, my idea of the sacred space within – cultivated by the eventual move from self-awareness to selflessness – centers on relinquishing the habitually dualistic self to the musical cosmos underlying the natural principle. On the flipside of the coin, the common notion of tension in musical performance may be a sign of the egocentric

---

9   My notion is in correspondence with the words of Thomas Matus: "The mystery of Jesus is specific to Christianity; it cannot be monopolized by Christian believers because it is universal" (Capra & Steindl-Rast, 1991, p. 56).

self that is isolated from the natural connectivity, resulting in the issues of the so-called performance anxiety and injury.

This contemplation indicates the current musical performance pedagogy focused on extrinsic outcomes (such as winning competitions) as a token of "successful" teaching and learning, yielding a mechanical, fragmented perspective on music and its pedagogy. This form of pedagogy reinforces the egocentric self – thereby desperately losing the pure meaning of education in music, for education is really about a process of searching for the true self that underpins the connectedness within.

Boyce-Tillman called to restore "musical wisdom"[10] in music education with an understanding of the connection between music and the cosmos. When applied to musical performance, in particular, the musical self's embodiment is an active way to cultivate "musical wisdom"; corporeal action is the essential pathway for understanding and regenerating self in belonging to the musical cosmos (or in its place within the musical cosmos). However, the embodied self is not the end but the door into *the sacred space within*, where music speaks solely for itself. Surrendering oneself does not result in emptiness but infinite possibilities connected to the principle of the universe. This is where *the sacred space within* begins.

Bibliography

Boyce-Tillman, J. (2016). *Experiencing music – Restoring the spiritual: Music as wellbeing*. Peter Lang AG; International Academic Publishers.

Capra, F. (2002). *The hidden connections: Integrating the biological, cognitive, and social dimensions of life into a science of sustainability*. A division of Random House.

Capra, F., & Steindl-Rast, D. (1991). *Belonging to the universe: Explorations on the frontiers of science & spirituality*. HarperCollins Publishers.

---

10 June Boyce-Tillman addressed the notion of "musical knowledge to musical wisdom" in her presentation at the International Society for Music Education Reboot conference in 2020.

Han, J. G. (2019). The somaesthetics of musicians: Rethinking the body in musical practice. *The Journal of Somaesthetics, 5*(2), 41–51.

Moore, R. L. (2001). *The archetype of initiation: Sacred space, ritual process, and personal transformation.* Xlibris Corporation.

Shusterman, R. (2004). Somaesthetics and education: Exploring the terrain. In L. Bresler (Ed.), *Knowing bodies moving minds: Towards embodied teaching and learning* (pp. 51–61). Kluwer Academic Publishers.

MARIA GIULIA MARINI

Interlude 2

Music: To Each Their Own When Illness Comes but Rhythm Is Universal

A Pre-Pandemic Survey on Musical Taste and Sound Considerations in COVID-19 Era

It is well established in scientific research that music stimulates the production of dopamine and endorphins in our brain. The former neurotransmitter is able to promote resiliency and a looking forward mind, and the latter to give us a sense of wellbeing. Music is a type of language with an intrapersonal effect, such as evoking past memories, developing empathy toward the very self and the other, interconnecting our mind and soul, depending on the contextual environment, health state, and personal taste. Our wish in 2017 and 2018 was to show the tastes of people with regard to music when facing difficult time, illness, fragility, and vulnerability. We never could have imagined the difficult time that we had to go through during 2020, and the resiliency which it demanded.

Pre-Pandemic Age

A survey on music was carried out from October 2017 to January 2018, in the pre-pandemic age, and was disseminated online through the website <www.narrativemedicine.eu>, and its Italian version <www. medicinanarrativa.eu>. This bilingual website is read by members of the patients' association, health care providers, students, and lay people from countries all over the world. In particular, the respondents came from Italy, UK, Chile, Switzerland, Israel, and USA. They were asked to write down the title of the ten preferred music, songs, ballads, concert, opera, sounds, or whatever of acoustic listening they want to listen in case of illness and vulnerability. They could also write the author's name, as songwriters, composers, and musicians. The answers were translated in English, and the titles of the songs were analyzed in their most recurrent words, represented by word clouds, and using the Natural Semantic Metalanguage analysis (Goddard, 2018). This linguistic theory attempts to reduce the semantics of all lexicons down to a restricted set of semantic primes. The primes are considered universal, since they have the same translation in every language, and they cannot be misunderstood moving from one language to another; they are also primitive, which means that they cannot be defined using other words. Among the sixty-five universal words were: *body, to feel, to live, to die, I, you, people, true, good, bad, to live, side, inside, to see.*

The survey had 115 participants, representative of four generations, where each generation encompassed roughly a period of twenty years, who reported overall 1,115 contemporary songs, classic music, melodies, anthems, "aria" of opera, ballet music, and sounds. Results, as shown in Figure I.1, displayed small clusters, recalling classic music – including Mozart, Bach, and Beethoven – or rock and pop – such as Beatles and Pink Floyd – but with a large divergence within the same cluster. Some answers mentioned the importance of silence in moments of fragility. However, the analysis of words evidenced some common trends. The most recurrent word from the titles was "you" (Tu, ti, te), while "I" was far less mentioned; the second most cited word was "love" (Amore, Amour, Amor), and the third was "life" (Vita, Vida Vie). The first and the third word belong to the Natural Semantic Metalanguage, therefore they are universal, breathing the spirituality of the alterity, the need of the other point of view, to create intersubjectivity among people, and the celebration of the beauty of life. Furthermore, the word "love" can be easily reduced to primes, through this linguistic approach: "I feel good things with you," "I feel good with you by my side," "My body feels good with you by my side."

Figure I.1. The word cloud of the participants' responses

The results of this study showed, at that time, the hypothesis that music plays an important part of human care, but it cannot be standardized since the single answers were extremely scattered. To use music as a therapy during times of fragility, one should respect the possible differences in personal tastes and needs, which are mirrors also of individual spiritual beliefs (Marini, 2017). The analysis of the titles unveiled that in times of vulnerability, there was a craving need for the "YOU," recalling a specific person who loves and takes care for. "LOVE" is a spiritual word, related to the feeling of experienced goodness, belonging and inclusion, strategically important for human beings and patients' coping (Marini, 2018). "LIFE" refers to the prime "to live," from the Natural Semantic Metalanguage, showing the attachment to living in case of fragility. People enjoyed different harmonies, and melodies, that anyhow, in the authors' chosen titles, were referring to these three universal or semi-universal words.

Paradoxically, since any music could have been mentioned with no censorship, the most emerging words could have been ironically *I (to be intended as Ego)*, *Death and Hate*, terms widespread in the titles of violent songs, representing indeed the opposite of healthy and positive spiritual beliefs. In July 2018, to reward the respondents of this musical survey, a comprehensive playlist of all the chosen music was realized; this playlist will never be inclusive of all the possible different tastes, variety of experiences, beliefs, and cultural contexts, following the concept "to each their own when illness comes." On the website <www.narrativemedicine.eu>, the results of the survey and the play list were the most visited blog in 2019, showing evidence of the choice of music over written language or figurative art posts.

Pandemic Age

We have asked art therapists, teachers of humanities and philosophers, and normal citizens at Home, and not in the setting of care – from worldwide countries as Italy, UK, Portugal, Spain, USA, Canada – to write down the pillars for wellbeing during the lockdown (period ranging in March–April 2020) according to the biological, psychological, social, and spiritual model. This was an upgrade by the World health Organization in 2015 of the bio-socio-psychological model. This matrix was chosen to overcome the reductionism of the biomedical model to promote wellbeing. It was very interesting to see that many "mental" tips were as well put in the "biological" part, since for these experts there is an interconnection between body and mind.

As for the spiritual part, some of our participants indicated the importance of social relations. In fact, the four dimensions are indeed interrelated, and it is very difficult to define clear borders among the four determinants. It is like an osmotic process, with no walls among the borders but biological membranes, where the reflections do belong, according also the reader's eyes to possible different sectors. Dance and singing (belonging the Music art) were classified mainly in two dimensions, the biological and the spiritual.

Biological reflects the effects of dancing and singing reverberating on body and mind. Spiritual reflects that music is somehow considered, together with *Being in the Nature*, as the Elected Language, which trespasses the ambiguity and limits of word communication and somehow generates peace and serenity into the turmoil of the most disruptive event in our Western countries after World War II. However, the people who contributed to the building of these pillars were indicating different kinds of Music, from disco for dancing to sacred anthems, again highlighting the importance of personal taste (Marini, 2020).

The Pandemic Hospital Settings

I was in contact almost daily with anesthesiologists and people in intensive care during the darkest days of March, April up to middle May. At the beginning in March, there was only time for silence among this overwhelming death in Bergamo, Milano and Brescia, with very few spoken words, in traumatized health care workers. They reported that in the hospital, to break this silence the only dominant sound was that of the ventilators. Doctors and nurses worked, exchanging technical words, trying to understand what to do, knowing that there were "no evidence-based protocol" to follow. Tears came out from the eyes of the operators as first signs of moving from a shock – tears made of sorrow and fatigue combined together, of seeing so much death around, as never seen before, with science in total confusion, and hope so far to reach.

There was no time for music in the first two weeks of March 2020 in the hospitals, only grief; everything was suspended, including the funeral rituals. No sacred anthems were sung and tears were shed in private homes. However, as time went by, the doctors found another way to cope with the cruel facts: One afternoon in middle March an intensivist, tired of this enduring silence, dared to put on a playlist, with Latin-American and disco music in intensive care, at a low volume as a soft background. Things suddenly changed: doctors and nurses were moving their bodies according to the rhythm – and even some patients who had enough energy to lift up only one finger, lifted up that finger. Rhythm was pervasive and was the right thing at the right time. The doctor when preparing herself to go away since her shift was over, turned off the music and went to say hello (as she used to do regularly) with the patients. One who could talk, in a whisper said to her: "Thank you, this afternoon was one of the most amusing times of my life."

Reporting this narrative, other intensive care units in Lombardia started to put the music on, and it worked indeed to cheer up the general mood allowing the body to move. "Body" is again another universal word, belonging to the Natural Semantic Metalanguage: The rhythm possibly has invited physical movements despite the stiff gowns, diving suits, and masks. Rhythm is thought to be the universal sound since the first sound we hear is the mother's heartbeat in her womb, even before our birth, together with the regular and constantly repeated sounds of maternal respiration (Teie, 2016). The drum is an instrument that was invented and adopted for use in music in every culture, and its amplitude contour is such that it conforms to the sound of the pulse as heard from the womb: It looks like that to counteract that huge ocean of sorrow, only the ancestral rhythm, played in the dance of the health care operators among the patients' bed. It was like a new beginning of human beings, a lively pulse to defeat the dying embedded in natural sounds. Before the pandemic, the listening of classic music in intensive and operatory theaters was quite a standard, but the COVID-19 had frozen this soothing tool, creating an apocalyptic silence on which only to build on, restarting from the universal rhythm of nature.

In May of this year, although very few randomized trials were conducted on drugs to fight COVID-19, in Italy a randomized study was undertaken to evaluate the effect of two playlists, a Breathing and an Energy playlist, on health care operators (Giordano et al., 2020). In the relaxation playlist (Breathing) music tracks were selected on the basis of the steady pulse; quiet mood; predictable melodic lines; little dynamic change; supportive bass line; stability in volume, timbre, rhythm, harmony, and pitch; simple structure; and clear form. The Breathing playlist was structured by selections from classical music of the Western tradition and modern selections with similar feature. By contrast, in the "stimulating" playlist (Energy) music tracks were more changeable in instrumentation and in dynamic flow, unpredictable in melodic lines, volume, timbre, rhythm, harmony, pitch, loose structure, and unclear form. Bass lines could range from supportive to non-supportive. All playlists were 15–20 minutes in length. A listening guideline was created for all the PLs ("*Find a quiet and comfortable space,*" "*close your eyes,*" "*focus on an image or a color,*" "*breathe slowly,*" etc.).

After one week of Standard playlists, all emotions on validated psychometric tools improved, but here, the last surprise to close the circle of this short writing: Customized playlists were prepared for the different health care professionals, and the results versus the standard playlist were striking. The customized Breathing Playlist generated a substantial variation in the emotional status with a significant decrease in the intensity of perceived sadness, increase in energy level, and increase in serenity level.

After the initial shock, which left most of us living in Lombardia speechless, and which required the universal beat of our mother's nature, things evolved up to the possibility to choose the sounds: to each its own music when illness comes. Not only for patients, but here, for doctors, nurses, and all carers. No words but sound.

Following our phylogenetic development of human kind, we have to bear this in mind: Sound can help us in this demanding and antifragility testing on our wellbeing, as a common language for creating kinship, overcoming political competitions, and promoting a universal feeling of wellbeing. This goes from the *first movement* – boosting in tears for all the recent and current pandemic of death and misfortune; *second movement* – the awareness that we are all part of the same galaxy and we are not alone; *third movement* – with a triumphal major musical note in the end of the composition: hope. On December 27, 2020, the European Union celebrated the *Vaccine Day*, as the utmost symbol of first light after this nightmare. We need anthems now, to mend our minds and bodies, and nourish our souls with enlightening beliefs and values.

Acknowledgments

Gratitude to the researchers who were able to carry out the music survey and to prepare the playlist with the most wished songs: Silvia Napolitano, Paola Chesi, and Matteo Nunner.

Bibliography

Giordano, F., Scarlata, E., Baroni, M., Gentile, E., Puntillo, F., Brienza, N., & Gesualdo, L. (2020). Receptive music therapy to reduce stress and improve wellbeing in Italian clinical staff involved in COVID-19 pandemic: A preliminary study. *The Arts in Psychotherapy*, *70*, Article 101688. <https://doi.org/10.1016/j.aip.2020.101688>

Goddard, C. (2018). *Ten lectures on natural semantic metalanguage*. Brill.

Marini, M. G. (2017, December 13). *The language of music, interview with June Boyce-Tillman*. Chronicle of healthcare and narrative medicine. <https://www.medicinanarrativa.eu/the-language-of-music-interview-with-june-boyce-tillman?utm_source=nl_37>

Marini, M. G. (2018). *Languages of care in narrative medicine*. Springer.

Marini, M. G. (2020). *The chart of humanities: An overview in the pillars of the bio-psycho-social-spiritual model to humanize isolation and care during COVID-19 pandemic*. Chronicle of healthcare and narrative medicine. <https://www.medicinanarrativa.eu/the-chart-of-humanities-an-overview-on-the-pillars>

Teie, D. (2016). A comparative analysis of the universal elements of music and the fetal environment. *Frontiers in Psychology*, *7*, Article 1158. <https://doi.org/10.3389/fpsyg.2016.01158>

KEITH D. THOMASSON

7 *Creative Spirit*

Conversations that Accompany Creativity in the Lives of Young People Who Are at Risk of Homelessness

Introduction

> Creativity is seen as accessing the deepest areas of the personality where […] the soul may be seen as residing. (Boyce-Tillman, 2016, p. 103)

In 2014 I joined Alabare Christian Care and Support as Senior Chaplain and Spirituality Advisor. Alabare supports young people and adults who are vulnerable. Such vulnerability stems from a number of sources and frequently is multilayered and complex: trauma, addiction, poor mental health, exposure to abusive relationships, little or no contact with other family members, homelessness, and debt. A colleague had recently written a song for fundraising purposes. The song was called "We will walk with you, everyday" (Alabare, 2014). It was composed by ear and became the source of a collective effort across Alabare. A range of people, staff and clients from across the charity, visited the underground recording studio in the homeless hostel, Alabare Place, in Salisbury. Backing vocals were written and recorded. A cornet obbligato was added. One client with experience of life on the streets told his story by rapping above an instrumental interlude. Those who played by ear were as welcome as those who played from notation.

This foray into music-making was liberating. It encouraged people's creativity and enabled them to give expression to their values and spiritual convictions. This led to several illuminating conversations for me as chaplain. Creativity and spirituality were clearly in the lifeblood of the charity. Gradually we would learn how to harness the potential of creativity and spirituality in the context of support working.

In this chapter I shall explore how support working, with young people who are at risk of homelessness and those leaving the care system, is being developed through developing the synergy between creativity and spirituality.[11] The project is called *Creative Spirit* (Alabare, 2019). When the young people engage in creative activities such as art, gardening, baking, and songwriting they do so alongside a support worker. This naturally can often lead to a conversation. These conversations grow in depth as the space where they take place is discovered, and understood, to be safe. Being alongside a staff member up to their arms in paint is less confrontational than facing them, as is the normal configuration for support sessions focusing on finances and housing issues. Rather, "alongside-ness" creates space for thoughts to be shared in a way that is non-threatening.

A new narrative emerges from these conversations. Past hurts are shared and sometimes understood more. This can enable the young person to let go of what is burdening them. From this fresh standpoint the young person can often begin to look forward with greater hope. Such encounters and conversations happen within the context of the wider care offered from within Alabare and in partnership with other agencies.

In terms of the structure of the chapter I begin by examining Genesis Chapter 1. This provides four ideas that help to illuminate what is taking shape within *Creative Spirit* working. I explore my understanding of creativity and how this enables the expression of suffering and spirituality, and I examine the relationship between them. I recall the story of how *Creative Spirit* evolved and developed. I analyze the input from staff colleagues who recount something of their experience of *Creative Spirit* before illustrating how the ideas are shaping work across the rest of the charity. Unfortunately I have not been able to gain permission to use any of the stories from the young people themselves. Nevertheless, there are several case studies in the

---

11   <https://www.Alabare.co.uk/youngpeople>. Alabare supports young people aged between 16–25 who are homeless, at risk of homelessness, leaving the care system, and those becoming new parents for the first time who have inadequate housing and family support.

booklet, *Creative Spirit* (Alabare, 2019) which is available on the Alabare website.[12] This may be downloaded. I encourage reading the booklet in tandem with the chapter.

Biblical Underpinning: Genesis 1

The four elements from Genesis Chapter 1 I wish to comment on are darkness, the breath of God, light, and the declaration by God that what he saw was "good." The elements provide a framework for the journey into creativity, conversation, and meaning making. We read, "the earth was a formless void and darkness covered the face of the deep" (NRSV, Genesis 1:2). Another reading translates it as "and the earth then was welter and waste and darkness over the deep" (Alter, 2004, p. 17). The Hebrew is *tohu wabohu*. There is waste, emptiness, and futility. As in a desert, there are no clear paths or tracks to follow. The word "welter" is equally powerful. It conjures up images of confusion, turbulence, and laying soaked in blood.

God is present in the waste and welter. We read of "God's breath hovering over the waters" (Alter, 2004, p. 17). Alternatively we hear that "a wind from God swept over the face of the waters" (NRSV, Genesis 1:2). Alter suggests that "the verb attached to God's breath-wind-spirit (*ruah*) elsewhere describes an eagle fluttering over its young and so might have a connotation of parturition or nurture as well as rapid back-and-forth movement" (Alter, 2004, p. 17).

I love the tension inherent in "hovering over" and "sweeping over." One is vast in its scope and the other suggests an intensity from remaining in one place. The waters have a "face." If we add the image of the eagle we have the laser vision the eagle employs to survey this expanse or "face" from above. We have the extraordinary idea of parturition or giving birth and the subsequent journeys back and to nourish the eaglets. This process resonates with the practice of pastoral supervision (Paterson, 2019).

---

12   <https://www.Alabare.co.uk/uploads/Creative_Spirituality_A5_-_November.pdf>

"Then God said, 'Let there be light'" (NRSV, Genesis 1:3). The text has moved from darkness to light. Light brings clear sight and understanding. It enables God to declare that what he saw was "good" (NRSV, Genesis 1:25). The Hebrew carries the idea of continued dependence on God, and his purposes (Zlotowitz, 1995, p. 52). This suggests to me that fruitfulness and flourishing are integral to God's creativity.

Frequently the Genesis text has been read in a Newtonian fashion. Underpinning my understanding here is that Genesis Chapter 1 may be read through the lens of emergence (Harle, 2012). Emergence and creativity are bound together. Out of chaos a new system emerges.

Creativity and Suffering

Although *Creative Spirit* is not a substitute for the array of arts therapies available, the place of creativity in supporting (young) people who are homeless can benefit from the insight of arts therapists. Levine (2009) is helpful in explaining artistic creativity. Levine writes of the "creative ground to human experience" (Levine, 2009, p. 42). Boyce-Tillman (2016), toward the end of an in-depth discussion of creativity comments, "The more universal view of the attribute of creativity sees the process as part of the flow of living and part of the process of growth and change" (p. 121). The artist shapes what they receive. This requires an openness that is made possible by an openness within oneself, to the world and to the Divine.[13] It involves, "an opening to the future, an attempt to find a new path beyond the eternal recurrence of the same" (Levine, 2009, p. 42).

Furthermore, the concept of liminality is important in describing how artistic creativity involves a safe space where a person is journeying from one place to another (Boyce-Tillman, 2016). The person exercising their creativity has an opportunity to rest and play. They can also experience

---

13   For an in-depth examination of creativity in relation to genius and inspiration see Boyce-Tillman 2016, pp. 114–121.

something that is "incredibly dynamic, leading to unexpected experiences of creativity" (Levine, 2009, p. 171).

It is also important that in a therapeutic relationship the client explores their creativity whilst the therapist is with them. This brings restoration and transformation. Levine explains this with reference to Heidegger's concept of "being-with others" (Heidegger, 1978; Levine, 2009, p. 45). This resonates deeply with Wells' idea of "being with" (Wells, 2017). The accompanier gives permission and encouragement. These enable a person to "tread the path of transformation" so that they can "inhabit an entirely new story" (Stockitt, 2015, p. 89).

Spirituality within Alabare

Alabare is a Christian charity that was formed nearly thirty years ago. A local group of churches was not equipped to support a "man of the road." They contacted the ecumenical Alabare Christian Community who agreed to take him in.[14] After this man left, the community received a call to support a young mother-to-be whose husband had just been convicted of an offense and was beginning a prison sentence. Due to this she had lost her accommodation. Whilst on the surface Salisbury is an affluent city clearly there was real need for support amongst those who were vulnerable. The charity Alabare Christian Care and Support began. The name Alabare comes from a Spanish song by Jose Pagan. It translates as, "I will praise (my Lord)."[15]

During the intervening years the charity has grown to support people who are at risk of homelessness and adults with learning disabilities. The original Christian ethos has remained. This is rooted in the idea of "abundant living" and "life in all its fullness" that we hear from the lips of Jesus (John 10:10). Within Alabare this has become "enabling a fulfilled life." Today the ethos is expressed in explicit and implicit ways. Explicit expression is

14   <https://www.Alabare.co.uk/about/how-we-began>
15   <https://susannawesleyfoundation.org/keith-thomasson-Alabare>

present through a network of Voluntary Christian Chaplains and a Fresh Expression of Church for adults with learning disabilities.[16] Implicit expression of the ethos is present in the social justice work and care for clients who are vulnerable. Central to this are the four values of care, compassion, generosity, and respect agreed by those involved in the charity, staff, clients, and wider family members. It is because of its Christian ethos that there is a commitment to inclusiveness where the gifting of all, and the worldviews of all enrich Alabare's commitment to serving those who are vulnerable (Wells, 2019).

The use of the word "spirit" in *Creative Spirit* is deliberate. It affirms the importance of spirituality within Alabare. Religion is part of how spirituality is understood (Swinton, 2002). It remains important that spirituality does "not become so narrow as to exclude religious ways of life" (Rankin, 2005, p. 12). Whatever one's standpoint, spirituality has "increasingly been recognized as a basic human need and a human right, which is a necessary component of both mental and physical health" (Swinton, 2004, p. 1).

Spirituality is notoriously difficult to define (Holloway, 2019). Even so it is worthwhile giving spirituality greater definition (Rowson, 2014). A person who is homeless has a lot of time to reflect on the meaning in their life. Meaning is often a central strand of how spirituality is understood (Swinton, 2001). This is the kernel that has formed my understanding of spirituality.

For the purpose of this chapter, I define spirituality as that which brings meaning to life, through creativity, community, the natural world, and world view. Underpinning this definition is the broad understanding of spirituality agreed upon within Alabare Christian Care and Support (Alabare, 2018). World view may be understood broadly and include ritual, and faith and its practice. This understanding is founded upon four touchstones: creativity, community, the natural world, and world view. My understanding

---

16   <https://freshexpressions.org.uk/about/what-is-a-fresh-expression/> Within Alabare the *Faith Saturdays* happen several times a year. About thirty clients and ten supporters (staff and chaplains) gather to eat, explore scripture through song with makaton, drama and craft, worship and eat again. Faith Saturdays also owe much to Messy Church <https://www.messychurch.org.uk/> and Faith and Light <https://www.faithandlight.org/>

of a touchstone is this. When you are involved in creativity, for example, you are busy with meaning in life (Rowson, 2014). For *Creative Spirit*, creativity is the primary touchstone. Nevertheless, there is overlap with the other three, especially community and the natural world. Whilst other themes such as "the psychological study of human nature" (Holloway, 2019, pp. xiii–ix) are seen as integral to spirituality, nonetheless community, the universe and the arts are frequently cited as ways in which the spiritual is encountered and through which spirituality is nurtured (Holloway, 2019).

Rowson (2014), who developed the notion of spirituality touchstones, has also developed the idea of spiritual sensibility. One cultivates a spiritual sensibility by "engaging deeply with questions of being, belonging, becoming, and beyondness" (Rowson, 2017, p. 17). Being, belonging, becoming, and beyondness are Rowson's four touchstones. They capture the essence of living. They connect with the four touchstones adopted by Alabare and indicate how the experience of grace and transcendence are integral to spirituality (Holloway, 2019).

It is appropriate to connect this broad discussion with what others understand by spirituality. Consequently, the Alabare Spirituality Working Group have asked staff and clients how they understand spirituality. The consultation findings were refined and formed the content of a *Spirituality Handbook* (Alabare, 2017). Of relevance here are the following sections, which I list with examples of content:

> *Spirituality is about ….*
> Enabling people to find meaning and purpose in life
> Living out values such as care, compassion, generosity, and respect
> Expressing yourself in creative ways
> Forgiving those who have wronged us, accepting forgiveness from others, forgiving ourselves for what we regret doing, and saying and realizing that forgiveness might be a repeated action
> Coming to terms with death and bereavement
> Working holistically in response to multiple traumas
>
> *Expressing Spirituality*
> Reflection groups for shared conversation and discussion
> Singing and making music together
> Reflecting on significant experience in our lives
> Telling one another our life stories, perhaps through art and conversation

Spirituality isn't …
Just about religious beliefs and practices
The sole responsibility of the chaplain

Christian Spirituality may be expressed through:
Living in the spirit of Jesus Christ
Praying and reading the Bible

Questions you might wish to ask as you support someone:
How do you feel about this now?
How do you make sense of what has happened?
What would you like to do about this?
How can I support you?

This approach emphasizes how spirituality is practical. This approach is rooted in the report "Lost and Found" (Gravell, 2014). This shares the results from extensive research into the place of spirituality in the lives of people who are homeless. Ideas came from established practitioner organizations in the homelessness field. Two of these ideas had been turned into practice, the "life conversation" and the "spirituality group." These caught the imagination of people at Alabare.

For the place of conversation, imagine a cozy fireside chat, underpins both practices. To enable a life conversation a skeletal framework of questions was devised. For a spirituality group Alabare's Spirituality Working Group devised a set of themes for conversation. These included the spirituality touchstones of creativity, community, the natural world, and world view. The spirituality group can become a safe space where people gather to share their stories and ideas of how they felt when being creative in whatever way was meaningful to them. These ideas became the launch pad for *Creative Spirit*. I shall return to this later. Now it is important to consider the connections, relationship, and synergy between spirituality and creativity.

Creativity and Spirituality

Corry et al. (2014) have produced research that illuminates the relationship between spirituality and creativity. They are writing in the context of mental health and have an eye to developing strategies to aid lifelong learning for wellbeing. The inner resources of creativity and spirituality may need cajoling out of a person yet they boost recovery and lead to greater wholeness. Creativity has an important role in enabling self-disclosure. "Whilst focusing on writing, painting or making music and so expressing one's emotion, one is led to a place of reflection and increased self-awareness" (Corry et al., 2014, p. 8). This enables change in a person's life story and perspective.

The creative drive comes from an inherent spirituality (Corry et al., 2014). The resulting synergy between creativity and spirituality enables change and as has happened in civilizations across time, brings healing. Either one may stimulate the other (Corry et al., 2014). "Artistic creativity can itself be understood as a form of soul-making which aims to restore sense to the world" (Levine, 2009, p. 45). Young people desire space to reflect (Rankin, 2005). Rankin (2005, 86) asks, "How can youth workers be encouraged to engage and journey with young people as they attempt to answer their spiritual questions and reflect on their spirituality?" Within Alabare we have framed a partial response through *Creative Spirit*.

The Evolution of *Creative Spirit*

A colleague and I devised and delivered a training course to invite colleagues to practice life conversations and spirituality group conversations. Two colleagues from the Alabare young people service attended. On returning to their work environment they devised their own innovative practice. This eventually became *Creative Spirit*.

Young people face many challenges, accessing education and work, and struggling with addiction. The colleagues discovered that by being creative themselves the young people would become curious and join them. The colleagues gardened, baked, walked along the canal, and knitted around the coffee table in the lounge. The space created was safe. The invitation was to participate rather than achieve a certain level of competence. Underpinning the activities was a belief that one could reshape life through engaging with the creative, by crafting (Corbett, 2017). Gradually a practice emerged and conversations began to happen.

These conversations were of a much higher quality and of greater depth than the conversations that took place in weekly support sessions. One factor was that the attention was not on the welfare of the client but it was elsewhere, for example, planting tomatoes. The conversations were not under the pressure of time nor were they face-to-face with a target in mind, for example, preparing a budget or applying for housing. As trust increased there was often an unfreezing within the young person: "The bad experiences of life, particularly those of childhood, can remain as it were frozen inside us, leading in severe cases to what would usually be regarded as mental illness" (Winnicott, 1958, quoted in Reed, 1978, p. 21).

With this in mind it is helpful to recall the four elements taken from Genesis. They may be loosely superimposed onto the *Creative Spirit* journey. The turbulence and darkness was present due to the trauma the young person had experienced. Coming alongside another resonates deeply with the behavior of the Holy Spirit who is also known as the "paraclete." The breath of God is life giving and sweeps over and hovers above the darkness in life. The fire of the Holy Spirit melts what is frozen. Through conversation the young person is able to work through something of what has happened to them. The engagement in creativity and the development of trust brings the opportunity for light to be shone upon deeply embedded feelings and issues. Life with more fulfillment and greater possibility ensues and is "good."

The concept of liminality connects with creativity (Boyce-Tillman, 2016). On arrival at Alabare the young person crosses a threshold into a safe and hospitable space. They have the opportunity to reflect through conversation when being creative. Alternative possibilities emerge and the young person has the potential to re-enter independent living and flourish.

The young people services are gradually integrating *Creative Spirit* into their systems of support. Practice is being shared and paperwork is being refashioned (Alabare, 2019, pp. 6–9). For example, in one location there is a staff member who uses music to support the young people. Drum, guitar, and keyboard lessons are offered. This is a one to one experience and a strong bond can develop. Once the importance of keeping lesson appointments is understood and honored a relationship of trust emerges. Through being with a young person, taking delight in them, and seeing their abundance the staff member enables their creativity.

Wells (2017) encourages his readers to take delight in the abundance within an individual. Within Alabare embracing such a paradigmatic shift has opened up a new dimension to the support relationship and has enabled the pursuit of creativity. Through being with (Wells, 2019) a number of young people, one on one, the musical staff member has frequently enabled them to explore that which holds them back. The young person arrives as a stranger within the service. Their identity is still being formed. The colleague hosts them as a guest and gradually the young person tells their story. In doing this the colleague becomes the guest to their story (Basil, 2019). For many young people this can be a liberating experience.

Creative Spirit: Staff Stories

The approach to using the *Creative Spirit* resource is rooted in the values of care (Noddings, 2013), compassion (Hendricks, 2018), generosity, and respect, the four values adopted by Alabare. Katy speaks of the importance of second chances and how this is demonstrated in nurturing the gifting of the young person (K. Mascall, personal communication, September 16, 2020). The staff take delight in, and see the abundance within, the young person. This contrasts with an approach that attempts to address deficit issues such as those associated with homelessness, poverty, broken relationships, and unhealthy addiction (Wells, 2017).

Staff member Katy recalls how she worked closely with a young person (K. Mascall, personal communication, September 18, 2020). She comments on the needs present at the beginning of the placement and the support work offered through cooking and baking. She comments on how the *Creative Spirit* approach was of benefit in the overall program of support. On reading Katy's account it is interesting to notice the importance of trust (Hendricks, 2018) and respect and how they developed during the conversations that accompanied the baking. The young person developed a network of values. She was generous and gave back to her home community by sharing her cooking and baking. The overall shape of this story is fairly typical and provides an insight into local practice shaped by *Creative Spirit* (Alabare, 2019). Katy writes (K. Mascall, personal communication, September 18, 2020):

> This young person came into the service at age sixteen and behaviors were so extreme the potential for eviction was a daily occurrence. Taking a variety of drugs, including class A's coupled with serious anti-social behavior towards property and others around them had led to the relationship breakdown with their parent. They were incredibly vulnerable due to their age, gender and risk-taking behavior. Unfortunately they were the witness of, and subjected to, traumatic events.
>
> Trust and rapport were developed through the young person's love of cooking and the ambition to become a chef later in life. Support staff built upon this ambition and through cookery they raised subjects such as self-esteem and self-worth and what the young person wanted for their life. Issues around the value the young person put on themselves as well as the perception of peers were discussed. There was no subject the support staff were unwilling to address and explore with the young person.
>
> The young person started to build positive steps and make them their core values to live by. These conversations gained trust, respect and honesty between the young person and staff and this meant the young person's behavior changed and reduced to a low level and drug taking stopped. They also make great cakes for everyone to share!

Within this account I detect resonance not only with the touchstone of creativity but also that of community. There is an experience of hospitality that is demonstrated by an openness to others (Pohl, 2012). An increased connectedness develops between the young person and Katy which creates space for vulnerability to be shared (Palmer, 2004).

Chaplain Heather captures the setting of a conversation she had the privilege of experiencing. Heather ascertained that a young person enjoyed walking. They walked side by side along the Kennet and Avon canal towpath on a beautiful summer day. Heather recalls, "There was plenty of time to hear about hopes for the young woman's future and the baby she was expecting, and to build a relationship" (Smith Serjeant, 2019, as quoted in Alabare, 2019, p. 14).

A number of young people have been encouraged to turn their story into a song as a way of coming to terms with past hurts. Elements of the story are explored and parts are selected for further development. These are worked up to create a chorus and several verses. Time is taken to develop a musical hook line, a chord sequence, and a riff. Gradually the elements required to form the basis of the song are ready. When the young person is confident with their song, tracks are laid down and recorded. In some instances a video recording is made of the young person singing their song. Some young people create a performance enhanced through lighting effects, a carefully crafted backdrop, particular choices around clothing, and the use of vivid makeup. Through such a creative process the young person works with the darkness they have experienced. They often appreciate the scale of their artistic achievement. Nevertheless it is the conversations that happen during the process that are important. Once the song is complete and shared with others the young person inhabits a new place. It is from here, with increased confidence, that new opportunities are sought by the young person, and a greater commitment to seeking further support is made.[17]

Nicky struggled with anger management (Alabare, 2019). Her interest in singing and modest keyboard facility enabled her support worker to encourage her to create a song. Nicky was able to communicate at a deeper level through writing down her feelings. The staff member recalled, "The very next session she brought a very emotional set of words, which gave me a real insight into the problems she was facing, notable being bullied at school" (Alabare, 2019, p. 10). Initially Nicky was too embarrassed to sing her song in front of the staff member. Nevertheless through feedback on the recorded song and further encouragement she wrote several more songs. Nicky then decided to sing with a band at school.

17   I have seen this happen a number of times as I have visited homes and hostels and spoken with staff and young people.

An Explosion of Creativity

"Creativity was found to be an important conduit for spiritual experience" (Swinton, 2004, p. 2). Whilst Swinton writes of people with learning disabilities this statement expresses what may be true for others. Today across Alabare clients of all ages together with staff are experimenting with creativity that encompasses not only music but coloring, glass jar painting, art groups, bush craft, and nail art.[18] Once again it is the accompanying conversation that is central to movement toward healing and wholeness. One client comments, "Alabare has given me a sense to give back" (Alabare, 2019, p. 15). Interestingly, giving is often identified as integral to wellbeing (Wright & Pascoe, 2015).

Creative Spirit can lead to change that happens weeks or months later. However, sometimes one-off workshops have an important role also. Colleague Lisa recalls (L. Thomas, personal communication, August 27, 2020):

> One example of a workshop that I enjoy running is a positivity jar workshop, in which residents can decorate a jar and then clients can jot down positive things that have happened. In a month or so afterwards people can look in their jars and see what they have achieved. Prior to the last workshop a resident had been in tears beforehand. She said that she had not got anything positive to say. We broke down the elements in her life and she found a lot of positives. She went off smiling, which was very pleasing to see. The other resident who came has children and a dual addiction. Again, she could not find anything positive to say, and I reminded her of her children. She then said "I was offered a room at Alabare."[19]

The benefits of spirituality include reducing vulnerability and increasing hope and meaning in addition to bringing an increased sense of connectedness (Brown, 2015; Corry et al., 2014). One Alabare chaplain

18   Within the learning disability strand of Alabare's work, singing with Makaton helps to build community and nurture faith. This is central to my work as senior chaplain and that of Chaplain Andrew.

19   Unity House is a hostel in North Wiltshire.

picks up the theme of hope in connection with an art class in an Alabare hostel. "It always comes down to the look in people's eyes. It tells you whether people are happy […] whether they are on a course that might lead to hope. Here people are on that course" (Quoted in Alabare, 2019, p. 15).

Conclusion

Spirituality is understood as bringing meaning to life, and this may be mediated through an engagement with a touchstone such as creativity. Conversations often accompany creativity and can lead to the processing of experiences that have become frozen within a person. This can be liberating and help the young person to move on with greater confidence. Within Alabare this has led to the initiative *Creative Spirit* that is reshaping support working. The story is in its infancy and will prove a rich seam for future research.

Bibliography

Alabare. (2014, December 9). *We will walk with you, everyday* [Video]. YouTube. <https://www.youtube.com/watch?v=0X3bj2PYK4o>

Alabare. (2017). *The spirituality handbook*. Alabare Christian Care and Support.

Alabare. (2018). *Policy 23: Spirituality*. Alabare Christian Care and Support.

Alabare. (2019). *Creative spirit: Case studies and guidance for Alabare staff*. Alabare Christian Care and Support.

Alter, R. (2004). *The five books of Moses: A translation with commentary*. W.W. Norton & Company.

Basil, P. (2019). *Be my guest: Reflections on food, community and the meaning of generosity*. Canongate.

Boyce-Tillman, J. (2016). *Experiencing music – Restoring the spiritual*. Peter Lang.

Brown, B. (2015). *Daring greatly: How the courage to be vulnerable transforms the way we live, love, parent, and lead*. Penguin Life.

Corbett, S. (2017). *How to be a craftivist: The art of gentle protest.* Unbound.

Corry, D. A., Lewis, C. A., & Mallett, J. (2014). Harnessing the mental health benefits of the creativity spirituality construct: Introducing the theory of transformative coping. *Journal of Spirituality in Mental Health, 16*(2), 89–110. <https://doi.org/10.1080/19349637.2014.896854>

Gravell, C. (2014). *Lost and found: Spirituality in the lives of homeless people.* Lemos and Crane.

Harle, T. (2012). The formless void as organizational template. *Journal of Management, Spirituality and Religion, 9*(1), 103–121. <https://doi.org/10.1080/14766086.2012.641100>

Heidegger, M. (1978). *Being and time* (J. Maquarrie & E. Robinson, Trans.). Wiley-Blackwell. (Original work published 1927).

Hendricks, K. S. (2018). *Compassionate music teaching: A framework for motivation and engagement in the 21st century.* Rowman & Littlefield Publishers.

Holloway, R. (2019). *Looking in the distance: The human search for meaning.* Canongate Books Ltd. (Original work published 2004).

Levine, S. K. (2009). *Trauma, tragedy, therapy: The arts and human suffering.* Jessica Kingsley Publishers.

Noddings, N. (2013). *Caring: A feminine approach to ethics and moral education: A relational approach to ethics and moral education* (2nd ed.). University of California Press.

Palmer, P. J. (2004). *A hidden wholeness: The journey toward an undivided life: Welcoming the soul and weaving community in a wounded world.* Jossey Bass.

Paterson, M. (2019). *Between a rock and a hard place: Pastoral supervision revisited & revisioned.* Amazon Fulfillment.

Pohl, C. D. (2012). *Living into community: Cultivating practices that sustain us.* Wm. B. Eerdmans.

Rankin, P. (2005). *Buried spirituality: A report on the findings of the fellowship in the spirituality of young people based at Sarum College, Salisbury.* Sarum College Press.

Reed, B. (1978). *The dynamics of religion.* DLT.

Rowson, J. (2014). *Spiritualise: Revitalising spirituality to address 21st century challenges.* Royal Society of Arts.

Rowson, J. (2017). *Spiritualise: Cultivating spiritual sensibility to address 21st century challenges.* Perspectiva.

Smith Serjeant, H. (2019). A chaplain's story. In Alabare (Ed.), *Creative spirit: Case studies and guidance for Alabare staff* (p. 14). Alabare Christian Care and Support.

Stockitt, R. (2015). *The roots of transformation: Negotiating the dynamics of growth.* Cascade Books.

Swinton, J. (2001). Spirituality and the lives of people with learning disabilities. *Updates 3/6*. The Mental Health Foundation.

Swinton, J. (2002). Spirituality and the lives of people with learning disabilities. *Tizard Learning Disability Review*, *7*(4), 29–35. <https://doi.org/10.1108/13595474200200037>

Swinton, J. (2004). Why are we here? Spirituality and the lives of people with learning disabilities. *Updates*, *5*(11). <https://www.stmichaelshospice.org.uk/LD_spirtuality_support.pdf>

The new revised standard version of the Bible (2003). Oxford University Press.

Wells, S. (2017). *Incarnational ministry: Being with the church*. W.B. Eerdmans.

Wells, S. (2019). *A future that's bigger than the past: Catalysing kingdom communities*. Canterbury Press.

Winnicott, D. W. (1958). *Collected papers through paediatrics to psycho-analysis*. Tavistock.

Wright, P. R., & Pascoe, R. (2015). Eudamonia and creativity: The art of human flourishing. *The Cambridge Journal of Education*, *45*(3), 295–306. <https://doi.org/10.1080/0305764X.2013.855172>

Zlotowitz, M. (1995). Bereishis Genesis: A new translation with a commentary anthologized from Talmudic, Midrashic and Rabbinic sources. Mesorah Publications Ltd. (Original work published 1986).Web Resources

Alabare. (2020, September 15). *Creative spirituality*. <https://www.Alabare.co.uk/uploads/Creative_Spirituality_A5_-_November.pdf>

Susanna Wesley Foundation. (2020, September 15). *Keith Thomasson-Alabare*. <https://susannawesleyfoundation.org/keith-thomasson-Alabare/>

LIESL VAN DER MERWE, JANELIZE MORELLI, AND
CATRIEN WENTINK

8 Exploring Lived Experiences of Relationality during Participatory Performances of Sacred Musics at a Care Home for the Elderly

Introduction

The Oak Tree Elderly Care Home is situated in a leafy suburb in a peri-urban town in the North West province of South Africa. The quiet streets are lined with trees and as you enter the facility you are greeted by a friendly security guard on the left, asking you to sign in and a little fish pond on the right. Inside, there is a sense of institutionalization. The walls are painted beige and adorned with portraits of influential community leaders, reminders to adhere to procedures, and slightly faded paintings. Down a steep wheelchair ramp, one enters the general hall, with the dining hall on the left and a lounge area on the right. This is where the music has been happening on Monday afternoons since February 2018. Three university lecturers, a postdoctoral fellow, and an undergraduate student go to Oak Tree Elderly Care Home to engage the residents in musicking activities. We open the concertina doors to the hall; move chairs out of their rigid row-like formation; and unpack lyric books, music stands, and instruments, all as part of our ritual within this space. Here we listen to music, play music instruments, improvise, and sing secular and sacred songs. For this chapter we report only on the participants' experiences of communally singing the sacred songs.

This particular weekly activity is part of a larger project supported by the National Research Foundation of South Africa investigating how engaging in community music-making facilitates social cohesion. The importance of relationality became a focal point in our search to understand the complexity of the dynamics of social cohesion through musicking better.

The importance of relationships for positive health outcomes and wellbeing for older adults is well documented. There is evidence suggesting that fewer supportive relationships and relational resources are associated with higher rates of depression and suicidal ideation amongst older adults (Vanderhorst & McLaren, 2005). The lack of social and emotional support for older adults poses serious challenges for assisted living facilities and elderly care homes. Park (2009) suggests that such institutions may contribute to the wellbeing of their residents by providing opportunities for enjoyable social interaction. In her study she focused specifically on the role mealtimes can play as a catalyst for meaningful relationship building. In this chapter we will focus on the role that sacred musicking played in the relational worlds of our participants.

Creech et al. (2013) assert that musicking continues to play an important role in identity development, emotional regulation, and wellbeing for aging participants. Furthermore, musicking, as an activity which promotes a shared focus, may contribute to wellbeing as a harmonious passion project (Rousseau & Vallerand, 2008). There is a plethora of research indicating that active musicking contributes in a variety of ways to subjective wellbeing in older adults (Clair & Memmott, 2008; Lai & Good, 2006; Sung et al., 2010, 2012). Our study contributes to the literature on this topic by combining an investigation of the important health and wellbeing outcomes of musicking for older adults with satisfying a curiosity about the relational implications of sacred musicking for older adults.

Therefore, the purpose of this narrative inquiry was to explore eight older adults' lived experiences of relationality, when singing sacred songs together during weekly musicking sessions at Oak Tree Care Home for the Elderly. We understand relationality as entailing a connection to self, others, the environment, and a transcendent Other (Van der Merwe & Habron, 2015).

Procedures

We collected storied data through open-ended interviews with eight women: Maria, Hannie, Carla, Susan, Bianca, Lorraine, Riana, and Jeanette, who wanted to share their stories. All the women were regular participants at our musicking sessions and all were residents at the Oak Tree Care Home for the Elderly. The data also included our weekly observation and reflection diaries over approximately fifteen months. Habron and Van der Merwe's (2020) narrative coding structure was used to analyze and co-code the stories and observations. Through our co-coding process three stories became salient as representative of some of the key findings in this study. We present these stories as micro-narratives. Each of the authors converted the data from one interview into a micro-narrative. These narratives reflect both the unique, individual experiences of the participants and the pluralist viewpoints of the authors (Frost et al., 2010). We maintain that embracing this pluralism in our divergent worldviews as researchers adds to the trustworthiness of our findings.

Maria "… And Still I Rise" – Arranged by Liesl

Let me tell you the story of Maria. Maria lives in South Africa in an institution, a care facility for the elderly, disabled or weakened. This facility feels like a hostel and hospital in one. When one enters, the smell of cooked food and disinfectant hangs in the air. Here flowers mean that another resident has passed away. Once, when I came to visit my grandfather, Maria was sitting in front of the building, howling her heart out. All she could get out was, "My family forgot me, … my husband and daughters forgot me …, they forgot to pick me up!" She had mixed up the days.

But her story does not start here. A terrible thing happened when she was only 3 months old. She told me the following story:

My father murdered my mommy. I had to live with this bastard. Not only did he murder my mother, he also raped my two sisters … his own children! and a school girl where he was headmaster. I am so sad and angry! We had to move around a lot. Now I cannot move how I want to any longer because I have a disease that is killing my brain cells. I cannot remember a lot anymore, but I know that I love children and music. You know, I had a choir, my first performance was in '97. There is music in this place.

Every Monday a group from the university comes to play bassoon and piano, it is so beautiful! A highlight for me at these sessions was when the little girl, Bea, sang. I miss dear Bea so very much. It is difficult for me to walk to these sessions because my body cannot do what I want it to do. But when we sing sacred songs my body calms down. Music is the apex of my life!

I come to the Monday music sessions to sing. I always sang and I always will sing. I love sacred music. I've always been a Christian. When we sing the sacred songs my body doesn't jerk so much and I am able to sing on pitch and in harmony, even though I cannot speak well anymore. God is a special God and the music makes my relationship with God better. Sometimes I feel crazy, but the sacred music heals my head. I need music.

Carla, Forever Young – Arranged by Catrien

You would not believe that Carla is 79 years old. She has blonde, shoulder-length hair that is neatly blow-waved and styled. Her makeup is always perfect and she is beautifully and neatly dressed in bright colors. The first time I saw Carla, I thought that she was too young and vibrant to be in an old-age care facility already. In our interview I could see that she actually shared these feelings: "I already lost three husbands. The last one died in March last year and that is the only reason why I am here, because my children don't want me to live on my own, but I still do everything myself. … I don't need any caring." Carla is a very proud lady and proud of the fact that she can still do everything herself, does not take any medication and exercises regularly: "I used to do aerobics at Virgin Active and I still run every evening." This causes a problem for Carla in her current environment as certain activities that are done with the immobile older adults irritate her. However, during our conversation, she mentioned a number of times that she really enjoys the music sessions, and she specifically asked that we should never stop these sessions. "If the music stops, I would feel very bad as it will leave a gap in my life." She also enjoys it to just "sit and listen to the music" and the different instruments.

For Carla the music sessions are a personal experience: "These sessions are doing a lot for me as a person." She experiences the sessions as "calming," the instruments as "soothing," and they are an "enjoyable distraction" each week.

Carla also has a very close relationship with God and she feels that the hymns "should definitely be part of the music sessions." "The Lord is very good for me and He is always with me. I am deeply religious and that is why I sometimes get a lump in my throat when we are singing these hymns. My heart feels full, because the songs are so beautiful." She specifically mentions the hymns "Nearer my God to Thee" and "Amazing Grace" as some of her favorites.

Hannie, a Leader Without a Congregation – Arranged by Janelize

You know, some days I can speak, but on most days I don't feel like it. I can tell you about myself, but I don't know if this will help …

Music has always been a part of who I am. Back when we were children my mother heard the voice of God and we always had to sing. We didn't sing wonderfully, but later in life, I even sang in church.

You see, the whole thing with the accordion started with Ben, my husband. He could play any instrument. He told me to start with the guitar and I tried, but it didn't work out. Then, I tried the accordion and it stuck. Later I stopped playing in church, it was just the nerves, but late at night I would sit and sing the hymns. When you sit alone you can take your time, you even forget how late it is. You don't want to go to bed because the Lord is working with you.

When I had to move, I don't know what happened to my file, all my songs … To move here … it is difficult. When I first got here I wanted to do something, something with music and something for the Lord, but in a way the people here are not receptive anymore. I struggle to remember all the stories, but many people here remember nothing ….

When I first got here, I was very depressed, with this whole moving business. You know, such a moving thing, it is horrible. You can see how horrible it is – some people don't even want to leave their rooms anymore. But then I decided to go to the music session and then I would feel better. When you come to sing – it takes all the depression away, it is something big. These music sessions are a different kind of gathering. It is not like church – there is a different feeling. You know how people are here, they do not want to come to things, they do not want to do things together, but music is wonderful! Sometimes a hymn just doesn't sing well, but when it does, it brings you a blessing – sometimes you sing so joyfully it feels like you are transported to heaven. Music, it used to be my life before moving here. It draws you closer, closer to each other. It makes you feel good, good toward someone else.

Findings

Music as Mediator

In our findings Music is the main character. Our participants actively an-thropomorphize music and allow it to take on the role of a person in their lives. This person mediates and facilitates their relationships with them-selves, others, their environment, and God. Music, as a person, facilitates their spiritual experiences. Carla is anxious that Music will go away and Lorraine says "I love Music very much." In Susan's experience, Music cre-ates "opportunities for more aesthetic and spiritual experiences." Music is credited with having active attributes: "Music shares love" (Bianca). Riana said "Music serves the people." Hannie feels that "Music pulls you closer to each other." Not only does Music facilitate the relationships between people, it also brings them closer to the Lord and the Holy Spirit. Music is also described as a friend: "Music calms me down" (Carla, Jeanette); "Music is good to me" (Lorraine, Bianca). They feel they can escape to Music, it "provides distraction" (Jeanette, Carla). Carla and Lorraine feel "touched" by Music. Music plays the role of a very important "person" in their lives and therefore they state that they "need Music." The intentions of the music makers might also play a role in the way the participants experience the Music.

The Intentions of the Music Makers

Boyce-Tillman (2016) rightly states that "in much of Western culture we have lost the notion of intention in musical performances." Intention is often considered an important part of the spiritual experience. Therefore, we reflected on our intentions. During these sessions it is Liesl's intention to share love and compassion through music. Catrien describes her intention as follows: "I want them to make music with us and thus give them something that they can be a part of. I try to use music that is beautiful and that they will enjoy or recognize. Ultimately, I just want to give them a music experience to look forward to every week." Janelize explained that she wants to engage them in active musicking of their choice. We also consider the participants as music makers. Some of their intentions are to show gratitude to God (Carla), to come and sing with others (Maria), to feel better, praise His name, and help someone else (Hannie).

Relationship with Their Environment

The institutionalized environment limits interaction, since the residents are mostly isolated in their rooms and when they sit outside there is limited space and they all have to sit in a row. For Hannie and Carla the move to this residence required a huge adjustment. Hannie lost her role in the church community and Carla, as an independent highly functional adult, feels she does not belong here. Carla and Susan both lost their husbands and therefore had to move to the residence. During the move everything got lost. However, Hannie explains how going to the music session takes all this depression away. Susan feels that Music takes her to a better place.

Relationship with Self

The participants struggle to adjust to their old age and disabilities. Maria cannot move the way she wants to and Hannie cannot hold her accordion any longer. Susan and Hannie do not always identify with our choices of traditional Reformed sacred music. Jeanette on the other hand identifies with the music, because it reminds her of the way she was brought up. Carla is a dancer and feels trapped in this institution. Despite these experiences, they find that music helps them negotiate their sense of self. Hannie feels a wonderful freedom in these music sessions, whereas Carla enjoys private aesthetic listening experiences. In Maria's case, the music is transformational and helps her to heal mentally.

Relationships with Others

Lorraine and Bianca said, "We go together" and Maria and Riana have made new friends with other people at the music sessions. Although interaction is difficult, mostly because of their hearing difficulties, everybody participates in the music sessions and for some it is the only time in the week that they leave their rooms. Bianca, Carla, and Susan enjoy the interaction with the musicians, and Maria cherishes the interaction with the musicians' children. Everyone enjoys singing together.

Relationship with God

Carla explains that the music is a way in which she can give thanks to God for her good health. "Nearer my God to Thee" is one of the sacred songs they most often choose to sing. This is their longing, to go to heaven and to be with God. Through the music they experience this closeness with God and Hannie sometimes feels like she rises up to heaven. Maria says that Music improves her relationship with God and when we sing "How Great Thou Art" Lorraine feels like she belongs to

Jesus and she feels safe with Him. The hymn, "Our Father Who Art in Heaven," also resonates with most participants because it was a part of their life history.

Discussion

Our notion of anthropomorphizing Music as a mediator resonates with Ansdell's (2014) findings that people relate to music as if it were a person. We took this one step further by discovering that this "person," Music, actively facilitates relationships with the environment, self, others, and God, and in doing so facilitates spiritual experiences. Quindag (2017) has explored a relational ontology to understand spiritual music. She focused on all the relationships that contribute to the creation and performance of spiritual music. We agree that musicking is a social act and that in making music, relationships are built and secured. However, we expand this idea and argue that Music plays the role of a person, a mediator, who helps to restore relationships, when the musicians have intentions that support spiritual experiences.

The metaphor of Music as a person emphasizes that music is an "interactive, relational [and] multi-modal activity" (Van der Schyff, 2015, p. 4). With this metaphor we also emphasize "praxis and personal histories for the development of musical meanings" (Van der Schyff, 2015, p. 4). Music as a person is only one of the possible roles that music plays in these eight older adults' lives.

When Boyce-Tillman discusses the domain of her phenomenography, namely expression, she describes "Music as Companionship" (2016, p. 172) and explains that music can fill a void, much like God does to help people through life's difficulties. We add to this notion that Music provides not only companionship, but that the personified agent, Music, can serve as mediator to connect us with the self, others, the environment, and the Transcendental Other, and in doing so creates opportunities for spiritual experiences, which aligns with the intentions of the musicians who facilitate the sessions. This view is supported in emergent research on anthropomorphism, which indicates that individuals who lack social connections may be more prone to anthropomorphize non-human agents (Waytz, Epley et al., 2010).

The act of anthropomorphizing Music may also indicate a specific kind of relationship between the individual and their environment. Waytz, Morewedge et al. (2010) assert that anthropomorphizing may be a coping strategy used by individuals to manage an environment which feels out of their control. This is confirmed by the ways in which participants explained their feelings of loss and helplessness, and highlighted the role music played in coping with these feelings. Given this insight, it is possible that the relational experiences mediated through musicking may have helped participants cope with their feelings of loss and helplessness.

It is also important to note that anthropomorphizing music does not just have implications for the participants. When we attribute human qualities and actions to non-human objects, ideas, or processes it has an impact on the agent (in this case music). By anthropomorphizing music, the participants are attributing social influence to music and also asserting that music is an agent worth moral and ethical consideration (Waytz, Epley et al., 2010).

We would like to end this chapter with an excerpt from the Jacques Brel song:

> *The old folks*
> The old folks dream no more
> The books have gone to sleep, the piano's out of tune
> The little cat is dead and no more do they sing
> On a Sunday afternoon
> The old folks move no more, their world's become too small
> Their bodies feel like lead
> They might look out the window or else sit in a chair

But when we make music on a Monday afternoon at 3:00 p.m., everything changes for these old folks.

Acknowledgments

This work is based on the research supported wholly by the National Research Foundation of South Africa (Grant Numbers: 118579).

Bibliography

Ansdell, D. G. (2014). *How music helps in music therapy and everyday life*. Ashgate Publishing, Ltd.

Boyce-Tillman, J. (2016). *Experiencing music – Restoring the spiritual: Music as well-being*. Peter Lang.

Clair, A. A., & Memmott, J. (2008). *Therapeutic uses of music with older adults*. American Music Therapy Association.

Creech, A., Hallam, S., McQueen, H., & Varvarigou, M. (2013). The power of music in the lives of older adults. *Research Studies in Music Education*, *35*(1), 87–102. <https://doi.org/10.1177/1321103X13478862>

Frost, N., Nolas, S. M., Brooks-Gordon, B., Esin, C., Holt, A., Mehdizadeh, L., & Shinebourne, P. (2010). Pluralism in qualitative research: The impact of different researchers and qualitative approaches on the analysis of qualitative data. *Qualitative Research*, *10*(4), 441–460. <https://doi.org/10.1177/1468794110366802>

Habron, J., & Van der Merwe, L. (2020). Stories students tell about their lived experiences of spirituality in the Dalcroze class. *British Journal of Music Education*, *37*(2), 125–139. <https://doi.org/10.1017/S0265051720000091>

Lai, H. L., & Good, M. (2006). Music improves sleep quality in older adults. *Journal of Advanced Nursing*, *53*(1), 134–144. <https://doi.org/10.1111/j.1365-2648.2006.03693.x>

Park, N. S. (2009). The relationship of social engagement to psychological well-being of older adults in assisted living facilities. *Journal of Applied Gerontology*, *28*(4), 461–481. <https://doi.org/10.1177/0733464808328606>

Quindag, S. (2017). Seeking oneness: Exploring a relational ontology of spiritual music. In Boyce-Tillman (Ed.), *Spirituality and music education. Perspectives from three continents* (pp. 87–102). Peter Lang. <https://doi.org/10.3726/b13177>

Rousseau, F. L., & Vallerand, R. J. (2008). An examination of the relationship between passion and subjective well-being in older adults. *The International Journal of Aging and Human Development, 66*(3), 195–211. <https://doi.org/10.2190/AG.66.3.b>

Sung, H., Chang, A. M., & Lee, W. L. (2010). A preferred music listening intervention to reduce anxiety in older adults with dementia in nursing homes. *Journal of Clinical Nursing, 19*(7–8), 1056–1064. <https://doi.org/10.1111/j.1365-2702.2009.03016.x>

Sung, H., Lee, W., Li, T., & Watson, R. (2012). A group music intervention using percussion instruments with familiar music to reduce anxiety and agitation of institutionalized older adults with dementia. *International Journal of Geriatric Psychiatry, 27*(6), 621–627. <https://doi.org/10.1002/gps.2761>

Van der Merwe, L., & Habron, J. (2015). A conceptual model of spirituality in music education. *Journal of Research in Music Education, 63*(1), 47–69. <https://doi.org/10.1177/0022429415575314>

Van der Schyff, D. (2015). Music as a manifestation of life: Exploring enactivism and the "Eastern perspective" for music education. *Frontiers in Psychology, 6*, Article 345. <https://doi.org/10.3389/fpsyg.2015.00345>

Vanderhorst, R. K., & McLaren, S. (2005). Social relationships as predictors of depression and suicidal ideation in older adults. *Aging & Mental Health, 9*(6), 517–525. <https://doi.org/10.1080/13607860500193062>

Waytz, A., Epley, N., & Cacioppo, J. T. (2010). Social cognition unbound: Insights into anthropomorphism and dehumanization. *Current Directions in Psychological Science, 19*(1), 58–62. <https://doi.org/10.1177/0963721409359302>

Waytz, A., Morewedge, C. K., Epley, N., Monteleone, G., Gao, J.-H., & Cacioppo, J. T. (2010). Making sense by making sentient: Effectance motivation increases anthropomorphism. *Journal of Personality and Social Psychology, 99*(3), 410–435. <https://doi.org/10.1037/a0020240>

GARETH DYLAN SMITH

9 *Mud Drums* and Magic

Spirituality and Collaborative Improvised Drumming

Introduction

This chapter accounts for the experiences of two drummers – Martin Urbach and me – realizing the *Mud Drums* project – a collaborative, improvised drum kit recording session in New York City on July 6, 2019. Martin, like this author, is a drummer, teacher, and scholar. He is also a social justice activist, and teaches high school in New York City. Our aim was simply to make music together; hopefully sparks would fly and there might even be magic. We experienced fulfillment and joy playing together, a feeling that remained when we listened back to the recording. We both felt we had created something special, and discussed how writing about this experience might deepen our understanding of what we do as drummers, as illustrated in this excerpt from a conversation one week after the session[20]:

> MARTIN: We write a paper on how improvising (musicking or whatever) together helps in expanding how we know what we know and how we theorize? Or something! Mainly I think academics need to hear that there are some folks who talk academia but also who just literally act like 15 year old fools who JUST got their first set of drums

---

20 We intended to co-author this chapter, but due to Martin's work and activism commitments, we agreed I would write it alone.

GARETH: I could not agree more
                       (Messenger chat, July 13, 2019)

In this chapter I describe some of our experiences of playing and listening to *Mud Drums*. I frame these using June Boyce-Tillman's five-part
model of spirituality, in which she explains how spirituality is a state or
event comprising four elements (Boyce-Tillman, 2004, 2009, 2011, 2020).
These components of spirituality are Materials, Expression, Construction
and Values. To the extent possible in this brief chapter, I also draw on others'
work to help situate our theoretical and experiential understanding of our
drumming practice as spirituality.

Boyce-Tillman (2011) asserts that "within Western society it is still
a basic human challenge to keep body, mind and soul together, and …
musicking offers immense possibilities here" (p. 240). We were excited
to rise to this challenge, and to meet it through playing drums. As educators, scholars, and otherwise busy adults, we spend much of our lives in
our heads – planning, conceptualizing, framing, and theorizing. The joy
of drumming on this occasion was that it was musically spontaneous and
wholly immersive – engaging our ears, our bodies, and our very souls.

A Framework for Exploring Spirituality

As Boyce-Tillman (2011) makes clear, there are numerous ways in which
spirituality is and has been understood, practiced, and experienced
throughout the history of humans trying to make sense of ourselves, the
world around us, and beyond. Boyce-Tillman's model of spirituality comprises the following, as also set out in Figure 9.1.

- Materials – the instruments, the body, and the technical aspects involved in producing sound as well as the acoustics of the space
- Expression – the feelingful aspects of the experience including those
  within the sounds themselves (intrinsic) and those locked onto the
  sounds by significant life experiences (extrinsic)

- Construction – the way music is put together – what is repeated, what is changed, the degree of contrast
- Values – the context of musicking and its cultural meaning

These combine to account for:

- Spirituality/liminality – a different way of knowing where time and space operate differently (Boyce-Tillman, 2020, p. 75).

This exploration of spirituality at the drum kit extends from recognizing what Boyce-Tillman (2011) refers to as "Descartes' error" (p. 140), that is, the notion that as humans, we think therefore we are. To understand our engagement with phenomena as purely cognitive and rational, however, is misguided. Martin and I do not play drums for rational reasons – indeed, as I have explained (Smith, 2017), often reasons for playing drums are quite *ir*rational. Martin and I do not play in order to satisfy cognitive ends or to improve cognitive function. We are attracted to drumming because of truths beautifully captured and articulated by Salome Voegelin (2010),

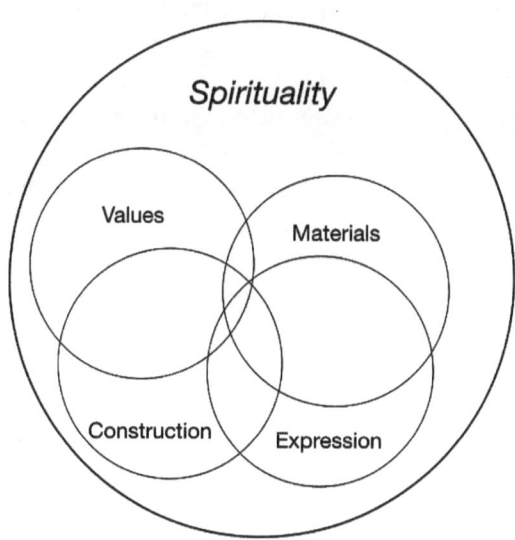

Figure 9.1. Boyce-Tillman's model of spirituality (2020, p. 74)

such as "the sonic now is … an expansion of experience in timespace" (p. 164) and "the aesthetic moment is the now in which sensation meets perception" (p. 182). Drumming feels good, and we feel something special and extraordinary when we do it. Richard Shusterman also refers to art-making in terms of "aesthetic experience," about which he says, "it is essentially valuable and enjoyable; it is something vividly felt and subjectively savoured, affectively absorbing us and focussing our attention on its immediate presence; it is meaningful experience, not mere sensation; it is at the core of what makes art, art" (Shusterman, 2000, p. 17). Boyce-Tillman acknowledges the validity of the "aesthetic" in accounting for such experiential phenomena, but, because of the particular ways in which "aesthetic" has been deployed in the Western classical music tradition (2011, p. 172), she eschews the term in favor of "spirituality."

Creating *Mud Drums*

Martin and I knew of one another from the music education scene and knew from a conversation over beers and macaroni and cheese in a Greenwich Village bar in April 2019, that we shared similar cultural references in terms of drumming heritage, and that each of us had relocated to one of the world's major cosmopolitan cities to pursue drumming as a career. While over the last fifteen years or so, other personal and professional responsibilities had come to occupy positions of priority in both of our lives, the burning flame of the deep need to play drums was not diminished in us. We set a date to meet up and play drums to share the spiritual satisfaction from doing so. I have called this type of fulfillment "autotelic," or intrinsically valuable (Smith, 2019a), an understanding I subsequently critiqued (Smith, 2021), explaining that I play drums not in order to play them, but because of the holistic, eudaimonic fulfillment I derive therefrom; that was what we sought on this day.

On Saturday July 6, 2019, Martin and I traveled independently to The James L. Dolan Studio in the Steinhardt School of Culture, Education, and Human Development at New York University (NYU) in Greenwich

Village, New York City. We set up a large acoustic drum kit (Gareth), a small electronic drum kit (Martin), and configured the studio's acoustic house drum kit. The recording engineer, Celia Yang, set up microphones and direct-inputs to capture the array of timbres and dynamics we hoped to produce. We had opted to play in a recording studio (instead, say, of a rehearsal space) because I had cost-free access to first-class facilities audio engineers at NYU. We took advantage of this in case it "worked" and we might wish to keep a record of it.

We recorded around ninety minutes of improvised drumming over about three hours, pausing somewhere in the middle for fresh air and to avail ourselves of falafel from the legendary Mamoun's, nearby. We exchanged few words during the day, limiting our discussion to suggestions such as "shall we try something a bit slower this time?" or "let's switch kits this time and see what happens." The idea was to not to plan, but to feel, listen, and hear – to *drum*. As saxophonist Chris Potter notes, "it can be hard to play with musicians who haven't really learned to play with you, and you haven't really learned to play with them" (Philip, 2013, p. 439). However, on this occasion, we were delighted to find that we met in a deep, mutual groove almost immediately and remained there for the whole day. We went our separate ways after recording, and stayed in touch via Facebook Messenger about the recordings Celia shared with us that evening. We agreed on some edits to the clumsiest parts of our jamming, cut about fifteen minutes in total, and agreed to leave the rest as a warts-and-all snapshot of the in-the-moment experience. We contacted audio engineer, Alasdair Kelly, who swiftly mixed and mastered the music to our taste. We uploaded the mixes to YouTube as the *Mud Drums* playlist[21] for us and for anyone else who might be curious.

We kept in touch occasionally, usually just to say how excited one of us was to listen again to the playlist. After deciding to write about the project for this book, we held a Zoom call on March 25, 2020 to discuss how we would approach it. I listened back to the Zoom recording and transcribed verbatim the sections where we discussed the recording and our experiences

---

21   The *Mud Drums* playlist can be accessed here: https://www.youtube.com/playlist?list=PLm1_1sLmHCYsixpr0TZlEPTGQkv4M3fWa

of and related to it. I then read back through our Messenger chat, and pasted into a document any discussion of our planning, realizing, and responding to *Mud Drums*. Due to time constraints, Martin permitted me to write this chapter alone, as noted above, but I shared the manuscript with Martin to review before submitting to the book's editors. He approved.

Elements of Spirituality in Making *Mud Drums*

This section is structured using Boyce-Tillman's (2020) five-part model of spirituality. In the subsections below, I interlace framing of Materials, Expression, Construction, and Values with descriptions of our experience and data from our conversations. I include dates for quotes from our ongoing Messenger chat, and timestamps from the Zoom call. In the final section of the chapter, I draw some conclusions regarding Spirituality and playing drums.

Materials

Boyce-Tillman (2009, p. 185) reminds us that "all music consists of concrete Materials drawn from the human body and the environment." I have explored the depth of the physical, bodily connection with my drums when playing them (Smith, 2017, 2019a, 2019b), echoing Auslander's observation that playing music is "an embodied event" in which "the physical body becomes one with the instrument and with the sound produced" (Stone-Davis, 2011, p. 162). The instruments Martin and I played were extensions of ourselves. For instance, my drums are twenty years old and have lived with me in seven homes in four cities in three countries; I have played them on hundreds of concerts and recordings, and know intimately the sonic potential of each drum and cymbal. We each brought our own drumsticks, key parts of the drumming experience that tend to be very personal to individual drummers. We also played the studio's house drum kit – a beautiful honey-brown, "satin natural" maple Gretsch kit (Gretsch, 2020) that complemented the mahogany wood tones of the studio floor – with the jazz department's sumptuous set of Zildjian K Custom Dark cymbals (Avedis Zildjian Company, 2020). These instruments – the drums and cymbals – are iconic brands and sounds in the history and culture of American jazz that we both love so well and in which we understood our collaboration to be rooted.

The studio environment was a familiar space to me as I had recorded here a handful of times with friends, and always with very pleasing results. There was something wonderfully inviting about the room. We loved the wooden floors, the acoustic paneling, the careful blending of woods and metals, and the finely crafted shape of the space with its high ceilings and sound-proofed windows and walls, so that we could make as unholy a drumming racket as we desired, yet be undetected by anyone on the floors above and below us, or even in the classrooms and bathrooms adjoining the walls of the studio. We were excited to work here as we could tell there was magic in these walls – the studio was alive with possibilities!

Expression

Boyce-Tillman explains that the domain of Expression "is concerned with the evocation of mood, emotion (individual or corporate), images, memories, an atmosphere on the part of all those involved in the musical performance. Here the subjectivity of all those involved in the musical event intersect" (2009, p. 186). Furthermore, she writes, "Expression … is important for the development of self-awareness and the development of authenticity – a person's sense of what constitutes The True for them" (Boyce-Tillman, 2011, p. 178). A large part of this collaboration was about establishing and reveling in a shared expression of joy, central to our respective and shared senses of self and purpose, as captured in these excerpts from our conversation:

> MARTIN: [making music is about] remembering … what are the things that make you feel alive inside, and reproducing that.
>
> (Zoom call, March 25, 2020, 23' 00")

GARETH: When it's good, it's REALLY good … the better you
            get, the better it gets … the love and the joy and the hard
            work, that's where the joy is, I think, that pursuit.

            (Zoom call, March 25, 2020, 26' 00")

Jazz drummer Brian Blade observes how "everybody wants to be lifted
up in their lives, in their experiences … It's great to find that balance between, okay, am I serving the situations, and am I giving what's needed,
and am I introducing something that feeds the fire of it?" (Blade, quoted
in Philip, 2013, p. 150). Drummer-scholar, Bill Bruford (2018) identifies
this approach as existing at the nexus of creativity and functionality, as
"mak[ing] the music work" and then "mak[ing] the music matter" (p. 17).
We both strongly empathize with jazz drummer Billy Hart's description
of how drumming "has always been a tremendous release" (Hart, quoted
in Philip, 2013, p. 124), a perspective reinforced by Boyce-Tillman (2011)
when she notes, how "music has profound effects on balancing relaxation
and excitement" (p. 247). Although in this instance Boyce-Tillman was
referring to religious choral music, her point rings very true in the context
of our collaborative improvised drumming as well.

    Our drumming functioned to facilitate a cathartic release that was also
engaging and thrilling. We reflected in our Zoom call as follows:

GARETH: I feel drumming is my meditation … when I feel whole
            again afterwards … [it can] centre everything, make me
            a better person, give me patience, calm me down, give
            me perspective, allow me to breathe again … recalibrate
            everything.

MARTIN: Yep, yep … it's ok to not get other things done as long
            as you're playing music and you're having fun and you're
            healing from the inside.

GARETH: Everything else gets better because you did this thing

MARTIN: Most of us, everything can wait, nothing is so urgent

GARETH: You can't rationalize it [spending a whole Saturday playing drums in a recording studio in Manhattan], there's no logical reason to do it … you do have to do it!

MARTIN: Right, you can't explain it

(Zoom call, March 25, 2020, 31' 00")

I play drums because "When I am drumming, this feeling in my body, and the conscious, embodied knowledge that I am core to the band creating and perpetuating the sound that I hear and feel around me, compel me to continue making the music, making and luxuriating in the perpetual now" (Smith, 2017, para. 22).

Construction

Boyce-Tillman writes that "in the domain of Construction, musical ideas are debated and explored; they are repeated and contrasted with one another … more circular structures of improvised traditions often sit uneasily with the terminology associated with the more linear traditions" such as Western art music (2009, pp. 186–187). There is a degree of "circularity" to the music Martin and I made, as it was groove-based, that is, consisting largely of repeated rhythmic patterns that we embellished with punctuation, call-and-response, metric modulations, and other elements characteristic of the broad jazz and popular music traditions in which our playing styles are rooted.

When we had initially met and discussed possibly drumming together, it immediately became clear how our drumming and respective senses of self were located in the heritage of that drumming tradition. We named shared influences from drumming lineage – icons such as Art Blakey, Ed Blackwell, and Rashid Ali, notably in Ali's almost unfeasibly intense duet recording with saxophonist John Coltrane, *Interstellar Space*. In the days leading up to the recording session, we messaged one another:

GARETH: Let's play drums to put the world to rights on Saturday

MARTIN: Yesssss. That's gonna be rad rad rad. Channel [jazz drumming icon] Elvin Jones meets [Muppet Show drummer] Animal

             (Messenger chat, July 3, 2019)

One of the exciting features of our collaboration was the "unpredictability of improvisation in practice" (Bramley & Smith, 2017, p. 443). This element of surprise within a shared cultural-historical framework of contemporary drum kit playing contributes to the "participatory discrepancies" that characterize such infectious and engaging participatory practice. We made this music for ourselves, and thoroughly enjoyed the "creative tensions," "relaxed dynamism," and occasional "out-of-syncness" (Keil, 1987, p. 275) that contribute to the participatory discrepancies constituting the music's "flesh and blood" (Keil, 1987, p. 279). In Boyce-Tillman's (2011) terms, "the combination of order and chaos offer the possibility of uniting the Apollonian and Dionysian elements of our culture," (p. 194). This flow process (Csikszentmihalyi, 1991), and the sense of fun and play with which we entered into and reveled in it (Gadamer, 2004; Huizinga, 1976), are what make this kind of musicking so compelling to do (Heble, 2000), and are what had us both grinning throughout the session and into the next day:

GARETH: Wicked day yesterday. Still buzzing.

MARTIN: Same here! I couldn't fall asleep at my regular time last night because I was so wired with energy! GREAT HANG!

             [a couple of hours later, having both listened to the raw studio recordings]

GARETH: Fuck, dude, wee were ON FIRE yesterday!! Dayam. This is so cool :) :)

MARTIN: Dayam. This duet sounds great!

             (Messenger chat, July 7, 2019)

Our improvised drumming fits what George E. Lewis terms an "Afrological" approach to improvisation – deeply rooted in memory and history, in opposition to "Eurological" improvisation, which he says "excludes history or memory" (1996, p. 147).[22] (Similarly, Dylan van der Schyff argues, "there is a strong sense in which improvisation may be seen as a meeting place for the present and the ancestral, the individual and the group, tradition and innovation" (2019, p. 319). We felt connected to our musical heritage, to one another, and a sense that we were creating something fresh and original in our drumming, improvising culture.

Values

Boyce-Tillman explains that "the domain of Values is related to the context of the music-making experience – the macro-area of culture and the micro-area of a particular event. Musical events contain both internal (within the musical structures) and external (the context of the music-making) Value systems" – what Lucy Green refers to as "inherent musical meaning" (Green, 2008a, p. 40) and "delineated musical meanings" (Green, 2008a, p. 44). Green (2008b, p. 91) also refers to the former as "inter-sonic" meanings, "by which [she means] exactly the same thing as 'inherent'" (Green, 2008a, p. xvi). Martin and I did not give much deliberate, conscious thought to intersonic meanings of the music we made, beyond listening intently and responding to one another to co-create something in real time. Our shared understanding, unarticulated on the day, was that we wanted to do something that sounded and felt like it was part of our culture as drummers. As Bruford notes, "Drummers think not only as individuals and human beings, but as members of a particular community with distinctive cultural traditions that allows us to ascribe meaning to creative experience, and to circulate and exchange that meaning" (2018, p. 17). I have called this drummers' cultural-psychological collective a "web," extending through history and cultures (Smith, 2013, p. 169).

---

22   Lewis is keen to emphasize that the concept and designation of "Afrological" is "historically emergent rather than ethnically essential" and that it accounts for "transcultural; and transracial communication" (Lewis, 1996, p. 133).

I noted, above, how Martin and I "clicked" instantly as co-improvising musicians. In this regard, it is perhaps noteworthy that Mickey Hart believes drummers to be "rhythmically related, and in drumming that's the same as blood" (Hart et al., 1990, p. 213). As I have noted elsewhere, "Hart thus invokes a notion of unity and a deep bond among drummers – we have rhythm, the groove, in our very DNA. Maybe drummers, as purveyors of rhythm, are more attuned to this elementally human phenomenon" (Smith, 2013, p. 100). Boyce-Tillman observed of the singing bowl tradition, that "this sound produced with reverence, an understanding of and connection with the 'feel' of a particular group and with the intention of calming and healing the people present, can have an amazing effect" (2011, p. 144). Our musicking on July 6, 2019 had just such an amazing effect on us. We discussed the importance of curating such experiences in order to nurture ourselves and our souls, and how this comprises part of our socio-cultural responsibility as musicians; we have a duty to nurture our musicianship:

MARTIN: We occupy a specific place in society, you know. Culture-
            bearers and musicians and culture creators – we have a
            very deep and honorable job, and we have to make sure
            that we step up to it … doing your life's mission benefits
            society.
            (Zoom call, March 25, 2020, 39' 35")

In Conclusion: Finding Spirituality through Mud Drums

Martin and I experienced our creation of *Mud Drums* as transcendent, and the recording, we feel, captures the process's essence. Our drumming was inherently worthwhile and of lasting value for us (I am listening to the playlist again while I draft these conclusions). It is reassuring, then, to read H. Stith Bennett's assertion that "the 'goal' of cultural work is … to share experiences of 'the good' which are intrinsically rewarding" (1980, p. 15). Martin and I affirmed this need in our Zoom chat:

MARTIN: When we get older we sometimes forget that this music thing changed our lives …

GARETH: gotta keep it alive

MARTIN: It's not even like you have to [keep it up]; you should

                      (Zoom call, March 25, 2020, 12' 21")

Later, I underlined this point:

GARETH: It's … stuff … that is just meaningful.

                      (Zoom call, March 25, 2020, 38' 30")

It is, moreover, the manner in which *Mud Drums* was rewarding and meaningful that is of particular salience here. Our drumming practice in creating *Mud Drums* affirmed Boyce-Tillman's assertion that "insofar as a musical experience takes us out of 'everyday' consciousness … and moves us into another dimension, we regard the musical experience as successful, whether we are a composer, performer or listener" (Boyce-Tillman, 2011, p. 266). I would add "player" to Boyce-Tillman's list of music makers, for it is often in non-performance contexts that drumming provides access to the Spiritual experience (Smith, 2021), as this account of *Mud Drums* affirms.

In this vein, Koji Matsunobu describes traditional Japanese musicians who "strive to assimilate themselves to the sound, become part of the cosmos, and achieve a state of unity with all things. Spiritual cultivation through sound, it is believed, may be attained through *otodamaho* by 'diluting' one's self and blending the body and mind in the universe" (Matsunobu, 2007, p. 1427). This is very much akin to Martin's and my respective and shared experiences of Spirituality with *Mud Drums*. As such, he and I concur with Boyce-Tillman's understanding of "Spirituality as the ability to transport the musicker to a different time/space dimension – to move them from everyday reality to 'another world'" (2011, p. 270). While it might be possible to explain the workings of liminal musical experience in terms of the brain's electro-chemistry and neuronal connections (Levitin, 2007; Sacks, 2008), this does not account for the actual lived experience, which is often perceived as otherworldly or magical.

Grateful Dead drummer, Mickey Hart, acknowledges the metaphysical realities of creating and improvising at the drums, titling his (1990) book, *Drumming at the Edge of Magic*; therein he identifies the seamless power of mutually realized rhythms as "the magic ride, the groove" (1990, p. 231). Drummer, Guy Richman, describes this as "a oneness" (Richman, in Smith, 2013, p. 98), and Bruford calls it "the most intense of feelings" (2009, p. 347). I have noted, elsewhere, that "we *are* the music. We drummers, we musicians, embody the music … Music is a magical thing" (Smith, 2013, p. 186, emphasis in original). Improvising musician and mentor to me, Keith Tippett, embodied liminality and transcendence in his music, captured in his solo piano performances and work with the bands *Ovary Lodge* and *Mujician* (Fordham, 2020; Smith, 2020,). Guitarist Jimi Hendrix aspired for his music to be "completely, utterly a magic science" (Henderson, 1981, p. 337), and Paul Clarke says Hendrix "proved himself something of a musical 'magician' in the ancient sense in that he attempted, through music, to mediate between order and disorder" (1983, p. 195). It is in this "ancient" sense that Martin and I experienced *Mud Drums* as magical – combining chaos and cohesion. Furthermore, it affirmed for us Kevin Shorner-Johnson's assertion that "musicians hold and encounter complexities of past, present, and future at a magical nexus" (2020, p. 62). *Mud Drums* is musical magic.

Bibliography

Avedis Zildjian Company, (2020). *K Custom cymbal set.* <https://zildjian.com/cymbals/k-custom-cymbal-set-dark.html>
Bennett, H. S. (1980). *On becoming a rock musician.* University of Massachusetts Press.
Boyce-Tillman, J. (2004). Towards an ecology of music education. *Philosophy of Music Education Review, 12*(2), 102–125.
Boyce-Tillman, J. (2009). The transformative qualities of a liminal space created by musicking. *Philosophy of Music Education Review, 17*(2), 184–202. <https://www.jstor.org/stable/40495499>
Boyce-Tillman, J. (2011). *Experiencing music: Restoring the spiritual.* Peter Lang.

Boyce-Tillman, J. (2020). An ecology of eudaimonia and its implications for music education. In G. D. Smith & M. Silverman (Eds.), *Eudaimonia: Perspectives for music learning* (pp. 71–89). Routledge.

Bramley, C., & Smith, G. D. (2017). Feral pop: The participatory power of improvised popular music. In G. D. Smith, Z. Moir, M. Brennan, S. Rambarran, & P. Kirkman (Eds.), *The Routledge research companion to popular music education* (pp. 438–450). Routledge.

Brennan, M. (2020). *Kick it: A social history of the drum kit.* Oxford University Press.

Bruford, B. (2009). *The autobiography: Yes, King Crimson, Earthworks, and more.* Jawbone.

Bruford, B. (2018). *Uncharted: Creativity and the expert drummer.* University of Michigan Press.

Clarke, P. (1983). "A magic science": Rock music as a recording art. *Popular Music, 3,* 195–213.

Csikszentmihalyi, M. (1991). *Flow: The psychology of optimal experience.* Harper Perennial.

Fordham, J. (2020, June 17). *Keith Tippett obituary.* The Guardian. <https://www.theguardian.com/music/2020/jun/17/keith-tippett-obituary>

Gadamer, H.-G. (2004). *Truth and method.* Bloomsbury.

Gooch, S. (1972). *Total man: Toward an evolutionary theory of personality.* Allen Lane; Penguin Press.

Green, L. (2008a). *Music on deaf ears: Musical meaning, ideology and education* (2nd ed.). Arima.

Green, L. (2008b). *Music, informal learning and the school: A new classroom pedagogy.* Ashgate.

Gretsch Drums. (2020). *Brooklyn series.* Gretsch Drums. <https://www.gretschdrums.com/drums/brooklyn>

Hart, M., Stevens, J., & Lieberman, F. (1990). *Drumming at the edge of magic: A journey into the spirit of percussion.* Harper.

Heble, A. (2000). *Landing on the wrong note: Jazz, dissonance and critical practice.* Routledge.

Henderson, D. (1981). *S'cuse me while I kiss the sky: The life of Jimi Hendrix.* Bantam Books.

Huizinga, J. (1976). Nature and significance of play as a cultural phenomenon. In R. Schechner & M. Shuman (Eds.), *Ritual, play, and performance: Readings in the social sciences/theatre* (pp. 46–66). Seabury Press.

Keil, C. (1987). Participatory discrepancies and the power of music. *Cultural Anthropology, 2*(3), 275–283. <https://doi-org.ezproxy.bu.edu/10.1525/can.1987.2.3.02a00010>

Matsunobu, K. (2007). Japanese spirituality and music practice: Art as self-cultivation. In Bresler, L. (Ed.), *International Handbook of Research in the Arts, volume 16* (pp. 1425–1437). Springer.

Levitin, D. J. (2007). *This is your brain on music: The science of a human obsession*. Penguin.

Philip, R. (2013). *Being here: Conversations on creating music*. Radhio.

Sacks, O. (2008). *Musicophilia: Tales of music and the brain*. Vintage.

Shorner-Johnson, K. (2020). Doing the common good work: Rebalancing individual "preparation for" with collectivist being. In I. M. Yob & E. R. Jorgensen (Eds.), *Humane music education for the common good* (pp. 54–65). Indiana University Press.

Shusterman, R. (2000). *Performing live: Aesthetic alternatives for the ends of art*. Cornell University Press.

Smith, G. D. (2013). *I drum, therefore I am: Being and becoming a drummer*. Routledge.

Smith, G. D. (2016). (Un)popular music making and eudaimonism. In R. Mantie & G. D. Smith (Eds.), *The Oxford handbook of music making and leisure* (pp. 151–168). Oxford University Press.

Smith, G. D. (2017). Embodied experience of rock drumming. *Music & Practice, 3*. <https://doi.org/10.32063/0304>

Smith, G. D. (2019a). Let there be rock! Loudness and authenticity at the drum kit. *Journal of Popular Music Education, 3*(2), 277–292. <https://doi.org/10.1386/jpme.3.2.277_1>

Smith, G. D. (2019b). *Garethdylansmith.com*. A drummer in all that I do. <https://drdrumsblog.wordpress.com/a-drummer-in-all-that-i-do/>

Smith, G. D. (2020, June 16). *Remembering Keith Tippett*. Thinking about Music. <http://thinkingaboutmusic.com/?author=227>

Smith, G. D. (in press). Eudaimonia and the autotelic drummer. In J. M. Pignato, D. Stadnicki, & M. Brennan (Eds.), *The Cambridge companion to drum kit* (pp. 248–258). Cambridge University Press.

Stone-Davis, F. J. (2011). *Musical beauty: Negotiating the boundary between subject and object*. Cascade Books.

Tuan, Y.-F. (1977). *Space and place: The perspective of experience*. University of Minnesota Press.

van der Schyf, D. (2019). Improvisation, enaction, and self-assessment. In D. J. Elliott, M. Silverman, & G. E. Mcpherson (Eds.), *The Oxford handbook of philosophical and qualitative assessment in music education* (pp. 319–346). Oxford University Press.

Voegelin, S. (2010). *Listening to noise and silence: Towards a philosophy of sound art*. Continuum.

ANNE T. JONES

Interlude 3

A Counselor's Search to Understand How Her Post-Traumatic Growth and Recovery Were Facilitated by Music

Relationship Counselor in Private Practice

The day the Prime Minister announced that we should all "stay at home" to contain the spread of COVID-19, there was a part of me that greeted the news with a shoulder shrug, confident that I could survive this latest upheaval. It was the third time in three years that everything in my diary was wiped-out overnight. Once again many of the familiar routines and rhythms of life had gone, with uncertainty about when they will come back.

Music has been a key component of holding me through these episodes of challenging times. This has been on multiple levels and reached into different domains of my life. This interlude is an exploration of my multifaceted experience of how learning to play the piano has aided recovery and growth. It is autobiographical inquiry, produced from reviewing themes occurring in journal writing. I learned to play the piano as a child but stopped as an adult with a thirty-year gap before resuming again. I am now preparing for ABRSM practical piano grade 5. These findings were originally gathered last year, two years after restarting the piano. I presented them as a poster for the International Symposium: Music, Spirituality, Wellbeing and Theology at the Tavener Centre, University of Winchester, in June 2019.

A Sense of Purpose and Achievement

There has been a sense of achievement and growing confidence in developing new skills. Throughout the last three years I have been steadily climbing the mountain of playing the piano. The lockdown provided an expansive opportunity to play; a sense that although other journeys may have ceased or been impeded, this one has been successful and becoming something more. Corlia Fourie (2019) presented her qualitative study of piano playing in five older adults at the Tavener Centre music conference. Her findings showed this sense of purpose and flourishing in the participants. We met at my poster and were both delighted with each other's experiences.

Others Blessed as Listeners

My journey started shortly after the first difficult life event. I was picking out Strauss' "The Blue Danube Waltz" on a piano in the corner of a lounge with other people present. I was very uncertain having not played for years. To my surprise a listener said she had been transported to a ball room in Vienna and how delightful that had been.

There have been multiple other special moments where family and friends tell me they have been moved as listeners. I often play for my mother and I enjoy her singing along to familiar melodies. It feels very precious and special.

Emotional Expression

The music I'm playing often becomes a soundtrack to periods of life. Hearing the music will bring back what I felt like during that those events. At the beginning of lockdown I was playing Chris Bowater's

(1989) beautiful worship song that uses the well-known last two verses of "Dear Lord and Father of Mankind." The lyrics "Drop Thy Still Dews of Quietness" seemed poignant as our busy world had an extraordinary pause.

Music that expresses the mix of both sadness and joy at the same time resonates with my real experience of grief. Very often when very difficult things have been happening, there have also been experiences of amazing kindness, new exciting opportunities or a heightened appreciation of beauty. Music with this bittersweet element such as Mozart's "Agnus Dei" from his first mass, expressed something that words cannot. Pieces that move from harmony to discord in the same piece also express the paradoxical mix of joy and pain. Crashing through the thunder-like section of Chopin's Prelude in Db major, "Raindrop," Op. 28, No. 15, seems like being forced to face the storm, but it is somehow therapeutic. I have very much valued the music of composer Pam Wedgwood (2001), whose music is very varied in style, so that I might go through different moods of music in one practice session.

Worshipping and Connecting to God

Using music to be in relationship with God works on multiple levels. First, there is the explicit one of playing and singing hymns and anthems. For example, leading others into worship through playing the piano for the church congregation. Before the pandemic I had just started being part of a group of musicians playing for a regular Taizé style service at my church. Second, making music is a creative act that is an expression of God abiding in my life. The Holy Spirit as the source of creativity is a theme in Julia Cameron's (1994) successful course in building creativity, *The Artist's Way*. I particularly like her description of creativity as listening and tuning into what God is doing, like dropping down into a well.

Helpful Metaphors and Life Lessons

June Boyce-Tillman (2000) talks about the healing process involving a daily reviewing of experiences in order to balance the self. She likens the process to the body's immune system, which works out whether an event is helpful or not. This may not be apparent initially; very difficult encounters may end up being fruitful and more promising ones may not lead anywhere.

The piano enables this experimentation and sifting of life lessons, principles that are relevant in other parts of life. It is different from hearing an idea without having the chance to put it into practice. As an example, when I am learning a difficult sequence my teacher says "go as slow as you need to." That's also a helpful approach in making important decisions and in other creative pursuits such as baking a cake.

Martin Lawrence (2020) has studied the experience and psychology of performance anxiety. He led a course I attended through Benslow Music called "Free up your playing." He takes this learning a step further by welcoming apparent blocks to progress or performance as useful information. In my case, tense shoulders as an invitation to play with more attitude.

A Sense of Abundance and Adventure

A sense that the world is a place of rich abundance has been helpful to me when life has appeared full of losses and holes. Martin Lawrence asked us during the course to pick three words to describe what we loved about our instrument. I chose "variety, beauty and joy." There are always many options and roads to follow when choosing music to play, giving a sense that maybe life is also full of possibilities.

Julia Cameron (1994) sees creativity as coming from an abundant God, as evidenced by the natural world. We can be sure that such a God is going to reward our moves toward creativity.

Relationship and Connection

Playing the piano has opened up opportunities and enabled me to connect to people.

Joining the church choir, where being able to read music is required; meeting with a friend who plays viola to encourage each other; playing to appreciative listeners; sharing an enthusiastic love of music with family and friends; discovering new music and sharing it with others. It has been helpful to be observed by my piano teacher, getting feedback on my manner and approach, showing me things to which I was blind – not something that generally happens in other parts of my life. This gives me a sense of being seen and supported in my music journey.

I am frequently surprised by listeners saying that I have inspired them to take up learning an instrument. This seems to be in line with the ideas of researcher and author Brené Brown (2012). She investigated the views of people who live wholeheartedly. Her interviews revealed how life affirming it is to have the courage to let yourself be seen together with your imperfections. In this case, I would be playing the piano for listeners as a beginner and not a concert pianist. Our authentic presence builds connections to others and encourages others to risk being vulnerable too.

Self-Care and Relaxation

It's an ethical principle for counselors to care for themselves. Tim Bond (2015) writes about the great demands placed on counselors through working with people experiencing difficulties. Counselors need to guard against burnout by maintaining their personal resources. Counselors also have serious events happen in their own lives. Julia Samuel (2017, p. 223) is a therapist who writes well about healing from grief. She cites several "pillars of strength" that are helpful. It seems that regular piano practice connects well to some of these, in particular: having a way to express grief;

activities that connect the mind and the body; and having a routine of self-care habits.

Everything I have written about so far could be thought of as building wellbeing and resilience. Music also provides self-care directly in using playing the piano to relax in the evenings. It is effective in being engaging, taking me away from the concerns of the day. It also helps me process my emotional reactions to the distressing situations I have just been hearing about. I often end my practice with pieces that finish with softness and beauty such as Beethoven's "Moonlight" Sonata, Op. 27, No. 2. It is an aid in preparing to sleep well.

Conclusions and Applications

I am seeking to apply these findings to my life in my local community and as a relationship counselor, engaging with the wellbeing of others. There are opportunities to choose pieces played for listeners to suit occasions such as to aid relaxation, worship, memories or celebration. I have recently been playing hymns for my mother and I to sing along to whilst the churches have been without congregational singing.

In client conversations, I listen for and encourage a variety of creative outlets and connections to the arts. It is interesting that this often then seems to connect my clients to others in their family or community. Several times clients have found a poem or song that resonates for them and shared it meaningfully with others. I can assist clients in the use of music for aiding emotional expression, spiritual connection, and change. It has been a helpful idea from trauma specialist Courtney Armstrong (2015) to have music playlists that bridge from songs that express the client's current emotion, such as sadness, through songs about letting go to songs about their desired emotional state.

I value and wish to participate in music within the local community such as singing in choirs and accompanying. These activities have been largely on-hold during the pandemic but I joined a community choir that was meeting on Zoom so that I could keep singing with others. It is an important philosophy for me that counselors can be part of the solution in creating the strong communities that we hear our clients need.

Acknowledgments

Grateful thanks for the patience and skill of my piano teacher Mike Rodgers. For my enthusiastic listeners and supporters: Rosemary Chapman; Helen and Nick Warwick; the Millichamp family; and guests at Holy Rood House, Thirsk. Thanks also to my good friend Eileen Padmore for help in writing this interlude.

Bibliography

Armstrong, C. (2015). *The therapeutic "Aha!"*. W.W. Norton.

Bond, T. (2015). *Standards and ethics for counselling in action* (4th ed.). Sage.

Bowater, C. (1989). *Drop thy still dews of quietness*. Lifestyle Ministries/Word Music.

Boyce-Tillman, J. (2000). *Constructing musical healing. The wounds that sing*. Jessica Kingsley Publishers.

Brown, B. (2012). *Daring greatly*. Penguin Life.

Cameron, J. (1994). *The artist's way*. MacMillan.

Fourie, C. (2019, June 14). *Positive aging with piano playing: A spiritual journey* [Conference presentation]. International Symposium: Music, Spirituality, Wellbeing and Theology, University of Winchester.

Lawrence, M. (2020). *Music performance anxiety as hidden desire and emerging self: The development and exploration of a conceptual lens for performers and practitioners* [Unpublished doctoral dissertation, University of London].

Samuel, J. (2017). *Grief works. Stories of life, death and surviving*. Penguin Life.

Wedgwood, P. (2001). *After hours: For solo piano*. Faber Music.

PART III

Therapy, Education, and Caring

10 Tracing Spirituality in Everyday Music Therapy Contexts

Methodological Reflections

Music therapy as a contemporary field of practice has rich and diverse spiritual roots that can be traced in the emergence of various music therapy approaches and initiatives. Examples include the development of approaches such as Creative Music Therapy (Nordoff & Robbins, 2007) and Guided Imagery and Music (Bonny, 2002), as well as initiatives such as the development of *Music Therapists for Peace* in the 1980s, which was informed by Boxill's view of music therapy as "love in action" (Boxill, 1997). More recently, values around social justice, citizenship, responsibility, and otherness have underpinned the growth of culture and community-oriented practices (Stige & Aarø, 2012). These values have also become increasingly significant in the emerging dialogues around colonization, oppression, and power in the field (Baines & Edwards, 2020; Norris, 2020).

Spirituality, however, remains an underdeveloped research area partly due to music therapists' endeavor to safeguard the legitimacy of their work within predominantly secular medical environments that are at odds with the seemingly unstable, paradoxical, and perhaps risky discourse of spirituality (Bradt, 2017; Tsiris, 2017). Additionally, the rapid increase of a "self-help" culture, which has led to the popularization and commodification of spirituality, has perhaps been a contributing factor to some music therapists' hesitant engagement with spirituality in their profession.

Despite this, a growing number of music therapists have started bringing spirituality to the fore in the last twenty years. In addition to clinical and theoretical explorations of spirituality (e.g., Aigen, 2008; Aldridge, 2003; Notarangelo, 2019; Potvin & Argue, 2014), a small number of empirical studies have been conducted to date (e.g., Marom, 2004; Masko, 2016; Potvin, 2013). Reviewing the literature, I have identified three common research areas: (a) the relationship between music therapists' spirituality and their practice, (b) music therapy's effect or impact on clients' spirituality, and (c) clients' and/or their families' experiences of spirituality in music therapy. Most studies are questionnaire or interview-based focusing on in-depth analyses of individual accounts. Such accounts tend to concentrate on positive aspects, such as peak or "magic" moments in music therapy and its beneficial effects on spirituality. Samples are usually small, homogeneous, and purposive (Tsiris, 2018, 2019).

While building on the existing music therapy knowledge base, there is a need to advance further our spiritual discourse. To this end, a critical engagement with our conceptual assumptions is crucial alongside an in-depth reconsideration of current methodological trends and orientations. Extending beyond reported effects of music therapy on wellbeing and spirituality, our discourse needs to foster a more nuanced contextual and ecological exploration of people's experiences, actions, and practices. Music therapy as a distinct, yet diverse and ever-growing profession, is uniquely placed within the broader field of music, health, and wellbeing, and it can be instrumental in (re)shaping our spiritual discourse with potential interdisciplinary influences.

Rooted in my research on spirituality and music therapy, I discuss in this chapter some key considerations which shaped my methodological stance. These considerations informed the implementation of a pilot international survey and of a subsequent ethnographically informed study in the UK. Instead of focusing on the findings of these two studies – which are available elsewhere (Tsiris, 2017, 2018) – I reflect on my methodological approach and consider its implications for future research.

Otherness and Messiness

Initially, I conducted an international online survey to explore music therapists' perceptions of spirituality and its potential relevance or irrelevance to music therapy. The basic premise of this pilot was to offer a welcoming space where music therapists could articulate *their* understandings of spirituality in relation to their practice and profession. To this end, and in contrast to other studies, I provided no working definition of spirituality. Instead, I invited each participant to set their own reference frame. This entailed a risk of generating messy data clashing with preconceived research ideals around control, accuracy, predictability, and replicability. This possibility for messiness, however, offered an open ground where the multiplicity, complexity, richness, elusiveness, and perhaps paradox of spirituality (or better, *spiritualities*) could be openly acknowledged and explored without imposing a preconceived, artificial unity.

Although a common research practice, the provision of working definitions to participants is not an innocent or unproblematic act. Definitions may bring a sense of clarity and order. This clarity and order, however, and their power in the formation of knowledge may close down different possibilities and reduce or even exclude "otherness." Such definitional issues are particularly relevant to spirituality as an elusive and complex area of music therapy, but they are rarely debated openly.

The definitional openness of my study aimed at inviting and documenting heterogeneous voices. It generated a welcoming space for otherness where practitioners provided their accounts of spirituality and its (ir)relevance to music therapy. This otherness included people's uncertainties, dilemmas, and potential disagreements regarding different aspects of spirituality and music therapy including training, practice, supervision, and professionalization matters.

From What to How

Music therapists' reported perceptions in the pilot survey pointed to spirituality as a multifaceted phenomenon with varying and, at times, conflicting appearances. These appearances depended on numerous contextual factors ranging from macro sociocultural influences to microprocesses of therapeutic musicking. Thus, my attention gradually shifted to the *experiencing* and the *doing* of spirituality. This orientation toward the "performance" of spirituality and its emergent character in everyday music therapy contexts (compared to the survey's focus on perception and self-report) shaped the focus of my subsequent, ethnographically informed study.

Instead of asking "what" spirituality means to individuals, I became more interested in "how" spirituality is experienced and manifested in everyday music therapy practices and contexts. This in-action and in-situ exploration broadened my analytic lens to include the people (e.g., music therapy participants, staff, and families), the material world (e.g., musical instruments and artifacts), the everyday events and rituals that take place in and around music therapy practice (e.g., multidisciplinary meetings) as well as the sociocultural characteristics of each music therapy context (e.g., the sociocultural background of people and organizations). This (re)orientation of my research toward *action* and *context* drew on pragmatic and eco-phenomenological thinking (Ansdell, 2014; Ansdell & Pavlicevic, 2010).

My stance was informed by pragmatism and its empirical commitment which resists abstraction, fixed principles, closed systems, and absolute truths. Pragmatism, rather, focuses on the actual lived realities and the *practical meaning* of values and beliefs. Understanding beliefs as rules for action, pragmatism looks for the utility or the "workability" of truths and interprets each notion by tracing its practical consequences (Menand, 1998; Morgan, 2007).

This approach brought in my study a balance between the "what" and the "how" of the multilayered performance of spirituality in music therapy. Instead of merely questioning "What does spirituality mean to you?" I also focused on exploring "How does spirituality work in this particular music therapy context?" This emphasis on "how" fostered a more open-ended and idiographic stance. I did not look for an essence but tried to understand where each phenomenon happened, when, for whom, why, for what purpose, and what it was achieving. As such, I tried to trace the practical meanings of people's spirituality including those of music therapists, music therapy participants, and of other people who were part of each context's ecology. This pragmatic tracing of spirituality entailed my ethnographic immersion in everyday music therapy settings and situations.

The Everyday

This re-orientation toward action and context spotlights the "everyday" as the natural stage where multiple meanings are constantly in the making and are (per)formed. The everyday calls for a broadening out of our focal points. It calls for an exploration of the extraordinary within the ordinary, with the hope to create space for "otherness."

In recent years, there has been an increased interest in exploring spirituality within everyday environments including their social, spatial, technological, and aesthetic worlds (MacKian, 2012, 2019). The emergence of "everyday spirituality" comes with a reappreciation of daily life. It urges us to re-cognize mundane, everyday actions and situations under a new light. Instead of confining spirituality to something inner or private, everyday spirituality brings to the fore people's relationships and their (inter)actions with their daily environments (Bartolini et al., 2017); a perspective that resonates with the concept of "spiritualities of the surface" (Hoyt & Combs, 1996). Without detracting us from the complexity of spirituality, everyday spirituality repositions its analytic attention to the surface of daily activity and highlights how spirituality may form and transform this very activity.

Interestingly, a similar focus on the everyday has been noticed in music sociology (DeNora, 2013), music psychology (Herbert, 2011), and in music therapy (Ansdell, 2014). The everyday though has weakly been featured in the study of spirituality in music therapy so far, and I hope my work has paved a path to this direction.

Tracing Spirituality

In my ethnographically informed study (Tsiris, 2018), I focused on three music therapy contexts in the UK: a hospice, a school, and a care home. My fieldwork at each site included participation in everyday situations, "hanging about," ad-hoc conversations with people, collecting artifacts, and, where appropriate, individual interviews. By observing and being part of daily practices in and around music therapy, I was able to trace spirituality in-action, in-situ and over a period of time. In all cases, I sought spirituality through a pragmatic prism by exploring the unobserved by the observed, and the intangible by the tangible. This process was supported by my appreciation of the particular case as source for rich descriptions and understandings that were "explicitly located" (Van Maanen, 1998, p. 28). Instead of measuring variables, I was *looking for* variables (Becker, 2014) while exploring how different elements, patterns, and frames that formed each case were played out.

This approach allowed space for understanding not only how spirituality was articulated by different individuals and organizations but also how it was "translated" for different audiences and purposes. The articulation of spirituality was often a challenge for participants and organizations irrespective of their background, spiritual orientation, and values. For some, the boundlessness of spirituality meant that anything could be potentially seen from a spiritual perspective. The uncertainties rising from this sense of boundlessness fueled multiple processes of naming and translating spirituality. Such processes appeared in diverse guises ranging from theoretical frameworks and organizational documents, to verbal and written communication between staff, and people's spontaneous narratives. Each organization's prevailing spiritual language offered a discursive framework that equipped music therapists with a language and a conceptual structure that was more or less accepted within each setting and had implications not only for their ways of speaking about their work but also for their ways of thinking and practicing.

The spiritual framework of each organization prioritized and cultivated certain beliefs, languages, concepts, and practices. Equally, it overshadowed, disabled, and marginalized other potential spiritualities. This included controversial, unspoken, and fragile spiritualities within and around music therapy, as well as multiple translations of spirituality within each organization. This observation became apparent not only in my fieldwork but also in the pilot survey findings.

Various survey respondents reported dilemmas and problems in terms of languaging spirituality within their professional environments. This included the perceived threat that discussions around spirituality could pose to their identity as professionals. These findings shed light on the processes of languaging spirituality in everyday contexts, including the challenges and power issues involved.

In my fieldwork these issues were often connected to the professionalization of spirituality and care, and the fit of music therapy within each organization. The notion of "spiritual care" emerged as the expression and attendance to people's spirituality, and for music therapists this was integral to their musical care practices. Spiritual care thus referred to what was intended, done, or experienced as spiritual in practice although it often remained unarticulated or unnamed as such. On many occasions, people talked about the "invisibles" to refer to such individual but also organizational spiritual care practices, experiences, and intentions. This invisibility was commonly the result of professionalizing the provision of spiritual care within organizations as well as the secularization of other professional services such as music therapy. Indeed, the music therapists often described their work as "spiritual care undercover" highlighting the unspoken spiritual care of music therapy. Music affords experiencing the spiritual without the need to name it. As the care home-based music therapist said:

> What I guess I am trying to do as a music therapist is using music to facilitate a deeper connection [...] the deeper connection would be the spiritual connection perhaps and it's often unspoken, I think. There is often a connection between people that doesn't rely on what they are saying to each other [...] and I think that's where the music really comes in and facilitates that. (Tsiris, 2018, p. 130)

A thread that connected different aspects of people's sense of undercover spiritual care had to do with the intention of their care actions. Although it often remained unarticulated, the invisibility of music therapists' care was not a random act. On the contrary, they talked about their intention to reach and support people through music not only during music therapy sessions but also in everyday situations within their work environment. Their intention was informed by their awareness and in-depth knowledge of their setting and of the people who were part of its ecology. This was insightfully reflected in the following account by the hospice-based music therapist:

Today at lunchtime I went across to the hospice to play the piano. We have live music in the Day Centre – large social space – each Sunday whilst visitors, families and patients have lunch together.

Checking emails before I started – not sensible – I realised someone – Maria – I've spent quite a lot of time with had come into the hospice. I bumped into someone who was looking for Maria and realised the chances were Maria would be coming down to the Day Centre across the lunch period. Whilst playing I looked up and saw the person I'd bumped into wheeling a lady in a chair across the room, I struggled because my brain was telling me it was Maria, the person I'd been working with but she herself was completely unrecognisable, so much worse, ravaged by her illness. I tried to look at Maria without her noticing me as I continued to play and when she smiled and waved at me, I still could not really believe it was her although I knew it was.

As I played, thoughts and wonderings about her completely overtook me. In my workplace I'm often spending time with people who have just the last drops left of themselves, physically and emotionally. Looking across at Maria, someone very close to me in age and someone I know a lot about I noticed her bright eyes and voice but also how shrunken she was, slipping away.

I thought about how my playing might support her. I became very aware of the silence within the music, around the edges of the phrases. Those silences can sometimes feel like caverns. The phrases of what I was playing seemed most important in fact – a structure to hang the emotional gestures of the music onto – something for me to hang on to as well. I was struggling and even though I'm well aware death is in the air all the time I sometimes get caught out. This was one of those moments.

She'd told me a lot about family dynamics – which were tricky – she was socially very isolated. Was this the particular sister I'd heard so much about with her now?

I wondered about the music offering her some safety to meet with some of these people she'd been having such difficult times with. I offered her the energy of the music. Alongside this intense sense of wondering about her and trying to meet her in my music the room was full of other families chatting and eating, volunteers calling across the room with food orders, a family of kids close by playing in the reclining chairs making the chair go back and forwards and then behind me in the garden an old man scooping fish out of our pond, standing in the pond wearing ridiculous rubber trousers. All of life together. I feel that putting music into this space helps make all this possible together – the mundane and the mystical and the fact that it can all be there together in the moment makes it all the more powerful. The music elevates and heightens possibilities. (Tsiris, 2018, pp. 137–138)

This account exemplifies the kinds of invisible, yet intentional, musical care that music therapists offered within their organizations. It also highlights how such musical-spiritual care was often an inextricable, yet fuzzy, part of everyday experience beyond the discrete time and space boundaries of music therapy sessions.

The openness of my methodological approach enabled me to follow musical "things" and people who made the ecology of each music therapy situation (Ansdell, 2014; DeNora & Ansdell, 2017). It also allowed my analytic lens to expand beyond immediate music-making situations to explore broader and multiple dimensions that shaped the performance of spirituality in and around music therapy within each research site. This included a consideration of organizational histories, discourses, and professional identities, as well as the music therapists' improvisatory and holistic work.

Music therapists' improvisational craft was linked to their ability to work with "amorphous" music and emerging musical forms. Spirituality was performed in the constant interplay between morphopoiesis and metamorphosis or, in other words, between the co-making of musical forms and people's experiences of transformation. These transformational experiences were described as everyday experiences of joy and transcendence (see also Boyce-Tillman, 2000; Robbins, 1993).

I understood the relationship between morphopoiesis and metamorphosis as implying some kind of outer-musical and inner-personal change, respectively, which forms a basis of music *as* therapy. Musical change was observed through people's ability to participate, express, and relate through and in music, whilst personal change was expressed in people's sense of beauty, purpose, and meaning. Expanding beyond the individual, this inner change included the person's social and cultural aspects of living.

Music therapists expressed their belief, recognition, and work to bring out the potential in people and situations. Their improvisatory stance was supported by a balanced sense of questioning and trust. Their questioning attitude fostered a sense of wonder, curiosity, and search for "the beyond." Simultaneously, they had a sense of trust that each person knows what they need in their therapeutic process, a sense of trust in "the unknown" as well as in music's capacity to bring change or some kind of metamorphosis in the person.

A Boundary Object?

My performative notion of spirituality helped to re-orient and refine my attention to the experiencing and the doing of spirituality, and to its emergent character in everyday music therapy contexts. However, both in the survey and the ethnographically informed study I wrestled with the challenges of exploring and articulating phenomena that were undefinable, multiple, and in constant flux. Despite my endeavor to avoid any fixation, a degree of "objectification" of spirituality (and of music therapy) as some-*thing* was in different guises present in my research. Initially, the reporting and somehow distant nature of the pilot's survey method pointed to this objectification of spirituality as an "it." My attempt to avoid such objectification in the follow-up study led partly to its ethnographically informed methodology. Nonetheless, even in my fieldwork I became aware of people (including myself) talking about spirituality as if it were a thing or something tangible.

As I followed participants' varied ways of talking about and doing spirituality, I became aware not only of the inevitability of such objectification but also of its usefulness. This objectification had partly to do with the processes of languaging spirituality and with the distance between experiencing and reporting or documenting. People like the school head – with no specific interest in spirituality – described spirituality as a fandangled, useless, or ornamental thing. Others – like the hospice-based music therapist – who were keen to comprehend and capture in words the meaning of spirituality, tried to describe "it" as an attitude, quality, or some kind of recognition or (musical) knowing.

By acknowledging and working with these challenges during my research, I realized that the processes of objectifying spirituality not only enabled people to translate their experiences of spirituality in music therapy but also generated a useful reflective space. This space helped people to articulate and make sense of their experiences. It also helped them to experience spirituality as some-*thing* that they could see, hear, smell, or touch. Most importantly, these reflective processes of objectification often renewed participants' experience of spirituality in their everyday lives. The music therapists, for instance, said that talking about spirituality increased their awareness of "it" and its performance in their everyday practice. This emphasized how their spiritual discourse influenced their practice-based performances too.

Based on my research and my performative understanding of spirituality, I argue that this objectification of spirituality is useful as long as it is recognized as a heuristic device and not assumed for the "thing" in itself. This perspective can offer a platform for a performative understanding of spirituality's objectification. Stepping beyond a performance-object dichotomy, spirituality can be theorized as a performative object in music therapy. This resembles the notion of "boundary object" (Star, 2010).

Conceptualizing spirituality as a boundary object can offer an elastic interpretative framework within which diverse, even conflicting, spiritualities can be explored and embraced without requiring ontological consensus. It can also raise awareness of spirituality's multiple translations and adaptations to local practices and contexts, as well as prompt us to trace its diverse manifestations and consequences in and around music therapy practice (Tsiris & Ansdell, 2019). This includes an exploration of the multiple contexts that surround spirituality to include the sociocultural, political, aesthetic, and material realities of music therapy as profession and discipline. I argue that the conceptualization of spirituality as a boundary object can enhance understanding of how those within the broader music therapy ecology create some shared understandings without losing sight of the diversity of their spiritualities. Indeed, the notion of the boundary object can be particularly helpful in situations where a degree of mutuality and coherence can be achieved without necessitating uniformity (Trompette & Vinck, 2009). From this perspective, spirituality can emerge both as something abstract and concrete, philosophical and material, inner and outer, otherworldly, and everyday.

Toward New Vistas

In this chapter, I have offered some methodological reflections drawing on my research endeavor to explore spirituality in music therapy. My focus has not been on research findings. Instead, I focused on the considerations that shaped my research stance and work with the hope to point toward new directions in the study of spirituality in music therapy and in related fields of practice.

Looking ahead, I propose the need for a hybrid spiritual discourse that can afford multiple and unfinished meanings as these are (co)created, negotiated, and enacted in everyday music therapy contexts. This entails a hybridity that "affords the co-existence of unfinished spiritualities as well as their multiple and heterogeneous translations" (Tsiris, 2018, p. i). Hopefully, this fluid, context-responsive, and emergent notion of spirituality in music therapy introduces a renewed confidence and trust toward what might be unknown, undefinable, or unpredictable. In fact, this trust in "the unknown" emerged as a key element of spirituality in music therapists' improvisatory work. Perhaps the proposed hybridity can introduce a similar improvisatory stance to our discourse and research practices too urging us to remain alert to the musical-spiritual potential of each situation, and to adapt our analytic lenses accordingly.

This proposed spiritual discourse resonates with the need for a "messy hybridity" that reflects the sociocultural and cosmological fusions required for contemporary music therapy as argued by Pavlicevic and Cripps (2015):

> Straddling the South and the Global North, we propose that Western (and at times bio-medically informed) healing and health practices might well consider reclaiming and re-sourcing their own, and other, traditional and indigenous healing cosmologies, whatever their respective and situated ideologies and ontologies. Despite apparent (and possibly intellectual and ideological) segmentations and separations of disciplines by Western scholarship and economics, we propose that "the ancestors" and "the aspirin" need to embrace rather than view one another with suspicion. Just possibly, each might become enriched (and discomforted) by the silenced coincidences of one another's desires to know and experience our common humanity through music. (Pavlicevic & Cripps, 2015)

This messy hybridity underscores the need for a spiritual discourse in music therapy which embraces different music therapy practices, cosmologies, geographies, languages, and discourses alongside their histories, politics, and their implicit and explicit values. This however can only be achieved through our readiness for critical, yet constructive, interdisciplinary dialogue, for un-learning and re-learning (Tsiris & Ansdell, 2019). Contemporary advancements in related fields, such as music and theology, can offer invaluable insights to music therapists and vice versa (Ansdell, 2005; Nickles, 1992). Such interdisciplinary exchange can promote a critical reconsideration of professional identities, practices, and languages, and support a re-examination of spirituality and its place in professional training, supervision, and codes of practice.

Bibliography

Aigen, K. (2008). The religious dimensions of popular music and their implications for music therapy. *British Journal of Music Therapy*, *22*(1), 24–34. <https://doi.org/10.1177/135945750802200104>

Aldridge, D. (2003). Music therapy and spirituality: A transcendental understanding of suffering. *Music Therapy Today*, *4*(1), 1–28.

Ansdell, G. (2005). Musicing, time and transcendence: Theological themes for music therapy. *British Journal of Music Therapy*, *19*(1), 20–28. <https://doi.org/10.1177/135945750501900105>

Ansdell, G. (2014). *How music helps in music therapy and everyday life*. Ashgate.

Ansdell, G., & Pavlicevic, M. (2010). Practicing "gentle empiricism" – The Nordoff Robbins research heritage. *Music Therapy Perspectives*, *28*, 131–139. <https://doi.org/10.1093/mtp/28.2.131>

Baines, S., & Edwards, J. (2020). Analysing gender oppression in music therapy research and practice. In S. Hogan (Ed.), *Arts therapies and gender issues: International perspectives on research* (pp. 37–54). Routledge.

Bartolini, N., Chris, R., MacKian, S., & Pile, S. (2017). The place of spirit: Modernity and the geographies of spirituality. *Progress in Human Geography*, *41*(3), 338–354. <https://doi.org/10.1177/0309132516644512>

Becker, H. S. (2014). *What about Mozart? What about murder? Reasoning from cases*. University of Chicago Press.

Bonny, H. (2002). *Music consciousness: The evolution of guided imagery and music* (L. Summer, Ed.). Barcelona Publishers.

Boxill, E. (1997). *The miracle of music therapy*. Barcelona Publishers.

Boyce-Tillman, J. (2000). *Constructing musical healing: The wounds that sing*. Jessica Kingsley Publishers.

Bradt, J. (2017). Threats to legitimacy? *Nordic Journal of Music Therapy*, *26*(4), 291–292. <https://doi.org/10.1080/08098131.2017.1328033>

DeNora, T. (2013). *Music asylums: Wellbeing through music in everyday life*. Ashgate.

DeNora, T., & Ansdell, G. (2017). Music in action: Tinkering, testing and tracing over time. *Qualitative Research*, *17*(2), 231–245. <https://doi.org/10.1177/1468794116682824>

Hadley, S. (Ed.). (2006). *Feminist perspectives in music therapy*. Barcelona Publishers.

Herbert, R. (2011). *Everyday music listening: Absorption, dissociation and trancing*. Ashgate.

Hoyt, M., & Combs, G. (1996). On ethics and the spiritualities of the surface: A conversation with Michael White. In M. Hoyt (Ed.), *Constructive therapies 2* (pp. 33–59). Guilford Press.

MacKian, S. (2012). *Everyday spirituality: Social and spatial worlds of enchantment*. Palgrave Macmillan.

MacKian, S. (2019). 'The constant hum of the engine …': A story about extraordinary interdisciplinary dialogues in spirituality and wellbeing. *Approaches: An Interdisciplinary Journal of Music Therapy, Special Issue*, *11*(1), 15–31. <http://approaches.gr/mackian-a20191124/>

Marom, M. (2004). Spiritual moments in music therapy: A qualitative study of the music therapist's experience. In B. Abrams (Ed.), *Qualitative inquiries in music therapy: A monograph series* (Vol. 1, pp. 37–76). Barcelona Publishers.

Masko, M. K. (2016). Music therapy and spiritual care in end-of-life: A qualitative inquiry into ethics and training issues identified by chaplains and music therapists. *Journal of Music Therapy*, *53*(4), 309–335. <https://doi.org/10.1093/jmt/thw009>

Menand, L. (Ed.). (1998). *Pragmatism: A reader*. Vintage Books.

Morgan, D. (2007). Paradigms lost and pragmatism regained: Methodological implications of combining qualitative and quantitative methods. *Journal of Mixed Methods Research*, *1*(1), 48–76. <https://doi.org/10.1177/2345678906292462>

Nickles, R. (1992). Integration of music therapy and theology: A preliminary approach. *Australian Journal of Music Therapy*, *3*, 52–56.

Nordoff, P., & Robbins, C. (2007). *Creative Music Therapy: A guide to fostering clinical musicianship* (2nd ed.). Barcelona Publishers.

Norris, M. S. (2020). Freedom dreams: What must die in music therapy to preserve human dignity? *Voices: A World Forum for Music Therapy*, *20*(3). <https://doi.org/10.15845/voices.v20i3.3172>

Notarangelo, A. (2019). Music therapy and spiritual care: Music as spiritual support in a hospital environment. *Approaches: An Interdisciplinary Journal of Music Therapy, Special Issue*, *11*(1), 88–103. <https://approaches.gr/notarangelo-a20191124/>

Pavlicevic, M., & Cripps, C. (2015). Muti music – In search of suspicion. *Voices: A World Forum for Music Therapy, 15*(3). <https://doi.org/10.15845/voices.v15i3.836>

Potvin, N. (2013). Spiritual belief as a predictor of theoretical orientation in music therapists. *Nordic Journal of Music Therapy, 22*(1), 25–45. <https://doi.org/10.1080/08098131.2012.690443>

Potvin, N., & Argue, J. (2014). Theoretical considerations of spirit and spirituality in music therapy. *Music Therapy Perspectives, 32*(2), 118–128. <https://doi.org/10.1093/mtp/miu022>

Robbins, C. (1993). The creative processes are universal. In M. Heal & T. Wigram (Eds.), *Music therapy in health and education* (pp. 7–25). Jessica Kingsley Publishers.

Star, S. L. (2010). This is not a boundary object: Reflections on the origin of a concept. *Science, Technology, & Human Values, 35(5)*, 601-617. <https://doi.org/10.1177/0162243910377624>

Stige, B., & Aarø, L. E. (2012). *Invitation to community music therapy*. Routledge.

Trompette, P., & Vinck, D. (2009). Revisiting the notion of boundary object. *Revue d'anthropologie des connaissances, 3*(1), 3–25. <https://doi.org/10.3917/rac.006.0003>

Tsiris, G. (2017). Music therapy and spirituality: An international survey of music therapists' perceptions. *Nordic Journal of Music Therapy, 26*(4), 293–319. <https://doi.org/10.1080/08098131.2016.1239647>

Tsiris, G. (2018). *Performing spirituality in music therapy: Towards action, context and the everyday* [Doctoral thesis, Goldsmiths, University of London]. Goldsmiths Research Online. <https://doi.org/10.25602/GOLD.00023037>

Tsiris, G. (2019, June 14–15). *Music therapy and spirituality: A systematic review of the research literature* [Symposium Presentation]. Music, Spirituality, Wellbeing and Theology, University of Winchester, UK.

Tsiris, G., & Ansdell, G. (2019). Exploring the spiritual in music. *Approaches: An Interdisciplinary Journal of Music Therapy, Special Issue, 11*(1), 3–8. <http://approaches.gr/tsiris-e20191124/>

Van Maanen, J. (1998). *Tales of the field: On writing ethnography*. University of Chicago Press.

JILLIAN SCHOFIELD

Interlude 4
Healing with Shamanic Drums

This interlude will explore how the drum supports the healing process in my integrative psychotherapy and shamanic practice. It will introduce the shamanic drum, the shamanic cosmos, and healing with the shamanic drum.

The most important shamanic tool is the drum. Drake (2002) states the drum is important as "its rhythm develops a oneness of feeling and purpose with the rhythms of the universe …. Rhythm is the heartbeat of life …. The drum's beat unites the shaman with all life forms into a single being, a single heartbeat" (p. 13).

The repetitive sound of the drum is fundamental to shamanic healing (Harner, 1990, p. 51). It is the repetitive sound that enables the drum, the shaman's horse, to take shamans into a trance state. In a trance state they journey to other worlds (Turner, 2016) for problem solving, wellbeing, and healing (York, 2005) and to acquire knowledge or power (Walsh, 1994). The drum has an energy of its own; the drum is usually made from an animal skin and a wooden hoop, the joining of these and the birthing of the drum give the drum its own energy, its own personality. Once birthed, the drum goes through an empowered ceremony (Rysdyk, 2014).

I have a few drums, including an 18-inch drum I birthed, a 12-inch drum and a drum birthed and empowered by a Siberian shaman.[23] They have very different energies. The 12-inch drum likes to travel and has been to Peru and to Lithuanian. It is an excitable drum that likes to move. I usually

---

23 The process of birthing a drum involves laying the wooden hoop on the hide, which has holes punctured at the edges, and threading a length of hide through the holes, around a stone, in a set design. The stone is used to hold the drum when it is being played.

find myself standing and swaying when I play that drum; it also likes to get close to people who are journeying, using its energy to assist with the person's journey. The drum from Siberia is more serious; it holds the tradition of shamanic drums. It likes to be used when the journey has depth and related to healing. The drum I birthed is powerful and playful, enjoying journeys out into the cosmos.

The joy of playing a shamanic drum is that you do not need to be a musician or require any training; the drum connects to the energy of the journey and plays itself. Furthermore, you do not need to be a shamanic practitioner to experience journeying. As Needham (1979) states: "One thing never ceases to amaze me that within an hour or so of drumming, ordinary city folk are able to tap extraordinary mythic realities that they have never dreamed of" (p. 312).

The drum enables people to enter a shamanic state of consciousness:

> There are two realities and the perception of each depends upon one's state of consciousness. Therefore, those in the ordinary state of consciousness perceive only ordinary reality those in the shamanic state of consciousness are able to enter into and perceive non-ordinary reality or spiritual reality. (Harner & Harner, 2000, p. 1)

Shamanic Cosmos

The shamanic cosmos consists of three worlds. Berger (2005) described the worlds as being linked through: "a world tree, pillar, or mountain" (p. 85) and Eliade (1964) calls the three worlds sky, earth, and underworld. Although they are usually represented as the higher, lower, and middle world.

The three worlds are represented in the shamanic drum (Peemot, 2017; Rydving, 2001). Shamanic drums are round, representing the whole universe. The top third of the drum represents the higher world, the middle third represents the middle world and the lower third the lower world.

The drum takes the shaman on a journey to the higher world for learning; it is the place where the angels, saints, ascended masters, our spiritual parents, guides, and the lord of time live. However, when healing is required then the drum will take the shaman to the lower world. The lower world is a place of healing; in the lower world, there are healing pools and guides. The Nepali shamans describe the lower world as a place of rivers, caves, monasteries, shrines, and places of fertility (Desjarlais, 1989). The drum will take the shaman to the middle world to connect with spirits and guides. Berger (2005) described the middle world as a place where "spirits, deities, sorcerers, demons and ghosts of the invisible world are capable of influencing human life" (p. 85). The middle world is the world which surrounds us, but our spiritual eyes are closed, and so we are unable to see these other-than-human beings.

Healing

The drum aids the shaman to focus on healing, psychologically and physically:

> Shamanic activities bring people efficiently and directly into immediate encounters with spiritual forces, focusing the client on the whole body and integrating healing physical and spiritual levels. This process allows them to connect with the power of the universe, to externalise their own knowledge, and to internalise their answers; it also enhances the sense of empowerment and responsibility. These experiences are healing bringing restorative powers of nature to clinical settings. (Drake, 2012, p. 74)

Shamanic practitioners perceive everything as made of energy. Not only are we made of energy but also our emotions, our thoughts, are all energetic. The concept of energy is particularly important in shamanism, as healing includes not only assessing the energy of the person, it also uses the energy of the drum to assist with the healing process. Rich (2012) stated: "mental, emotional and physical illnesses all have a spiritual component" (p. 337), describing two categories of ill health; the first category is the loss of one's soul (energy). The second is due to a magic object or a spirit in a person's energy. This notion is supported by Eliade (1964) who stated that the: "Vast majority of illnesses have a spiritual cause – that is, they involve either the flight of the soul or a magical object introduced into the body by spirit" (p. 327).

Interestingly, the Coast Salish and Chinook native Americans perceived illness as spirit sickness, and disease as causing spirit powers and soul loss, which can occur when you offend your spirit power. Therefore, they perceive the healthy self is defined by spiritual and human relationships, with healers seeking to restore these relationships (O'Brien, 2013). When we do not connect to ourselves and nature, we are blind to ourselves and the world around us. This lack of connection causes low mood, low energy, and anxiety (Ingerman, 2008). Harner (1990) described shamanic healing as aiming to restore and maintain a person's spiritual, personal power, to return balanced and harmonious consciousness.

Therefore, the drum assists the healing process through being the horse which the shaman rides to places in the cosmos to retrieval soul parts, healing the soul. The drum heals emotions; as Drake (2002) identified, the drum relieves anger, gives courage, and provides solace. Furthermore, it is used to assist clients to meet guides and power animals, which can help them undertake shamanic journeys or give them strength to manage their daily life, to help them connect to themselves and to nature.

The Beats of the Drum

Harner (2013) and Drake (2002) state that the way to play the drum is through a steady monotonal beat. Maxfield (1994) researched the impact that the beat of the drum has on the mind; she found that the steady beat enables people to enter a trance-like state. I have found the steady monotonous beat useful when journeying; however, what I find more powerful is allowing the drum to lead the journey. I start with a steady, monotonous beat of three to four beats per second; this is the beat recognized in most shamanic practices and is the beat that Maxfield (1994) researched. It allows the person to enter a trance-like state. I do this for six beats; this allows the person to start their journey and the drum to connect. I then allow the process of the spirit of the drum connecting with the spirit of the journey to impact on the beat. The drum connects to the journey and plays itself. For example, when I am drumming, I find that the drum changes the beat and the speed; it becomes quiet or loud; it may want to include movement, all depending on the need of the journey or the person. I give my drum free rein rather than playing it at a set beat. This is supported by Porath (2013) and Li (1992), who observed shamanic rituals and found that the timbre, rhythm, volume, and tempo of the drum changes. For me, this is where the magic happens.

The drum supports the person in their journey, whether it speeds up when they are stuck or gives a stronger beat when more energy is needed. An example of this would be when I was drumming for a woman who had in her own energy some energy that did not belong to her. The energy was stuck, and she needed to push and push to get it out; she needed strength to keep going; the drum became louder, the beats stronger, as it shared its energy with that of the woman to help her push that energy out. When I am drumming for a group, there is a group energy to which the drum connects, helping people in their journeys, occasionally focusing in on one person's journey, especially when they are stuck and need that extra connection. It is incredibly powerful when the drum is fully involved in a person's journey and healing.

Bibliography

Berger, C. R. (2005). Interpersonal communication: Theoretical perspectives, future prospects. *Journal of Communication*, *55*(3), 415–447.

Desjarlais, R. R. (1989). Healing through images: The magical flight and healing. Geography of Nepali shamans. *Ethos*, *17*(3), 289–307.

Drake, M. (2002). The shamanic drum: A guide to sacred drumming. Talking Drums Publications.

Drake, M. (2012). *Shamanic drumming: Calling the spirits*. Talking Drum Publications.

Eliade, M. (1964). *Shamanism: Archaic techniques of ecstasy* (Bollingen series LXXVI). Princeton University Press.

Harner, M. (1990). *The way of the shaman*. Bantam New Age Books.

Harner, M. (2013). *Cave and cosmos: Shamanic encounters with spirits and heavens*. North Atlantic Books.

Harner, M., & Harner, S. (2000). Core practices in the shamanic treatment of illness. *Shamanism*, *13*(1–2), 19–30.

Ingerman, S. (2008). *Shamanic journeying: A beginner's guide*. Sounds True.

Li, L. (1992). The symbolization process of the shamanic drums used by the Manchus and other peoples in North Asia. *Yearbook for Traditional Music*, *24*, 52–80.

Maxfield, M. (1994). The journey of the drum. *ReVision*, *16*(4), 157–163.

Needham, R. (1979). *Symbolic classification*. Goodyear.

O'Brien, S. C. (2013). *Coming full circle. Spirituality and wellness among native communities in the Pacific Northwest*. University of Nebraska Press.

Peemot, V. (2017). Fractures of the whole: A depiction of the shamanic universe on Kaca drums brought by J. J. Sederholm from Siberia in 1917. *Studia Orientalia Electronica*, *5*, 27–45. <https://doi.org/10.23993/store.59323>

Porath, N. (2013). "Not to be aware anymore": Indigenous Sumatran ideas and shamanic experiences of changed states of awareness/consciousness. *Anthropology of Consciousness*, *24*(1), 7–31. <https://doi.org/10.1111/anoc.12001>

Rich, M. L. (2012). Integrating shamanic methodology into the spirituality of addictions recovery work. *International Journal of Mental Health and Addiction*, *10*(3), 330–353.

Rydving, H. (2001). The saami drums and the religious encounter in the 17th and 18th centuries. In T. Ahlbäck & J. Bergman (Eds.), *The Saami shaman drum* (pp. 9–27). The Donner Institute for research and Cultural History.

Rysdyk, E. C. (2014). *A spirit walker's guide to shamanic tools: How to make and use drums, masks, rattles, and other sacred implements*. Weiser Books.

Spinelli, E. (2009). *Tales of unknowing: Therapeutic encounters from an existential perspective*. Duckworth.

Turner, K. (2016). *Sky shamans of Mongolia: Meetings with remarkable healers*. North Atlantic Books.

Walsh, R. (1994). The making of a shaman: Calling, training, and culmination. *Journal of Humanistic Psychology*, *34*(3), 7–30.

York, M. (2005). Shamanism and magic. In C. R. Berger (Ed.), *Witchcraft and magic* (pp. 81–101). University of Pennsylvania Press.

11 Music, Meditation, and Mandalas

Re-Enchanting the Care Home

Introduction

This chapter describes an exciting project initiated by Meta Killick[24] and Alistair Clarkson (in a duo entitled *Living in Harmony*), which brings music together with a number of other areas that might be considered liminal or spiritual with the aim of transforming the atmosphere in a care home. This survey will examine these elements – music, visual art, and mindfulness – separately before bringing them together in a description of project itself. It starts by examining briefly the relationship between music and medicine and then music and the liminal space, which leads to the relationship between music and mindfulness. The use of mandalas addresses the use of visual images with music. The project under discussion brings all of these areas together powerfully to enrich care homes, physically, emotionally, and spiritually.

This project draws on the duo *Living in Harmony's* considerable experience in the area of music in care homes (Clarkson & Killick, 2016). Their previous project was entitled *What Good Looks Like* (Hopkinson et al., 2015; Oates, 2018) and was rooted in an innovative approach to safeguarding using art, drama, and music. The underlying hypothesis of this previous project maintained that if the overall atmosphere within the care home could be improved by means of establishing relationships characterized by mutuality, abuse would be reduced. In this case, they used

---

24 I am grateful to Meta Killick for her contribution to this chapter. <https:// livingwithharmony.net/>

active shared music-making between duo *Living in Harmony* and the staff and patients; this was seen to improve mood and enrich relationships. The aim to build safer, happier, and therefore safer care homes was effectively achieved. Most of the homes engaging in the project described in this chapter were already in trusting relationships with the musicians through this previous project. These homes welcomed the chance to engage in the new project described in this study.

The Context

Western culture with its competitive basis and stress on assessment has generated a great deal of stress. The caring professions are under particular pressure in situations where they feel undervalued and overstretched. It is often cited by employees as a reason for sickness absence, increasing stress on patients and families (Subothini et al., 2015). If prolonged, stress leads to mental and physical illness, including heart disease, back pain, headaches, gastrointestinal disturbances, and alcohol and drug dependency. There is a general reduction in the quality of life in general and depression and fatigue become regular occurrences. It is in the context of a desire to produce an environment that is supportive and encouraging that this project is rooted.

Music, Health, and Medicine

Once in European history music, health, and medicine were seen to be interrelated (Boyce-Tillman, 2000a). Apollo, for example, was God of music and medicine. In the Hebrew Scriptures, David is said to have played for King Saul as a method of lifting depression. The link was still alive in the Middle Ages in Europe, with figures such as Hildegard of Bingen (Boyce-Tillman, 2000b) and in indigenous cultures (Meiklejohn-Free &

Peters, 2015). In the times of the COVID-19 outbreak many people are using music in similar ways. Although much has been gained through scientific medicine methodologies in a materialist approach to healing and evidenced based ways of confirming truth, something has been lost, particularly in the relationship between the arts and healing. This project is one of many projects seeking to restore music as a healing force for both staff and patients in a health-care context.

One of these contexts was the *Elevate* arts program in Salisbury Hospital; here in the context of an arts program for patients, members of the hospital staff were actively observed taking part in the artists' sessions with patients, with small gestures such as singing a song with the musicians, or improvising a little dance in the middle of the bay in the ward. Subsequently staff were observed using music to distract the patients from the procedure they were carrying out (Preti & Boyce-Tillman, 2015, p. 24).

Wright and Sayre-Adams (2009, p. 29) described music as a soul food, along with art, nature, and scripture. They summarize the history of music in healing contexts:

> From the relaxation effect of soft background music, to patient participation in musicmaking, there are many opportunities for carers to find a path for music in holding the sacred in right relationship. Music, the "food of love" has inspired people to the heights of human achievement, and has been used in all cultures as a meditative and contemplative tool to alter states of consciousness, from the repetitive drumming of the shaman to the ragas of India and the complex and intricate qawaal songs of the Sufis. Latterly, we have witnessed some of the most ground-breaking work in the care of the dying with the application of music at the point of death in the Chalice of Repose Project led by Dr Therese Schroeder-Sheker. A whole new (some might argue, renewed) science and art is emerging of "music thanatology" (Schroeder-Sheker, 1994) bringing prescriptive music to the dying and seriously ill, with profound beneficial and spiritual effects being reported. (Wright & Sayer-Adams, 2009, p. 94)

Within some of the new thinking we have the concept of being able to hold a sacred (transformative) space by means of music. New singing groups have arisen – for the homeless, for the mentally ill, people with memory loss and stroke victims. Examples are the Seaview singers in Kent for people with dementia (Vella-Burrows, 2012, pp. 11–13), Recovery Choirs (2020) for people with mental health problems and Threshold choirs singing with the dying.[25]

The ArtsCare *Elevate* program in Salisbury hospital saw the following effects, which are very relevant to this study:

- The mediation of the artists through the program's activities promoted socialization between the patients in the same location through singing, experimenting with small and gentle movements, reciting a poem, or creating a story based in the natural world, seen in this project in how the music and mandalas established a strong sense of communitas (spiritual community) (Turner, 1969, 1974).
- The symbolic language of arts appeared to be a gentle aid for the patients to reconnect positively with their past, seen below in the ability of the mandalas to establish a relationship with participants' life journey.
- The experience improved the patients' perception of their hospital experience and made them more relaxed, even if they were undergoing stressful treatments, seen below in the peaceful attitude created.
- Staff engaged with the patients at a more personal level such as short conversations about musical taste and memories, seen below in the interaction between staff and patients sharing the mandala activity.
- Artists used their art forms to elicit physical, cognitive, social, and emotional responses from their patients, seen below in the willingness of people to participate in the project.
- Hospital administrators supported the program and were aware of its impact, seen below in the desire of care homes to purchase the project (based on Preti & Boyce-Tillman, 2015, pp. 5–6).

The data from Salisbury project indicated that music was not only a distraction from suffering but facilitated the work of the hospital. The arts genuinely supported the care of older people in this context. The project was in a hospital where, according to the Department of Health, older people occupy two thirds of general and acute hospital beds in the UK (Pope, 2012). These people will often be affected by dementia, either vascular, Alzheimer's or Parkinson's disease. Depression, psychosis and agitation, or aggression, are often symptoms associated with dementia (Shub

25   See <https://thresholdchoir.org>

et al., 2010) exacerbated when people are put in a situation that they cannot manage emotionally (Rockwood et al., 2014).

An admission to a care home requires a set of psychological and behavioral skills that a frail and often sick individual may not possess (Inouye et al., 1998). In this context where the most frequent activity is "waiting" (e.g., for mealtimes, for such tasks as washing and dressing, for treatment, for some visitors) boredom may well turn into depression (Hayes, 2014). Admission to a care home in the life of an older person is also associated with approaching death (Inouye et al., 1998). I wrote this poem to see how important music may be in this confusing and diminishing world:

A Cry from the Depths of Memory Loss

> 1. Hold me! My eyes are dim, my memory faltering;
> My sense of past and future now are fused;
> I cannot recognize much any longer,
> Except the music that the choir intones.
> 2. Help me! My limbs are frail and arms that once worked strongly
> Hang limp and useless, will not respond to me;
> I cannot understand the puzzling world around me,
> Except the music that the choir intones.
> 3. Hear me! My earthly usefulness is fading
> And nurture that I once gave freely, now I need;
> I can make sense of little any longer,
> Except the music that the choir intones.
> 4. Heal me! You whom I loved and who once loved me!
> How can I feel that caring love right now?
> Where can I still lay hold of warm acceptance -
> Ah! In the music that the choir intones.
> So now I flow within the river of that song.[26]

26 Unpublished poem by June Boyce-Tillman (2016).

At present, there is no cure for dementia and associated illnesses (e.g., Parkinson, Alzheimer's disease); therefore, psychosocial interventions are valued as therapeutic allies to improve the daily care of older people, including those with dementia (Vernooij-Dassen & Moniz-Cook, 2014). Examples of psychosocial interventions include occupational therapy, cognitive stimulation therapy, and support programs for caregivers (Cohen-Mansfield, 2001). Arts interventions are now part of a range of non-pharmacological programs that can be offered to older people. Even if some of the sessions are not intended as therapy, nonetheless their outcomes can be therapeutic (Vasionytė & Madison, 2013). Music was seen in Salisbury Hospital to work with the elderly as an extremely important way of unlocking painful memories – making the private more public so that it can be healed. Patients would request a song that they were keen to hear, such as "The White Cliffs of Dover," "It's a Long Way to Tipperary," "Edelweiss," or "Oh, What a Beautiful Morning." The varied repertoire of the artists allowed patients to engage actively with the songs, singing along, recognizing the tunes. In these cases, the transformative properties of the spiritual/liminal space are clear (Preti & Boyce-Tillman, 2015, p. 19). Although such practices were not part of the project under review, some of the shapes of the mandalas might fulfill a similar function.

The value of music in the lives of older people has begun to emerge through evidence-based research (Clift, 2012; Cohen, 2006). In relation to the effects of music on older people, the literature suggests that listening and being actively engaged in music activities (recorded or live) can:

- decrease stress and promote relaxation (Spintge, 2012)
- reduce agitated behavior (Gerdner, 2000; Lou, 2001)
- decrease behavioral and psychological symptoms of dementia (i.e., delusions, agitation, anxiety, apathy, irritability, and night-time disturbances) (Raglio et al., 2008)
- promote the recall of personal histories (Lord & Garner, 1993)
- improve mood, orientation, remote episodic memory and to a lesser extent also general cognition (Särkämö et al., 2013)
- enhance caregiver wellbeing, when they are engaged in the singing activities (Särkämö et al., 2013).
- impact positively on the quality of life of the residents in nursing homes (O'Shea et al., 2014)

- facilitate the discussion of death/dying and deep personal issues that sometimes older people are not able to discuss with anybody (Pope, 2012).

However, despite all of these findings, there is little evidence for the use of listening to music in care homes as in this project, either for general relaxation or as distraction from painful procedures (Zengin et al., 2013). Preti and McFerran (2015, p. 380) produced a helpful map indicating the interacting worlds of the patient in hospitals and care homes. Any project needs to evaluate the impact on and make its choices of appropriate activities:

- all the participants involved: patients, caregivers, hospital staff, and artists
- the quality of the relationships between the different participants

We see this below when the duo *Living in Harmony* describe the need for an intuitive grasp of the context as a whole. This social ecology model (Figure 11.1) suggests that individual behavior simultaneously shapes and is shaped by the complexity of this environment (Bronfenbrenner, 1979; Preti, 2013). The material will have connections with the socio-cultural identity of the patients involved in the program (MacDonald et al., 2002). In this model the hospital is a meta-level that will reflect the socio-cultural characteristics of the levels that it embraces: the patients and their families (including their caregivers), the community, and the wider society. Although the diagram was designed to illustrate work in hospitals, it is likely that care homes could be put in the oval containing hospital to reveal similar interactions in the care home sector.

The Chief Executive of Salisbury NHS Foundation Trust affirmed the impact on the hospital in general:

> It has a very positive impact on the environment both for the individual patient and the patients around them and the staff on the ward and the environment, and it also leaves behind a kind of lasting footprint … So all in all, in terms of motivating our patients, and a by-product being motivation of our staff, it's incredibly effective. (Preti & Boyce-Tillman, 2015, p. 33)

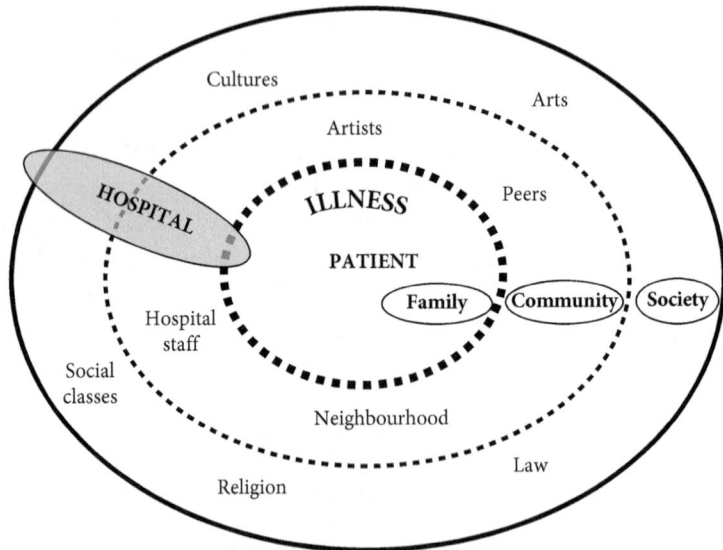

Figure 11.1. A socio-ecological model of factors involved when music is played in a
health care setting (adapted from Preti & McFerran, 2015)

Complementary therapists have seen music as one of their tools for
longer than allopathic medicine; sitting often in New Age spiritualities,
they are more likely to use the word spiritual to describe its effect:

> In holistic medicine, spiritual concerns rank with those of mind and body … In the
> struggle to make sense of life, certain activities create a supportive framework that
> connects us to our inner selves, to each other and the world. These activities include
> art, literature, music, community, family, worship and play and they are especially
> important when illness presents us with the reality of vulnerability, limitations and
> dependency. Broadly speaking, this is the realm of spirituality. (Woodham & Peters,
> 1998, p. 80)

Although it has proved difficult to fit music into the pattern of randomized control trials as proof of effectiveness, musicking projects in the
area of music and health are developing in the contemporary world. This
poem is included to illustrate the range of experiences that can accompany
a listening experience that may regarded as liminal/spiritual:

On Hearing Chaminade's *Automne*[27]

A silver birch sways proudly above the garden in a gentle breeze
There is a deep longing reaching to my roots
A sadness for time past
memories of lost dreams and relationships –

And yet there is a strange mystical hope –
Not for the past – not for the future
but for the present
A longing for a beyond in the now
The heavenly in the earth

The tears flow with the movement of skilled fingers on smooth ivories
The soul of a distant animal transmuted to a drawing room
To a world where women get lost in a field of men

The storm breaks
The tree swings dangerously to and fro
Insecure
Waving
Maybe drowning
Will it survive
Or will it be uprooted in the fury of the winter?

The mist swirls around the delicate trunk and branches
It clings on
Bending and yielding to survive
The valley of the shadow of death
Insecure
At risk
Circling, circling
Circling – to what purpose?
Why?
How?

Miraculously the storm subsides
Nostalgia fills the air –
A memory of a former peace

27   Unpublished poem by June Boyce-Tillman May 12, 2020.

> but this time is reduced
> only a brief healing -
> before a time of rest
> In an eternal now

As in this poem, the musical experience can enable the contemplation of life's meaning and purpose:

> Art uproots us into virtual reality … Time in the standard sense of *khronos* is suspended, and space is irrelevant because the viewer/listener/reader is encapsulated in the art, the virtual space provided by the artists. (Galtung, 2008, p. 54. Author's italics)

This use of music to create sacred space is found in reviews of music in health contexts: "Sacred space, and its instruments – beauty, stillness, music and so on – inspires and uplifts us" (Wright & Sayre-Adams, 2009, p. 13).

It "fills us with awe, with joy, with wellbeing, that which adds meaning to our lives" (Agwin, 1998, p. 6). These are part of my definition of spirituality as the musicker is transported into a different time/space dimension – to move them from everyday reality to "another world." Liminality would be another possible term, as defined by Turner (1969, 1974; see also Boyce-Tillman, 2016). It brings various parts of a person together in what Damasio calls "the neurobiology of consciousness" (Damasio, 2000, p. 11). It represents the reintegration of the body, the emotions, the intellect, and the culture. There is some agreement that these time/spaces are potentially transformative (Boyce-Tillman, 2009). Csikszentmihaly (1990) saw the connection between flow, religion, and the spiritual seeing a connection with ordering consciousness (p. 76). Turner (1969, 1974) saw the liminal space as transpersonal and consciousness-changing. It included the quality of communitas, which transforms what might be regarded as an individualized state into a lostness in a wider reality that includes the rest of the cosmos. This is often fleeting and transient:

> A moment of insight which was … like the moment when a tightly-coiled spring begins to release its energy, and then a violent explosion of pure happiness which passed so rapidly that I became conscious of it and identified it only as something that was already fast receding and becoming forgotten. I found myself snatching at it as it slipped away, melting though my fingers. (Cupitt, 1998, p. 8)

Isabel Clarke's (2005, p. 93) notion of the transliminal way of knowing has to do with our porous relation to other beings which re-establishes a cosmic relationship. People often require that the arts take them into this other way of knowing (Jackson, 1998). John Sloboda (2000) describes what he calls "non-judgemental contemplation," which means responding on a moment-to-moment basis to the unfolding music, a state with clear relationship with mindfulness as described below. It is clear in this account:

> For the first twenty-five minutes I was totally unaware of any subtlety ... whilst wondering what, if anything, was supposed to happen during the recital. What did happen was magic! After some time, insidiously the music began to reach me. Little by little, my mind all my senses it seemed –were becoming transfixed. Once held by these soft but powerful sounds, I was irresistibly drawn into a new world of musical shapes and colors. It almost felt as if the musicians were playing me rather than their instruments, and soon, I, too, was clapping and gasping with everyone else ... I was unaware of time, unaware of anything other than the music. (Dunmore, 1983, p. 20–21)

In summary, I have suggested that there is a potential domain of spirituality/liminality within the experience of music (Boyce-Tillman, 2016, 291–292) which links it with meditative practices.

Meditation

One of the strategies that people today are using in their search for spirituality is a practice called mindfulness. The spiritual experience in music in its processes has much in common with notions in mindfulness; some people can get close to the state of mindfulness by means of music, particularly music involving some degree of repetition and where its texture is thin enough to allow for the thoughts of the experiencer (Boyce-Tillman, 2016, p. 291). Mindfulness has great popularity with its sense of a non-judgmental resting in the present. It is often defined as "paying attention on purpose moment by moment without judging" (Kabat-Zinn, 1990). Concentration on the present moment and calm acceptance of feelings and memories often bear remarkable similarities to the transformative power of music:

> It can support the development of our inner resources to respond rather than react, to stress, anxiety, depression and chronic illness and pain ... Mindfulness training offers us alternative skills to manage the difficulties that life inevitably brings. Correspondingly we learn to be fully present to our happy and pleasant experiences and thus take more pleasure in them. (Mindfulness practice, 2012)

Jon Kabat-Zinn's description of the state of mindfulness concentrates on stopping completely, accepting paradox without anxiety and discord, outside of time and consisting of pure feeling (Kabat-Zinn, 2012). The mind is quietened and stress is reduced. There are, on the market, a number of recordings designed for use in meditation, which often contain a great of repetition and have an improvisatory character, similar to those used in this project.

Although in a hospital context and in mental health treatments mind-fulness is increasingly offered and practiced it is not regularly available in residential or nursing homes. Because of this, it is not entirely clear how successful it would be; for some people the period of silent contemplative meditation is not peaceful but filled with uncomfortable and challenging thoughts. The combination with mandalas in this project provides an additional way of holding the space alongside the music. The use of two holding techniques – both music and mandalas – means that the meditative practice is perhaps more likely to be peaceful and relaxing. It is possible, therefore, that this combination of music, mandalas, and meditation may have immense possibilities for improving the character of interactions in care homes and the general wellbeing of everyone involved within them, including people with or without cognitive impairment.

The Use of Mandalas

Mandalas are becoming very popular in meditative practices. They were a regular part of Hindu and Buddhist practices where they were seen as

Figure 11.2. The Labyrinth design in Chartres cathedral

linking the outer world (macrocosm) with the inner world (microcosm) with overtones of weaving (Madhu, 1979, pp. 12–22). Now mandalas have been embraced in Jewish, Christian, Pagan, and other religious traditions today. In Sanskrit the word means circle and it represents the cosmos as well as the spiritual journey of the meditator reminding them that the journeyer is a part of a never-ending circle which includes living and dying – recalling the earth, the moon, the sun, and so on – often with connections to sacred geometry.

As we have seen above, for older people the ability to contemplate living and dying is important for which opportunities are lacking in contemporary society. There were mandala type shapes within the Christian tradition in shapes like the Celtic cross (see Figure 11.3), the rosary, the halo, the crown of thorns on Jesus's head, the rose window (Painton, 2005) and the labyrinth as found in the floor of Chartres cathedral (see Figure 11.2).

So, for some older people with a Christian heritage, it may recall memories from their religious past.

Psychotherapy embraced these shapes in the hands of Jung, who through his personal experience (Fincher, 1991) used art as a way of accessing his own unconscious. He saw his daily mandalas as reflecting his state of mind. He found that it was often the circle that appeared spontaneously and found these in his exploration of traditions from the Indian subcontinent:

Figure 11.3. A Christian Celtic cross

> I sketched every morning in a notebook a small circular drawing, … which seemed
> to correspond to my inner situation at the time. … Only gradually did I discover
> what the mandala really is: … the Self, the wholeness of the personality, which if all
> goes well is harmonious. (Jung, 1961, pp. 195–196)

He saw that these were related to times of intense personal growth and an
essential part of the rebalancing of the psyche.

The mandala has been used in art therapy. This developed into therapists seeing mandalas as giving outward expression to inward experience
(Bonny & Kellogg, 1977). They offered an ordering and integration of
emotionally intense material (Henderson et al., 2007; Levick, 1980; Tucci,
1961) and saw them as offering a sense of liberation. Fincher (1991) saw the
drawing of a spontaneous mandala as accessible as a form of art. Various
schemes of assessing them have been created. Bush (1988) included the use
of color as well as the image in his view that this revelation of the deepest
parts of the client offered the possibilities of enduring changes. Joan Kellogg
(Barhar, 2012) developed a scheme of interpretation following an in-depth
study of many mandalas and developed her understanding, given to her
initially in a dream. It parallels nature circling through times of growth,
stagnation, and death. She developed MARI – *Archetypical Stages of the
Great Round* and includes such stages as *The Void* (akin to the black soil
of creation), *Dragon Fight* (A time of inner conflict during which we give
birth to a new sense of self), *Gates of Death*, and *Transcendental Ecstasy*.

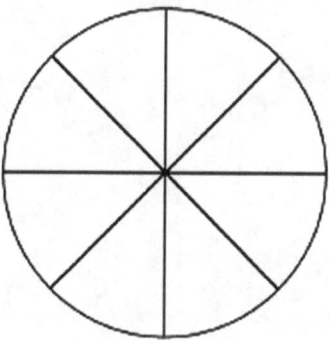

Figure 11.4. Basic mandala shape

It shows how humans reflect the cycles of nature repeat these stages over and over again (Barhar, 2012).

It is clear that such rebalancing is essential at such a momentous moment in a life journey as admittance to a care home – finding a purpose in a new form of life. Other writers like David Fontana (2005) developed the place of mandala in healing in books with titles like *Meditating with Mandalas – 52 New Mandalas to Help You Grow in Peace and Awareness* Healing mandalas became part of many courses designed to awaken wisdom, bring about calmness and aid focus and concentration.[28] So they became a centering device. The contemplation of ancient or modern mandalas have proved very helpful, as well as the process either of coloring within them or drawing one's own. One basic shape is shown in Figure 11.4. But this can be made much more complex and decorated in a variety of ways such as in Figure 11.5.

The symmetry of a mandala has been seen to create a sense of order for the mind – letting go of the thinking mind and entering a liminal space. Coloring a mandala has already been shown to bring improvements in wellbeing in the more general population as the number of coloring books

---

28   <https://lonerwolf.com/mandala-meaning/> Mandalas: How the sacred circle helps us reconnect with ourselves by Aletheia Kuna.

Figure 11.5. Example of a plain and colored mandala

on sale proliferate containing mandala shapes designed to produce peace and tranquility (Gogarty, 2013).

Music Therapy

These findings were brought together with the practice of music therapy through Guided imagery to Music Therapy (GIM).[29] Madelaine Ventre

---

29   Developed by Dr. Helen Bonny, the GIM process "is a music-centered, transform-ational therapy, which uses specifically programmed classical music to stimulate and support a dynamic unfolding of inner experiences in service of physical, psy-chological, and spiritual wholeness" (Association for Music and Imagery, 1990). A GIM session is approximately two hours long and usually contains four sections that naturally flow one into the other. A prelude begins the session. This is a period of focusing on what will be the work of the session. It is usually verbal and may include a sharing of events since the previous session, dreams, mandalas, in-sights, and questions. The induction that follows is a fine tuning of this focusing so that the client is more internally focused and the issues can more completely form his/her center of concentration. It is during the music segment of the ses-sion that in-depth work with the issues occurs. The music in the GIM session is experienced in an alternate state of consciousness, and this factor has great impact on how the music is heard and perceived. This state-receptive and open, yet focused

(1994) used mandalas in association with this therapy to explore the territory of the archetypal mother, using the MARI model in the process of integration and individuation to contact both the personal and collective unconscious. It is a way similar to myths and fairy tales. In this context the therapist appears to have asked clients to choose appropriate images from the MARI set of cards as well as drawing their own. Heather Wagner (2012) used mandalas in GIM with music therapists to understand their practice and in her processes of self-reflexivity.

Ritual is becoming a greater part of music therapy. Carolyn Kenny – a therapist with American indigenous roots – included in her concept of The Field of Play (Bruscia, 2018). Her two core constructs were love and the creation of beauty divided into seven fields (Bruscia, 2018). Later she (Kenny, 1999) works through these topics: aesthetics, intersubjectivity, empathy, uniqueness and the representation of our experiences through symbols, analogies, and metaphors (Bruscia, 2018). In the way in which this project under review in this chapter is set up many of these characteristics appear. Aesthetic judgment is necessary in both the choice of musical style and the mandala shapes chose. Intersubjectivity is present as the coloring of the participants interfaces with Anja Stacey's designs in the mandala shapes. Empathy is there in all involved and the intuitive interchange between them Because each person chooses their own colors, there is scope for uniqueness within a communal project.

Musical Construction and Meditation

In Europe, a new philosophy of the functionality of music developed with figures such as Erik Satie in the 1920s, who invented the idea of Musique d'ameublement or Furniture Music (Lanza, 2007, p. 18). This was meant

---

on issues of personal importance to the client – enhances the innate tendency of the music to produce imagery of various kinds. A postlude, in which creative processing of the issues takes place and a re-focusing on the external environment is affected, concludes the session (Ventre, 1994, pp. 19–20).

to be nothing more than a background music with no subject matter; pieces such as *Gnossiennes*, were not intended to attract attention in any way. It was in the 1970s, when Brian Eno invented ambient sound which was intended to induce calm and a space to think, as in Brian Eno's 1978 *Music for Airports*. It used a great deal of repetition; but uncertainty was also there sometimes, as in *Discreet Music*, a piece consisting of repeated chord progressions not rooted in any set key (Lanza, 2007, p. 210). Many of these pieces have proved very popular for meditation, peace, and relaxation; in the music for the project in this chapter similar characteristics can be seen.

Improvised music is more likely to have these characteristics and therefore a different feel from notated pieces. Olu Taiwo examines the relationship between the way time functions in literate (Western linear time) and orate (Return Beat) musical traditions:

> Western linear time and the curved time of the flux of the Return Beat. My becoming is contained and expressed in my kinesphere or personal space, which prepares me for the unborn/future … this idea stretches into the notion of temporal existence, where the world of the living (the present) is seen, in a metaphysical sense as sharing the same spatial and temporal context as the world of the ancestors (the past) and the world of the unborn (the future). (Taiwo, in press)

This view of past, present, and future coalescing in the present makes improvised music as having properties of the mandala examined above where people are exploring the journey of life in a very circular way which is reflected in the concept of time in the music.

The Practice of Music, Mindfulness, and Mandalas

This project[30] combines the elements discussed above in a new way. Although various schemes of interpreting mandalas have been created (Fincher, 1991; Kellogg et al., 1977), in this project it is the process rather

30   <https://www.youtube.com/channel/UCsgZ6uql3zXNmm92PI66THQ>

than the interpretation that is considered important. The process of creating music and image simultaneously can be extremely engaging.

> [One of my sons] used to do something I called "singing-drawing." He would have a piece of paper and a pencil and be tracing a line over it, singing or humming all the time. He could amuse himself for a long time meditating in this way. (Boyce-Tillman, 2018, p. 304)

Drawing on this experience this activity was included in a number of music workshops with people drawing or doodling while humming or singing. It created a magical meditative atmosphere.

The way this project works is that the care homes indicate their desire to engage with the project and then receive the mandala shapes by email, which are printed off by the care home. The mandalas given as part of the project to the care homes for coloring in advance are by Anja Stacey (see Figure 11.6).

When the time for the session is fixed, the staff of the care home have the mandala shapes printed and set them out with colored pencils and pens for the patients and the staff to use. Different levels of complexity of mandala are available. Both care staff, support workers and service users have the opportunity to choose a mandala which would engage and interest them. People can choose a less complex mandala should they require it. It is important that the mandala is meaningful and appealing to the person coloring it as in the MARI project above with the multiple potential meanings. Authentic engagement with the practice can create a powerful mood of mindfulness that is shared round the room; this means engaging with a variety of interacting contexts as in Figure 11.1. Making the practice genuinely useful for supporting staff as well as the vulnerable adults is essential to the success of the session. The music is played live through the computer screen. It is improvised and therefore is part of an orate musical tradition rather than literate musical traditions which are reproducing written musical scores with the characteristics explored above.

Combining listening to improvised music with the opportunity to color a mandala is the essence of this practice. Coloring a mandala with improvisatory music using repeated motifs in a circular musical shape creates a musical cradle, gently holding the meditative mood; it is a simple and

Figure 11.6. Mandala shapes used in the project

possible path to the health benefits of mindfulness for vulnerable adults as it combines the powerful tools described earlier – music, mandalas, and mindfulness. Done in a group characterized by non-judgmental acceptance, the associated tranquility is shared in a profound sense of togetherness and shared mindfulness.

At the time of writing this chapter, the project has been delivered in six care homes. In these, the duo *Living in Harmony* with Alistair Clarkson and Meta Killick improvise on harp and guitar using repetitive motifs with calming expressive character. Both of them have trained as music therapists. This training taught them to listen to and respond to/flow with the sounds and moods around them. In this project, this means entrainment to the rhythms and tones in the care homes as we saw in Figure 11.1. They have developed a style of music-making that reflects the rhythms of the coloring and is also soothing to the mood. They describe their improvisation as intuitive, sourcing energy.[31] We have already seen above that in various contexts these properties for music have been observed from earliest human history.

The overall aim was to create the meditative mood. The *Living in Harmony* duo in this project sought to create music of a character between beautiful and boring – pleasing enough to hold the ear yet not so nice that it causes activation – similar to some of the aims of ambient music above – such as singing along, tapping to the rhythm and so on, which might be a goal of other uses of music therapy, in which participants are asked to engage musically. The music in this project is intended for listening and promoting mandala activities. They describe that, now the project is delivered online, getting a sense of appropriate tones and rhythms which is highly intuitive is more complex. However, because *Living in Harmony* see all human beings as intuitively connected, their underlying understanding is that if in their improvisation they themselves are drawn into a liminal space, others will be drawn into that way of knowing as described above; this is aided by the mandalas which, as described above, are also a potential gateway to the meditative space.

The duo improvises music without lyrics to promote these relaxing and liminal experiences. The guitar and harp have similar string tones and mostly they duet without offering too much contrast. The keyboard and voice are sometimes used to offer sustained sounds; in an hour-long session they see the need for variety to maintain the participants' connection to the present in the care home. They produce gentle soothing cycles of sound, created and present in the moment – ephemeral and passing. The soothing improvised music has small melodies and repeated small intervals. They frequently create a drone or add a pedal note to give a sense of continuity. They often explore three-beat rhythms; this is often followed by a five-beat rhythm with the attention of creating a more liberating feel in the sound scape and a sense of uncertainty that we say in Brian Eno above. The key is often something which the duo agrees on in advance. They

31   Unpublished email from Meta Killick August 18, 2020.

use changing modes that evolve as the improvisations move forward. The Mixolydian is a favorite, as is the pentatonic, because of the major thirds in it which they associate with positive mood; the absence of the leading note makes less possibility of dissonance. The Phrygian is also a favorite for transitions. Chord changes follow the musical flow. Any harmonic dissonance is used to push toward the release in consonance. There is much use of the tonic/dominant polarity. There is a great deal of repetition but not so much structure that listeners can get attached to particular phrases. The musicians are expressing musically the circle of life in the same way as the mandalas. In the care homes staff and patients can color together to promote all the characteristics described in the sections above on music, meditation, and mandalas – discovery of meaning, contentedness, happiness, relaxation, and understanding.

Meta Killick writes about the atmosphere they are trying to set:

> The music is in happy speech range. That is, it is functioning as reassuring communication to the receiving ears (and brain) no dramas or excited phrases to worry about, but human contented presence saying "all is well" this soothing calming others are doing fine so the group is safe.[32]

So the players see the music as supportive of the participants' mindful activity of coloring a mandala, keeping a balance through the music delivered through the television/computer screen. With the understanding that moods transmit between people – both staff and patients – those who are able and willing to color a mandala are encouraged to do so, while others who are able to sit in the session are able to observe and absorb the atmosphere. This allows the maximum number of people the possibility of entering a quieter, more tranquil meditative space in a ritual way that includes people with underlying health conditions as well as less vulnerable people. It could in time be extended to include administrators and family members and even members of the wider community.

---

32   Unpublished email from Meta Killick August 18, 2020.

The Outcomes

An open training and evaluation session of music and mandalas has recently been delivered at a Sutton nursing home. Representatives from five other residential, supported living and nursing services attended. A simple mood scale was used at the start and the end of the session. Staff had some explanation of the purpose of the session. Twenty-two people (staff and residents) completed before and after mood scales. Analysis of the results showed an improvement in mood. This result is substantial and highly likely to be due to the music and mandalas practice. Evaluation in greater depth is in the process of being pursued.

The less formal feedback from the participants was also positive. Staff reported preferring this session to other music sessions. One resident who can be very disruptive was noticed to have engaged and remained calm. A carer of one who engaged in coloring commented that she had not seen her engage in an activity with such intention before. The practitioners facilitating the session, said that the calm mood was palpable and a contrast to day-to-day mood of the home. The musicians felt relaxed and calm at the end of the session too.

Their intention is to extend the practice as a useful way of increasing mental health and wellbeing uniting mind, body, and soul and enabling contemplation of the journey of life as described above. With little risk of harm from the intervention and potentially significant gains for those who live and work in residential settings, it has many possibilities for development. The care home sector is often characterized by stress and depression in both staff and patients. The use of both visual art and music to create a liminal space provides a powerful ritual for all present. This project entitled *Music and Mandalas* is an accessible mindfulness practice for those with or without cognitive impairment.

Conclusion

The combination of two art forms that promote entry to a liminal/ spiritual/meditative space as a way of alleviating stress, raising mood, self-awareness, contemplating dying and relaxing is an innovative practice with considerable potential, drawing on previous experiences of the musicians and the increasing research in this area. The capacity to deliver this electronically, via the internet, in care homes offers a real possibility of effective musical interventions during the time of the COVID-19 virus. This could be useful and expandable in non-COVID times. Extension and greater evaluation is needed to examine its potential. It is hoped that in the area of safeguarding it will be seen as transforming the mood of staff, family, patients, and the wider community. This would restore cultural faith in the role of music in complex health care contexts and in the care home as a place of protection and nurture.

Bibliography

Agwin, R. (1998). Creating sacred space. *Positive Health*, *24*, 6–7. <http://www.positivehealth.com/article/meditation/creating-a-sacred-space>

Barhar, T. (2012, August 21). *Archetypal stages of the great round of mandala: A guide to life's cyclical nature.* <https://tamarabarharlmt.wordpress.com/2012/08/21/archetypal-stages-of-the-great-round-of-mandala-a-guide-to-lifes-cyclical-nature-by-tamara-barhar-lmt-htcp/>

Bonny, H., & Kellogg, J. (1976). Guided imagery and music and the mandala: A case study illustrating an integration of music and art therapies. *Proceedings of 7th Annual Conference of American Art Therapy Association*, 71–76.

Boyce-Tillman, J. (2000a). *Constructing musical healing: The wounds that sing*. Jessica Kingsley.

Boyce-Tillman, J. (2000b). *The creative spirit: Harmonious living with Hildegard of Bingen*. Canterbury Press.

Boyce-Tillman, J. (2009). The transformative qualities of a liminal space created by musicking. *Philosophy of Music Education Review*, *17*(2), 184–202.

Boyce-Tillman, J. (2016). *Experiencing music, restoring the spiritual: Music as wellbeing*. Peter Lang.

Boyce-Tillman, J. (2018). *Freedom song: Faith, abuse, music and spirituality: A lived experience of celebration*. Peter Lang.

Bronfenbrenner, U. (1979). *The ecology of human development*. Harvard University Press.

Bruscia, K. E. (2018). The enduring concepts of carolyn Kenny. *Voices: A World Forum for Music Therapy, 18*(3). <https://doi.org/10.15845/voices.v18i3.2569>

Bush, C. (1988). Dreams, mandalas, and music imagery: Therapeutic uses in a case study. *The Arts in Psychotherapy, 15*, 219–255. <https://www.barcelonapublishers.com/resources/QIMTV7/Wagner2012.pdf>

Clarke, I. (2005). There is a crack in everything, that's how the light gets in. In C. Clarke (Ed.), *Ways of knowing: Science and mysticism today* (pp. 90–102). Imprint.

Clarkson, A., & Killick, M. (2016). A bigger picture: Community music therapy groups in residential settings for people with learning disabilities. *Voices: A World Forum for Music Therapy, 16*(3). <https://doi.org/10.15845/voices.v16i3>

Clift, S. (2012). Creative arts as a public health resource: Moving from practice-based research to evidence-based practice. *Perspectives in Public Health, 132*(3), 120–127. <https://doi.org/10.1177/1757913912442269>

Cohen-Mansfield, J. (2001). Nonpharmacologic interventions for inappropriate behaviors in dementia: A review, summary, and critique. *The American Journal of Geriatric Psychiatry, 9*(4), 361–381. <https://doi.org/10.1097/00019442-200111000-00005>

Cohen, G. D. (2006). Research on creativity and aging: The positive impact of the arts on health and illness. *Generations, 30*(1), 7–15. <https://hsrc.himmelfarb.gwu.edu/son_ncafacpubs/2>

Cowen, P. (2005). *The rose window*. Thames & Hudson.

Csikszentmihalyi, M. (1990). *Flow: The psychology of optimal experience*. Harper & Row.

Cupitt, D. (1998). *The revelation of being*. SCM.

Damasio, A. R. (2000). *The feeling of what happens: Body, emotion and the making of consciousness*. Houghton Mifflin Harcourt.

Dunmore, I. (1983). *Sitar magic, nadaposana one*. Editions Poetry.

Fincher, S. (1991). *Creating mandalas: For insight, healing, and self-expression*. Shambhala.

Fontana, D. (2005). *Meditating with mandalas*. Duncan Baird Publishers.

Galtung, J. (2008). Peace, music and the arts: In search of interconnections. In O. Urbain (Ed.), *Music and conflict transformation: Harmonies and dissonances in geopolitics* (pp. 53–60). Tauris.

Gerdner, L. A. (2000). Music, art, and recreational therapies in the treatment of behavioral and psychological symptoms of dementia. *International Psychogeriatrics, 12*(S1), 359–366. <https://doi.org/10.1017/S1041610200007286>

Gogarty, J. (2013). *The mandala colouring book: Inspire creativity, reduce stress, and bring balance*. Adams Media.

Hayes, N. (2014). Boredom is the enemy. *Nursing Older People, 26*(3), 5–6. <https://doi.org/10.7748/nop2014.03.26.3.5.s1>

Henderson, P., Rosen, D., & Mascaro, N. (2007). Empirical study on the healing nature of mandala. *Psychology of Aesthetics, Creativity and the Arts, 1*(4), 148–154. <https://doi.org/10.1037/1931-3896.1.3.148>

Hodgkinson, T. (1996). Siberian shamanism and improvised music. *Contemporary Music Review, 14*(1–2), 59–65. <https://doi.org/10.1080/07494469600640161>

Hopkinson, P. J., Killick, M., Batish, A., & Simmons, L. (2015). "Why didn't we do this before?": The development of making safeguarding personal in the London borough of Sutton. *The Journal of Adult Protection, 17*(3), 181–194. <https://doi.org/10.1108/JAP-12-2014-0045>

Inouye, S. K., Peduzzi, P. N., Robison, J. T., Hughes, J. S., Horwitz, R. I., & Concato, J. (1998). Importance of functional measures in predicting mortality among older hospitalized patients. *JAMA, 279*(15), 1187–1193. <https://doi.org/10.1001/jama.279.15.1187>

Ireland, M. S., & Brekke, J. (1980). The mandala in group psychotherapy: Personal identity and intimacy. *Arts in Psychotherapy, 7*(3), 217–231. <https://doi.org/10.1016/0197-4556(80)90028-3>

Jackson, P. W. (1998). *John Dewey and the lessons of art*. Yale University Press.

Jung, C. (1961). *Memories, dreams, reflections* (A. Jaffé, Ed.). Fontana Press.

Jung, C. (1964). *Man and his symbols*. Dell.

Kabat-Zinn, J. (1990). *Full catastrophe living: Using the wisdom of your body and mind to face stress, pain, and illness*. Delta Trade Paperbacks.

Kabat-Zinn, J. (2012, August 10). A poem on mindfulness. *Mindfulness for Dummies*. <https://mindfulnessfordummies.blogspot.co.uk/2010/08/poem-on-mindfulness-by-jon-kabat-zinn.html>

Kellogg, J., Mac Rae, M., Bonny, H., & di Leo, F. (1977). The use of the mandala in psychological evaluation and treatment. *American Journal of Art Therapy, 16*(4), 123–126. <https://psycnet.apa.org/record/1979-11275-001>

Kenny, C. (1989). *The field of play: A guide for theory and practice in music therapy*. Ridgeview Publishing.

Kenny, C. (1996). The dilemma of uniqueness: An essay on consciousness and qualities. *Nordic Journal of Music Therapy, 5*(2), 87–96. <https://doi.org/10.1080/08098139609477876>

Kenny, C. (1999). Beyond this point there be dragons: Developing concepts for general theory in music therapy. *Nordic Journal of Music Therapy, 9*(2), 127–136. <https://doi.org/10.15845/voices.v3i2.129>

Khanna, M. (1979). *Yantra: The tantric symbol of cosmic unity*. Thames and Hudson.

Lanza, J. (2007). *Elevator music: A surreal history of muzak, easy listening and other moodsong*. University of Michigan Press.

Le Marechal, C. (2015, September 4). 'Addiction choir' sings at Bristol's recovery festival. BBC. <https://www.bbc.co.uk/news/uk-england-bristol-34121360>

Levick, M. (1980). Group dynamics of dependency and counter-dependency manifested in drawings of graduate art, movement, and music therapy students. *The Arts in Psychotherapy, 7*(2), 87–96. https://doi.org/10.1016/0197-4556 (80)90014-3

Lord, T. R., & Garner, J. E. (1993). Effects of music on Alzheimer patients. *Perceptual and Motor Skills, 76*(2), 451–455. <https://doi.org/10.2466/pms.1993.76.2.451>

Lou, M. F. (2001). The use of music to decrease agitated behaviour of the demented elderly: The state of the science. *Scandinavian Journal of Caring Sciences, 15*(2), 165–173. <https://doi.org/10.1046/j.1471-6712.2001.00021.x>

MacDonald, R. A. R., Hargreaves, D. J., & Miell, D. (2002). *Musical identities*. Oxford University Press.

Meiklejohn-Free, B., & Peters, F. K. (2015). *The shamanic handbook of sacred tools and ceremonies*. Moon Books.

Mindfulness Practice. (2012). <www.mindfulpractice.co.uk/2005/05/search/label/5.benefitsofmindfulness>

O'Shea, E., Devane, D., Cooney, A., Casey, D., Jordan, F., Hunter, A., & Murphy, K. (2014). The impact of reminiscence on the quality of life of residents with dementia in long-stay care. *International Journal of Geriatric Psychiatry, 29*(10), 1062–1070. <https://doi.org/10.1002/gps.4099>

Oakes, P. (2018). Making safeguarding musical: How music is being used to create safer happier homes for vulnerable adults. *PMLD LINK, 30*(2), Issue 90, 8–13. <http://www.pmldlink.org.uk/wp-content/uploads/2018/09/PMLD-Link-Issue-90.pdf>

Pope, T. (2012). How person-centred care can improve nurses' attitudes to hospitalised older patients. *Nursing Older People, 24*(1), 32–37. <https://doi.org/10.7748/nop2012.02.24.1.32.c8901>

Preti, C. (2013). Live music as a bridge between hospitals and outside communities: A proposed research framework and a review of the literature. *UNESCO Multi-Disciplinary Research in the Arts, 3*(3), 1–18. <https://www.researchgate.net/publication/259694642_UNESCO_Observatory_Multi-Disciplinary_Journal_in_the_Arts_International_perspectives_on_the_development_of_research-guided_practice_in_community-based_arts_in_health>

Preti, C., & Boyce-Tillman, J. (2015). Elevate: Using the arts to uplift people in hospitals. *ArtCare*. <https://doi.org/10.13140/2.1.4269.0880>

Preti, C., & McFerran, K. (2015). Music to promote children's well-being during illness and hospitalization. In G. E. McPherson (Ed.), *The child as musician* (pp. 373–385). Oxford University Press. <https://doi.org/10.1093/acprof:oso/9780198744443.003.0020>

Preti, C., & Welch, G. F. (2011). Music in a hospital: The impact of a live music program on pediatric patients and their caregivers. *Music and Medicine, 3*(4), 213–223. <https://doi.org/10.1177/1943862111399449>

Raglio, A., Bellelli, G., Traficante, D., Gianotti, M., Ubezio, M. C., Villani, D., & Trabucchi, M. (2008). Efficacy of music therapy in the treatment of behavioral and psychiatric symptoms of dementia. *Alzheimer Disease & Associated Disorders, 22*(2), 158–162. <https://doi.org/10.1097/WAD.0b013e3181630b6f>

Rockwood, K., Fay, S., Hamilton, L., Ross, E., & Moorhouse, P. (2014). Good days and bad days in dementia: A qualitative chart review of variable symptom expression. *International Psychogeriatrics, 26*(8), 1239–1246. <https://doi.org/10.1017/S1041610214000222>

Särkämö, T., Tervaniemi, M., Laitinen, S., Numminen, A., Kurki, M., Johnson, J. K., & Rantanen, P. (2013). Cognitive, emotional, and social benefits of regular musical activities in early dementia: Randomized controlled study. *The Gerontologist, 54*(4), 634–650. <https://doi.org/10.1093/geront/gnt100>

Schroeder-Sheker, T. (1994). Music for the dying: A personal account of the new field of music-thanatology: History, theories, and clinical narrative. *Journal of Holistic Nursing, 12*(1), 56–64. <https://doi.org/10.1177/089801019401200113>

Shub, D., Ball, V., Abbas, A.-A. A., Gottumukkala, A., & Kunik, M. E. (2010). The link between psychosis and aggression in persons with dementia: A systematic review. *Psychiatric Quarterly, 81*(2), 97–110. <https://doi.org/10.1007/s11126-009-9121-7>

Sloboda, J. (2000). Music and worship: A psychologist's perspective. In J. Astley, T. Hone, & M. Savage (Eds.), *Creative chords: Studies in music, theology and Christian formation* (pp. 110–125). Gracewing.

Spintge, R. (2012). *Clinical use of music in operating theatres.* Oxford University Press.

Subothini, S., Aggarwal, N., & Vassilou, V. (2015). Tuning the heart with music. *Journal of the Royal Society of Medicine, 108*(11), 462–464. <https://doi.org/10.1177/0141076815600906>

Taiwo, O. O. E. (in press). *The return beat: Interfacing with our interface: A spiritual approach to the golden triangle.* Peter Lang.

Tucci, G. (1961). *The theory and practice of the mandala* (A. H. Brodrick, Trans.). Rider & Company.

Turner, V. (1969/1974). *The ritual process: Structure and anti-structure.* Penguin Books.

Turner, V. (1982). *From ritual to theatre: The human seriousness of play.* PAJ Publications.

Vasionytė, I., & Madison, G. (2013). Musical intervention for patients with dementia: A meta-analysis. *Journal of Clinical Nursing, 22*(9–10), 1203–1216. <https://doi.org/10.1111/jocn.12166>

Vella-Burrows, T. (2012). *Singing with people with dementia.* Canterbury Christchurch University.

Ventre, M. (1994). Guided imagery and music in process: The interweaving of the archetype of the mother, mandala, and music. *Music Therapy, 12*(2), 19–38. <https://doi.org/10.1093/mt/12.2.19>

Vernooij-Dassen, M., & Moniz-Cook, E. (2014). Raising the standard of applied dementia care research: Addressing the implementation error. *Aging & Mental Health, 18*(7), 809–814. <https://doi.org/10.1080/13607863.2014.899977>

Wagner, H. (2012). The use of music and mandala to explore the client/therapist relationship in a therapeutic day school. *Qualitative Inquiries in Music Therapy, 7*, 1–32. <https://www.barcelonapublishers.com/resources/QIMTV7/Wagner2012.pdf>

Woodham, A., & Peters, D. (1998). *Encyclopaedia of complementary medicine.* Churchill Livingstone.

Wright, S. G., & Sayre-Adams, J. (2000/2009). *Sacred space: Right relationship and spirituality in healthcare.* Sacred Space Publications.

Zengin, S., Kabul, S., Al, B., Sarcan, E., Doğan, M., & Yildirim, C. (2013). Effects of music therapy on pain and anxiety in patients undergoing port catheter placement procedure. *Complementary Therapies in Medicine, 21*(6), 689–696. <https://doi.org/10.1016/j.ctim.2013.08.017>

LAURA BENJAMINS

12 Facilitating Relational Spaces of Musicking
A Music Educator's Practice of Care

Introduction

Within a variety of contexts of music teaching and learning, both within and outside of the formal school classroom, relationships can be seen as being cultivated and developed through one's engagement in music-making (Small, 1977/1996, 1998). Although many students' musical experiences can be seen to be of significant value, some prevalent models of North American music education continue to emphasize the end musical product and notions of ability and excellence over the cultivation of relationships and students' musical growth (Bucura, 2020). In response to realities of exclusion, elitism, and a focus on purely technical skill development in the music classroom, recent discourses in music education have emerged surrounding issues of social justice in terms of inclusion, participation, accessibility, engagement, and student voice (Benedict et al., 2015; Wright, 2015, 2018). This literature tends to place value on students' experiences and relational engagement with one another through musicking (Small, 1977/1996, 1998), over final musical products or performances alone.

If we choose to look beyond the trends of standardization, curricular goals, and normative structures of schooling to insights, ideas, perspectives, and abilities, as well as spaces in which these attributes could be encouraged (Emmanuel, 2011), then we are, in Conroy's (2004) terms, focusing on "promot[ing] the flourishing of both individual and community" (p. 73). When education is thus seen as a means through which humans explore and develop answers to fundamental life questions, subject areas such as music should be spaces for students to engage in experiences that might contribute to a deeper understanding of human existence (Palmer, 2006). The arts, in particular, are uniquely positioned as nondiscursive and nonliteral phenomena which hold and express meaning separate from normal spoken language (Yob, 2011). It is therefore necessary to consider how musical experiences as nondiscursive phenomena may contribute to students' encounter with one another in the relational space. When students enter into relational spaces through musicking, it is possible that these spaces might nurture opportunities for dialogue, encounter, and meeting, thus contributing to the generation of deeper relationships and community in the classroom.

It is the role of the educator, then, to promote opportunities for students to enter into relational spaces and open the time for dialogue and reflection. Providing space for awareness and mindfulness takes time and effort in order for students to see and understand the world around them (Yob, 2011). I argue that through an educator's practice of care–incorporating elements of modeling, dialogue, practice, and confirmation–students may be better positioned to enter into relational spaces of music-making and learn to encounter the world in a new and different way. I begin by exploring literature related to themes of relationality, liminality, and education. In current music educational literature, relational spaces in which students' perspectives, ideas, and possibilities can be nurtured are often linked to a notion of the spiritual, a relational encounter "with the ineffable" (Yob, 2011, p. 42), in a world "other than the commonplace" (Boyce-Tillman, 2007, p. 1410). Separate from themes of religion, ethics, and morality (Van der Merwe & Habron, 2015), the spiritual is typically understood as a "between," or relational space of meeting the other. For some, including myself, the encounter with the other is an expression of God-given relationality, but is not equivalent to an encounter with God. I will, therefore, continue to refer to a liminal space of encountering the other as relationality, rather than spirituality, throughout the chapter.

I address Noddings's (1984, 1992) four components of nurturing the caring relation in the classroom through the lens of a music educator, providing practical examples of how they may be accomplished in musicking environments. I then explore concepts of spirituality and relationality in connection with liminality in greater detail, in order to describe relational experiences that students may undergo when musicking. Building on Silverman's (2012) research, I suggest, therefore, that students' engagement within relational spaces can lead to social cohesion and an increased sense of student wellbeing in the classroom. The chapter concludes with possible limitations and implications for future research.

Review of Literature

Spirituality and Music Education

The study of spirituality in academic discourse beyond theology and religious studies has increased in prevalence more recently (Boyce-Tillman, 2017; Van der Merwe & Habron, 2015). Themes of spirituality have been understood as integral in various contexts of education such as early childhood education (Adams et al., 2016; Pedraza, 2006), adult learning and education (English et al., 2003; Tisdell & Tolliver, 2003), and higher education (Chickering et al., 2006; Judge, 2016). Scholars who address spirituality and education often differentiate between spirituality and religion, noting that spirituality is a broad and universal term, not necessarily pertaining to the religious (Van der Merwe & Habron, 2015; see also Carr, 2008; Palmer, 2006). In addressing the pluralistic and increasingly diverse state of many schools today, there appears to be a sensitivity in promoting one religion over another in a multifaith public school classroom context (Yob, 2011). Spirituality is thus often kept separate from the religious in educational literature.

The arts have been linked to spiritual education in literature, associating music in particular with spiritual experience or growth (Bogdan, 2003; Boyce-Tillman, 2007; Carr, 2008; Yob, 2011). Carr (2008) and Yob (2011) both mention how music can be used to explore emotion in the classroom, "affording unique access to insights or experiences that somehow transcend the purely empirical" (Carr, 2008, p. 27). In a multifaith, multicultural classroom context, an educator's primary task is to guide, providing opportunities for learners to "discover and construct meaning" (Yob, 2010, p. 151) through the facilitation of their learning. The educator's role can therefore be seen as one that will involve an intentional knowing and caring for one's students in order for them to enter into this relational space. "Caring for," according to Noddings (1984), implies a direct action or presence by the one caring. The one caring is reactive and responsive to the needs of the cared-for (p. 19). While several scholars have distinctly connected care ethics to moral education (Charney, 2002; Johnston, 2006; Noddings, 2002; Stengel & Tom, 2006), this chapter is focused on the connection between care ethics and students' entrance into a space of relationality, contributing to their overall sense of wellbeing and social cohesion.

Liminality and Relationality in Music Education

As students enter musical engagements together, their experiences may be connected to a notion of relationality. In her writings, Boyce-Tillman (2007) "reestablish[es] a notion of spirituality as relationality within the musical experience" (p. 1405). Spirituality, for Boyce-Tillman, exists within the relationality between four domains of the musical experience–Materials, Expression, Construction, and Values – each contributing to the experiencer's movement to a different time/space dimension, away "from everyday reality" (p. 1410). Noddings's (1984) description of relation as "a set of ordered pairs generated by some rule that describes the affect–or subjective experience–of the members" (pp. 3–4) similarly aligns with Boyce-Tillman's description of relationality, where relationality is associated with or leads to the spiritual in certain contexts.

Literature has also connected themes of relationality and the musical and/or religious experience to a variety of concepts such as flow (Custodero, 2002, 2005), intuition (Noddings & Shore, 1984), ecstasy in terms of the "holy" (Otto, 1923), and liminal spaces (Turner, 1969, 1974; see also Tuan, 1977). The liminal is a space that is "ambiguous, neither here or there, betwixt and between all fixed points of classification" (Turner, 1974, p. 232), or a "between" space of meeting. I define liminality as Conroy (2004) does, that is, as a metaphor "which points to a space that is neither inside or outside but lies at the threshold of our social, political, cultural and educational spaces" (p. 7). Liminality, according to Conroy, may therefore "offer the possibility of deliberately displacing our understandings, beliefs, and ideals outside the realm of others, or indeed our own, socio-psychological containment in order to view them afresh" (p. 7).

Thus, I explore liminality in conjunction with relationality in order to describe students' engagement in a space where community and relationships and attributes – such as perspectives, ideas, and possibilities (Emmanuel, 2011) – might be developed and sustained in the classroom. Tuan (1977) describes "place" as "an organized world of meaning" (p. 179) in where, I suggest, student-musicians can construct liminal spaces of meeting and, ultimately, meaning. Through an educator's practice of care in developing a conducive classroom place, then, students may be able to enter into the liminal and meet one another through music. In transforming a particular classroom space into a place of belonging, educators might encourage students' practices of mutual care and concern (Hendricks, 2018), finding commonalities while also valuing difference in the space of "otherness" or "between." This exploration is significant in terms of aiding students in their construction of meaning and understanding of the world, as well as promoting student wellbeing and social cohesion.

Enacting a Caring Relationship through Music

As Noddings's ethic of care is concerned with the caring relationship between "the one caring" and the "cared for," various scholars have explored how a caring relation between an educator and student might be enacted in a practical sense. Characteristics that focus on open-ended, communal, empathetic, and dialogical processes of teaching and learning are often linked in literature to a "care-based" pedagogy (Bates, 2004, 2009; Silverman, 2012; van der Schyff et al., 2016). Within a care-based relation, educator–student relationships can be seen to move away from that which is "grounded in a fixed or depersonalized hierarchy" (van der Schyff et al., 2016, p. 95), and instead emphasize practices of active listening and interest for another. As Noddings (2012) explains, "it is important not to confuse what the cared-for wants with that which we think he should want. We must listen, not just 'tell,' assuming we know what the other needs" (p. 773). Caring, then, begins with an open-ended relationship and encounter between an educator and the student. Caring involves compassion, a "relationship of *experience-sharing*" in which one might support the other "based on a shared understanding of feelings, hopes, and/or desires" (Hendricks, 2018, p. 5). Following Noddings's work, one's act of encountering the other within a caring relationship may be accomplished through classroom musicking. I therefore examine Noddings's (1984, 1992) four means of nurturing the ethical ideal in the classroom–modeling, dialogue, practice, and confirmation–through the lens of a music educator's practices.

Modeling

An educator begins the music class without saying anything and simply hums a consistent note to the class. As students quiet down and begin to notice the educator, (s)he motions for them to join in. Initially everyone sings the same pitch until the educator points at one group of students and motions for them to move a few notes up, while motioning to others to move several notes down. As the educator circles their arms, students begin to understand that the educator is opening up a space for vocal improvisation. (S)he starts moving around the room, encouraging students to also walk around freely, opening up a space to move while they improvise. The class joins together musically, pitches ebbing and flowing in relation to those around them. After a few minutes of improvisation, the educator diminishes in volume, and others follow their lead, eventually resulting in a space of pure silence.

> This example demonstrates how an educator modelled practices of care to students by creating a space that encouraged active listening and musical response to others. The educator started the class by capturing students' attention, engaging them in a practice in which they needed to listen and interact with their classmates. As students entered into this relational space, the educator modelled how this might be

accomplished, but then took a step back, resulting in an open-ended relationship between students, where each listened and met with one another in the musical space.

Dialogue

Students are placed in small instrumental groups in which they are asked to listen and respond musically to group members' musical excerpts. Each student has a musical excerpt picked out ahead of time, plays it, and other group members start to respond musically, contributing to a "call-and-response" type of composition. Students begin to engage in dialogical musicking as the initial student responds and meets the other in the musical space, collaborating as an intimate group.

> In this example, students are asked to actively listen and engage in musical dialogue as they connect through a caring relation. Through the creation of a healthy, trustworthy, environment by the music educator, students will ideally take risks and express themselves musically in response to what they are hearing. Similar to Noddings's (2002) description of dialogue, neither student knows the outcome of their dialogue preceding their interaction. They act and respond in the moment, adapting and shifting according their engagement in musicking.

Practice

A music educator provides opportunities for each student to act as a facilitator or leader in their small popular music ensemble. Asking each group to choose a recording on which to base their performance, students take turns leading their group in their musical choices and decisions. The educator steps back and lets the music students have a significant amount of freedom in their assignment. Students "jam" together, entering into a space of relation as they interact with one another musically, listening to each other's suggestions, comments, and ideas.

> Here, students are assigned groups to engage in "caring apprenticeships," as mentioned by Noddings (1984), providing them with opportunities to practice their skills in caregiving. Since students are asked specifically to lead their groups, creating

an open-ended space for them to engage in decision making and dialogue, group leaders are encouraged to practice being "carers" for others. They are encouraged to think about their choice of language in the way they pose questions and comments to other group members. Since students are given quite a bit of freedom in their assignments, this may contribute to their sense of creativity in terms of improvisation and ability to enter into a relational space.

Confirmation

Following each student's completion of a musical composition assignment, the class is asked to sing each other's compositions in small groups alongside one another. As each student-composer shares their work, they are encouraged to also engage in a time of self-reflection, sharing with their group a variety of musical possibilities and ideas that were considered in their compositions, as well as what they were envisioning when composing. Fellow classmates then respond to one another, encouraging each other in their musical process as they continue to musically explore each composition as a group.

> In this example, students are encouraged by other classmates in their musical journeys as they share their personal compositions with one another. As students sing compositions as a group, this musical experience may be seen to contribute to students' encounter with one another. As Noddings (1984) explains, a relation of trust grounds confirmation, where the dialogue then begins. Both the sharing of compositions and the time of critical self-reflection must occur in a space of trust, to which a music educator contributes.

Each of these practical examples of nurturing the ethical ideal in the classroom point toward the importance of establishing safe, communal, trustworthy spaces for students to deeply engage in dialogue with one another. As Hendricks (2018) suggests, practices such as demonstrating personal integrity, reducing students' sense of vulnerability, and celebrating experimentation while supporting risk are all strategies that one might adopt in developing a trusting environment for music teaching and learning. The creation of these trustworthy educational spaces takes time and in order to genuinely make connections with others, certain levels of personal authenticity, integrity, and vulnerability are necessary (Hendricks, 2018). Through an educator's practices, then, students may be better positioned to enter into relational spaces of music-making. In accordance with Silverman's (2012) assertion, these relational spaces can thus result in greater opportunities for "transformative musical-affective experiences, for positive interpersonal relationships, and for democratic agency" (p. 112).

Liminality and Relational Musicking

In the following section, I explore the concept of relationality in connection with liminality (Turner, 1969), in order to describe students' relational experiences that they may undergo when musicking. When teaching for spirituality through music, Yob (2011) recommends teaching students to go "beyond technicalities of a performance or musical work to the meaning and experience of that work" (p. 46). Yob's (2011) description of teaching for spirituality can be connected here to a class's relational engagement in musicking (Small, 1977/1996, 1998). Together, music students actively perform music of different genres, share musical experiences, as well as their values, beliefs, and understandings.

As students enter into a space of relationality through musicking, they can be seen to initially leave their secular, hierarchical social structure of classes and ranks, which separates one person from another as "more or less" (Turner, 1969). A *limen* or threshold is crossed, and boundaries are dissolved as individuals move from ordinary knowing and being to a sense of encounter and opening up (Boyce-Tillman, 2009). The liminal, "between" space of being, is one that is unstructured and undifferentiated, "open to the play of thought, feeling, and will … where suppositions, desires, hypotheses, possibilities, and so forth, all become legitimate" (Turner, 1969, p. vii).

Within the liminal space, students' perspectives, ideas, and possibilities are welcomed without restrictions in a variety of forms such as musicking. In accordance with Small's (1977/1996, 1998) definition of musicking, students' music-making may be seen to be tied to the set of relationships surrounding them within the liminal. Students actively share musical experiences, as well as their values, concepts of ideal relationships, and who they are as individuals, finding a sense of place and value as they meet with one another in the liminal. Tuan's (1977) investigations support this connection between space and place, for "what begins as undifferentiated space becomes place as we get to know it better and endow it with value ... each pause in movement makes it possible for location ... to be transformed into place" (p. 6). A liminal, temporal pause in a musical space, then, has the ability to create place, further connecting musickers as a community of learners. Both students as well as the music educator can find commonalities in this "between" space, meeting and finding value in their "otherness."

Turner (1969) further connects the liminal to the concept of *communitas*, which describes the relationships and social bonds created in the liminal space. These bonds are "undifferentiated, equalitarian, direct, extant, [and] nonrational" (p. 274), where participants eliminate their typical roles and statuses. Communitas as a part of ritual, thus, is essential to a community's survival and flourishing in an orderly fashion, as the liminal provides a space for healing from traditional social hierarchies of everyday life (Turner, 1974). Similarly, communitas within the liminal space, as part of classroom musicking, is also essential to the classroom community's flourishing, social cohesion and further development. Within the liminal space, both teachers and students might develop a greater awareness and understanding of one another, meeting each other and contributing to a shared sense of belonging.

Figure 12.1 shows a model of the conceptual framework outlined in this chapter thus far. It is necessary to note that the process described is flexible and adaptable according to the particular classroom environment, taking shape according to student–teacher relationships and practices. Rather than a linear process, the purpose of this model is to provide a visual representation of how the concepts presented might fit together.

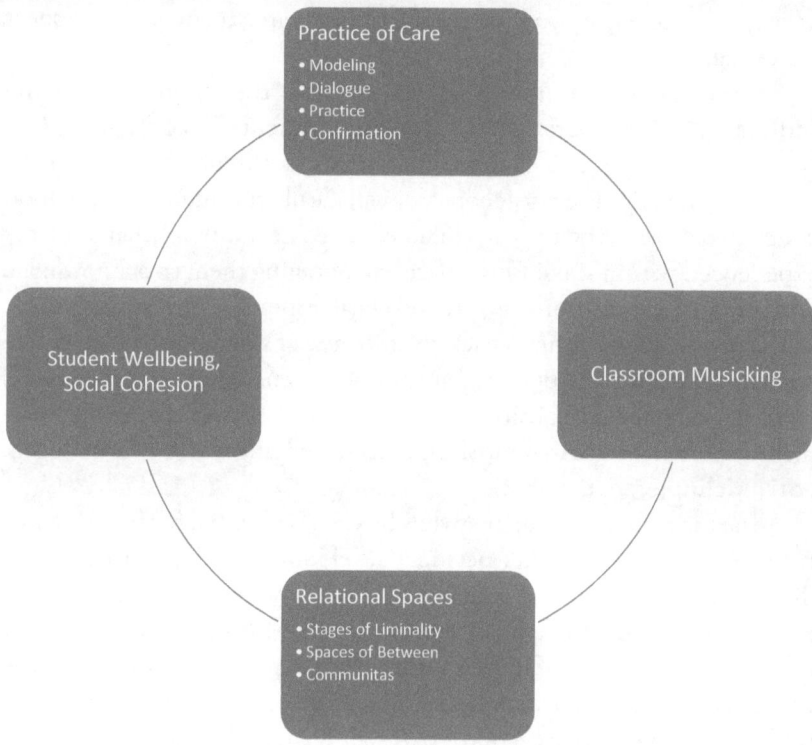

Figure 12.1. Conceptual framework

Student Wellbeing and Social Cohesion

Students are both cared for and care for each other as they continuously enter a relational, liminal space with others through musicking. Within this space, they can be seen to experience a variety of personal and collective emotions, interpersonal engagements, and a greater understanding of living with and for others (Elliot & Silverman, 2014). Students practice meeting fellow students, recognizing the "otherness" of each person (Noddings, 2002), building commonalities, and sharing experiences. These actions may be foundational to students' flourishing, as they learn to engage in lifelong practices of care, dialogue, and respect (Silverman, 2020).

Although communitas is not necessarily a "transformation" among individuals who experience the liminal, moments of communitas do contribute to "equitable relations" that can be scaffolded and built upon (Emmanuel, 2011). The music educator will ideally continue to reflect upon the shared sense of belonging (Baumeister & Leary, 1995) that students experienced within the liminal space, encouraging them to acknowledge and sustain these relationships. This cyclical responsive process, as evident in the model above, returns back to an educator's practice of care, where students' strengths and potential are promoted, encouraging each learner's "positive personal self, positive social self, and their spiritual self to optimally experience human flourishing in a challenging world" (Cruywagen, 2018; McEntee, 2013, p. 154;).

The caring relationship may thus be seen as essential for further classroom learning and students' personal development and growth to occur. Silverman (2012), however, clarifies that the "goods" of teaching are not entirely relational. Rather, music education "must include the development of students' awareness of their responsibilities as democratic citizens, the enhancement of their artistic and academic growth, [and] their personal wellbeing." None of these "goods" of teaching, though, "can grow or thrive in an uncaring school environment" (p. 111). By establishing a sense of care and trust first in the classroom, students can then enter into a relational space of vulnerability and honesty, learning to engage in radical hospitality toward the other, valuing them for who they are as individuals. Only after that process can music education focus on goals such as the development of democratic citizens, personal and musical growth, and wellbeing (p. 111).

Concluding Thoughts

This chapter explored themes of spirituality, relationality, and liminality in relation to Noddings's ethic of care as expressed in the music classroom. In particular, I explored how an educator's practice of care may create a conducive classroom place for students to enter into the relational space of the liminal, meeting one another through music. I suggest that as students encounter one another in their musicking, they may build commonalities, explore possibilities, and value difference, contributing to students' sense of wellbeing and social cohesion.

This examination of students' musical engagement in the liminal leading to wellbeing and social cohesion has its limitations. The conceptual framework presented assumes that students will be able to enter into the liminal, encounter the other, and be positively impacted in the process. Relationships among students are not always equitable, and will not necessarily be "fixed" in the process. An educator may want to instead use these learning experiences to critically reflect on situations where relations are not equitable among students, interrogating perspectives and possibilities for why this may be so and how these relations might be negotiated. There are certainly always limitations of time and resources too, as well as other factors such as power imbalances and lack of student participation.

When exploring relational spaces of liminality, it is also necessary to understand that an educator's practice of self-examination is also critical in building community. Emmanuel (2011) suggests that educators must "place [their] values side-by-side with those of [their] students in nonjudgmental ways that [they] can work toward mutual understanding, build relationships, and move toward community in the liminal space" (p. 59). As the liminal involves a loss of social hierarchy and distinctive boundaries, one must be prepared to direct students in interactions that may become uncomfortable and unpredictable to allow for community to emerge. Because certain school settings do not typically allow for a prevalence of equality, shared power, and ambiguity (Emmanuel, 2011), I am therefore not recommending a lack of direction or leadership from the educator. I am, however, encouraging an increased critical awareness of all interactions and decisions that are occurring within the music classroom, including an awareness of the educator's status and perceived structures of power.

Finally, it is important to note that themes of spirituality, relationality, and liminality together have received minimal attention in music education literature. The spiritual, in particular, is difficult to define in terms of its multidimensional, subjective, complex nature (Van der Merwe &

Habron, 2015, 2020). In order to better understand how students might enter into a relational space of meeting and encountering one another in the classroom, future research exploring these themes would be beneficial. As music educators continue to look to the future of classroom musicking, spirituality, liminality, and relationality may be critical areas of exploration to consider, ultimately contributing to a greater understanding of students' sense of community, relational engagement, and authentic connection in the classroom.

Bibliography

Adams, K., Bull, R., & Maynes, M. L. (2016). Early childhood spirituality in education: Towards an understanding of the distinctive features of young children's spirituality. *European Early Childhood Education Research Journal*, *24*, 760–774. <https://doi.org/10.1080/1350293X.2014.996425>

Bates, V. (2004). Where should we start? Indications of a nurturant ethic for music education. *Action, Criticism, and Theory for Music Education*, *3*(3). <http://act.maydaygroup.org/articles/Bates3_3.pdf>

Bates, V. (2009). Human needs theory: Applications for music education. *Action, Criticism, and Theory for Music Education*, *8*(1). <http://act.maydaygroup.org/articles/Bates8_1.pdf>

Baumeister, R. F., & Leary, M. R. (1995). The need to belong: Desire for interpersonal attachments as a fundamental human motivation. *Psychological Bulletin*, *117*(3), 497–529. <https://doi.org/10.1037/0033-2909.117.3.497>

Benedict, C., Schmidt, P., Spruce, G., & Woodford, P. (Eds.). (2015) . *The Oxford handbook of social justice in music education*. Oxford University Press.

Bogdan, D. (2003). Musical spirituality: Reflections on identity and the ethics of embodied aesthetic experience in/and the academy. *Journal of Aesthetic Education*, *37*(2), 80–98. <https://doi.org/10.1353/jae.2003.0011>

Boyce-Tillman, J. (2007). Spirituality in the musical experience. In L. Besler (Ed.), *International handbook of research in arts education* (pp. 1405–1422). Springer.

Boyce-Tillman, J. (2009). The transformative qualities of a liminal space created by musicking. *Philosophy of Music Education Review*, *17*(2), 184–202. <https://doi.org/10.2979/PME.2009.17.2.184>

Boyce-Tillman, J. (Ed.). (2017). *Spirituality and music education: Perspectives from three continents.* Peter Lang.

Bucura, E. (2020). Rethinking excellence in music education. *Visions of Research in Music Education, 36*(1). <http://www.usr.rider.edu/~vrme/v36n1/visions/3607_Bucura.pdf>

Carr, D. (2008). Music, spirituality, and education. *The Journal of Aesthetic Education, 42*(1), 16–29. <https://doi.org/10.1353/jae.2008.0005>

Charney, R. S. (2002). *Teaching children to care: Classroom management for ethical and academic growth, K-8.* Northeast Foundation for Children.

Chickering, A., Dalton, J., & Stamm, L. (2006). *Encouraging authenticity and spirituality in higher education.* John Wiley & Sons.

Conroy, J. (2004). *Betwixt and between: The liberal imagination, education and democracy.* Peter Lang.

Cruywagen, S. (2018). "Flourishing with music": From music students to well-rounded musicians of the 21st century. *Koers: Bulletin for Christian Scholarship, 83*(1), 1–15. <https://doi.org/10.19108/koers.83.1.2306>

Custodero, L. (2002). Seeking challenge, finding skill: Flow experience in music education. *Arts Education and Policy Review, 103*(3), 3–9. <https://doi.org/10.1080/10632910209600288>

Custodero, L. (2005). Observable indicators of flow experience: A developmental perspective of musical engagement in young children from infancy to school age. *Music Education Research, 7*(2), 185–209. <https://doi.org/10.1080/14613800500169431>

Elliott, D., & Silverman, M. (2014). Music, personhood, and eudaimonia: Implications for educative and ethical music education. *The Journal for Transdisciplinary Research in Southern Africa, 10*(2), 57–72. <https://doi.org/10.4102/td.v10i2.99>

Emmanuel, D. (2011). Liminality as thought and action. *Action, Criticism, and Theory for Music Education, 10*(1), 47–68. <http://act.maydaygroup.org/articles/Emmanuel10_1.pdf>

English, L., Fenwick, T., & Parson, J. (2003). *Spirituality of adult education and training.* Krieger.

Hendricks, K. (2018). *Compassionate music teaching: A framework for motivation and engagement in the 21st century.* Rowman & Littlefield.

Johnston, D. K. (2006). *Educating for a caring society: Classroom relationships and moral action.* Teachers College Press.

Judge, J. (2016). *Spirituality in higher education: A narrative analysis of its use for decision-making* [Unpublished doctoral dissertation, Minnesota State University].

McEntee, M. (2013). Human flourishing: A natural home for spirituality. *Journal of Spirituality in Mental Health*, *3*, 141–159. <https://doi.org/10.1080/19349637.2013.799410>

Noddings, N. (1984). *Caring: A feminine approach to ethics and moral education.* University of California Press.

Noddings, N. (1992). *The challenge to care in schools: An alternative approach to education.* Teachers College Press.

Noddings, N. (2002). *Educating moral people: A caring alternative to character education.* Teachers College Press.

Noddings, N. (2012). The caring relation in teaching. *Oxford Review of Education*, *38*(6), 771–781.

Noddings, N., & Shore, P. J. (1984). *Awakening the inner eye: Intuition in education.* Teachers College Press.

Otto, R. (1923). *The idea of the holy: An inquiry into the non-rational; factor in the idea of the divine and its relation to the rational.* Oxford University Press.

Palmer, A. (2006). Music education and spirituality: Philosophical exploration II. *Philosophy of Music Education Review*, *14*(2), 143–158. <https://doi.org/10.1353/pme.2007.0007>

Pedraza, L. (2006). *"Because they are spiritually discerned": Spirituality in early childhood education* [Unpublished doctoral dissertation, Ohio State University].

Silverman, M. (2012). Virtue ethics, care ethics, and "The good life of teaching". *Action, Criticism, and Theory for Music Education*, *11*(2), 96–122. <http://act.maydaygroup.org/articles/Silverman11_2.pdf>

Silverman, M. (2020). The Hull house: A case study in eudaimonia for music learning. In G. D. Smith & M. Silverman (Eds.), *Eudaimonia: Perspectives for music learning* (pp. 30–43). Routledge.

Small, C. (1977/1996). *Music, society, education.* Wesleyan University Press.

Small, C. (1998). *Musicking: The meanings of performing and listening.* University Press of New England.

Stengel, B., & Tom, A. (2006). *Moral matters: Five ways to develop the moral life of schools.* Teachers College Press.

Tisdell, E., & Tolliver, D. (2003). Claiming a sacred face: The role of spirituality and cultural identity in transformative adult higher education. *Journal of Transformative Education*, *1*(4), 368–392. <https://doi.org/10.1177/1541344603257678>

Tuan, Y. (1977). *Space and place: The perspective of experience.* University of Minnesota Press.

Turner, V. (1969). *The ritual process: Structure and anti-structure.* Cornell University Press.

Turner, V. (1974). *Dramas, fields, and metaphors: Symbolic action in human society.* Cornell University Press.

Van der Merwe, L., & Habron, J. (2015). A conceptual model of spirituality in music education. *Journal of Research in Music Education, 63*(1), 47–69. <https://doi. org/10.1177/0022429415575314>

Van der Merwe, L., & Habron, J. (2020). Exploring lived experiences of spirituality amongst five Dalcroze teachers. *Psychology of Music, 48*(2), 163–181. <https:// doi.org/10.1177/0305735618785011>

van der Schyff, D., Schiavio, A., & Elliott, D. J. (2016). Critical ontology for an enactive music pedagogy. *Action, Criticism, and Theory for Music Education, 15*(5), 81–121. <http://dx.doi.org/10.22176/act15.5.81>

Wright, R. (2015). Music education and social reproduction: Breaking cycles of injustice. In C. Benedict, P. Schmidt, G. Spruce, & P. Woodford (Eds.), *The Oxford handbook of social justice in music education* (pp. 340–354). Oxford University Press.

Wright, R. (2018). Envisioning real Utopias in music education: Prospects, possibilities and impediments. *Music Education Research, 21*(3), 217–227. <https://doi. org/10.1080/14613808.2018.1484439>

Yob, I. (2010). Why is music a language of spirituality? *Philosophy of Music Education Review, 18*(2), 145–151. <https://doi.org/10.2979/PME.2010.18.2.145>

Yob, I. (2011). If we knew what spirituality was, we would teach for it. *Music Educators Journal, 98*(2), 41–47. <https://doi.org/10.1177/0027432111425959>

KARIN S. HENDRICKS

13 Authentic Connection in Music Education
A Chiastic Essay

Acknowledgment of Land and Privilege

I wrote this chapter during the COVID-19 pandemic, tucked away at home in Foxborough, Massachusetts, a land long inhabited by the Wampanoag tribe who were overtaken by my own European ancestors. Members of the Wampanoag were almost completely eradicated by diseases that the European immigrants brought with them to this land (Wampanoag Tribe of Gay Head, Aquinnah, n.d.). Just as that epidemic squashed the future and promise of many Indigenous people, the contemporary pandemic has interrupted life as we once knew it, while similarly disproportionately taking the lives of Black, Indigenous, and People of Color in my home country (Moore et al., 2020). I dedicate this chapter to the Wampanoag, while also reflecting on the injustices that continue to this day in the United States. I also acknowledge that my reception into this scholarly endeavor – including the privileges of a quality computer, library access, high-speed internet, and many social network opportunities – did not come from my own merits alone, but also from the White privilege into which I happened to be born. As I recognize this privilege, I also recognize that there is much to do to promote equity, healing, and human connection.

Authentic Connection: The Ultimate Quality of Compassion

Authentic connection is one of the qualities of compassion that I discussed previously in my framework for compassionate music teaching

(Hendricks, 2018a). It was the last quality I introduced, as the ultimate compassionate quality that would presumably follow after effective demonstrations of trust, empathy, patience, inclusion, and community. In that prior presentation, I first described the essence of human connection, as it relates to heart/mind coherence, authenticity, integrity, and vulnerability. I then offered general instances of authentic connection in music learning settings, such as peer-to-peer interaction, outreach and in-reach, self-expression and self-connection, and shared expression.

In this chapter I further elaborate on the essence of authentic connection in music education, to offer a more nuanced view of the ways in which musicking and authentic connection in education stimulate and reinforce one another. I do so, however, by first placing authentic connection within a broader societal context, describing the ways in which authentic connection is currently stymied through political division, notions of supremacy, truth denial, and the COVID-19 pandemic. The chapter is written as a chiastic essay, using parallel and symmetrical writing structures inspired by chiasmus in ancient scripture (Lund, 1930; Welch, 2020).[33] The central point of the chapter – confession and rising up with purpose – highlights the essence of vulnerability and integrity, which I argue are essential for authentic connection (see Figure 13.1).

Virtual Connection, Physical Separation

Currently, in this time of COVID-19, we live in an unprecedented era of virtual connection juxtaposed with physical and spiritual separation.

---

33   Although I do not use a perfectly symmetrical structure, the essay contains material in a general "X" form with the central focus point of the X being "falling to our knees" and "rising up." Several themes are revisited in both sides of the X as parallels and/or opposites, including supremacy/superiority; racism/antiracism; I can't breathe/breath; cycles/circles; disconnection/connection; denial/honesty, integrity, vulnerability; false innocence/authenticity, vulnerability; pathoadolescence/transformation.

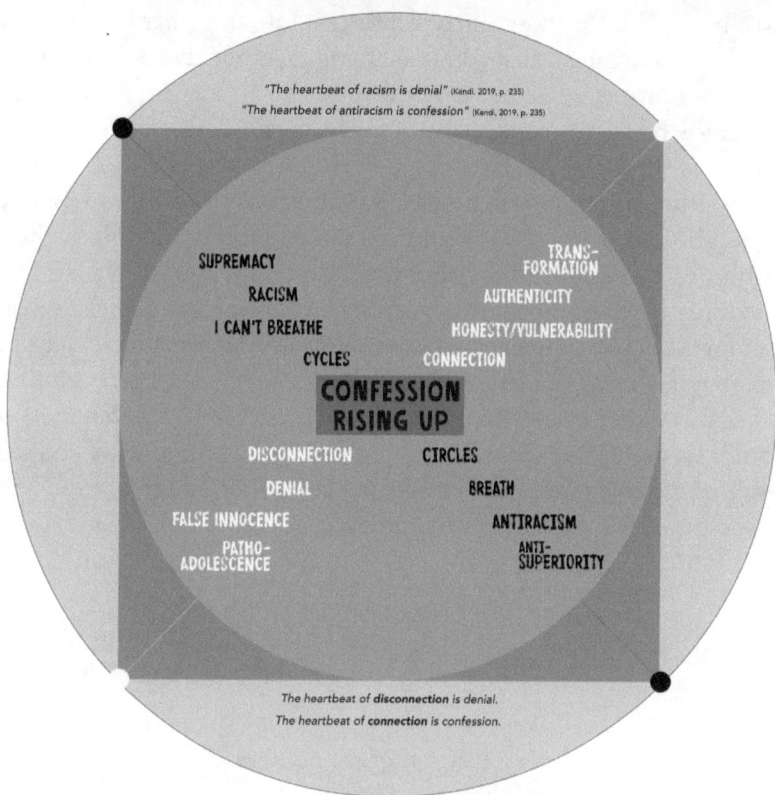

Figure 13.1. Essay themes in chiastic form

We are simultaneously required to isolate physically from one another, while sharing a common global health threat that requires us to rely on one another's actions and choices to stay safe. Despite technological advancements that can bring us instantly together wherever we are in the world, movements of nationalism threaten to keep us apart spiritually. Notions of supremacy, selfishness, and entitlement have found their way into everyday life – even in debates regarding public health and safety. Our spiritual separation is illustrated in a musical sense, by the inefficacy of our present videoconferencing technology to support synchronous music-making. Even in instances where it is safe to gather together, the risk of infection means that communal singing is not always allowed.

A few days after the murder of George Floyd, an African American man, at the hands of – or, more accurately, the knee of – a White police officer, I awoke in the middle of the night, hearing George Floyd's words "I can't breathe" still ringing in my ears. I shuddered in a cold sweat as I recognized how these same words are spoken much too often throughout communities of color, where life breath is literally suppressed through police brutality; disproportionate exposure to and lack of sufficient treatment for COVID-19; pollutions associated with environmental injustice; and inhumane confinement in prison cells due to unjust incarceration. As musicians we do not take breathing for granted; however, even more so as humans, we recognize that breathing is necessary for survival and that breathing well is the essence of freedom. We cannot be a free world until all of us have an opportunity to breathe freely.

Suffocating Supremacy

White supremacy is suffocating all of us, no matter our skin color. The history of racism reveals that it is neither hate nor ignorance, but self-interest, that has formed and fueled racist ideas (Kendi, 2019). Pride, considered the deadliest of the cardinal sins, involves the belief in superior worthiness. This belief in superiority is necessary to satiate greed and gluttony, such as in the case of imperialism that led to colonization and slavery (DiAngelo, 2018; Kendi, 2019). Racist ideas were developed centuries ago to justify inhumane practices founded in greed (Kendi, 2016). Supremacist beliefs are further aided by abstraction and segregation, where empathy is suppressed and obscured due to imposed lack of familiarity. As legal scholar Thomas Ross described:

> The power of black abstraction is that it obscures the humanness of black persons. [White supremacists] can more easily think of black persons as not fully human so long as [they] do not see them in a familiar social context [...] The great power of black abstraction is its power to blunt the empathetic response. (Ross, 1990, p. 6)

Just as segregation and abstraction interfere with empathy, so does a false or misguided sense of piety or religious innocence, which too easily allows those of us who are uncomfortable with difficult truths and difficult conversations to shift the blame elsewhere and – whether knowingly or unknowingly – perpetuate a cycle of disconnect from reality and spiritual separation from others (Brooks, 2020).

The lack of empathy can further reinforce a belief of superiority and entitlement, and encourage an unhealthy filtering of information (whether fact or fiction) that supports our worldviews as well as our addictions. Such lack of empathy and accompanying self-selection of information also stymies the ability for authentic connection, damages integrity, and degrades morality (Brooks, 2020). Black author James Baldwin described this false perception of innocence as a kind of White entrapment:

> They have destroyed and are destroying hundreds of thousands of lives and do not know it and do not want to know it … it is the innocence which constitutes the crime … these innocent people […] are in effect still trapped in the history which they do not understand and until they understand it, they cannot be released from it. (1963, p. 21)

Denial and Confession

Denial for the sake of preserving self-interests is a part of what Plotkin (2008, as cited in Smith, 2021) has attributed to an egocentric rather than soulcentric orientation. In the former, one is "unaware of the soul's purpose" whereas in the latter one is "aware of their ultimate place in both the ecological and social worlds and is therefore able to embody their unique psycho-ecological niche" (Smith, 2021, p. 7). Those who deny the truth and put down others for the sake of their own gain – whether through greed, racist policies, or harmful ecological practices, as addressed by both Smith and Plotkin – may be stuck in a kind of egocentrism and "pathoadolescence" that may signal the lack of healthy human maturation, including perhaps from individual and collective traumas that have not been healed (Smith, 2021). Greed spawns false narratives of superiority, which leads to harm, which relates to denial, and the cycle continues.

"The heartbeat of racism is denial" (Kendi, 2019, p. 235).

"The heartbeat of antiracism is confession" (Kendi, 2019, p. 235).

I can't breathe, say my brothers and sisters of color whose oppression did not stop with the emancipation of slavery.

I can't breathe, say those in COVID-19 intensive care units gasping for air.

We can't sing together, we cry as we feel our separation so tangibly. Could it be that we, like an addict who is running out of options, might finally fall to our knees?

Falling to Our Knees, Rising up with Purpose

It is beyond time to rethink our own positions and places in the various human interactions that are critical to save us and this planet. I am just one music educator, but I am a member of a larger human ecology. Although I recognize my limitations, I do what I can – which includes interrogating ways for fostering authentic connection in my own field of music education. I offer my small part, inspired by the words of Parker Palmer:

> The darkness around us is deep. But our great calling, opportunity, and power as educators is to shed light in dark places. In a world that needs new professionals – true professionals – in every institution, let us resist the temptation to respond with a fearful "no" or an elusive "maybe" and allow our lives to speak a clear and heartfelt "yes." (2017, p. 214)

I am further motivated by the words of Amanda Gorman:

> What can we do?
> Open your eyes.
> Know that the future of
> this wise planet
> Lies right in sight:
> Right in all of us. Trust

this earth uprising.
All of us bring light to exciting solutions never tried before
For it is our hope that implores us, at our uncompromising core,
To keep rising up for an earth more than worth fighting for. (2018, para. 13)

My point of departure – of rising up – begins with challenging notions of superiority that exist in the field of music education, and then revisiting what it means to connect authentically within music-learning spaces.

Challenging Notions of Superiority

Popular media are saturated with images of teachers, often caricatured as larger-than-life figures who are either villainous or heroic. Neither of these extremes is accurate nor fair, and both are used at different times by politicians and other influential policymakers to push an individual agenda. In the case of the villain, teachers may be viewed as aloof, boring, lacking emotional control, and/or tyrannical. Heroic narratives also abound, not only in popular media but are also commonplace in societal perceptions of teachers. However, I have argued previously that embracing the "hero" narrative can lead to the same kind of superior/inferior relationship alluded to previously, and interfere with authentic connection:

> The "hero" teacher narrative is one that we have come to take for granted, often without questioning what it truly means for us or the students we serve. Although our egos might salivate at the idea of playing Superman or Wonder Woman in the classroom, such an approach […] demonstrates an inherent and ironic problem with power: Not only are students seen as inferior and helpless, but teachers are, in a sense, expected to act the role of benefactor, generously teaching out of the goodness of their hearts without adequate compensation or personal respect. (Hendricks, 2018a, p. 14)

Instead, we might choose to celebrate the humanity of music teachers, honoring the strengths, mistakes, and strivings that are a part of our common lived experience. We can simultaneously resist the notion of teachers being either totally terrible or practically perfect, instead recognizing us all as human and giving space for all of us to continually learn and grow along with our students. By taking a viewpoint wherein students and teachers each bring particular strengths to the learning process, we allow authentic connections to forge between them, including authentic expressions of music and self.

Connection: Caring For, About, and With

Care, compassion, and connection go hand in hand (Hendricks, 2018a; Noddings, 1984) – and music is one way that we may come to better understand our shared humanness (Bowman, 2006; Elliott, 2020). Meaningful musical connections can emerge over time through "a rich and diverse web of intersubjective relationships" (Silverman, 2013, p. 33) as people engage in musicking together. Particularly, musical meaningfulness exists as one cares for, and about, other people within shared musical activities that they collectively care about – and, in turn, having others within that musicking experience care for and about them (Silverman, 2013).

In her celebrated writing on an ethic of care, Noddings (1984) describes the essence of empathy in the relationship between carer and cared-for. She sometimes uses the term "engrossment" to explain the way in which a carer might become immersed in the world of a cared-for. She explains the concept: "When I receive the other, I am totally with the other" (Noddings, 1984, p. 51). This conception of engrossment is derived in large part from the work of Buber (1970), whose spiritual treatise on the essence of the I-You relationship articulates a kind of unification of two souls when one (the "I") comes to truly see and honor another (the "You").

Another term that Noddings (1984) uses to describe a caring relationship – in a way that may be somewhat problematic for our purposes – is that of "displacement of interest" (p. 34), to describe the carer's act of putting their needs or interests aside when caring for another. Citing Buber (1957/ 1970), Noddings explains the essence of caring-for as that "the other 'fills the firmament.'" (1984, p. 51). She then points to such "displacement" and the potential for carers and cared-for to be "at risk of losing themselves" (p. 51) when caring is out of balance. For this reason she suggests that "there is a characteristic and appropriate mode of consciousness in caring" (p. 51) that involves the balancing of rational thought with sympathetic feeling to maintain appropriate balance. I have offered a similar caution to avoid becoming overly caught up in students' lives and worlds, as is possible when affective empathy is not balanced with its cognitive counterpart (Hendricks, 2018a).

Buber's interpretation of relationship might also be viewed differently. If the You were to completely fill the circle of relation, then it is not an I–You relationship, but rather a hollow, empty You. Rather than viewing the I–You relationship as one in which the needs and interests of the I might get lost or subverted, I perceive Buber's description of the I–You relationship as the essence of spiritual communion – as authentic connection. The You that "fills the firmament" (*Himmelskreis*[34] in the original; Buber, 1974, p. 14) does not become everything at the expense of the I. Rather, the You becomes everything at the loss of the *It*. When one enters into an authentic I–You relationship (as opposed to an I–It experience), the "I" becomes unified with the "You" in such a way that the "it" characteristics of the person are eclipsed by the essence of the encounter – "not as if there were nothing but he [sic]; but everything else lives in *his* light" (Buber, 1957/1970, p. 59).

> Even as a melody is not composed of tones, nor a verse of words, nor a statue of lines – one must pull and tear to turn a unity into a multiplicity – so it is with the human being to whom I say You. I can abstract from him [sic] the color of his hair or the color of his speech or the color of his graciousness; I have to do this again and again; but immediately he is no longer You. And even as prayer is not in time but time in prayer, and the [offering][35] not in space but space in the [offering ...] I do not find the human being to whom I say You in any Sometime and Somewhere. I can place him there and have to do this again and again, but immediately he becomes a He or a She, an It, and no longer remains my You. (Buber, 1957/1970, p. 59)

34 *Himmel* = heaven, *Kreis* = circle, including sphere of association or relationship.
35 In this English version, Kaufmann translated *Opfer* as "sacrifice." I prefer "offering" for this context, while also honoring the historical significance of sacrifice in ancient Jewish texts.

Revisiting an ethic of care from this interpretation of Buber, I propose a third kind of caring – caring *with* – where the discussion of relationship is one of spiritual communion rather than roles to be performed, and where neither I nor You need be superior nor inferior.

I alluded to the concept of caring *with* in previous writing, in the context of compassionate music teaching (Hendricks, 2018a). I cited Tibetan Buddhist nun Pema Chödrön (2004, 2007) to explain that compassion might be defined as "shared human experience between equals" (Hendricks, 2018a, p. 5). Although these equals may bring different strengths and experiences to a music learning space (such as in the case of an adult and child), they are neither greater nor lesser than one another, and they connect through a common sense of purpose. This essence of caring about, for, *and* with, in a music learning context, is also reflective of musical meaningfulness (Silverman, 2013) as described above, and plays a role in the pursuit of human flourishing (Smith & Silverman, 2020).

Authenticity: Honesty, Vulnerability, and Integrity

When describing the empathy that exists in the act of caring, Noddings (1984) acknowledges the level of vulnerability that a carer might experience: "It is clear that my vulnerability is potentially increased when I care, for I can be hurt through the other as well as through myself" (p. 52). Her solution to this concern – as mentioned previously – is to maintain a balance of thinking and feeling so as to avoid being too permissive or, conversely, to avoid manipulating the cared-for "into some mold" (p. 77) that suits the purposes of the carer.

It may be, however, that the practice of authenticity – as vulnerable as it may make us feel – may eliminate the need for a tug of war in the first place. In his description of reality pedagogy, Emdin (2016) bemoans how pre-service teachers are taught to fear students before they even know them, indoctrinated into a no-nonsense system of rote classroom management strategies – meant as a firewall to prevent systemic breakdown – that can suck the life out of teaching:

> We were both told not to express too much emotion with students or be too friendly with them. I was told to "stand your ground when they test you," … and "remember that there is nothing wrong with being mean." Unfortunately, this same mantra required us to remove all emotion from our teaching. It turned us from passionate educators into automatons who worked to maintain the school's structures and inequities. Rather than face our fears, the mantra helped us to mask them. And because being in touch with one's emotions is the key to moving from the classroom (place) to the spaces where the students are, our students were invisible to us. (pp. 36–37)

This kind of inauthenticity – which often comes as teachers attempt to avoid admitting weaknesses or confronting fears – can lead to a disconnect in the classroom that separates teachers from students, and becomes an unhealthy model for students to similarly avoid feeling vulnerable. Such inauthenticity restricts connection between teachers and students – and, as an extension, between students and their peers – in spaces where they feel a need to be on guard. Learning may take place, but not learning about, and love for, music in ways that well-meaning teachers had in mind. Rather, students might learn techniques and skills, both musical ones as well as those of self-preservation, which may carry forward into anxious musical performances with hollow expression.

"Tone has a living soul," violin pedagogue Shinichi Suzuki emphasized (see Hendricks, 2011). But allowing that soul to live freely in our music requires vulnerability. It requires facing our fears.

According to Parker Palmer (2017), there are four fears that can lead to shutdown and inauthentic disconnectedness:

1. The fear of a live encounter; especially one that might introduce us to "otherness" and cause us to question our own worldviews;
2. The fear of conflict, which might lead to a situation of winning and losing;
3. The fear of losing identity, or sense of self, when our ideas or knowledge systems are challenged; and
4. The fear that confronting difference might change our lives.

Yet this kind of life-changing process is precisely what Black feminist scholar bell hooks (1994) advocates in her vision for education as the practice of freedom – an educational practice that is embodied, holistic, open, and dialogical. In this vision teachers and students alike are free to bring their whole selves to the learning space. As such, they encounter one another's authentic self, and courageously challenge one another's and their own ideas in the collective pursuit of critical consciousness that leads to individual, collective, and even societal transformation.

hooks's (1994) vision of emancipated education is polar opposite from director-centered music education practices that Allsup and Benedict (2008) claim have reinforced themselves throughout music education's history through systematic control, lack of self-reflection, and a prioritization of fear. The authors describe how school-based instrumental education particularly has bolstered a tradition of the teacher as militaristic leader who motivates students through fear of failure and works so efficiently that there is little time for expressions of satisfaction, let alone dialogue. Suppressed dialogue maintains the status quo and colonizes the external as well as the internal landscape, in everything from director-centered music approaches to supremacist structures in society at large (Hendricks, 2018b). Dialogue requires vulnerability, as does expressive music-making (Hendricks, 2018a).

> How can we move beyond the fear that destroys connectedness? [...] By reclaiming the connectedness that takes away fear. [...] For all the fearful efforts we make to protect ourselves by disconnecting, the human soul yearns eternally for connection [...] We can get into the circle [of spiritual life][36] that is already within us by abandoning ourselves to the yearnings that run just behind, or ahead of, our fears. (Palmer, 2017, pp. 59–60)

Perhaps we might alter Kendi's (2019, p. 235) aforementioned words on racism and antiracism for our purposes of connection to say,

> The heartbeat of *disconnection* is denial.
> The heartbeat of *connection* is confession.

---

36   The brevity of this quotation does not do justice to the eloquence of Parker's description of the way that spiritual life moves in circles. Here I am also reminded of the *Himmelskreis* in Buber's I-You relationship. Parker writes of spiritual circles within each of us, while Buber writes of spiritual circles that surround us in an authentic encounter. Despite their different conceptions of spiritual circles, both reference the spiritual circle that exists through authentic connections with others.

Rather than distancing ourselves emotionally and spiritually from students in the classroom – and in some instances even devaluing students as potential troublemakers from whom we need to defend ourselves – Emdin's (2016) reality pedagogy proposes that we self-reflect on our power dynamics in the classroom, envision how we are similar to students, and consider how an earlier version of ourselves might respond to the way we are teaching. As Debrot (2021) described of her own self-reflection journey,

> Contemplation led me to question my pedagogical practices and power relationships in my classroom. I discovered that teaching and learning could be joyful and meaningful, and that "music was a pathway for me to be alive and more importantly *be alive with others*." (Vũ, 2020, p. 41)

Being alive and alive with others – what a breath of fresh air!

Music teachers have fostered such "collective effervescence" (Emdin, 2016; see also Durkheim, 1912) in their classrooms by promoting student-directed and co-teaching experiences in a space and place of collective trust, responsibility, and musical risk-taking (Hendricks, 2018a). The process of musical entrainment has served for millennia as a means of unifying communities (Boyce-Tillman, 2000), and energy exchanges between humans are tangible and measurable (see Hendricks, 2018a, p. 145). Music may, then, offer unique avenues for authentic connection by the sheer essence of this vibroacoustic art, where musickers can not only see and hear, but also *feel* the vibrations of their collective endeavor.

Conclusion

Authentic connection can flourish between humans in spaces of radical openness and hospitality. It thrives where compassion is less about pity and more about shared experience. It thrives where empathy is less about imagining others' needs from one's own perspective and more about attunement to another person's values and worldviews. It occurs when inclusion is an act of common sense rather than a quota, and where diversity and difference are viewed as welcome opportunities for everyone to grow and learn from one another.

Authentic connection is the essence and backbone of communal music-making. As Custodero (2009) has articulated:

> Through music, we learn about ourselves and about our relatedness to the world; our engagement with melodies and rhythms provides opportunities for appreciating sound, people and ideas. Such sympathetic understanding is a product of interaction, a connection (or collision) between perception and experience, between social context and individual disposition. We make meaning through shared experiences of musical time and space; we find personal solace and inspiration from our own and others' individual interpretations within those dimensions. Through the compelling qualities of organized sound and the rewards of making such sound, we are drawn to others through revelations of our common humanity, and drawn to artistry through realizations of uncommon accomplishments. (p. 513)

Yet authentic connection in music is even more than mere "musical companionship," more than "sympathetic human company." It is a collective and intimate musical experience that is biophysical as well as musical, where dynamics of power give way to ebb and flow of sound, and control gives way to contribution. It is where we breathe together.

I have elsewhere defined authenticity as "connection with our true selves, as well as the integrity we display in our interactions with others" (Hendricks, 2018a, p. 148). Authenticity is the essence of presence with ourselves, or self-alignment, that allows utmost honesty and genuineness in interactions with others. Authentic connection in music-making requires a fair amount of vulnerability and risk-taking among the musickers. Risk-taking, in turn, requires a feeling of safety and trust.

Authentic connection is necessary in a disconnected and troubled world, and music-making offers one opportunity to move beyond theorization of humanity toward the practice of it. As Niknafs (2020) recently proposed, "it is only through our humanity and efforts, sense of self-worth, and care for others that we might be able to avoid, ever so slightly, the human suffering happening around us" (p. 15). By opening ourselves up to authentic connection, we might embody a vision of shared passions and possibilities.

Bibliography

Allsup, R. E., & Benedict, C. (2008). The problems of band: An inquiry into the future of instrumental music education. *Philosophy of Music Education Review, 16*(2), 156–173.

Baldwin, J. (1963). My dungeon shook: Letter to my nephew on the one hundredth anniversary of the Emancipation. In *The fire next time*. Dial Press.

Bowman, W. (2006). Educating musically. In R. Colwell & C. Richardson (Eds.), *MENC handbook of research methodologies* (pp. 63–84). Oxford University Press.

Boyce-Tillman, J. (2000). *Constructing musical healing: The wounds that sing*. Jessica Kingsley.

Brooks, J. (2020). *Mormonism and White supremacy: American religion and the problem of racial innocence*. Oxford University Press.

Buber, M. (1970). *I and Thou* (W. Kaufmann, Trans.). Simon & Schuster. (Original work published 1937)

Buber, M. (1974). *Ich und Du*. Random House GmbH.

Chödrön, P. (2004). *Start where you are: A guide to compassionate living*. Shambhala Publications.

Chödrön, P. (2007). *The places that scare you: A guide to fearlessness in difficult times*. Shambhala Publications.

Custodero, L. A. (2009). Intimacy and reciprocity in improvisatory musical performance: Pedagogical lessons from adult artists and young children. In S. Malloch & C. Trevarthen (Eds.), *Communicative musicality: Exploring the basis of human companionship* (pp. 513–529). Oxford University Press.

Debrot, R. (2021). Singing the good life. In J. Boyce-Tillman & K. S. Hendricks (Eds.), *Living song: Singing, spirituality, and wellbeing* (pp. 219–233). Peter Lang.

DiAngelo, R. (2018). *White fragility: Why it's so hard for white people to talk about racism*. Beacon Press.

Durkheim, É. (1912). *The elementary forms of the religious life*. Allen & Unwin.

Elliott, D. J. (2020). Eudaimonia and well-doing: Implications for music education. In G. D. Smith & M. Silverman (Eds.), *Eudaimonia: Perspectives for music learning* (pp. 107–120). Routledge.

Emdin, C. (2016). *For white folks who teach in the hood … and the rest of y'all too: Reality pedagogy and urban education*. Beacon Press.

Gorman, A. (2018). *Earthrise*. North American Association for Environmental Education (published January 9, 2019). <https://naaee.org/eepro/blog/earthrise-poem-amanda-gorman>

Hendricks, K. S. (2011). The philosophy of Shinichi Suzuki: "Music education as love education." *Philosophy of Music Education Review, 19*(2), 136–154. <https://doi.org/10.2979/philmusieducrevi.19.2.136>

Hendricks, K. S. (2018a). *Compassionate music teaching: A framework for motivation and engagement in the 21st century.* Rowman & Littlefield.

Hendricks, K. S. (2018b). Gaga spirituality. In K. S. Hendricks & J. Boyce-Tillman (Eds.), *Queering freedom: Music, identity and spirituality* (pp. 243–260). Peter Lang.

Hooks, B. (1994). *Teaching to transgress.* Routledge.

Kendi, I. X. (2016). *Stamped from the beginning: The definitive history of racist ideas in America.* Nation Books.

Kendi, I. X. (2019). *How to be an antiracist.* One World.

Lund, N. W. (1930). The presence of chiasmus in the Old Testament. *The American Journal of Semitic Languages and Literatures, 46*(2), 104–126.

Moore, J. T., Ricaldi, J. N., Rose, C. E., Fuld, J., Parise, M., Kang, G. J., Driscoll, A. K., Norris, T., Wilson, N., Rainisch, G., Valverde, E., Beresovsky, V., Brune, C. A., Oussayef, N. L., Rose, D. A., Adams, A. E., Awel, S., Villanueva, J., Meaney-Delman, D., Honein, M. A., COVID-19 State, Tribal, Local, and Territorial Response Team. (2020, August 21). *Disparities in incidence of COVID-19 among underrepresented racial/ethnic groups in counties identified as hotspots during June 5–18, 2020 – 22 states, February–June 2020.* Centers for Disease Control and Prevention. <https://www.cdc.gov/mmwr/volumes/69/wr/mm6933e1.htm>

Niknafs, N. (2020). Music education as the herald of a cosmopolitan collective imperative: On being human. *International Journal of Music Education, 38*(1), 3–17. <https://doi.org/10.1177/0255761419859635>

Noddings, N. (1984). *Caring: A feminine approach to ethics and moral education.* University of California Press.

Palmer, P. (2017). *The courage to teach: Exploring the inner landscape of a teacher's life* (3rd ed.). John Wiley & Sons.

Plotkin, B. (2008). *Nature and the human soul: Cultivating wholeness in a fragmented world.* New World Library.

Ross, T. (1990). The rhetorical tapestry of race: White innocence and Black abstraction. *William and Mary Law Review, 32*, 1–40. <https://scholarship.law.wm.edu/wmlr/vol32/iss1/2>

Silverman, M. (2013). A conception of "meaningfulness" in/for life and music education. *Action, Criticism, and Theory for Music Education, 12*(2), 20–40. <http://act.maydaygroup.org/articles/Silverman12_2.pdf>

Smith, G. D., & Silverman, M. (Eds.). (2020). *Eudaimonia: Perspectives for music learning.* Routledge.

Smith, T. D. (2021). Music education for surviving and thriving: Cultivating children's wonder, senses, emotional wellbeing, and wild nature as a means to discover and fulfill their life's purpose. *Frontiers in Education, 6,* 648799. <https://doi.org/10.3389/feduc.2021.648799>.

Vũ, K. T. (2020). My body was left on the street: Making pathways toward home. In K. T. Vũ & A. de Quadros (Eds.), *My body was left on the street: Music education and displacement* (pp. 34–48). Brill Sense. <https://doi.org/10.1163/9789004430464>

Welch, J. W. (2020). *Chiasmus in antiquity*. Wipf and Stock Publishers.

14 "Only When I Think the Light…"
Teaching Religion Inclusively in a Camphill SEND Setting

The Sheiling Ringwood

This chapter offers glimpses of a pathway toward teaching religion inclusively in a special-needs setting. The particular pathway presented here has been taken by the authors, Michele Keim and Fabian Lochner, who, over the last ten years, have been team-teaching weekly religion lessons at The Sheiling Ringwood, a Camphill Special School and College on the Hamsphire/Dorset border. Our students, aged 16 to 19, had a wide range of complex, moderate to severe learning difficulties relating to a spectrum of conditions such as autism, Downs syndrome, fragile-X, cerebral palsy, and others. The student profile at our school has shifted over the years. Currently, most students are offered one-on-one support by in-class learning assistants. We worked with a combined group of three upper school classes, with new intake at the beginning of each year and some departures at the end, each student remaining in our program for three years on average.

Developing and teaching the curriculum described here has been a hugely inspiring journey for both of us. We felt that in trying to approach the teaching of religion in a new way something important was happening that could perhaps offer inspiration to teachers and students beyond our own school. We do not presume to provide a ready-made model for others to follow but hope to stimulate new thoughts and fresh creativity.

Our approach is much indebted to our accumulated experience within Steiner education and Camphill special education.[37] Throughout this chapter, we have made every effort to use language that will not exclude anyone less familiar with Steiner and Camphill concepts. We will briefly discuss the aims, principles, and ethos of our lessons before going on to describe their content and our pedagogical approach in some depth. At the end, we will ask some broader questions about the inclusive teaching of religion and about the possible transferability of our approach to other settings. The Appendix, posted on the Music, Spirituality and Wellbeing International website, <https://musicspiritualitywellbeinginternational.wordpress.com/>, offers a descriptive table and summary of our yearlong curriculum with sources.

Analysis of student assessments is beyond the scope of this chapter, as it would necessitate much detailed discussion of individuals' background and personal profiles. The global experience of our students will, of course, be central in our discussion. Likewise, we are unable to engage here with scholarly research and other background literature.

Guiding Ethos and Aims

Camphill schools have traditional roots in a non-denominational form of Christianity.[38] In more recent times, the Sheiling School has put much effort into becoming an inclusive organization on every level, and this

---

37 Michele is a trained eurythmist and has been active as a teacher and therapist in Steiner SEND settings in the UK for over twenty years. Fabian taught music for many years at Sunbridge College, a Steiner teacher education college in New York, and has led music and drama programs in Camphill setting in the US and the UK. The Sheiling Ringwood has been following various adapted and updated versions of the Steiner curriculum since its founding in 1951.

38 The founder of the Camphill movement, Dr. Karl König (1902–1966), built on Rudolf Steiner's esoteric approach to Christianity, with a strong emphasis on the universality of the "Christ being," conceived independently of religious belief, and on the relation between cosmic powers and individual soul experience. Traditional

has created the opportunity to re-evaluate the place of religion within the school. We were grateful to have been given the chance to develop and renew the teaching of religion in the upper school within that context.

From the outset, we were clear that the aim of our lessons would never be to inculcate specific religious beliefs. This would be inappropriate on account of the diversity of our students alone, who come from families of many faiths and none. But neither did we want to take a narrowly intellectual approach, imparting information or prompting comparative analyses of various belief systems and practices.[39]

A Focus on Students' Inner Needs

In line with the mission of our special educational needs and disabilities (SEND) school, we wanted to keep our focus firmly on the developmental needs of our students. It seemed to us that our religion lessons could become a platform for addressing the needs of their inner life in particular. There is, of course, a definite inner dimension to many school activities across the board. Keeping students safe, supporting them in their social interactions, building their skills and academic learning or just having fun together by definition also supports students' centeredness, their ability to process experiences, their capacity for making choices, etc. One might say that in special education the inner needs of the students are more immediately obvious because with many SEND students, social conventions or the capacity for dissimulation are not present to obscure the expression of inner needs, as they often are with mainstream children.

Camphill communities offer a weekly "Bible evening," Sunday services and a full round of festivals with pageantry throughout the year.

39 This is in keeping with the general ethos of Steiner education which places much emphasis on children developing confidence in their own thinking and in finding their own solutions to problems, rather than merely absorbing and applying ready-made knowledge. We will return to the importance of discovering meaning in open and un-predetermined ways.

The SEND educator will therefore always be specially focused on students' wellbeing and inner states, even while teaching practical skills or academics.

We wanted to focus this general orientation toward the inner life more sharply and give it a spiritual home, as it were. As our lode star we chose the educational aim that has been at the heart of Steiner education for over a hundred years: to awaken inside each young person a sense of awe and wonder. This, then, was our plan for teaching religion inclusively: to expose our students to some of the great religious imaginations of humanity, hoping thus to generate in them an inner experience of devotion or reverence for an awe-inspiring reality larger than themselves, in other words, a genuine religious feeling.

Religion, the Seasons, and the Performing Arts

All this needed to be accomplished without indoctrinating or imposing on our students in any way. We therefore chose the passing of the seasons of nature as the central theme for a curriculum designed to be repeatable year after year, with room for variations and development. The theme of the seasons had the double advantage of leading straight into the subject of religion on account of the profound connection of religious festivals, stories, and rituals with the seasons of the year while at the same time offering an immediate link to our students' own daily experience of their natural surroundings. Our choice was the more obvious because the Sheiling School has been, from its inception, deeply committed to celebrating the seasons through a yearly round of assemblies and elaborate community festivals. The seasons are used in the curricular design of other classes as well, especially in arts classes and in the so-called "main lessons," a central feature of Steiner education. The Sheiling School is also fortunate in being located on a beautiful estate which allows students to have immediate, sometimes spectacular experiences of the changes in nature during the year, as they walk from building to building, attend outdoor crafts, physical education, or gardening lessons or simply enjoy the swings.

In delivering our curriculum the path of the performing arts was a natural choice for us, not only because of both our backgrounds as performers but also because of the affinity between the performing arts and religious ritual, sacred tales, spirit journeys, and inner transformation. The idea was to draw in each lesson on the performative aspects of religion without it forming an act of worship, or being intended as such. Thus, we set about weaving together a diverse array of age-appropriate stories, dances, and songs from different spiritual traditions, for live presentation by us teachers, enriched by carefully designed and facilitated activities for students to participate in, each story being allowed to unfold over a number of weeks. Eurythmy was to be included both for performance and for students to participate in.[40] Achieving the right balance between student receptiveness and activity was crucial if our plan was to succeed.

Balancing Polarities

On the side of receptiveness, a calm listening space needed to be established that would help our students to settle, focus, and engage. At the beginning of each lesson, we set the mood with the help of a ceremony involving the lighting of a candle and the speaking of a verse, as described below. For the presentations proper we held our students' attention principally by artistic means: a carefully crafted script, thoroughly rehearsed and delivered, as much as possible, with integrity and passion.

40   Eurythmy, the art of movement created by Rudolf Steiner between 1911 and 1924, is not to be confused with eurythmics created by Émile Jaques-Dalcroze, also developed in the early twentieth century. Eurythmy works with both live speech and music and has artistic, pedagogical as well as therapeutic applications. Steiner conceived it as a renewal of Greek temple dance. The style of movement is gently expressive in a range from complex choreographies down to very simple forms such as circles and straight lines that are immediately accessible to untrained participants. Eurythmy depends very much on the interaction between the person and the space around, below and above them which makes it an ideal medium for conveying and facilitating inner experiences. At the same time, it ritualizes social interactions in a way that makes it accessible even to people with severe contact difficulties.

Opportunities for students to become active had to be carefully integrated into the mood of each session, allowing them to process what they had absorbed and to respond to it by making individual and collective contributions. Sometimes, students would take turns at acting out a scene and/or taking on the role of specific characters. At other times, the whole group was engaged in singing, dancing or eurythmy. We took care to recalibrate the balance between active and receptive modes in each lesson to reflect the changing character of the seasons and subjects. Examples of this are given below.

The Classroom as Temple

Over the years, students' and teachers' contributions seemed more and more to meld into one single endeavor. To judge by their attentiveness and engagement, it appeared that our students had some sense of this as well. In the most special moments, each of us seemed able to connect, or reconnect, to something that united us all, something profound and invaluable, not easily accessed in our workaday lives, a sort of *re-ligio*.[41]

We also became aware, as hoped for, of the extent to which our religion lessons offered our students a uniquely powerful opportunity to enhance their personal growth and wellbeing. We know how difficult it is, at the best of times, for "mainstream" children and adults alike to find inner calm and quiet, unpressured focus, to be ready for delighted yet not over-stimulated engagement; how much more difficult it proves for special-needs students to generate or maintain such states out of their own resources, as so many are prey to obsessions and anxieties that can overwhelm their inner lives! The magic of the religious/artistic experiences provided in our lessons seemed to give our students a chance to "come to themselves" by conjuring up the quiet and centering surroundings of a church or temple, the submersion in the multisensory richness of a traditional liturgy and the excitement and high adventure of a mystery drama.

---

41   Latin, from *religare*, to bind fast.

Description and Analysis of Curriculum

Our description here is very much focused on the imaginative content, sequencing, and overall experience of our curriculum with its integrated array of stories in drama, music, and movement. Much more could be said regarding the choices and effects of individual pieces of music or of particular eurythmy choreographies. This, however, would go beyond the limitations of our presentation and must therefore be delayed to a future occasion.[42]

The Physical Setting

Our lessons were held mostly in a large school assembly hall with a proper stage and ample floor space and, between the two, shallow steps across the whole width for easy front stage access. There was a stage curtain, back curtain, and a drawable mid-stage scrim, as well as a multicolor lighting system controlled from a cabin in the back of the hall. This setup allowed us to create a theatrical space for onstage presentations by us teachers. For the more interactive pieces we also made use of the floor area, with seating arranged in a semicircle along the edge.

During most sessions, the house curtains would be drawn. Dimmable house lights allowed us to create a gentle twilight or a blackout as needed. Only in the summer term, when the weather was fair, did we open the house curtains to let the sunlight stream in through the large hall windows. To one side of the stage, there was a small table, draped with different fabrics of various colors according to the seasons. On this was placed the candle used for the opening and closing ceremonies described below.

Costuming for students usually consisted of easy-fitting accessories such as hats, scarves, and cloaks. As presenters, we would often wear more

---

42   Source references to stories, selections from classical and modern classical piano repertoire, as well as songs and incidental music are given in the MSWI website Appendix.

elaborate costumes such as gowns with belts and headpieces, a crown or a *kippah*,[43] for example. When presenting eurythmy on stage, Michele would wear variously colored eurythmy dresses with added silk veiling, at times changing into different costumes between scenes. In the *Myth of Persephone*, Michele embodies all three aspects of the triple goddess: the maiden Kore in pink with green veiling, mother Demeter in red with orange, and Persephone the dreaded crone in black with a long gray veil covering the head, face, and upper body. For all this we were fortunate to be able to draw on the extensive contents of the Sheiling School's long-established costume cupboards.

We did not use large stage sets; rather, small or medium-sized props would indicate the surroundings, for example, a makeshift manger for the stable in Bethlehem in the story of Bridget's starry cloak, a little live oak tree for the hermit's forest in Gods' Throne and a giant boulder for Grandfather Rock to emerge from, built from a pile of chairs covered in cloth. Michele draped such objects artfully with colored silk scarves and fabric remnants to evoke a forest floor, a royal throne, the portal of a temple. All incidental music was performed live and unamplified. We were very fortunate to have access to a fine grand piano in our hall, placed near the stage. Fabian played this regularly, both for solos and for accompanying Michele's eurythmy.[44] Besides the piano, Fabian also used a *Choroi* flute in C and an array of small percussion instruments such as hand drums, tambourines, and rattles, the latter mostly for sound effects.

Beginnings and Endings

Before the start of each lesson, students would gather in the lobby and sit quietly with their carers and supporters on benches along the walls until everyone had arrived. When the door opened each student was welcomed and greeted individually by name, with a warm smile, eye contact

---

43   A ceremonial Jewish skullcap.

44   For specific selections from classical and modern classical piano repertoire, see the MSWI website Appendix.

and, wherever appropriate, a handshake. Upon entering, students were invited to find their own seats in the softly lit room. When all had settled we both stood quietly in front of the class. Michele turned to the side table to light the candle. Then, we both motioned for all to stand. We all crossed our arms over the chest, palms resting lightly on the heart area, to speak a verse together. At the end of the lesson, the same was done in reverse order: standing for the verse, sitting down, extinguishing the candle, individual goodbyes, and quiet exit.

The verse we used sums up the ethos of our classes.[45]

> *Only when I think the light, my heart begins to shine.*
> *Only when my heart does shine, the earth becomes a star.*
> *And when the earth becomes a star, then I am a true human being.*

The choice of such a metaphysical verse for a class of special-needs adolescents may seem surprising. Yet, almost all our students joined in consistently. Those who could not speak (or chose not to) would join in the gestures. Many picked up at least some of the words. Some surprised us, after a while, by speaking out clearly and loudly, with a palpable sense of pride. One reason for this may be that the practice of choral declamation tends to draw attention to certain key words rather than the meaning of whole sentences. *Light, heart, shine, star, earth, human*: These are evocative words that can take on a power of their own, gathering meaning to themselves over time while allowing a fine web of inner connections to emerge in the soul, little by little.

The overall meaning of the verse, while far from vague, is not meant to be one-dimensional or predetermined. We left it unexplained so that,

---

45   The words by Herbert Hahn (1890–1970), written originally in German, were intended specifically for use in the non-denominational religion lessons of the first Steiner school in Stuttgart, Germany (from 1919). The unpublished verse has been passed on from teacher to teacher for generations but has been posted in some Steiner school magazines and other online resources (e.g., <https://spreuken. antrovista.com/erst-wenn-ich-lichtes-denke>). It is popular as an inspirational verse and formed the central tenet of Edith Fraenkel (1922–1944), the Jewish resistance fighter during the Nazi era, who was a former pupil of the Steiner school in Berlin. See Scheer (2004). We have slightly altered the received English translation.

with each repetition throughout the year, there was a chance for the words to resonate anew, to accrue meaning, in different ways. Rather than acting as a corporate "prayer" that would assert a definite set of beliefs, the verse thus provided the first step on a journey into the living substance of our own souls.

In what follows, we will be guiding the reader through a part of that journey. We will describe the curriculum of the first term of the academic year in more depth to give an idea of the overall progression. For the second and third terms we will pick out certain highlights. Again, sources for stories and music can be found in the MSWI website Appendix.

From Autumn to Winter

At the beginning of the school year all of us, students and adults alike, find ourselves facing the excitement and anticipation of a new beginning but also worries and fear of the unknown. How can we address such feelings and not become overwhelmed by them? In the natural world around us we are entering the season of autumn. The seeds of summer's fruits and flowers are falling to the earth. Leaves are shed and life begins its sinking down into roots. As nature's outward activity appears to lessen, cosmic forces enter into the earth. We can draw on these forces to find qualities within ourselves that will help us face our anticipation and our fears alike: qualities of strength, stamina, and courage.

Near the beginning of the school year, on September 29, the festival of Michaelmas is celebrated. The festival of the Michael the Archangel falls near the autumn equinox, a moment of cosmic balance between day and night, light and dark. This is the time when we take up the story of Michael's battle with the seven-headed dragon, according to the Book of Revelation from the New Testament. Students are stirred into inner activity by watching and listening as the drama of the contest unfolds on stage before their eyes and ears.

After the presentation a moment of quiet is kept. Then each student is called individually to stand up, step forward and cross the floor on their own in front of their classmates to view a traditional icon of Michael and the dragon displayed near the stage. The silence in the room deepens as students are gently asked to identify various details in the picture (the figure of Michael, his sword, the dragon, the hand of God coming out of a cloud) and to find the courage to touch the figure of the dragon.

Touching and being touched is of course a live issue in SEND education – as it is elsewhere. By creating a situation where students are allowed to explore ritualized touch we are linking to broader educational aims around personal boundaries. These links, however, are not overt in our lesson, so that the emergence of unpremeditated meaning from the delicate, quasi-devotional experience of touching a "sacred image" is not disrupted. Both the performance and the activity before the icon are built up progressively over a number of weeks.

The harvest with all its activity is now drawing to an end and the days are getting noticeably shorter. As the darkness of winter deepens, the earth takes within herself the seeds of autumn, caring and protecting them in anticipation of next year's spring. Cosmic forces are getting active within the earth. The individual strength and courage gained during the Michaelmas season now help us to look inward toward our soul life, kindling a small inner light in the ever-increasing darkness around us.

It is often hard to stay cheerful and purposeful at this time of year. While some animals might hibernate and birds might fly to warmer climes, humans must take care of their inner soul light. As we share that light in encounters with the people around us we begin to develop qualities of empathy needed for working together.

It is a time when we often tell the story of Grandfather Stone. This myth from the North American Seneca culture is about how stories first came into the world. During a harsh winter, a young hunter travels far to seek food for his tribe. Tired from the chase, he sits down to rest against a huge stone and is nearly startled out of his wits when the stone begins to speak to him! The young hunter listens spellbound to the words of the stone spirit. He learns that people do not "live by bread alone" but need stories to nourish their souls as well. Grandfather Stone teaches the young hunter about the creation of the four worlds, the various relations of humans, animals, and spirits and the mischief of Old Man Coyote. Each of the four parts of the story is punctuated by an interactive dance song with animal gestures (eagle, salmon, firefly, buffalo), enjoyed by the whole class.[46]

As November days become still shorter, we move to the first part of the Myth of Persephone. This story from ancient Greece tells of the loss of eternal spring and the coming of the very first winter. Kore, the lovely spring maiden, is abducted by Hades, Lord of the dead. She becomes Persephone, the fearsome queen of the underworld. As at Michaelmas, the students sit, watch, and listen to our story unfolding onstage. This time, however, after the presentation is over, we all form a circle together in the floor space and move on an inward-winding spiral toward the central point of maximum contraction to meet the dark, like Kore-Persephone. Having gained courage from the cosmic forces and from our individual experience of Michael's battle with the dragon we are now ready to face the coming darkness, ready to awaken in our souls the will to engage together in purposeful activity.

As we approach the winter solstice, a mood of expectancy arises. At the Sheiling, as in many Steiner schools, we mark this with a very special ceremony in early December, referred to as the Advent Garden. This ceremony is not strictly part of our religion lesson curriculum; however, it is a key event in the year and the whole school comes together as if engaged in a religion lesson! Students and staff members alike are invited to walk one by one into the center of a spiral of moss laid out on the assembly hall floor, carrying a single unlit candle. When the person arrives at the center of the spiral, they light their own small candle from a larger candle placed there. As they walk out again, they place their candle somewhere along the mossy way, resulting in a growing spiral of living flames, a stunning sight and memorable highlight of the year for students and staff members alike.

Working with candles around children obviously requires some precautions with respect to health and safety. Yet, it can be done safely by keeping the candles as a central focus of attention. Our special needs students have always shown themselves able to step up to the situation, and there have been no incidents involving candles at the Sheiling within living memory. The surrounding darkness and the soft singing help them to relax and to focus. Those who need extra support have a staff member walking with them. If

---

46   "Hey wichy-chayo," See MSWI website Appendix.

someone cannot manage at all, then a staff member will carry the candle and walk the spiral on their behalf.

The candles, of course, symbolize the light we nurture within ourselves. Our inner, spiritual light also enables us to grow closer to the world of the angels. In our curriculum, we now move to the story of the Annunciation of Gabriel the Archangel to Mary, as told in the New Testament.[47] For this piece, we wanted to create an overall mood of stillness and intense listening, of gentle giving and receiving. This is often the moment in the year when those students who have been previously reluctant to take part in activities begin to feel able to participate. Therefore, student interaction now becomes a central focus in the lesson.

The session opens with a solemn, quasi-liturgical reading from the gospel of Luke. Then students watch as we teachers create a *tableau* on stage, modeled on medieval and Renaissance depictions of the Annunciation. Mary in her blue mantle sits to one side, bathed in soft many-hued stage light. The angel Gabriel enters gently from the other side. From a vase positioned center stage he picks a silk lily, lifts it up, kneels before Mary, stretches out one hand in blessing and sings the medieval chant, *Ave Maria gratia plena dominus tecum.*[48] Mary bows slightly as she accepts the flower from the angel. The angel departs and Mary rises up slowly to place the flower back into the vase.

Having viewed this scene once, students are now asked, two-by-two, to replay it with our support, with a blue cloak for Mary and a white silk scarf for the angel Gabriel. In choosing their role some students quite naturally take the opportunity to cross gender. As our students embody their characters on stage, limitation and aspiration are poised in delicate balance.

---

47 Even though liturgical traditions celebrate the feast of the Annunciation in the spring, on March 25, counting back nine months from the date of the birth of Jesus at Christmas on December 25, Annunciation carols are traditionally sung around Christmas, as they belong to the Nativity cycle from the Gospel of Luke. The date of Christmas itself is not biblical, of course, but was set close to the winter solstice as Christ replaced the *Sol invictus*, the "unconquered sun" of the Mithras cult, which was closely associated with the Roman emperors at the time of the rise of Christianity.

48 Latin, "Hail Mary, full of grace, the Lord is with you."

Strength and vulnerability are revealed in equal measure in a setting that dignifies and even "sanctifies" both. Over the years, supporting staff have often mentioned to us how deeply moved they were by the exquisite stillness achieved so often in this particular production and by the ability of our students to shine within it.

In the depth of darkness, as many people are getting ready to celebrate Christmas, the winter solstice arrives at last, one of the great turning points of the year. The sun is "born again," the longest night is followed by a new dawn, and the small light we have taken into our souls now becomes ever clearer and brighter to carry us, students and adults alike, into a new year.

From Winter to Spring

When students return in January it is often hard for them, after the excitement of Christmas, to readjust to school life.[49] The days are lengthening but this is not obvious at first. How will we get through these dark winter months? Can we really imagine spring coming? All the while, the activity concentrated within the earth is beginning to be released and we begin to see the first flowers, snowdrops and crocuses, appearing. At this time the inner light we have nurtured and cared for can slowly begin to meet the increasing light shining in from the cosmos.

Around the time of Candlemas (February 2) and the Celtic festival of Imbolc we now tell the story of Brigid of Ireland with her magic cloak and her great wish to free the earth from eternal winter. The story includes a dream sequence in which Brigid experiences herself at the stable in Bethlehem, helping Mary to cradle her child, a lovely link for our students to the familiar Christmas story. Blessed by Mary, Brigid's star-spangled cloak magically spreads over the frozen earth, shining its light into the waiting seeds, thereby re-awakening life and ending the harsh rule of winter.

---

49   Although for many students with special needs, this can also be accompanied by a
      sense of relief at being able to settle back into familiar routines after the "upheaval"
      of the festival time.

As we approach the spring equinox the days are lengthening noticeably at last. Students begin to become aware of the changes in the natural world around them, seeing the daffodils, the new buds on the trees and hearing the spring songs of the birds. This is when we tell the second part of the Myth of Persephone: Demeter has forced Zeus and Lord Hades to work out a compromise that will allow Persephone to return to her mother, to be Kore again for two thirds of the year, bringing back life, youth, and beauty to the earth. In Demeter and Kore's joyful embrace our students can recognize their own sense of wellbeing in this season of hope. Our inner light meets the new light pouring in through our senses.

Finally, close to the time of the spring equinox, we come to the story of Passover. Cosmic hope and renewal are followed by the escape of the people of Israel from tyranny and slavery in Pharaoh's Egypt. As we move from winter into early spring, so we shift from myth into history. Accordingly, for our Passover lesson the balance is tilted again toward more active participation, drama, dance, and song.

From Spring to Summer

After the spring holiday the days become increasingly longer. All around us nature is teaming with life and it is easy for us to feel slightly out of ourselves. This is true for all of us familiar with spring fever but especially so for many special-needs students who have difficulties with being alert and focused under any circumstances. How do we help them to be able to be more present, not to lose themselves in the overstimulation coming from their environment at this time?

In the story of God's Throne, the knights assembled at Arthur's Whitsun gathering in Camelot are asked to give account to the king of their exploits over the past year. Each knight approaches the king, speaking of a good or valorous deed they have accomplished. As the students/knights step forward the king gazes down at them and gently touches them on the shoulder, "seeing" their true being, confirming their strength and dignity – a very special moment for our youngsters.

When one knight begins to tell of a vision he has had the assembled knights erupt in laughter. King Arthur calls his jeering courtiers to order and listens with deep interest to the young knight's tale of a vision he had while serving an old hermit in the forest. "I have seen God's Throne here on earth," he says. "The divine that lives in nature and the divine that lives within us are connected," he seems to be implying. The forces of nature don't have to overwhelm us. On the contrary, they can help us to find ourselves.

Another Arthurian tale is that of the Fisher King. This adventure story is especially beneficial for more able students. Everyone can take the part of a courtier at Camelot but some students may also dare to step out of the chorus to take on more challenging and substantive roles. Beside the young Prince Arthur, there is the wise and noble King, Uther Pendragon, or his beautiful Queen, Igraine. There are Arthur's two companions, the powerful magician Merlin and the brave knight Gawain.[50] Acting out these characters is not only great fun but can help students to feel grounded and develop confidence in themselves. We have moved a long way from the first gentle attempts of acting out the Annunciation to starring in a full-blown tale of heroic initiation!

Now we are approaching the second great turning point of the year, the summer solstice. At this time we can feel at one with the sun, riding high in the sky during the long days, and with the starry heavens, shining in glorious majesty at night. We are fully expanded but we can't remain that way, or rise any higher without danger. Somehow we must find the way back to ourselves after touching the excitement of our peak experiences.

This is when our students encounter the ancient Greek myth of Icarus and Daedalus. Once more we walk together the in-winding and out-winding spiral, symbol of the sun, shape of the labyrinth at Knossos in Crete. Once more we hear of captivity and flight into freedom, thanks this time not to the divine leadership of a Moses but to the human ingenuity of the architect Daedalus – though young Icarus's headlong flight into the sun costs him his life. At the end of the story Daedalus, the grieving father, beholds Apollo, god of the sun, revealing himself in splendor as the Lord

50   Evil or threatening characters like the witch Morgana or the dragons of the Perilous Land are mostly not appropriate for our students to act out – though they very much enjoy seeing them and interacting with them when they are played by us teachers.

and master over "the way in and the way out," over beginnings and endings, over life and death.

After the intensity of the build-up to Midsummer a certain mood of relaxation should prevail throughout the remainder of the term. Students and staff members alike can find it hard to concentrate in the month of July and all are looking forward to the end of the school year. A light-hearted Native American story tells How Grandmother Spider Stole the Sun. All the animals work together to acquire a piece of the sun to brighten their dark world. Sister Buzzard, the star of the story, carries the new sun into its zenith position but is badly disfigured in the process. Brother Fox may laugh at her but we all learn that heroes are to be praised for their service and sacrifice, not mocked for their missing feathers! Thus we end the year with a sense of contentment and appreciation for the beauty, dignity, and preciousness of the world we live in.

During the long summer holiday the experiences of the whole year are allowed to sink down into forgetfulness while the soul is spread out among the warmth and light of the elements. As the season contracts and autumn announces itself, students and staff members alike begin to get ready for a new year, a new cycle and further growth, with Michael and the dragon returning to mark the threshold.

Concluding Questions

At the beginning of this chapter we stated our intention of stimulating new thoughts and fresh creativity rather than offering ready-made answers. In keeping with that intention we would like to leave our readers with a set of questions and reflections regarding our presentation.

Annual Repetition

Typically, our students would experience the same curriculum during each of their 3 years in the upper school. The educational soundness of such repetition may well be questioned in other contexts. Yet in our case we have found that returning to the same materials year after year felt very much like being welcomed more deeply into the eternal turning of the familiar seasons. Changes in the student body would certainly offer variety aplenty to us teachers while for many of our students there was a real sense of progression in terms of their ability to listen with increasing maturity to familiar stories and to participate more fully in familiar routines, even to the point of helping and supporting others.

Curricular Diversity

As it stands, our curriculum is no doubt less culturally and religiously diverse than it could be. Western and Native American stories abound but the absence of African stories is glaring. The choice of religious traditions is heavily weighted toward Christianity, Judaism, ancient religion, and shamanism. While a Buddhist story is included, the absence of Muslim and Hindu traditions is felt.

These admitted limitations were not the result of intentional exclusion. Certainly, our choice of building our curriculum around the solar year has meant less emphasis on some cultures that are more centered on moon cycles. On the other hand, we did feel it important to include a number of Arthurian stories as a way of connecting with the sacredness of the land and the country our students inhabit (our school being located in the Southwest of England). The potential one-sidedness in our curriculum, we felt, was balanced out by the inclusion of a rich array of world cultures in other classes and assemblies also held in our school, involving the same students. For example, Fabian used a comprehensive world music curriculum in his music lessons. His weekly choir sessions in both upper and lower school also placed much emphasis on African songs and included the annual celebration of Divali and Eid.

Is It Religion?

Some may question whether what we have done is exactly "teaching religion." After wrestling with the question time and again and trying out a number of alternative names, we decided to retain "religion," and with conviction. After all, our baseline was the recognition that religious experience is fundamental to the development of every human soul, regardless of the particulars belonging to different historic forms of religion. Surely no one would deny that "religious experience" is a central part of "religion"?

While we have set aside any claims of absolute truth and religious normativity we have at the same time affirmed the inherent worth of each spiritual tradition we worked with. There has been no attempt at leveling, rationalizing, or denying the essence of these traditions. On the contrary, we strove to bring their individual character to the fore in a rich and powerful way, as true images of a universal human-divine journey, each tradition offering a different facet of an emerging whole. Some may feel that we placed too much importance on religious feeling and on artistic presentations, thereby missing the moral side of religion, the *vita activa*. Where is the teaching of compassion, one may ask, where are acts of mercy, where is the forming of character to the pattern of goodness?

One answer is in the stories themselves. Spiritual art, as we conceived it, is neither mere entertainment nor a superfluous luxury or indulgence but rather a necessary nourishment for the soul. The bravery of Arthur, the leadership of Moses, the compassion of the Shell Maiden all create powerful presences in the moral imagination of those who encounter them.[51]

Another answer lies in the integrity of our own stance or presence as teachers. Whatever our personal limitations, flaws, or distractions, which we know to be legion, we worked on the strong belief that by genuinely intending to project a moral presence in the classroom and by imbuing every detail of our delivery and our "classroom management" with a healing intention we did as much as we could do to draw our students into a moral sphere for them to inhabit and make their own.

---

51   It is not by chance that contemporary atheistic thinkers are pointing to religious art as something that addresses universal "needs of the soul" – and therefore something to be learned from, even when the religious doctrines that underpin it are left behind. See De Botton (2012).

Adaptability and Transferability

Is what we have done transferable to other educational settings? We have
stressed before that we do not wish to uphold our curriculum in its specifics as a model for others to follow. Nonetheless, we believe that a central focus on the spiritual year could provide a potentially unifying factor
in many contexts where inclusivity and spirituality are both valued. The
choice of material is almost unlimited and can easily be adapted to local
needs. Having said that, other worthy and workable themes could no
doubt be found.

    Could our curriculum be transferred to mainstream children? The
experience of Steiner schools gives an affirmative answer. We do realize
that our approach does best in a teaching environment that allows a certain degree of freedom from the pressures of testing based on intellectual
recall. For any experience and arts-based approach to succeed it is vital that
meaning be allowed to emerge in an open and un-predetermined way, much
the way it happens naturally in music.[52] This is not to say that creative ways
of student assessment could not be found within a school environment
committed to standard testing, perhaps by adapting well-tried approaches
for assessment in projects-based arts, music, and drama courses.

Bibliography

Boyce-Tillman, J. (2017, November/December). A biomechanical universe? Music
    and Humanity. *ISM Music Journal*, 15–17.
de Botton, A. (2012). *Religion for atheists: A non-believer's guide to the uses of religion.*
    Hamish Hamilton.
Scheer, R. (2004). *Im Schatten der Sterne: Eine jüdische Wiederstandsgruppe.*
    Aufbau-Verlag.

52   This is one of the great insights promoted by the Rev Professor June Boyce-Tillman.
    See, for example, Boyce-Tillman (2017), 17.

15 Gerotranscendence and Music Therapy Supporting a Transpersonal Dimension to Aging

Over the last eight years, I have been reading, reflecting, presenting, and writing on ideas related to transpersonal gerontology, gerotranscendence, and the roles that I believe music can play in supporting this facet of aging. As a clinician trained from a transpersonal orientation, this has been done as a personal labor of love, and the chapter you are reading is the current synthesis of my thoughts on gerotranscendence and music. It is meant to build upon my thoughts previously published as a paper called "Music and gerotranscendence: A culturally responsive approach to ageing" (2019b). It is my hope that this present writing will encourage music therapists working with older adults to apply a transpersonal lens to their work that can be integrated with any other theoretical approach from which they may be working. Doing so, I believe, will allow them to expand their understanding of this phase of life, the people for whom they provide services, and how they can approach their own aging process.

Using the transpersonal lens is important because the spiritual, which I interpret as the transpersonal dimension of being, is believed to be an area that allows for continued growth and development, in spite of the other declines and losses that can come with aging (Achenbaum, 2001; Atchley, 2001, 2011; Erikson & Erikson, 1997; Mowat, 2010; Tornstam, 2005, 2011; Wacks, 2011). Therefore, awareness of this dimension of being opens up opportunities for music therapists to support their older adult clients on deeper, more meaningful levels within their aging experience. One reason for this is because music can facilitate transcendent experiences that can expand a person's worldview and deepen their understanding of who they are (Boyce-Tillman, 2000; Crowe, 2017; Rugenstein, 1996).

Another reason is that music can support people in being able to come to terms with painful memories and life experiences, which can allow them to gain a greater sense of meaning and purpose in their lives (Boyce-Tillman, 2000; Bright, 1996). The ability to do so is vital to the process of becoming an integrated self, considered to be the final stage of human development (Crowe, 2017; Erikson, 1980; Erikson & Erikson, 1997).

Tornstam's (2005, 2011) gerotranscendence theory of aging suggests that the transpersonal dimension of being is part of our development as humans. As such, the process of developing gerotranscendence can lead to the integration of self in ways that go beyond one's limited sense of self-identity. As a theory, it also provides a lens through which transpersonal experiences can be seen and understood by care providers working with older adults (Tornstam, 2005, 2011; Wadensten & Carlsson, 2003; Wang et al., 2011). Gerotranscendence involves three dimensions, each relating to a different aspect of being: the cosmic dimension, the self-transcendent dimension, and the social selectivity dimension (Tornstam, 2005, 2011). Seen as a theory of aging that embraces elements of both the disengagement and activity theories of aging, Tornstam describes gerotranscendence "as the final stage in a natural process towards maturation and wisdom. It defines a reality different than the normal midlife reality which gerontologists tend to project on old age" (Erikson & Erikson, 1997, pp. 123–124).

The development of mature gerotranscendence can be enhanced or hindered by one's unique life experiences and the personal meaning they make from those experiences (Read et al., 2014; Tornstam, 2005, 2011). These factors include education levels, socioeconomic class, language, as well as societal norms and constraints (Tornstam, 2005, 2011). It is worth noting the parallels that such factors have with other social determinants of health, such as race, gender, sexual orientation, experiences of trauma, attachment style, and geographic location, on the health and wellbeing of older adults in the United States (Ferraro et al., 2017; Hoy-Ellis et al., 2016; McCarthy & Davies, 2003). A study by Read et al. (2014) suggests that negative life events can promote gerotranscendence in the second half of life, and other cross-cultural studies on the topic suggest that increases in gerotranscendence, particularly increases within the cosmic dimension, can lead to increased life satisfaction (Braam et al., 2010; Thomas, 2001; Wang, 2011).

Because music impacts us in multidimensional ways that can support and facilitate a spectrum of transpersonal experiences (Rugenstein, 1996), it is my belief that music holds great potential for supporting the development of mature gerotranscendence of today's older adults. Music has long been used in spiritual or religious contexts within different cultures, and it is known to be able to facilitate non-ordinary states of consciousness as well as peak experiences. As Boyce-Tillman writes, "[M]usic can be a trigger for the spiritual, because qualities within the experience … may be regarded as self-transcending or mystical," and she further recognizes "that an experience of the spiritual is important for realizing our full humanity" (2016, p. 44). Additionally, music is commonly used within eldercare, settings which for some, bring up painful feelings around the loss of independence, autonomy, sense of dignity, or sense of identity.

With this chapter, it is my argument that music and the intentional use of it through therapeutic practices such as music therapy can be an effective, accessible, and culturally responsive way of supporting the development of mature gerotranscendence in today's older adults, and in particular those of the Baby Boom generational cohort. In making this argument, I will provide further context into the significance of the topic of aging and the transpersonal dimension of being, as well as a bit more about my background and what led me to study this topic. Following that will be a closer examination of gerotranscendence, specifically the three dimensions of gerotranscendence, which I think can help clarify ways in which music therapists can support the mature gerotranscendence of today's diverse older adults in America. From this framework and understanding I further examine ways in which I believe music can contribute to this development.

The Origins of My Investigation of This Topic

To begin, it may be helpful to provide some background as to who I am, why this topic interests me, and the facets through which my thoughts on this topic have been informed. I currently live in Colorado where I moved to study transpersonal counseling psychology and music therapy at Naropa University in Boulder, the Buddhist-inspired university founded in 1974 by the controversial Tibetan Buddhist teacher, Chögyam Trungpa Rinpoche. Other well-known spiritual thinkers and thought leaders in the areas of aging and transpersonal psychology, such as Rabbi Zalman Schachter-Shalomi and Ken Wilber, have also lived in the Boulder area and their works have been influential in my professional training and ongoing development. The famous Caribou Ranch recording studio, active from 1972 until 1985, is nearby up in the mountains outside of Boulder, and it has in part contributed to the development of vibrant intergenerational musical communities. As well, the world-famous Red Rocks Amphitheatre is further south in the Foothills near Denver. Needless to say, I live in an area rich with access to diverse spiritual practices and belief systems, cutting-edge thoughts on aging, and world-class music.

My Experiences Working with Older Adults

As a counselor and music therapist, I have worked with older adults in a variety of contexts and settings over the course of my career. In my private practice as a mental health provider, I have worked with well-older adults who were needing support working through the life transitions they were facing, including retirement, managing chronic health conditions, and coming to terms with their changing identities. As a music therapist, I have worked in hospice and end-of-life care where I use music and therapeutic presence to enhance the quality of life for those with terminal illness and supporting them in coming to a sense of peace about the life they have lived. Additionally, I have worked as a team supervisor for an elder home health care company based upon the Windhorse Model developed by psychiatrist Dr. Edward Podvoll, the founder of the Contemplative Psychotherapy program at Naropa University. I also provide music for New Thought spiritual services with congregations made up of older adults holding various New Age beliefs. All of these roles and experiences have influenced my thoughts on this topic.

Early Reflections on Transpersonal Gerontology and Gerotranscendence

The topics of gerotranscendence and transpersonal gerontology have fascinated me since 2012 when I first received an issue of *The Journal of Transpersonal Psychology* highlighting transpersonal gerontology. At that time, I was working full-time in hospice and serving diverse patients in the Metro Denver area as a music therapist. Reading about gerotranscendence made me think differently about some of the situations I was encountering in the course of my work. Could visits that were declined be interpreted through the lens of the social selectivity dimension? Might I better understand patients with dementia if I viewed their statements through the lens of the cosmic dimension? I first put down my thoughts and reflections about the topic in a blog post on my private practice website (Halverson-Ramos, 2012).

Reflecting on the Aging of the Baby Boom Generation

Thinking about gerotranscendence led me to wonder more specifically about how gerotranscendence might be relevant to the aging experiences of those from the Baby Boom generation. How would those from a generation formed around youth, and whose desires and insecurities have been marketed to them since childhood, experience themselves and their aging process? How would the discrimination, traumas, and victories of those directly affected by the Civil Rights movements of the 1960s and into the 1980s shape how they view themselves within the world as older adults today? For some, what role might the use of mind-altering substances and/or spiritual exploration during one's formative years, and perhaps continuing on into their elder years, have on their aging process?

More than anything, though, I wondered what role popular music and pop culture might play in the aging process of older adults from the Baby Boom generation, and in facilitating experiences that could lead to the development of gerotranscendence. The impact of twentieth-century popular culture and popular music on our larger culture cannot be overstated, as Bennett (2013) writes:

The beginning of the 21st century marks an interesting and highly significant period in contemporary popular music history. Almost every living generation in the Westernized world has grown up in an age during which popular music has been a pivotal element of the global media and cultural industries, be it the advent of rock 'n' roll during the mid-1950s, the psychedelic and politicized rock of the late 1960s, the punk backlash of the mid-1970s, or the dance music explosion of the late 1980s. (p. 1)

With the development of transistors after World War II, music became portable and more accessible. Music became amplified. These developments created wide-ranging cultural changes. Popular music contributed to people's sense of identity and composed a soundtrack for their formative experiences (Bennett, 2013) in ways unlike for previous generations.

Likewise, with fewer people identifying as "religious," including older adults (Pew Research Center, 2012, 2015), what role could popular or secular music play in addressing the existential questions that are inevitably a part of life and aging in the twenty-first century? In hospice many of the elderly patients with whom I worked took great comfort in the old, familiar hymns of their childhood, but based on my personal interactions with members of the Baby Boom generation, I had reason to suspect that such music would not be considered as comforting. How might popular or secular music be used to provide this same sense of existential comfort and facilitate the development of greater life meaning and purpose to those who were "spiritual, not religious" or who had no affiliations at all? These were questions I thought could be answered by looking more deeply into transpersonal gerontology and gerotranscendence.

Why This Topic Is Important Today

Collectively, we are at an interesting time as a species. Between the COVID-19 pandemic, climate change, and the worldwide cries for social justice and change, humanity is facing a unique existential crisis. For people aged 65 or older especially, this has been a trying time as public health responses to the pandemic have led to isolation away from loved ones. In some instances, this isolation was self-selected, whereas for others it was enforced upon them. For those who were already lacking a social support system, their feelings of isolation may have become greater. Facing such unprecedented existential challenges, coupled with the feelings of powerlessness that come with those challenges, can force one to question the deeper meaning and purpose to one's life (Bright, 1996).

Exacerbating this for today's older adults is that the aging process itself inevitably comes with losses that can raise existential questions. These losses can be related to one's physical and/or cognitive abilities, their self-identified roles, and their meaningful relationships as one moves closer to the end of life. One's ability to manage the increasing complexities and vulnerabilities of aging can lead to having a greater sense of meaning and purpose in life (Baars, 2010; Erikson & Erikson, 1997; Westerhof, 2010). The effectiveness of how one manages this affects the process of becoming an integrated self. Integration requires a recognition and an acceptance of all facets of one's self and lived experiences, "including the primitive, the negative, and the ugly. It is the birth of the true self" (Crowe, 2017, p. 20).

However, a person's ability to become an integrated self may be complicated by a variety of factors. Some reasons include, but are not limited to: the general loss of autonomy that can come with aging (Bright, 1996), the challenges involved with managing complex and chronic health conditions (Gillespie, 2015), unresolved trauma (Heller & LaPierre, 2012; Wilson et al., 2006), attachment style and attachment relationships (McCarthy & Davies, 2003), discrimination and its associated health disparities (Coley et al., 2017; Foglia & Fredriksen-Goldsen, 2014), or a poor social support system (Goldman & Cornwell, 2018; Population Reference Bureau, 2014). The ability to become an integrated self can be negatively affected if one does not have access to effective supports and support systems.

Accessing the Transpersonal Dimension of Being

One way that integration can be supported is through accessing the transpersonal dimension of being. The transpersonal relates to those transcendent experiences that take us beyond the limits of our egos and personalities; experiences that take us beyond our narrow and rigidly defined perceptions of ourselves and the world within which we live. By accessing this dimension, we can recognize a deep interconnectedness that exists between ourselves and others, as well as between ourselves and the planet. As a result, we gain a new perspective on our lives that leaves us generally feeling satisfied and at peace. We can gain a greater sense of meaning and purpose to life that goes beyond attaining material goods and satisfying our individual egoic, self-centered desires.

These transcendent experiences are available to us all, and though these types of experiences may be viewed by some through the cultural lens of religion, religious beliefs are not necessary. However, they can involve a certain mindset that one might broadly understand as being "spiritual" in the way that Atchley (2011) describes as "a region of experience" (p. 156). He broadens this understanding by identifying that spirituality can take on three basic forms: "intense awareness of the present, transcendence of the personal self, or a feeling of connection with the ground of being – variously conceived as all of life, the universe, a supreme being, a great web of being, and many other conceptions" (p. 157). Such an understanding is important to keep in mind given the great diversity of belief systems, cultural backgrounds, and formative experiences of older adults in the twenty-first century (Drury, 2011; Pew Research Center, 2009, 2012, 2015; Wilber, 2000).

Gerotranscendence

The aging theory of gerotranscendence provides a framework for understanding these internal shifts that can occur within older adults as they come to recognize and experience themselves in ways that transcend the limited and narrowly defined sense of individual ego that they may have held when younger (Tornstam, 2005, 2011). These shifts can be experienced and expressed in three different levels or domains, with each related to different aspects of being: cosmic (time and space), self-transcendent (body and sense of self-identity), and social selectivity (social roles and relationships). These dimensions can be helpful in categorizing and conceptualizing different aspects of transpersonal experiences that older adults may undergo as part of their aging and integration process. I further outline each dimension below.

Cosmic Dimension

The cosmic dimension pertains to how a person experiences themselves in space and time. What this means is that a person may have an altered sense of time where the distance between the past and present disappears (Tornstam, 2005, 2011). They may feel a generational connection between past and future generations (Tornstam, 2005, 2011). As well, the person comes to a place of acceptance around death, while still rejoicing in life (Tornstam, 2005, 2011).

Self-Transcendent Dimension

The self-transcendent dimension relates to how one perceives themselves. With the self-transcendent dimension, one engages in self-confrontation that allows them to make an honest and objective review of their life (Tornstam, 2005, 2011), much like that which is required with integration. With this, there can come the development of new skills or the recognition of previously repressed or unexpressed skills. There can also be a decrease in self-centeredness where the individual is able to shift their needs and concerns away from themself and toward others, such as children and grandchildren (Tornstam, 2005, 2011). Additionally, a body-transcendence can occur in which one establishes a healthy relationship with one's body and physical condition (Tornstam, 2005, 2011).

Social Selectivity Dimension

Relationships and one's social roles are at the heart of the social selectivity dimension. With this dimension, one may find that they have a disinterest

in superficial relationships and there might also be an increased desire to
have time alone for contemplation (Tornstam, 2005, 2011). The idea of
one's authentic self versus the social roles they may have played in life is
also highlighted with this dimension (Tornstam, 2005, 2011). With this
can come an emancipated innocence where one cares less about how
others perceive them. Likewise, one's worldview can shift away from a
right/wrong duality and evolve into becoming more broadminded and
tolerant.

Using Music to Support Mature Gerotranscendence

Although I have been unable to find studies specific to gerotranscendence
and music, I have found in the literature support for my belief that
music could play a role in the development of gerotranscendence.
Tornstam (2005) himself describes music as being "a bridge to a transcendent experience of the whole" (p. 73). While not in direct reference
to gerotranscendence, Boyce-Tillman (2000) seems to be describing the
self-confrontation that can occur as part of the self-transcendence dimension when she describes music's ability to facilitate maturity through its
"capacity to express and awaken hidden aspects of the personality" which
has "a way of gaining a wider acceptance of painful private areas of human
experience and aids the process of maturity: to know how to use music to
express private events publicly can lead to maturity" (p. 46).

While such statements illustrate in general a role for music in addressing gerotranscendence, music therapists working in eldercare must
know how to intentionally use music therapeutically with people of varying
physical abilities and neurological/cognitive functioning. How could therapeutic musical experiences already employed by music therapists working
in eldercare be viewed in ways to address gerotranscendence? To clarify
ways that music therapists could address gerotranscendence in ways that
allow them to meet the diverse needs of the older adults with whom they
work, I examined my own uses of common receptive and active therapeutic
musical experiences used in music therapy practice with older adults and

outlined how I believed these experiences fit within the three dimensions in Table 15.1. My explanations for using these interventions follow below.

The Cosmic Dimension and Music

Because music can facilitate moments of transcendence, aesthetic pleasure, and awe, it is apparent that music can support the cosmic dimension. Examples of therapeutic musical activities I have used in my work include active music-making, music-facilitated life review, guided meditation with music, and intergenerational music groups where children and older adults come together in music. These kinds of experiences with music can induce feelings of connectivity, "flow" and life recall (Halverson-Ramos, 2019a).

The Self-Transcendent Dimension and Music

In addressing this dimension, it is important to think about ways in which music can support a person in further understanding and accepting who they are. Activities that I have used to promote healthy aging and ego-integration include music discussion, songwriting, music-facilitated life review, active music-making, guided meditation with music, and intergenerational music groups. Such experiences allow for people to engage in the self-confrontation necessary for ego-integration, while also providing opportunities for accessing and/or developing new skills and experiencing new ways of being.

The Social Selectivity Dimension and Music

With its focus on re-evaluating relationships and social roles, I believe that addressing the social selectivity dimension through music can be paradoxical at times. Sometimes music plays an active role, and sometimes it is a person's ability to refuse engaging with others through music

Table 15.1. Addressing the Three Dimensions of Gerotranscendence through Music

Dimension	Musical Experiences	Rationale
Cosmic dimension	AMM MFLR GMWM IGMG	Induce feelings of connectivity, "flow" and life recall
Self-transcendent dimension	MD SW AMM MFLR GMWM IGMG	Promote healthy aging and assist in processing the aging experience
Social selectivity dimension	MD SW AMM MFLR	Assist in re-evaluating relationships and social roles

This table, adapted from Halverson-Ramos (2019a), illustrates ways in which the three dimensions of gerotranscendence can be addressed through music. Abbreviations for musical experiences are as follows: AMM = Active music-making, GMWM = Guided meditation with music, IGMG = Intergenerational music groups, MFLR = Music-facilitated life review, MD = Music discussion, and SW = Songwriting.

that is key. Therapeutic musical experiences I have used to address this dimension include music discussion, music-facilitated life review, song-writing, and active music-making. Such experiences provide opportunities for contemplative self-reflection, as well as for engaging with oneself and others in ways that can lead to emancipated innocence.

Closing Thoughts

In exploring this specific topic, I recognize that there are other variables affecting human development that are worth further exploration in order to see what sort of impact they may have on one's ability to develop mature gerotranscendence. For example, how might one's attachment style and adverse childhood experiences impact one's aging process and ability to access transpersonal dimensions of being? There is an identified need for more research in this area (Chopik et al., 2013; McCarthy & Davies, 2003), and I think that it would be worthwhile for music therapists to be part of transdisciplinary research in these areas. Likewise, specifically to gerotranscendence, studies have not included looking at the role of ethnicity or sexual orientation, which may be worth further examination.

While I have tried to make the case for why music should be considered a tool for facilitating the mature gerotranscendence of older adults from diverse backgrounds, and outlined ways that music therapists can do so, ultimately this is not a topic limited to older adults. As it has been suggested that this transpersonal dimension of being exists for us all, people at any age can benefit from taking time to tap into this dimension of being. For music therapists, viewing your work and your own aging process through a transpersonal lens can help you to see your clients and yourself more fully. It is my hope that more of us taking the time to tap into the transpersonal dimension of ourselves and life can lead to the creation of a more healthy, sane, and empathic society.

Bibliography

Achenbaum, W. A. (2001). The flow of spiritual time amid the tides of life. In S. H. McFadden & R. A. Atchley (Eds.), *Aging and the meaning of time* (pp. 3–19). Springer Publishing Company, Inc.

Atchley, R. C. (2001). The influence of spiritual beliefs and practices on the relation between time and aging. In S. H. McFadden & R. A. Atchley (Eds.), *Aging and the meaning of time* (pp. 157–170). Springer Publishing Company, Inc.

Atchley, R. C. (2011). How spiritual experience and development interact with ageing. *The Journal of Transpersonal Psychology, 43*(2), 156–165.

Baars, J. (2010). Aging as increasing vulnerability and complexity: Towards a philosophy of life course. In J. Bouwer (Ed.), *Successful ageing, spirituality and meaning: Multidisciplinary perspectives, studies in spirituality supplement 20, Titus Brandsma Institute* (pp. 39–51). Peeters.

Bennett, A. (2013). *Music, style, and aging: Growing old disgracefully.* Temple University Press.

Boyce-Tillman, J. (2000). *Constructing musical healing: The wounds that sing.* Jessica Kingsley Press.

Boyce-Tillman, J. (2016). *Experiencing music: restoring the spiritual: Music as well-being.* Peter Lang.

Braam, A., Deeg, D., van Tilburg, T., Beekman, A., & van Tilburg, W. (2010). In J. Bouwer (Ed.), *Successful ageing, spirituality and meaning: Multidisciplinary perspectives, studies in spirituality supplement 20, Titus Brandsma Institute* (pp. 53–69). Peeters.

Bright, R. (1996). *Grief and powerlessness: Helping people regain control of their lives.* Jessica Kingsley Publishers.

Chopik, W., Edelstein, R., & Fraley, R. (2013). From the cradle to the grave: Age differences in attachment from early childhood to old age. *Journal of Personality, 81*(2), 171–183. <https://doi.org/10.1111/j.1467-6494.2012.00793.x>

Coley, S. L., Mendes de Leon, C. F., Ward, E. C., Barnes, L. L., Skarupski, K. A., & Jacobs, E. A. (2017). Perceived discrimination and health-related quality-of-life: Gender differences among older African Americans. *Quality of Life Research, 26*(12), 3449–3458. <https://doi.org/10.1007/s11136-017-1663-9>

Crowe, B. J. (2017). *A transpersonal model of music therapy: Deepening practice.* Barcelona Publishers.

Drury, N. (2011). *Wisdom seekers: The rise of the new spirituality.* O Books.

Erikson, E. H. (1980). *Identity and the life cycle.* W. W. Norton.

Erikson, E. H., & Erikson, J. M. (1997). *The life cycle completed.* W. W. Norton.

Ferraro, K. F., Kemp, B. R., & Williams, M. M. (2017). Diverse aging and health inequality by race and ethnicity. *Innovation in Aging, 1*(1), 1–11. <https://doi.org/10.1093/geroni/igx002>

Foglia, M. B., & Fredriksen-Goldsen, K. I. (2014). Health disparities among LGBT older adults and the role of nonconscious bias. *Hastings Center Report, 44*(October), s40–s44. <https://doi.org/10.1002/hast.369>

Gillespie, L. (2015, December 17). *Baby boomers set another trend: More golden years in poorer health.* Kaiser Health News. <https://khn.org/news/baby-boomers-set-another-trend-more-golden-years-in-poorer-health/>

Goldman, A. W., & Cornwell, B. (2018). Social disadvantage and instability in older adults' ties to their adult children. *Journal of Marriage and Family, 80*(5), 1314–1332. <https://doi.org/10.1111/jomf.12503>

Halverson-Ramos, F. (2012, June 6). *Examining a transpersonal view of aging.* SoundWell Music Therapy Blog. <https://soundwellmusictherapy.com/examining-a-transpersonal-view-of-aging/>

Halverson-Ramos, F. (2019a, June 14–15). *Gerotranscendence, music, and the Baby Boom generation* [Poster presentation]. International Symposium: Music, Spirituality, Wellbeing and Theology, Winchester, England. <https://issuu.com/theuniversityofwinchester/docs/07431_-_tavener_prog_2019_v2>

Halverson-Ramos, F. (2019b). Music and gerotranscendence: A culturally responsive approach to ageing. *Approaches: An Interdisciplinary Journal of Music Therapy, 11*(1), 166–179. <http://approaches.gr/special-issue-11-1-2019/>

Heller, L., & LaPierre, A. (2012). *Healing developmental trauma: How early trauma affects self-regulation, self-image, and their capacity for relationship.* North Atlantic Books.

Hoy-Ellis, C. P., Ator, M., Kerr, C., & Milford, J. (Summer 2016). Innovative approaches address aging and mental health needs in LGBTQ communities. *Generations: Journal of the American Society of Aging, 40*(2), 56–63.

McCarthy, G., & Davies, S. (2003). Some implications of attachment theory for understanding psychological functioning in old age: An illustration from the long-term psychological effects of World War Two. *Clinical Psychology and Psychotherapy, 10*(3), 144–155. <https://doi.org/10.1002/cpp.365>

Mowat, H. (2010). Ageing, health care and the spiritual imperative: A view from Scotland. In J. Bouwer (Ed.), *Successful ageing, spirituality and meaning: Multidisciplinary perspectives, studies in spirituality supplement 20, Titus Brandsma Institute* (pp. 109–120). Peeters.

Pew Research Center. (2009, December 9). *Many Americans mix multiple faiths.* [Data file and code book]. <http://www.pewforum.org/2009/12/09/many-americans-mix-multiple-faiths>

Pew Research Center. (2012, October 9). Religion and the unaffiliated. [Data file and code book]. <http://www.pewforum.org/2012/10/09/nones-on-the-rise-religion/>

Pew Research Center. (2015, November 3). U.S. public becomes less religious: Modest drop in overall rates of belief and practice, but religiously affiliated Americans are as observant as before. <http://www.pewforum.org/2015/11/03/u-s-public-becoming-less-religious/>

Population Reference Bureau. (2014, March 6). Unmarried baby boomers face disadvantages as they grow older. <https://www.prb.org/baby-boomers-and-disability/>

Read, S., Braam, A. W., Lyyra, T. M., & Deeg, D. J. H. (2014). Do negative life events promote gerotranscendence in the second half of life? *Aging and Mental Health, 18*(1), 117–124. <https://doi.org/10.1080/13607863.2013.814101>

Rugenstein, L. (1996). Wilber's spectrum model of transpersonal psychology and its application to music therapy. *Music Therapy, 14*(1), 9–28. <https://doi.org/10.1093/mt/14.1.9>

Thomas, L. E. (2001). The job hypothesis: Gerotranscendence and life satisfaction among elderly Turkish Muslim. In S. H. McFadden & R. A. Atchley (Eds.), *Aging and the meaning of time* (pp. 207–227). Springer Publishing Company, Inc.

Tornstam, L. (2005) *Gerotranscendence: A developmental theory of positive aging.* Springer Publishing Company, Inc.

Tornstam, L. (2011). Maturing into gerotranscendence. *The Journal of Transpersonal Psychology, 43*(2), 166–180.

Wacks, Q. V. (2011). The elder as sage, old age as spiritual path: Towards a transpersonal gerontology. *The Journal of Transpersonal Psychology, 43*(2), 127–155.

Wadensten, B., & Carlsson, M. (2003). Theory-driven guidelines for practical care of older people, based on the theory of gerotranscendence. *Journal of Advanced Nursing, 41*(5), 462–470.

Wang, J. J. (2011). A structural model of the bio-psycho-social-spiritual factors influencing the development towards gerotranscendence in a sample of institutionalised elders. *The Journal of Advanced Nursing, 67*(212), 2628–2636.

Wang, J., Lin, Y., & Hsieh, L. (2011). Effect of gerotranscendence support group on gerotranscendence perspective, depression, and life satisfaction of institutionalized elders. *Aging and Mental Health, 15*(5), 580–586.

Westerhof, G. (2010). Personal meaning and successful ageing: A psychogeronotological perspective. In J. Bouwer (Ed.), *Successful ageing, spirituality and meaning: Multidisciplinary perspectives, studies in spirituality supplement 20, Titus Brandsma Institute* (pp. 73–90). Peeters.

Wilber, K. (2000). *The theory of everything: An integral vision for business, politics, science and spirituality.* Shambhala.

Wilson, R. S., Krueger, K. R., Arnold, S. E., Barnes, L. L., Mendes de Leon, C. F., Bienias, J. L., & Bennett, D. A. (2006). Childhood adversity and psychosocial adjustment in old age. *American Journal of Geriatric Psychiatry, 14*(4), 307–315. <https://doi.org/10.1097/01.JGP.0000196637.95869>

PART IV

Ecology

16 Recovering Our Humanity
What's Love (and Music) Got to Do with It?

Introduction

Music might be a potent resource for recovery in a number of ways. Not only as a resource for improving or recovering individual health and wellbeing, but in a more holistic sense, as a resource for our evolution as a more sustainable species on an increasingly fragile planet. The sympathetic entanglement of musical and neurobiological mechanisms and their implication in both musical performance and human intimacy is not coincidental. As the world recovers from the shocks of the first global zoonotic pandemic, musicking might prove a valuable resource to guide and shape the kind of world we want to recover to, emphasizing our capacity as human beings to bond with others in a spirit of fellowship and love.

In this chapter, I trace the origins of the postwar humanist project and its current precarious state in a dehumanizing neoliberal global system. Recognizing love as an essentially human characteristic, I explore some of the ways in which the neurobiological underpinnings of human attachment might be sympathetically entangled with our musical instincts. I proceed to suggest the positive role that musicking (Elliott, 1995; Small, 1998) might therefore have as part of a necessary re-humanization in order for humans to evolve into a more sustainable future.

The Rise and Fall of the Human

In 2019, Europe commemorated the seventy fifth anniversary of D-Day, the Allied invasion of northern Europe, which ultimately led to the end of "World" War II, and the resulting postwar project to rebuild Europe in such a way that the partisan interests of its nation states could never again threaten the fundamental rights of its human citizens. For me, and I suspect for many others, there was quite a cognitive dissonance seeing the leaders of the retreat from the European project – Donald Trump's increasingly isolationist United States, and the Prime Minister of "Brexit" Britain – standing side by side with the European leaders fighting to keep the historic union alive.

The horrors of World War II brought with it "the shock of coming face to face with the moral horror of nation state actors and their citizens" (Caruso & Flanagan, 2018, p. 1), and led to a postwar human existential crisis that "expressed the genuine worry that humans might simply not be up to living morally or purposefully" (p. 4). This crisis led to global attempts to "regain a positive, less anguished, more hopeful image of persons" (p. 1), which we can see in the foundation of the United Nations in 1945 and the subsequent Universal Declaration of Human Rights (United Nations, 1948), with powerful perspectives of survivors (e.g., Frankl, 1946) providing a moral lead toward human recovery from the crisis. Thus was the modern humanist project born, and developed over the following decades to build a common understanding of what was common to all humans on the planet regardless of the specifics of their existence, that is, "life itself, natality and mortality, worldliness, plurality, and the earth" (Arendt, 1977).

Of course, the world we live in now is quite a different one to the one that even our recent ancestors knew. For one thing, in the intervening years the human population has exploded. In 1945, there were approximately 2.5 billion people on the planet. In just seventy-five years, that figure has tripled to 7.7 billion now, and is likely to have quadrupled to 9.6 billion by 2050 (Roser et al., 2013). This sudden rise of the human in terms of our sheer unsustainable numbers on the planet's limited resources is paradoxically coinciding with challenges to the institutions (e.g., the United

Nations, European "welfare state" systems, the European Union itself), which were set up to guarantee the rights necessary to underpin this explosion of human population. The second half of those seventy-five years has also been characterized by neoliberalism, an international consensus on economic policy emphasizing market deregulation, and limitation of state interests. For its critics, forty years of neoliberalism has been "in practice an assault on humanism, [enforcing] the reduction of human nature to economic competition, and [suppressing] all attempts to experiment with alternatives" (Mason, 2019, p. 1404).

And now, "our house is on fire" (Thunberg, 2019). Along with the stark reality of our current climate emergency, the collapse of the neoliberal project in 2008, with the promise of markets' self-regulation betrayed by the state bailouts of the banking system (Mason, 2019, p. 2203), had already led us into a unique and unsettling period of "hysteresis" (Bourdieu, 1977, p. 83) – a simultaneously stagnant and chaotic phase of a transition into a new world order. And then in 2020, the world's first global pandemic pitched us into renewed turmoil as a species, this time bringing us face-to-face with the moral horror of our destruction of global animal habitats and the inevitable resulting spread of zoonotic diseases, which are only likely to intensify (*Preventing the next Pandemic – Zoonotic Diseases and How to Break the Chain of Transmission*, 2020). As a result, we currently stand at a critical moment in human history, in the midst of an existential crisis of our own times.

Having evolved over millennia from bands to tribes to chiefdoms and finally to states only five and a half thousand years ago (Diamond, 2013, p. 12), we now find ourselves ill equipped to make the next evolutionary leap into the global geopolitical order that neoliberalism had promised us. In place of the emancipation of the human condition, we find its substitute: "countless forms of melancholy" (Bourriaud, 1998, p. 12), some of which arise as part of the paradox of digital hyper-connectivity and corresponding social isolation (Twenge, 2017). Tech giants thrive on the affordances of global networks, while nation states retreat to the soil of their geographical boundaries and reinforce those borders to keep the future out rather like the medieval villagers building walls to keep the cuckoo in. That bird has already flown. Globalization is increasingly both an unavoidable technological reality whilst simultaneously a geopolitical and ecological uncertainty.

The European postwar humanist project feels threatened precisely because neoliberalism required us to forget the one thing that could help us deal with the current uncertainty, and that we had only so recently learned – our humanity. If we want to recover it, we have to remember what makes us human; we have to know what *love* is.

I Want to Know What Love Is

Theories of love often start with a reference to the ground-breaking work that John Bowlby and Mary Ainsworth developed from the 1960s (Bowlby, 1969, 1973, 1980) and that has led to the widespread recognition of "attachment theory," a theory that argues that "our adult romantic and other intimate relationships develop out of, or are scaffolded by, our early experience of mother–infant relationships" (Dunbar, 2013, p. 16). This "maternal love" – a healthy attachment to our mother – gives us the "secure base" we need to launch ourselves in to the world and form other attachments, but if that maternal attachment is not secure, it can have profound and complex ramifications on our psychological development, and our experience of the world. "Romantic love," by contrast, is to do with the attachments we form with those to whom we find ourselves sexually or romantically attracted. This gives us two distinct types of love, which are similar in many ways but also quite different (p. 17). As well as these more singular types of intense love, we also have substantial networks of friends and family whom we may also love (p. 14).

At the heart of all these diverse kinds of close relationships – if they are functioning healthily – is the sense that our parents, our life partner, our close friends and family, see us for "who we are": the real "us." Dan Siegel describes this "sense that our internal world is shared" with another as "feeling felt" (Siegel, 2011, p. 10). Or we might recognize it as the "unconditional positive regard" found in the person-centered approach to psychotherapy of Carl Rogers (Rogers, 1951) and his followers, characterized by, "an outgoing positive feeling without reservations, without evaluations" (Rogers, 1961, p. 62). Although Maslow's hierarchy of needs is "not nearly as rigid" (Maslow, 1943, p. 27) as its title suggests, having these basic needs of "feeling felt" or being loved unconditionally are important foundations upon which the higher orders of needs – esteem and ultimately self-actualization (Maslow, 1943, pp. 20–23) – can be established; it is hard to imagine having a sense of wellbeing whilst simultaneously feeling unloved.

What Is Love Anyway?

Social bonding is not something that is restricted to humans – all mammals have evolved similar ways of strengthening the bond between mother and infant, which extends to developing cooperative "communities" (Lewis et al., 2001, p. 25). The means through which these strong attachment bonds are formed and sustained are complex, but include the part of the brain which mammals possess, but which other animals – reptiles, for example – do not: the limbic system.

"The limbic area lies deep within the brain" (Siegel, 2011, p. 17), and "drapes itself around the [Reptilian Brain] with a languid ease" (Lewis et al., 2001, p. 24). Dan Siegel explains that, "It evolved when small mammals first appeared around two hundred million years ago," and "works closely with the brainstem and the body proper to create not only our basic drives but also our emotions" (Siegel, 2011, p. 16). In Siegel's "hand" model of the brain, if you make your hand into a fist, the limbic area is where your thumb is, tucked underneath your fingers and sitting on top of your wrist. He elaborates:

> The limbic regions help create the "e-motions" that "evoke motion," that motivate us to act in response to the meaning we assign to whatever is happening to us in that moment. The limbic area is also crucial for how we form relationships and become emotionally attached to one another. (Siegel, 2011, p. 16)

The limbic system is described as an "open-loop arrangement" that only functions healthily in an individual when it is attuned to the limbic system of another (Lewis et al., 2001, p. 85). This kind of interpersonal "limbic regulation" is an important factor in maintaining homeostasis. When it is disrupted, the results can be catastrophic, especially for dependent animals. Universally, an infant mammal separated from its mother will cry in protest (p. 76), but if it fails to be reunited with them, will sink into the second stage of separation, a more lethargic, despondent, dejected, and miserable despair, from which it may not recover (p. 78).

Limbic regulation is therefore significant for our general health and wellbeing (Siegel, 2011, p. 27). Siegel refers to this as a core part of our "resonance circuitry" which explains "how we can come to resonate physiologically with others – how even our respiration, blood pressure, and heart rate can rise and fall in sync with another's internal state. This is the pathway that connects us to one another" (p. 71). In other words, neurobiology is interpersonal: "the internal states of others – from joy and play to sadness and fear – directly affect our own state of mind" (p. 71). Siegel explicitly connects this to the idea of love:

> When we see the mind of another person, we bring the qualities of being present – curiosity, openness, and acceptance – into our relationships. These qualities seem to me to be the essence of that overused, often misunderstood word: love. I propose that this stance of curiosity, openness, acceptance, and love is at the heart of secure attachments. (Siegel, 2011, p. 188)

If love is integral to our understanding of what make us human, you might now be asking …

What's *Music* Got to Do with It?

I believe there are a number of related reasons why music might have something to do with both love and our shared humanity. Like interpersonal attunement, music is a system which requires us to "tune in" to the internal world of others, through the process of musical entrainment, "a phenomenon in which two or more independent rhythmic processes synchronize with each other" (Clayton et al., 2004, p. 1). It is likely, therefore, that the Mirror Neuron System (MNS) – also part of Siegel's "resonance circuitry" – is implicated in "feeling felt" both emotionally and musically (Molnar-Szakacs & Overy, 2006), and in music, this leads to the phenomenon of "self-other merging," where the corresponding release of endorphins help to "create and strengthen social bonds amongst interacting group members" (Tarr et al., 2014, p. 1). In other words, the simple act of being musical with other people is sympathetically entangled with the neurobiological mechanisms that underpin social connection, and we might therefore consider it as a form of "love-as-action" (Silverman, 2012).

Musical Communication

Unless we are practicing music on our own, music is generally something that we do with other people, and therefore involves collaboration to make a good sound together. Because music is what Daniel Barenboim terms a "simultaneous dialogue" between voices – "each one expressing itself to the fullest while at the same time listening to the other" (Barenboim, 2009, p. 20) – it means accounting for the "other," not just one's own expression. This naturally leads to a situation where our own expression "feels felt" by others, whether that's the group leader, other members, or indeed an audience. As a communicative medium, music also has what Ian Cross and Ghofur Woodruff refer to as a "socio-intentional" dimension (Cross & Woodruff, 2009, p. 8). Rather than necessarily communicating information (language is much better at that), the act of musicking helps us to communicate our social intent, as a form of "shared intentionality" (Tomasello, 2019).

In participatory music, another dimension often comes into play, that of "non-auditioned" participation. Although previous experience is always beneficial, participants in a "non-auditioned" group are welcomed for who they are and what they can bring to the group, that is, "encouraging people to join in regardless of the quality of their contributions" (Turino, 2008, pp. 31–36). This is significant, because it represents a fundamentally "unconditional" acceptance of everyone's contribution. For many, especially older musicians who may have grown up believing that they aren't "good enough" to take part in musical activities because of previous negative experiences at school (Bithell, 2014, p. 51), this in itself can be a powerful affirmation. Rather than being judged on the quality of sound they can currently produce, participants can "feel felt" before they even produce a note.

Also, although some music may use words or lyrics, it is predominantly a sonic experience, where meaning is communicated through non-linguistic means. Our imagination may be captivated by the beauty of sounds in space, or our bodies may be moved to dance by the rhythms created through music, and music's capacity for creating "strong" experiences (Gabrielsson, 2011; Lamont, 2011) is well known, as is its capacity for affecting our emotions (Juslin & Sloboda, 2011; Sloboda, 2004; Västfjäll et al., 2013).

As well as being predominantly non-linguistic, a significant part of music's power might also be considered to be pre-linguistic, in the sense that it is a form of communication that language cannot be a substitute for (Camlin et al., 2020, p. 10). Being profoundly moved by music may render us literally speechless, because it speaks to a part of us deeper than language. These important aspects of music's power point toward music's function as a form of "communicative musicality" which lies at the heart of the bond between mother and infant (Malloch & Trevarthen, 2010). The prosodic communication – known variously as "baby talk," "motherese," or "infant-directed speech" (IDS) – that occurs between mother and infant in all known human cultures serves a number of key developmental functions, and is explicitly musical in nature (Mithen, 2007, p. 74). Hence, our most formative experiences of being loved or "feeling felt" are contained in these musical exchanges with our primary carer before we have learned the rudiments of language, and goes some way to explaining why we can be so profoundly affected by musical experiences which transcend our ability to describe them in words.

Evolutionary biologists now seem to concur that, far from the "useless" trait which Steven Pinker dismisses it as in evolutionary terms (Pinker, 2003, p. 528), music serves an important evolutionary function around promoting pro-social behavior and cooperation across large groups (Dunbar, 2012; Mithen, 2007, p. 229). The size of social groups amongst apes – our

nearest primate relatives – is restricted to the small number of other individuals a relationship can be maintained with by physical "grooming"
(Dunbar, 2012, p. 212; Mithen, 2007, p. 146), whereas our hominid ancestors typically cooperated across much larger groups. Part of the reason for
this difference, Aiello and Dunbar (1993) explain, derives from the "vocal
grooming hypothesis," which suggests that musical communication in
the form of "enhanced vocalization" may have evolved as "an expression
of mutual interest and commitment that could be simultaneously shared
with more than one individual" (Aiello & Dunbar, 1993, p. 187).

In evolutionary terms, musical communication with those in one's
immediate social group may help to reassure group members that they are
under no direct threat from each other, and hence help them to experience others in a positive and trusting way rather than as potential threats
to health or security. Stephen Mithen refers to this kind of primal cooperative communication system as "holistic, multi-modal, manipulative
musical and mimetic" (Mithen, 2007, p. 183). Or "hmmmm" for short. He
suggests that this kind of vocal communication has been present not just
throughout our history as a species, but also in that of earlier Hominid
species (i.e., Neanderthals) for a lot longer. Music in this sense is part of
the metaphorical glue that bonds Hominid societies together, enabling
cooperation. Notwithstanding some of the ways in which this phenomenon can be deployed to negative effect – for example, the use of music in
Nazi Germany (Turino, 2008, pp. 190–210) – music as a form of "bonding
social capital" (Putnam, 2001) is a universal biological characteristic of the
human species. As such, when we sing or make music together, we are participating in a form of social bonding that is at least as old as our species,
and probably much older (Mithen, 2007, pp. 241–243).

Fellowship of Hill and Wind and Sunshine

Although detailed studies have yet to be undertaken to test the hypothesis that musical entrainment and interpersonal neurobiology are entangled in the way I suggest, when people talk about their experiences of

music, they certainly point to such a connection. In 2018, I led a project involving three "scratch" choirs – each consisting of fifty to sixty singers many of whom had not previously met – onto the summits of the Lake District fells in Northern England as part of a project to commemorate the gift of land to the nation by a group of local mountaineers. Between them, the Fellowship of Hill and Wind and Sunshine sang a song cycle on each of fourteen summits over three separate weekends (National Trust, n.d.). We used a research method called Sensemaker© (Snowden, n.d.) to invite participants to share and interpret a story about their experience, and subsequently compared these with the stories of singers who had not been involved in the project (Camlin et al., 2020).

When asked to interpret their story against three equally weighted dimensions of "me," "my people," and "my place," most of the singers – from both groups – said that their story was about "my people," that is, connecting with the other singers. This tendency was most noticeable in the female respondents, but still very noticeable in all of the stories (Camlin et al., 2020, p. 6). For the mountain singers, this came as a surprise, as we were expecting a stronger emphasis on "my place" because of the connections the project was making with a specific – and very beautiful – landscape. More of the mountain singers' stories *did* attribute meaning to "my place," but not at the expense of "my people." If anything, the potent shared experience of the mountain location could be seen as another resource to amplify the social bonding effect of the group singing.

Similarly, when interpreting their stories against the equally weighted dimensions of "physical," "spiritual," or "emotional/mental" health, the vast majority of singers located the significance of their experience in the spiritual and emotional dimensions. For the mountain singers, this was again a surprise, owing to the challenging physical nature of climbing mountains to sing on them. Although there *was* more emphasis in the mountain singers' stories on the physical dimensions of the activity, it was not at the expense of the spiritual/ emotional dimensions of the activity. They talked about the sense of feeling "uplifted" by the group singing, and the resulting sense of "communitas" (DeNora, 2000, p. 149; Turner, 2012), that is, "showing up" for each other (Camlin et al., 2020, p. 10). This uplifting sense of unity and common purpose through the music is perhaps what helped to divert their attention away from any aches and pains they might have been experiencing as a result of the hard physical effort required to climb the mountains.

But is it love?

Is This Love that I'm Feeling?

A recent UK report exploring the independence and mental wellbeing of older people concluded that group activities should be at the heart of any effective approach, and top of the list of group activities was group singing. The committee behind the report "discussed the evidence on singing and noted that it is unclear whether it is the singing itself that produces the benefit, the group-based nature of the activity or something else" (NICE, 2015).

When we explored the stories of the singers from the Fellowship project in a focus group of respondents, a similar elusive quality of the experience was revealed:

- We talked a lot about the feeling, about how sometimes – well, certainly for me, the stronger the feeling and the sensation was about that [social] connection, the less able I was to articulate it in the stories.
- You become more and more interconnected as people and with the place and with the sound. And all of a sudden, something starts happening in your brain. I was driving home thinking, "What is that feeling like?"
- Singing with others takes me out of myself into another space. Singing on Great Gable was an almost mystical experience.[53] I felt my precious sense of self drifting away on a wave of harmony.

This is a common experience when it comes to talking about the powerful, almost transcendental effects of music on the self. A form of "self-other merging" (Tarr et al., 2014), such "magic moments" occur when "the group is in peak flow," and the "social-musical improvisation [seems] to

---

53   Mountain Summit in Cumbrian Lake District, UK.

be known within and between all minds and bodies as one, complex, phenomenon" (Pavlicevic, 2013b, p. 102) or where "identities are dissolved (or shared) in the interests of being people together in music in this place and in this time" (Pavlicevic, 2013a, p. 197). As another of the respondents expressed it, "The choir knits us together. We sing, we laugh, we cry, and all is held."

In this sense, when they perform, the choir are not just performing musical works – they are also literally performing the relationships that underpin the music and give it its vibrancy (Camlin et al., 2020; Camlin, in press-a, in press-b; Small, 1998, p. 13). This is not to suggest that group singing is simply a musical kind of "relational aesthetics" in the sense that Bourriaud describes, with Art as "a site that produces a specific sociability" (Bourriaud, 1998, p. 15). Rather, the performance of relationship is so much a part of the musical "moment" that we might think of the musical works and the human relationships which underpin them as interdependent, a creative tension of co-subjectivity, united through the paramusical effects of such a union. This idea of relationship imbricated within the music itself resonates so strongly with the idea of "feeling felt," that the inference is hard to resist: What if the elusive "something else" of the NICE report turns out simply to be love? A complex entanglement of interpersonal neurobiology amplified through musical entrainment?

Music as Polyvalent System

If we think of music as a system "able to sustain [...] polyvalent significance" (Cross & Woodruff, 2009, p. 2), we recognize that it operates across a number of interlinked dimensions, and pinning its potency down to any one of them is potentially to miss the complex ways in which it achieves its effects. It is perhaps the elusive and slippery character of its meaning which *gives it* its potency. Yes, its power may derive from the effect of the sounds in the air resonating with our emotions, *or* the interplay of our neurobiology as we "feel felt" through the process of entrainment, *or* through the power of expressing our personal or cultural identities and histories, *or* the uplifting effect of a range of hormonal activations (Altenmuller & Schlaug, 2013; Bernatzky et al., 2013; Fancourt, Perkins et al., 2016; Fancourt, Williamon et al., 2016; Koelsch & Stegemann, 2013; Kreutz et al., 2013; Macdonald & Macdonald, 2010; Salimpoor et al., 2011; Tarr et al., 2014). Or all of the above and more. Interdisciplinarity is therefore an essential "turn" if we are to advance our understanding of music's power from the ephemeral language of "magic" to a more sophisticated articulation of its complex and polyvalent potency.

Of course, the sheer complexity of this interconnected and polyvalent system would make it difficult to validate the truth of the hypothesis – that our neurobiology becomes entangled with others' through the process of musical entrainment, and that we feel it when it occurs, in the "magic moments" of uplift and transcendence which characterize the experiences of those who participate in it. There would be perhaps insurmountable methodological complexity in attempting to measure these complex interdependencies.

However, it may also be true that we have a sophisticated research instrument capable of making sense of them already: the human body-mind. As participant narratives attest, we *feel* these transcendental, spiritual moments when they happen. Perhaps that's enough? Shouldn't anyone who wants it be able to mobilize the power of music in their lives, to experience how music can help us to connect with others, and "feel felt?" Because, frankly, we *need* as many ways as we possibly can to feel connected to our fellow humans, to re-establish our common humanity in order to face our future with a global spirit of communitas.

What the World Needs Now

Re-humanization

Poised on the edge of a "posthuman" world (Hayles, 1999), musicking (Elliott, 1995; Small, 1998) provides an increasingly rare opportunity to experience an idealized form of empathic human relationship that can be mobilized in people's everyday lives (Camlin et al., 2020, p. 12). Similar to Bourriaud's "interstices," musicking offers us "free spaces and periods of time whose rhythms are not the same as those that organize everyday life, and they encourage an inter-human intercourse which is different to the 'zones of communication' that are forced upon us" (Bourriaud, 1998, p. 16).

Moreover, if neoliberalism compromised our humanity, the humanity that can be recovered in a "post-everything" world can be presupposed on the basis of our common neurobiology, rather than on more contingent socio-cultural or biological characteristics – such as gender, race, belief, bodily capacity or sexual orientation, which have been activated historically by a more paternalistic conception of humanism as a means of discrimination and subjugation. Human rights may be continually under threat, but the fact that they are also continually contested is an indication of how far the postwar humanist project has already come.

Similarly, the tensions between aesthetic and participatory dimensions of artistic creativity – of music especially – reveal not just how much of our humanity can be recovered when we emphasize the participatory dimension, but also how much the aesthetic "turn" of the last few centuries has given us ever more sophisticated ways to manipulate human-produced sound to achieve more potent effects for listeners and participants. To do so is, as Shannon Jackson (2011) expresses it, "not only to take a community stance on the arts but also to take an aesthetic stance on community engagement" (Jackson, 2011, p. 212). As social prescribing comes online, there is enormous potential for music to make a difference in the lives of many people across our fragmented and polarized societies, including the formation of "healthy publics" (Hinchliffe et al., 2018) and especially for the prospect of "mutual recovery" (Crawford et al., 2013, pp. 137–152) where it is not just those with a medical diagnosis, but their health and social care professionals, family, and indeed, the wider community whose health and wellbeing might benefit from the collective act of musicking.

At the time of writing, many of these benefits of group musicking have become less accessible because of the restrictions worldwide surrounding social gatherings, especially those activities involving singing together.

While the benefits may survive as potent memories within the hearts and minds of pre-pandemic participants, there is a clear risk that their impact will lessen over time unless they are able to be "re-charged" through the act of face-to-face musical entrainment outside of the technological limitations of the digital world. Just at the time when we need all of the resources we can muster as a species to support our evolution through these turbulent times, one of those key resources – musicking – is rendered more distant from us. It does not mean that we have to stop being musical. Indeed, we cannot; being musical is part of our biological inheritance. Rather, we need to explore the constraints and limitations of what separates us to find new ways of connecting through music in a digital age, whether through the development of more sophisticated "immersive" technologies to more closely resemble "real" musical experiences, by organizing ourselves in more local and sustainable communities of music, by building international communities of online musicking despite the limitations, or a combination of all of the above.

Even as a potentially important part of a global recovery to a more harmonious and sustainable future, there is also a risk that musicking – especially if we are talking about it in terms of its capacity for supporting bonds of trust and attachment, and more nebulous qualities like love – can be dismissed by its critics (Bishop, 2006) as simply "feel good" leisure activities which "[neutralize] the capacity of critical reflection" (Jackson, 2011, p. 47). Or worse, "do good" activities which "risk becoming overly instrumentalized, banalizing the formal complexities and interrogative possibilities of art under the homogenizing umbrella of a social goal" (p. 47). In this case, the greater risk is that the real power of music becomes subverted into a pale shadow of its full potential, a proxy for people's actual rights as human beings, and simply a return to a more instrumentalized version of the all-too-familiar "social impact of the arts" paradox – as Claire Bishop expresses it in an interview with Jennifer Roche – "a cost-effective way of justifying public spending on the arts while diverting attention away from the structural causes of decreased social participation, which are political and economic (welfare, transport, education, healthcare, etc.)" (Roche, 2006).

For musicking to be radical and progressive, we cannot let it simply become a means of *coping* with the privations of living in the attenuated conditions of late capitalism, climate emergency, and the pandemic age. In order to fully harness music's capacity for social change and human potential, we need to continue to resist the ideological drive to co-opt "everyday creativity" (Hunter et al., 2016) into another part of the life-support system for an economic order that is already past its sell-by date. Instead, we have to believe that it gives us a glimpse into the "universe next door" into which we might *change* our present reality. In this way, we might consider it to be a political and dissensual act of "re-humanization" – "a division inserted in [the] 'common sense'" of the neoliberal consensus (Ranciere, 2003, p. 69), which "suggests possibilities for exchanges other than those that prevail within the system" (Bourriaud, 1998, p. 16). Literally, "singing the rights we do not possess" will help us to re-establish our humanity as we navigate an uncertain future as a dominant species co-existing on a fragile planet (Camlin, 2017).

Ultimately, we need to view our musicality as a uniquely human characteristic that we can put to service as part of our evolution beyond the constraints of the current political orthodoxy of nation states, and which will support our emergence as a global species, able to transcend the geographical, cultural, religious, political, and physical boundaries that continually threaten to divide us. We need to view our musicality as something which helps us to retain that precious quality which makes us unique as a species – our common humanity, and our capacity for empathy and love.

Bibliography

Aiello, L., & Dunbar, R. (1993). Neocortex size, group size, and the evolution of language. *Current Anthropology*, *34*(2), 184–193. <https://doi.org/10.1086/204160>

Altenmuller, E., & Schlaug, G. (2013). Music, brain and health: Exploring biological foundations of music's health effects. In R. MacDonald, L. Mitchell, & G. Kreutz (Eds.), *Music, health and wellbeing* (pp. 532–941). Oxford University Press.

Arendt, H. (1977). *The human condition* (M. Canovan, Trans.). University of Chicago Press.

Barenboim, D. (2009). *Everything is connected: The power of music.* Phoenix.

Bernatzky, G., Strickner, S., Michaela, P., Franz, W., & Kullich, W. (2013). Music as non-pharmacological pain management in clinics. In R. MacDonald, L. Mitchell, & G. Kreutz (Eds.), *Music, health and wellbeing* (pp. 257–275). Oxford University Press.

Bishop, C. (2006). The social turn: Collaboration and its discontents. *Artforum*, 179–185.

Bithell, C. (2014). *A different voice, a different song: Reclaiming community through the natural voice and world song.* Oxford University Press.

Bourdieu, P. (1977). *Outline of a theory of practice* (J. Goody, Ed.; R. Nice, Trans.). Cambridge University Press.

Bourriaud, N. (1998). *Relational aesthetics.* Les Presse Du Reel.

Bowlby, E. J. M. (1969). *Attachment and loss: Vol. 1. Attachment* (Rev. ed.). Vintage Digital.

Bowlby, E. J. M. (1973). *Attachment and loss: Vol. 2. Separation: Anxiety and anger.* Vintage Digital.

Bowlby, E. J. M. (1980). *Attachment and loss: Vol. 3. Loss: sadness and depression.* Vintage Digital.

Camlin, D. A. (2017). Singing the rights we do not possess. In A. Banffy-Hall & B. Hill (Eds.), *Community music: Beitrage zur theorie und praxis aus internationaler und Deutscher perspektive* (pp. 137–148). Waxmann.

Camlin, D. A., Daffern, H., & Zeserson, K. (2020). Group singing as a resource for the development of healthy publics. *Nature.* <https://doi.org/10.1057/s41599-020-00549-0>

Camlin, D. A. (2021). Encounters with participatory music: In M. Dogantan-Dack (Ed.), *The chamber musician in the 21st century.* Oxford University Press.

Camlin, D. A. (2021). Organisational dynamics in community ensembles. In H. Daffern, F. Bailes, & R. Timmers (Eds.), *Together in music.* Oxford University Press.

Caruso, G., & Flanagan, O. (Eds.). (2018). *Neuroexistentialism: Meaning, morals, and purpose in the age of neuroscience.* Oxford University Press.

Clayton, M., Will, U., & Sager, R. (2004). In time with the music – The concept of entrainment and its significance for ethnomusicology. *ESEM CounterPoint*, *1*, 1–84.

Crawford, P., Lewis, L., Brown, B., & Manning, N. (2013). Creative practice as mutual recovery in mental health. *Mental Health Review Journal*, *18*(2), 55–64. <https://doi.org/10.1108/MHRJ-11-2012-0031>

Cross, I., & Woodruff, G. E. (2009). Music as a communicative medium. In R. Botha & C. Knight (Eds.), *The prehistory of language* (Vol. 1, pp. 113–144). Oxford University Press.

DeNora, T. (2000). *Music in everyday life*. Cambridge University Press.

Diamond, J. (2013). *The world until yesterday: What can we learn from traditional societies?* Allen Lane.

Dunbar, P. R. (2013). *The science of love and betrayal*. Faber & Faber.

Dunbar, R. (2012). On the evolutionary function of song and dance. In N. Bannon (Ed.), *Music, language and human evolution* (pp. 201–214). Oxford University Press.

Elliott, D. J. (1995). *Music matters: A new philosophy of music education*. Oxford University Press.

Fancourt, D., Perkins, R., Ascenso, S., Carvalho, L. A., Steptoe, A., & Williamon, A. (2016). Effects of group drumming interventions on anxiety, depression, social resilience and inflammatory immune response among mental health service users. *PLoS One*, *11*(3), Article e0151136. <https://doi.org/10.1371/journal.pone.0151136>

Fancourt, D., Williamon, A., Carvalho, L. A., Steptoe, A., Dow, R., & Lewis, I. (2016). Singing modulates mood, stress, cortisol, cytokine and neuropeptide activity in cancer patients and carers. *Ecancer*, *10*(631). <https://doi.org/10.3332/ecancer.2016.631>

Frankl, V. E. (1946). *Man's search for meaning: The classic tribute to hope from the holocaust* (New ed.). Rider.

Gabrielsson, A. (2011). *Strong experiences with music: Music is much more than just music*. Oxford University Press.

Hayles, K. (1999). *How we became posthuman*. University of Chicago Press.

Hinchliffe, S., Jackson, M. A., Wyatt, K., Barlow, A. E., Barreto, M., Clare, L., Depledge, M. H., Durie, R., Fleming, L. E., Groom, N., Morrissey, K., Salisbury, L., & Thomas, F. (2018). Healthy publics: Enabling cultures and environments for health. *Palgrave Communications*, *4*(1), 57. <https://doi.org/10.1057/s41599-018-0113-9>

Hunter, J., Micklem, D., & 64 Million Artists. (2016). *Everyday creativity*. 64 Million Artists. <http://64millionartists.com/everyday-creativity-2/>

Jackson, S. (2011). *Social works: Performing art, supporting publics* (1st ed.). Routledge.

Juslin, P. N., & Sloboda, J. (Eds.). (2011). *Handbook of music and emotion: Theory, research, applications* (Reprint ed.). Oxford University Press.

Koelsch, S., & Stegemann, T. (2013). The brain and positive biological effects in healthy and clinical populations. In R. MacDonald, L. Mitchell, & G. Kreutz (Eds.), *Music, health and wellbeing* (pp. 436–456). Oxford University Press.

Kreutz, G., Quiroga Murcia, C., & Bongard, S. (2013). Psychoneuroendocrine research on music and health: An overview. In R. MacDonald, L. Mitchell, & G. Kreutz (Eds.), *Music, health and wellbeing* (pp. 457–476). Oxford University Press.

Lamont, A. (2011). University students' strong experiences of music: Pleasure, engagement, and meaning. *Musicae Scientiae, 15*(2), 229–249.

Lewis, T., Amini, F., & Lannon, R. (2001). *A general theory of love* (Reprint). Vintage Books.

Macdonald, K., & Macdonald, T.-M. (2010). The peptide that binds: A systematic review of oxytocin and its prosocial effects in humans. *Harvard Review of Psychiatry, 18*(1), 1–21. <https://doi.org/10.3109/10673220903523615>

Malloch, S., & Trevarthen, C. (2010). *Communicative musicality: Exploring the basis of human companionship*. Oxford University Press.

Maslow, A. H. (1943). *A theory of human motivation*. Wilder Publications.

Mason, P. (2019). *Clear bright future: A radical defence of the human being*. Allen Lane.

Mithen, S. (2007). *The singing neanderthals: The origins of music, language, mind, and body*. Harvard University Press.

Molnar-Szakacs, I., & Overy, K. (2006). Music and mirror neurons: From motion to 'e'motion. *Social Cognitive and Affective Neuroscience, 1*(3), 235–241. <https://doi.org/10.1093/scan/nsl029>

National Trust. (n.d.). Songs on the summits 1918–2018. *National Trust*. Retrieved March 14, 2018, from <https://www.nationaltrust.org.uk/borrowdale-and-derwent-water/features/songs-on-the-summits-1918-2018>

NICE. (2015). *Older people: Independence and mental wellbeing* (Guidelines No. NG32; NICE guidelines). National Institute for Health and Care Excellence. <http://www.nice.org.uk/guidance/ng32/resources/older-people-independence-and-mental-wellbeing-1837389003973>

Pavlicevic, M. (2013a). Between beats: Group music therapy transforming people and places. In R. MacDonald, G. Kreutz, & L. Mitchell (Eds.), *Music health and wellbeing* (pp. 196–212). Oxford University Press.

Pavlicevic, M. (2013b). Let the music work: Optimal moments of collaborative musicing. In B. Stige, G. Ansdell, C. Elefant, & M. Pavlicevic (Eds.), *Where music helps* (pp. 100–123). Ashgate.

Pinker, S. (2003). *How the mind works* (1st ed.). W. W. Norton & Company.

Putnam, R. (2001). *Bowling alone: The collapse and revival of American community* (New ed.). Simon & Schuster Ltd.

Ranciere, J. (2003). *Dissensus: On politics and aesthetics*. Bloomsbury Academic.

Roche, J. (2006). *Socially engaged art, critics and discontents: An interview with Claire Bishop*. American Community Arts Network. <https://contextualpractice.files.wordpress.com/2011/08/bishopinterview.pdf>

Rogers, C. (1951). *Client centred therapy: Its current practice, implications and theory* (New ed.). Constable.

Rogers, C. (1961). *On becoming a person* (New ed.). Constable.

Roser, M., Ritchie, H., & Ortiz-Ospina, E. (2013). World population growth. *Our World in Data*. <https://ourworldindata.org/world-population-growth>

Salimpoor, V., Benovoy, M., Larcher, K., Dagher, A., & Zattore, R. (2011). Anatomically distinct dopamine release during anticipation and experience of peak emotion to music. *Nature Neuroscience, 14*(2), 257–262. <https://doi.org/10.1038/nn.2726>

Siegel, D. (2011). *Mindsight: Transform your brain with the new science of kindness.* Oneworld Publications.

Silverman, M. (2012). Community music and social justice: Reclaiming love. In G. McPherson & G. Welch (Eds.), *Oxford handbook of music education* (Vol. 2, pp. 155–167). Oxford University Press.

Sloboda, J. (2004). *Exploring the musical mind: Cognition, emotion, ability, function* (1st ed., Later Printing). Oxford University Press.

Small, C. (1998). *Musicking: The meanings of performing and listening.* Wesleyan University Press.

Snowden, D. (n.d.). SenseMaker®. Cognitive Edge. Retrieved December 1, 2016, from <http://cognitive-edge.com/sensemaker/>

Tarr, B., Launay, J., & Dunbar, R. (2014). Music and social bonding: "Self-other" merging and neurohormonal mechanisms. *Frontiers in Psychology, 5*(1096). <https://doi.org/10.3389/fpsyg.2014.01096>

Thunberg, G. (2019). *Our house is on fire.* World Economic Forum, Davos.

Tomasello, M. (2019). *Becoming human: A theory of ontogeny.* Harvard University Press.

Turino, T. (2008). *Music as social life: the politics of participation.* University of Chicago Press.

Turner, E. (2012). *Communitas: The anthropology of collective joy.* Palgrave Macmillan.

Twenge, J. (2017). *Igen: Why today's super-connected kids are growing up less rebellious, more tolerant, less happy – and completely unprepared for adulthood – and what that means for the rest of us.* Atria Books.

UN Environment Programme. (2020). *Preventing the next pandemic – Zoonotic diseases and how to break the chain of transmission.* <http://www.unenvironment.org/resources/report/preventing-future-zoonotic-disease-outbreaks-protecting-environment-animals-and>

United Nations. (1948). *Universal declaration of human rights.* <http://www.un.org/en/universal-declaration-human-rights/>

Västfjäll, D., Juslin, P. N., & Hartig, T. (2013). Music, subjective wellbeing, and health: The role of everyday emotions. In R. Macdonald, G. Kreutz, & L. Mitchell (Eds.), *Music, health and wellbeing* (pp. 405–423). Oxford University Press.

Interlude 5

This Holy Adventure

A Meditation in Loving Memory of Paul Robertson

It was with a shock of sadness, though not with any surprise, that I learned in Summer 2016 of Paul Robertson's death. However, the paramount feeling was of immense gratitude and appreciation for ways in which he impacted my life – and indeed the Soul-Voyagers Network – during the last two years of his life.[54] Paul was a world-famous violinist, leader for over forty years of the Medici Quartet, one of the most respected ensembles of his generation. But he also had a deep interest in non-ordinary states of consciousness and the power of music to enable progressive access to transpersonal realms.

I first encountered him in the magical environs of Tintern, when he was the chief presenter at a Scientific and Medical Network event which culminated in a superb concert under the stars at Tintern Abbey. The program included music by Tavener, Pärt, Gorecki and Britten, and culminated in a performance of *Towards Silence*, the Near-Death-Experience-inspired piece, written by Sir John Tavener for Paul, and with Paul and the Medici Quartet specifically in mind as leading performers. The piece grew out of Sir John and Paul's deep interest in altered states of consciousness – including the transforming potential of the death experience, of which they both

---

54   The Soul-Voyagers Network is open to all those working in transpersonal fields who would like to deepen their experience and practice by connecting with like-minded others. It seeks to expand and promote the deep healing facilitated by regression, holotropic breathwork, ancestral and constellation work, psychodrama, bodywork, shamanism, and other transpersonal therapies and spiritual paths.

would *later* have personal experience. Quite remarkable synchronicities – The Divine does indeed have an exquisitely ironical sense of humor!

I was greatly taken, not only with the profundity of the experience communicated, but also by the lightness of touch, the humor, and the ego-puncturing self-deprecation Paul demonstrated as he shared his experiences with us. He also generously offered concessionary tickets for another imminent concert. It was to take place at the Westminster Synagogue, specifically to promote peace in the Middle East, with music by Mozart and Beethoven, but with pride of place given to the UK premiere of Sir John Tavener's final work, *Scatter Roses Over My Tears*, composed for Paul and the Medici. Only recently following its world premiere by them in Austria, this was a most moving occasion – "Scatter roses over my tears" is a quotation from a poem by Rumi, and it was read in Farsi by a woman in full Islamic dress – right there in the heart of the synagogue! – and in a week of July 2014 when Palestinian children were being bombed on a beach in Gaza. There has to be another way – and this concert was demonstrating it.

Those who were at the Soul-Voyagers Retreat last year will appreciate how influential these experiences were on our program. Bold as it was, I wrote to Paul and his wife, Chika, who jointly directed the Music Mind Spirit Trust, to ask if they would consider being guest presenters at our retreat – and they accepted! So "Healing in the Middle East" became our theme, leading to wonderful inclusions of guitarist Sam Muir playing *Chant* by Sir John Tavener, and Sama Mara demonstrating his Islamic take on "what music would look like if you could see it" – a melding of Jewish, Christian, and Islamic influences into one rich and satisfying whole. Not only that but, because Chika is Japanese, we incorporated a healing flame of love and forgiveness directly from Hiroshima into our rituals, complete with Japanese ancestral music.

Since then, I have had two opportunities to encounter Paul and Chika again. I learned with delight that Paul was to introduce *Towards Silence* again – this time in my hometown – at the Sherborne Abbey Festival in early May. They arrived on time to attend Sam's guitar recital, also part of the Festival, and we were shocked to see how very ill he looked after the journey from Surrey. But by the next day he had rallied, and gave, as ever, a delightful and self-possessed performance. It was a great pleasure, at lunch afterwards, to be able to introduce Paul to my husband, Richard, also a musician of note. They struck up an instant rapport and I know they would have got on famously had they had an opportunity to get to know one another better. In a future life perhaps?

As our retreat approached last year, Paul was in such a precarious state of health that right up to the last moment it was uncertain whether he would actually be able to come. I therefore enlisted the help of some notable distant healers amongst our Network and – coincidence or not (?!) – Paul was able, not only to be with us, but to talk and play with inspired energy.

After seeing his frail state of health at the Sherborne event, I contacted Sharon Mehdi and Pam again to enlist further support, saying:

> He is now faced with two events that will tax his strength and energy so he could do with maximum support. On Sat 4th June, he is to give a lecture in the Wigmore Hall in London about the strains and stresses of ensemble playing (and the Medici Quartet will be giving its, most likely, very final performance) and, in the Autumn he very much hopes to be still around for the publication of his book *Soundscapes*. When we spoke this week he felt he was rather unlikely to make both events – but can we make our very best efforts to ensure that he does?

Pauline Compton-Tough, who had attended the Sherborne event with me, completed the healing quartet at this time. Sharon responded immediately:

> His energy is huge and pure. I can feel it from here … The magic and wonder of music is that it never dies. Every note Paul has ever played will play unto eternity. I am so honored to be loving Paul and Chika along with you. It's the only "healing" they, or any of us, truly needs. Thank you, dear friend, for letting me be part of this holy adventure.

Paul's lecture at the Wigmore Hall was, indeed, a great success. It was called "Cavatina: The Inner Life of Ensemble," where he offered his perspective on the inner workings and emotional dynamics of ensemble playing. He was wearing no rose-colored spectacles; he said that it was a huge challenge because of the intense emotional ambivalences the players experience with the music, and occasionally between themselves – but when it does work it makes all the striving worthwhile – as in the transcendental

Medici experience of *really* playing Beethoven's "Cavatina" – of which he spoke with tears in his eyes.

He had come full circle, returning "home" to the Wigmore Hall, the scene of many triumphs in his professional career, and surrounded by the other members of the Medici Quartet who had traveled from various ends of the earth to be there with him.

When I reported on the success of his lecture to Sharon and asked if we could continue to send healing until his book was published, she responded: "Of course I will continue sending healing love to Paul and Chika. As always, it is an honor. His light keeps getting brighter and brighter. It's quite thrilling. He appears to be living in two dimensions, if not simultaneously, sequentially and at will. What his physicality lacks right now is more than made up for by the purity of light he carries."

As ever, Paul was more than skeptical about the "purity" of his "light!" But he did send this most appreciative email to us (although he was unaware at that point of Pauline's involvement):

> Dearest Jen, Pam and Sharon,
>
> Blessings upon you for your wonderful prayers, insight and goodwill.
>
> I must tell you that I do indeed feel as prepared as possible to leave – in fact impatient to do so.
>
> However, I imagine this impatience is a sign that there are still things to complete.
>
> I can hardly tell you how grateful I am for your spiritual support –believe me I will need all the help I can to stand a chance of making it to a final safe haven. Would it were not so.
>
> If there are others you know of who are sharing and creating this golden web for me please thank them from the bottom of my being.
>
> Much love and gratitude,
>
> Paul
>
> After all: "We are the Music, whilst the music lasts." (T. S. Eliot)

And to this perfect final communication, Sharon responded equally perfectly:

Not to worry, precious one, that safe haven is ready and waiting. No judgement, just joy. Love is all there is. Everything else is just illusion. All the illusions you have known and loved will disappear like the nothingness they are and voilà! – HOME.

So Paul did not stay in his increasingly frail and uncomfortable body until his book appeared. *Soundscapes: A Musician's Journey through Life and Death* was published on September 1, 2016. Do buy it if you would like to hear his voice again.

In a moving interview he was able to give to Christina Patterson, a *Sunday Times* journalist, in June, he whispered, "My only hope is to be able to leave the world with the lightness of a small bird."

I feel confident that his wish will have been granted.

Bless you, Paul, for all your wonderful legacies to us.

P.S. When I shared the draft of the above with Chika, feeling it should not be shared, even with Soul-Voyagers, without her permission, she sent the following reply:

Paul did, in actual fact, leave this world with the lightness of a bird! His final tortured breath was replaced by a long peaceful breath at exactly the same moment as *Towards Silence* ended, simultaneously as our daughter Calista finished reading from three cards she had written to Paul over the years. Within the sudden still and peaceful atmosphere (I hardly dared breathe!), a blackbird suddenly swooped down to the French doors and sang a most heavenly song as the sun continued to rise. It flew away and the children laughed, as it had been such an utterly charming and unexpected display. As you will see in the book, Paul's wish was to die to the sound of birdsong and children's laughter – which he did. I'm sure it will be of no surprise to you that he had, indeed, scripted his own perfect passing!

I had a wonderful sensation that I was receiving a message on the ninth and tenth mornings after his death. He was very excited, ecstatic even, and wanted me to know that he had arrived safely and that it was "more beautiful than anyone could possibly imagine."

This afternoon I noticed there was something on my bed. I walked up to it and was amazed to find a lovely, glossy dark feather … perhaps off a blackbird? There were rays of light dancing from an angel-shaped form onto the bed. In between this light and the feather were diamond-shaped rays of flashing sunlight. I'm not even sure how a bird would have gotten into the room to leave a feather …

When I contacted her, yet again, to ask if this could be shared, she added:

> Thank you – I would be honored and grateful if you would like to pass on any messages from Paul, via us, to fellow friends and dear, kindred spirits at Soul-Voyagers. I should add that his initial message began with, "I am safely ensconced!"

I also wanted to thank and let the Quartet of Healers know, as well, that Sharon's words were very comforting to Paul and our family while caring for him. He was, indeed, inhabiting both domains and his light *was* becoming purer and brighter. I still can't work out how a bird would have gotten into the bedroom to leave a feather …

As a final P.S. you might like to know that, although it could not actually *explain* how a blackbird feather might have made its way onto Chika's pillow, she was greatly comforted when I was able to tell her that Blackbird, in Druid/Celtic shamanic mythology, is the Gateway bird to the Otherworld.

Bibliography

Robertson, P. (2016). *Soundscapes: A musician's journey through life and death*. Faber & Faber.

17 Re-Imagining Ritual, Creating Communitas

This study, stemming from my professional practice as a community musician, explores the relationship between the rituality of the one-off participatory care home concert and the social wellbeing these performances intend to improve. In such concerts, I often felt something missing. I was too afraid of being patronizing to truly engage residents as active participants, too nervous to experiment with ideas, and too shy to talk freely to participants. In short, my performances were just that: performances. A feeling of "us and them" or "I-It" (Buber, 2019/1958) developed that made mutual musical vulnerability impossible and authentic connection rare. Both audience and performer longed for more, to be drawn into the power of an I–Thou relationship:

> As experience, the world belongs to the primary word *I–It*. The primary word *I-Thou* establishes the world of relation. [...] I do not experience the man to whom I say *Thou*. But I take my stand in relation to him, in the sanctity of the primary word. (Buber, 2019/1958, pp. 5, 7)

In this chapter, I explore the concept of communitas to articulate what was missing in these participatory concerts. Communitas is an intense bond formed between passengers in a rite of passage. It emerges within a liminal space, the central, transitionary phase of such rites, where socio-cultural classifications or hierarchies from the previous or coming states cease to apply (V. Turner, 1969). It has since been identified in a wide variety of settings: festivals and sport (E. Turner, 2012), raves (Rill, 2006), and times of disaster or revolution (E. Turner, 2012). The exact requirements for communitas remain elusive, though Turner (2012) explores its probable optimal conditions, of which one is a musical event.

In my search for its optimal conditions within the context of a one-off participatory care home concert I engage with Ronald Grimes' (2010) notion of ritual criticism, and his seven steps to reinventing ritual: attending, imagining, studying, inventing, improvising, evaluating, and reinventing (Grimes, 2000, p. 83). With prior personal experience of attending concerts, community music projects, and Christian services, this chapter begins by studying the potential health benefits of an interdisciplinary approach to community music. I then dissect the concert experience, comparing it with the Christian Eucharist, a ritual in which the significance of liminality is prominent, to understand pre-existing ritual expectations of participants. In this analysis I identify three key issues: musicians as outsiders, the performer-audience hierarchy, and the lack of transitionary space.

The chapter concludes with a participatory concert model optimized for the creation of a liminal space, and therefore communitas, centered on two overlapping rites of initiation. First, the musicians are initiated into the community of the residents, before the residents are initiated into the community of musickers. This leads to a novel and important liminal phase that I have coined the post-preliminal crossfade. It is my hope that this model will serve early-career community musicians, as well as those more experienced who may have lapsed into routine. The model draws specifically on seven sessions in homes around Shropshire and the West Midlands, between January and March 2020, in which versions of the model were explored.

Studying

The positive relationship between engagement with music and increased wellbeing is well documented (MacDonald et al., 2013; Paton, 2012; Smith, 2002). Similarly, it is well known that older people are particularly vulnerable to social isolation or loneliness (Windle et al., 2011) and that this can have a detrimental effect on health (Courtin & Knapp, 2017). This supports the view of health as a relational phenomenon, not simply located within an individual but equally in the "quality of the interaction and activity that humans engage in" (Stige, 2004, p. 96). In entering into communitas with others, participants are engaging with both the music and each other more fully (E. Turner, 2012, p. 3), thus enjoying the social and health benefits of participation to their fullest. These benefits are likely to be longer lasting if communitas is achieved: "The benefits of communitas are quick understanding, easy mutual help, and long-term ties with others" (E. Turner, 2012, p. 3).

Many scholars have also drawn connections between liminality, communitas, and music, illustrating its usefulness in relation to music and wellbeing. Evan Ruud (1998) first introduced the concept into the field of music therapy in relation to improvisation and it has since become a cornerstone of the community music therapy movement as both a means and an end (Pavlicevic & Ansdell, 2004). Furthermore, Edith Turner (2012) notes that music is a "fail-safe bearer of communitas" (p. 43), and connects with the theory of communicative musicality (Malloch & Trevarthen, 2009). It is this engagement with one's intrinsic communicative musicality that allows for the unspoken intersubjectivity of communitas to arise.

However, the optimal conditions for communitas within a musical context are under-researched. Frequently, the feeling and transformative effects of communitas are better documented than the process of getting there. The sense of oneness, the "essential We" (Buber, 1961, p. 214), can be so strong that the focus lies in what happens within this space, and its effects going forward. Communitas is ephemeral: "It comes unexpectedly, like the wind" (E. Turner, 2012, p. 3). This means that it is impossible to define and formulate, but should not dissuade us from seeking it out.

Some authors have made steps to seeking out the optimal conditions for communitas within a musical context. Most notably, June Boyce-Tillman (2009) argues for the transformative possibilities of a liminal space created through musicking, and how such a space may be accessed. Her identification of the four domains of musical experience (Expression, Values, Construction, and Materials) and how these must be engaged by the musicker, provide a framework for creating a fully immersive, musical, liminal space:

- Expression is "concerned with the evocation of mood, emotion (individual or corporate), images, memories, and atmosphere on the part of all those involved in the musical performance" (Boyce-Tillman, 2009, p. 186).

- Values contextualize a musical event against socio-cultural standards and hierarchies both on a macro level (the particular event within a culture) and a micro level (a musical moment within the event).
- Construction describes the constitution of the musical work. In Western classical tradition, concepts such as form and motivic development would be found within this domain.
- Materials refers to the physical apparatus (drawn from both the environment and body) that creates the musical performance (pp. 186–187).

Boyce-Tillman (2009) argues that to fully engage with each of the four domains of the musical experience is to access a transformative liminal space. In encountering each domain, the musicker is drawn into a state of flow between themselves and the "otherness" of the music (p. 185). The practical application of these domains as relating to my duo "Filkin's Drift" is discussed later in the chapter, but first it is important to understand the ritual expectations of the participant in a care home concert.

Concert as Ritual

When live music is brought to a care home, residents are often anticipating a performance. They may not be expecting to join in and certainly won't be seeking communitas in those specific terms. How, then, can a musician meet these expectations while gently encouraging them to enjoy a fuller participatory experience? First, I consider pre-existing expectations surrounding public performances and identify key areas in which the participatory care home concert differs from this template. I compare this with the Christian Eucharist, where the significance of liminality is prominent, to illuminate further ritual expectations and alternative practices.

Christopher Small, in his examination of the concert space, identifies it as "sacred" (Small, 1998, p. 24). Furthermore, without using the term, he identifies many ritual stages of the concert. Upon arriving at any venue, the first things that one attunes to are social groupings: "Will my friends be there already?" or "I hope they haven't gone in without me" Then there is the importance of the foyer as a "transitional space" (p. 22), a space that separates us from our everyday lives. Here, the concert is primarily a social experience where a distinction can be made between those "who are privy to [the concert's] rituals, and those who are not" (p. 23). Less-frequent attendees may behave more self-consciously and quietly, while experienced concertgoers display behaviors that signal relaxation and ease with the occasion.

Small also writes of the ritualized behavioral manners undertaken in the auditorium: "If the foyer was a place for socializing, this is strictly a place for looking, listening and paying attention" (p. 26). Indeed, the spatial design encourages these behaviors: "Since all the seats face in the same direction, we can talk only to our neighbors in the same row" (p. 26). Our attention is directed to the stage and away from our social group. We may continue to talk quietly for a time, but once the lights go down, signaling the start of the performance, a complete hush falls on the auditorium.

The participatory care home concert is a much different experience. There is no sense of arrival at a different venue surrounded by strangers. The residents may have been seated in the performance space for a number of hours already that day, meaning no spatial separation between listening and socializing. Many homes arrange furniture to draw attention to a central space, but this is not a given, and there are often some participants facing away. There can be no clear way to distinguish the beginning or end of a performance (such as the dimming or raising of the lights) and residents and staff may come and go throughout, disturbing the ritual.

Boyce-Tillman (2019) notes how certain aspects of the concert ritual can be found within a church service. The rows of chairs in a concert, directing attention to the stage and away from neighbors, bears much relation to pews found in most Christian churches, where attention is drawn to the front where the altar, pulpit, and lectern are positioned. The program is the order of service, and the musicians wear a costume to distinguish them from the audience much like clerical robes (Boyce-Tillman, 2019, p. 50). In addition, there is often a social, transitionary space before and after the service helping to separate the ritual from the everyday.

In all of these settings the key issue is the performer and audience dynamic. In concerts, the sanctity of the musical object, particularly but not exclusively within the field of Western classical music, can produce a hierarchy, or as Small (1998) calls it a one-way "flowchart of communication" (p. 6): composer, performer, and audience. What this omits is feedback from listener to performer, and engagement from listener to listener (p. 6). This dynamic can arise particularly within a care home context where the musicians are outsiders to the situation, not privy to the rituals of the home in question.

However, there are many moments when participation is invited in the Eucharist, and herein lies the key difference: In the Eucharist, the congregation will engage in liturgy, sung hymns, and the consuming of Holy Communion. In a Western classical concert, the audience contributes their applause at the end of each work, but this is all. Indeed, in treating the music itself as an object, both performer and audience member are treating the other as such and are entered into an I–It relationship (Buber, 2019/1958) not the I–Thou of communitas that is desired.

The above analysis of the concert experience identifies three main problems in seeking communitas within the care home context. The first is that the musicians are outsiders to the situation and may be treated warily. The second is the assumed audience and performer hierarchy, exaggerated by the outsider relationship. Third, the lack of transitionary space gives no spatial separation between socializing and listening and no clear signal for the performance to begin. With these ritual expectations considered, I now turn to the reinvention of the care home concert ritual, tackling these three issues, and creating a fully participatory concert experience.

Inventing

When turning this theory into a practical model I pay careful attention to two main areas: the social/transitionary space, and the concert itself. When discussing the social/transitionary space, I will primarily be dealing with the issue of musicians as outsiders, and begin to address the audience–performer dynamic. The musical event then aims to strengthen the bond between musickers and to eradicate the us–them, I–It relationship as far as possible. This is largely based on Boyce-Tillman's (2009) theory of the four domains of musical experience. In both sections I draw upon Grimes's (2000) writing on initiation rites, viewing the experience as two overlapping rites. First, the musicians are initiated into the community of the care home; then, the residents are initiated into the community of musickers.

In presenting this model I will be employing a version of Arnold van Gennep's (1960) tripartite model of liminality. On a macro scale, the model can be seen as a single, overarching rite with three phases: separation (preliminal), transition (liminal), and incorporation (postliminal), relating to entrance and introductions, musical event, and exit and goodbyes, respectively. However, I also argue for a period of intense liminality within the musical event itself, and for viewing introductions and goodbyes as their own rites. This leads to an overlapping of rites in what I have coined a post-preliminal crossfade, described below. Table 17.1 shows how the macro and micro ritual models align and overlap.

In dealing with the macro preliminal phase, the entrance and introductions, the musicians as outsiders is the main issue to overcome. At this stage, it is the musicians' aim to be accepted into the community of residents before the musicking begins. The concept of initiation rites resonated with this notion. Initiation rites indicate a change in social status (Grimes, 2000, p. 103) and normally refers to a change in age (child to adolescent; adult

Table 17.1. Overlapping Ritual Processes

Macro Liminal Phase	Micro Liminal Phase	Description
Preliminal	Preliminal	Entrance
	Liminal	Introductions
Liminal	Post-preliminal crossfade	Music begins
	Intense liminality	Participation introduced
	Post-preliminal crossfade	Participatory musicking
Postliminal	Liminal	Goodbyes
	Postliminal	Exit

to elder) but in this case the change is either from stranger to co-musicker, or non-musician to musicker. Grimes lists a number of component parts found in many initiation rites from around the world. Some would be inappropriate in the present context, ("being hazed, subjected to painful or unpleasant treatment") while others ("showing respect, displaying subservience or obedience") (p. 106), form an important part of the model that follows.

First, the musicians go through the necessary rites of separation (micro preliminal) consisting of meeting staff members, signing in, and washing hands. This shows respect and builds trust with both residents and staff and is an essential part of being accepted into the community. The musicians are then shown to the performance space where the micro liminal rites begin. Here, they are strangers entering someone's home. The performance space is often a communal living area meaning displays of respect and obedience to the residents are vital. Entering the room as a concert hall or an audition room misjudges the real social dynamic of the situation. This can lead to a sense of distance from residents, either through annoyance at their loud and brash presentation, or through apathy at a timid entrance, fearing judgment. In either case, an "I–It" dynamic may be established from the outset.

Instead, the musicians should enter the room as though meeting a new family, taking the time to meet every individual and learn as many names as possible before setting up. Every individual will have a different way of engaging with new people: Some may be uncomfortable with physical or even eye contact, whereas others will approach immediately to shake hands. It is important to let the resident lead, and to match their greeting. The musicians are strangers in this territory and that must be acknowledged in the preliminal phase. I began to improvise with the ritual here and found some good opening questions: Have you lived here long? Where are you from originally? Do you play an instrument? What sort of music do you listen to? This macro preliminal stage can be particularly challenging because musicians are often entering a situation in which a strong sense of community already exists. However, if the introductions are managed carefully, the optimal conditions for communitas begin to appear.

Once every resident has been greeted, it is necessary to turn to the performance space. Many residents may have been in the space for some hours that day, which may be a barrier to the alternative, transitionary space necessary to achieve communitas. However, familiarity with the space can lead to a more relaxed atmosphere among participants, who are then more willing to engage with the musicians. Furthermore, with a number of small changes, the space can become quite transformed.

First, the layout of seating is significant. This is where the layout differs from both the concert hall and the church. In these layouts, rows divide the community into subgroups and the hierarchical relationship between audience and performer or congregation and clergy is emphasized. Instead, the chairs of a care home concert should draw attention to the central space (as in church pews) but not separate and restrict engagement between participants through numerous rows. There should also be room for the musicians to move around the room and engage with each participant individually.

A final aspect of room layout that can transform the space from the everyday is what I call the percussion altar. This is a surface with an attractive cloth cover on which the musicians display an array of participatory instruments. The addition of a new and different item of furniture at a focal point of the space signals that something out of the ordinary is about to take place, giving a sense of occasion. It also indicates the significance of these instruments so that their use in the musical event becomes a special moment, not an afterthought.

Grimes (2000) argues that van Gennep's tripartite model of rites of passage has its problems (pp. 105–107). It can both over-simplify and over-complicate a ritual passage. Indeed, in the present context I believe a new liminal phase appears. In an introductory rite the musicians go through a period of separation from the old world (preliminal) and begins to transition into a new community with the residents of the home (liminal). However, the final incorporation into this community (postliminal) only occurs once the musicking has begun. It is this that consolidates the position and purpose of the musicians in this new group. Simultaneously, the musicking signals the separation from the resident's old world (preliminal). This leads to what I refer to as the post-preliminal crossfade (Figure 17.1).

In this phase, the musicians perform standard repertoire from their genre, setting out who they are as players and people. This has the concurrent

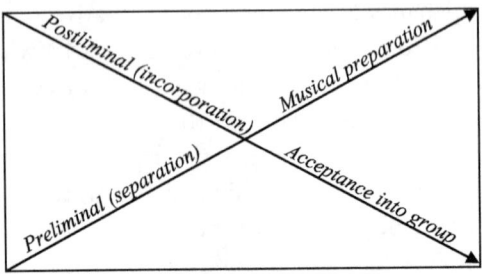

Figure 17.1. Post-preliminal crossfade

effects of establishing the musicians' place within this new community (postliminal/incorporation) while preparing residents to become co-musickers by removing them from their everyday (preliminal/separation).

From this moment, the musicians' aim is to initiate residents into their community of musickers. The next step on this path is to meet the participants where they are musically. In the care home, this often means playing music from the residents' formative years. At present, this includes standards such as "What a Wonderful World" or early Elvis such as "Hound Dog." This helps participants to feel heard and able to participate in a low-pressure situation, laying the foundations for more participation to come. The musicians must also begin to gently encourage the residents to engage with the four domains of musical experience (Boyce-Tillman, 2009). For example, they may exhibit the domain of Expression through phrasing, body language, or storytelling, while encouraging engagement with the domain of Materials (the instruments themselves) by moving into closer proximity to participants, playing softly and intimately.

With this sense of mutual understanding established, it is then possible to move into a period of intense liminality. Here, the musicians must consider ways in which residents may engage more actively with the four domains of musical experience. As an example, I will use a performance of "The Water is Wide" by my folk duo "Filkin's Drift." First, we talk of what the song means to us personally (Values). Then, we encourage engagement with both Expression and Materials by creating a sonic backdrop akin to waves rising and falling by gently rubbing our hands together, making a "shh" sound, and handing out rainsticks and an ocean drum to participants. We use careful instrumentation to distinguish sections (Construction) within the song, that is, an acapella first verse, introducing the guitar second verse and so on. We also ensure that the song has a clear high point and that it builds to this gradually. Not every song will engage with each of the four domains equally, but it is important not to neglect any one domain throughout the concert.

At this point, the participatory instruments may begin to be handed out from the percussion altar. These instruments will have been displayed prominently throughout the concert and therefore be a natural climax to the ritual. Grimes notes that "[b]ecoming acquainted with sacred objects, [...] assuming new responsibilities [...] [and] mastering difficult tasks" is an important part of many initiation rituals. In being entrusted with these important instruments and learning how to use them, the residents are making a vital step in their musical initiation.

Although a liminal space is itself conducive to collaborative forms of leadership, encouraging a non-hierarchical approach from the outset can create, or enhance, liminality (Boyce-Tillman, 2019). For this reason, it is important to include activities in which musickers may conduct or improvise. For example, a participant might use a conductor's baton to control the dynamics and/or tempo of the performance or could lead an antiphonal improvisation with fellow musickers. The equal plane created by this collaborative leadership lays important foundations for the micro postliminal phase in which participants are accepted into our community of musickers.

In this final phase, participants are given instruments and are free to use them as they wish. Little instruction is given, as they are trusted to act appropriately following their initiation into our community. Again, Grimes (2000) notes that "[h]aving one's status elevated; passing through initiatory levels or degrees [and] being allowed access to secrets; gaining access to previously off-limits areas" (p. 106) is common in initiatory rites around the world. Here, the residents are beginning to solidify their position in our musical community and may feel that they have been elevated from audience member to performer. This moment signals the beginning of a post-preliminary crossfade similar to the opening of the concert.

This final phase sees a return to standard repertoire and familiar songs. By this point, every musicker will have an instrument and may be able to join in singing. Here, the residents are accepted into the community of musickers (postliminal/incorporation), as the musicians relinquish some control. By finishing with similar repertoire to the opening, this phase acts as a preliminal rite for the musicians, separating them from the perform-ance itself. Finally, the post-event conversations become the transitionary, liminal phase for the musicians and signing-out incorporates them back into wider society, completing the postliminal phase.

This macro postliminal phase of pack-down and goodbyes, is often easier to negotiate than the preliminal as the musicians and residents have a common experience (the preceding musical event) to discuss. However, although this phase may feel more comfortable, it still requires attention. Before the musicians leave, each resident should be connected with, how-ever briefly, mentioning something musical that they accomplished during the session. This places value upon their contribution, placing them at an equal musical level to the professional musicians, while consolidating their contribution in memory. "[T]elling stories about initiatory experience" (Grimes, 2000, p. 106) is an important final phase of many initiation rites. By recognizing their contribution, they are encouraged to relay their ex-perience to friends or relatives.

By combining the research above with real-world tests, I can present the following model for a participatory performance (Table 17.2). As a base, I found this model conducive to experimenting with activities that I had previously been too nervous to attempt. For example, we incorp-orated conducting and improvisation into the set where we had avoided this in past and found that a more collaborative form of leadership led to a greater sense of freedom both in us and our co-musickers. This feeling of freedom and experimentation enhanced our ability to improvise and alter the plan within the given model. Finally, I felt a much closer connection to our co-musickers both personally and musically than in previous sessions. Each session finished feeling like a community of equal musicians rather than performers and audience.

Table 17.2. Concert Model

Macro Ritual Phase	Micro Ritual Phase	Activity	Description
Preliminal	*Preliminal*	Entry	Sign-in, handwashing, entry to performance space.
	Liminal	Introductions	Speaking to each of the residents. Learning names. Follow-up questions: Have you lived here long? Do you play an instrument? Where are you from originally? This section begins to build trust with participants and allows for easier ongoing interaction.
Liminal	*Post-Preliminal crossfade*	Standard repertoire and familiar songs	Being accepted into their community while setting out who you are as musicians (in genre and personality) and meeting audience members where they are musically with familiar songs. Giving context (Values) and meaning (Expression) is important here.
	Liminal	Participatory and improvised	Gradually increased participation and experimentation including, but not limited to, the following: • Introducing handheld instruments (engaging with Materials) • Conducting and/or improvising with participants (non-hierarchical approach to music-making) • Creating improvised sonic landscapes with particular instruments (e.g., rain sticks/ocean drums for the sea)

(*continued*)

Table 17.2.   Continued

Macro Ritual Phase	Micro Ritual Phase	Activity	Description
	Post-Preliminal crossfade	Standard and familiar repertoire with enhanced participation	Return to familiar songs and standard repertoire. Participants are incorporated and accepted as co-musickers and freely use percussion and voices.
Postliminal	*Liminal*	Goodbyes	Speaking personally to each musicker, acknowledging a particular moment from the event.
	Postliminal	Exit	Sign-out, pack-down and exit.

Evaluation

Through engagement with the notion of ritual criticism (Grimes, 2010), dissecting the concert experience, and aligning with certain areas of the Christian Eucharist and the four domains of musical experience (Boyce-Tillman, 2009), I have reinvented the ritual of the participatory care home concert. This new concert model provides probable optimal conditions for liminality and communitas within the one-off participatory care home concert. Putting the model into practice, I have found it to be conducive to more confident collaborative musicking and an increased social bond between musickers, contrasting greatly with the previously distant performances that I had delivered.

However, the process is ongoing. Further steps to fully verify the model will include interviews and data collection from participants after a session, and to assess whether the model works for musicians in another genre. There may also be gains to be made by looking for inspiration to rituals with which I am less familiar, from different religions or non-Western cultures.

These rituals may project new ideas and practices onto an already firm foundation, helping to keep the model fresh: "Rites are not givens; they are hand-me-downs, quilts we continue to patch" (Grimes, 2000, p. 12).

It is my hope that through seeking out communitas, the present model will allow community musicians to forge deeper connections during their participatory concerts, allow care home residents to form new, long-lasting ties with others, and that both may enjoy improved health as a result. This model simply provides the needle and thread by which others may patch their own meaningful, ever-changing musical quilts.

Bibliography

Aasgaard, T. A. (2004). Pied piper among white coats and infusion pumps: Community music therapy in a paediatric hospital setting. In M. Pavlicevic & G. Ansdell (Eds.), *Community music therapy* (pp. 147–163). Jessica Kingsley Publishers.

Boyce-Tillman, J. (2009). The transformative qualities of a liminal space created by musicking. *Philosophy of Music Education Review, 17*(2), 184–202. <https://doi.org/10.2979/pme.2009.17.2.184>

Boyce-Tillman, J. (2019). The Western audience as congregation. In J. Boyce-Tillman, J. Erricker, & S. Roberts (Eds.), *Enlivening faith* (pp. 45–66). Peter Lang.

Buber, M. (1961). *Between man and man* (R. G. Smith, Trans.). Collins.

Buber, M. (2019). *I and Thou* (2nd ed.). (R. G. Smith, Trans.). Bloomsbury. (Original work published 1958).

Courtin, E., & Knapp, M. (2017). Social isolation, loneliness and health in old age: A scoping review. *Health & Social Care in the Community, 25*(3), 799–812. <https://doi.org/10.1111/hsc.12311>

Grimes, R. L. (2000). *Deeply into the bone: Re-inventing rites of passage.* University of California Press.

Grimes, R. L. (2010). *Ritual criticism: Case studies in its practice, essays on its theory.* Ritual Studies International.

MacDonald, R., Kreutz, G., & Mitchell, L. (Eds.). (2013). *Music, health, and well-being.* Oxford University Press.

Malloch, S., & Trevarthen, C. (Eds.). (2009). *Communicative musicality: Exploring the basis of human companionship.* Oxford University Press.

Paton, R. (2012). *Lifemusic: Connecting people to time*. Archive Publishing.

Pavlicevic, M., & Ansdell, G. (Eds.). (2004). *Community music therapy*. Jessica Kingsley Publishers.

Rill, B. (2006). Rave, communitas, and embodied idealism. *Music Therapy Today, 7*(3), 648–661.

Ruud, E. (1998). *Music therapy: Improvisation, communication and culture*. Barcelona Publishers.

Small, C. (1998). *Musicking: The meanings of performing and listening*. Wesleyan University Press.

Smith, R. (2002). Spend (slightly) less on health and more on the arts: Health would probably be improved. *British Medical Journal, 325*, 1432–1433. <https://doi.org/10.1136/bmj.325.7378.1432>

Stige, B. (2004). Community music therapy: Culture, care and welfare. In M. Pavlicevic & G. Ansdell (Eds.), *Community music therapy* (pp. 147–163). Jessica Kingsley Publishers.

Turner, E. (2012). *Communitas: The anthropology of collective joy*. Springer.

Turner, V. (1969). *The ritual process: Structure and anti-structure*. Aldine.

van Gennep, A. (1960). *The rites of passage*. Routledge.Windle, K., Francis, J., & Coomber, C. (2011). *Preventing loneliness and social isolation: interventions and outcomes* (pp. 1–16). Social Care Institute for Excellence.

TAWNYA D. SMITH

18 Spiraling to Life

Listening and Sounding toward a Life-Sustaining Society

As a music educator deeply concerned about environmental degradation and climate change (IPCC, 2018), I consider the possibility that music engagement might need to serve different purposes in the future than it has in the past during times of relative environmental stability. Although I expect that performed and communal music-making will continue to serve humanity as it has during other times of change, I wonder if our musical skills, sensitivities, and ways of knowing might also be relevant in interdisciplinary efforts to adapt to the changing climate, restore degraded lands, and create sustainable practices – all of which will be essential for our individual and collective healing and wellbeing.

I draw upon the work of ecophilosophers Joanna Macy and Molly Brown to consider ways that music might serve as a vehicle for such healing. In their book *Coming Back to Life* (2014), the authors describe how they have empowered groups to work toward a life-giving society where human practices are both sustainable and equitable. They characterize our current society as an Industrial Growth Society that views the earth as "supply house and sewer" (p. 2) with an intention to maintain the exponential growth of markets. This mindset has resulted in a global corporate empire that requires military occupations, modern slavery, and other abuses to perpetuate such growth. Conversely, the authors envision a Life-Sustaining Society that "operates within the carrying capacity of its life-support system, … both in the resources it consumes and the wastes it produces" (p. 4).

Macy and Brown (2014) suggest that there are three meta-narratives at play at this time. The *Business as Usual* narrative is supported and maintained by The Industrial Growth Society, and the central plot of this perspective is to get ahead or even profit from climate disruption. The second narrative is *The Great Unraveling*, which is typically the story of environmental scientists and activists who point to the evidence of environmental degradation and climate change. The third narrative, *The Great Turning*, is offered by those who acknowledge the Great Unraveling and who wish to work toward community solidarity and actions to transform current practices toward sustainable ones.

Macy and Brown's (2014) *The Work that Reconnects* is an example of a program to foster and expand the narrative toward actions of The Great Turning. Those author's process for fostering The Great Turning can be conceived of as a spiral with four phases. The first phase, *coming from gratitude*, involves centering in "our love for life on Earth" to stimulate empathy and confidence (p. 67). *Honoring our pain* is the second phase where one honestly acknowledges feelings about the suffering of others and the destruction of the natural world. The third, *seeing with new eyes*, is an opportunity to expand awareness of one's relatedness to all aspects of the self-organizing world as well as to past and future generations. The fourth phase, *going forth*, is characterized by inspired actions that are aligned with one's unique situation and gifts. The overall spiral is intended to heighten awareness, to help individuals face difficult issues without going into denial or numbing out, to reclaim blocked energy so it can be directed toward informed action, and to help individuals discern their strengths and situatedness so that they are better prepared to embrace their unique role in the Great Turning.

Although Macy and Brown (2014) include a number of activities for each stage of the spiral, my background in the expressive arts and art-based research (McNiff, 1995) has led me to consider an adapted musical approach that is intended to foster an expanded exploration of non-verbal knowings and expressions. In order to explore this possibility, I undertook a self-study where I experimented with musical means to make sense of my experiences of deep listening and active engagement with the natural soundscape. My intention for engaging in this sound interaction was to begin a process of healing of the sense of separation that I often feel with the natural world. Macy and Brown (2014) assert that the ecological crises we have created are born of dualistic thinking; specifically, that we are somehow separate from the natural world. Even using the term "environment" might suggest that we are "in" but not "of" the natural world. Although sometimes I am aware that I am a part of the natural world, I also acknowledge that I have been socialized to perform a type of anthropocentric individuality that is pathological, ultimately destructive, and contributes to the ecological crises we are facing (Smith, under review).

Our musical structures often mirror such dualistic thinking as is represented in the distinctions between the performers and audience, in our language around musicians and non-musicians, and in our privileging of anthrophony (human-made sounds) over the biophony (animal sounds) and geophony (sounds made by air, water, and landscape) (Krause, 2016). Macy and Brown (2014) also point out that The Industrial Growth Society is held in place by power-over strategies of domination. An example in music education is offered by Bradley (2012), who speaks of the prevalence of musical colonialism enacted when those in power assume the moral superiority of Western classical music as compared with other traditions and keep structures in place to maintain the dominance of the genre in the conservatory and primary and secondary schools.

Although Western classical music remains stunningly beautiful to me, I fear that basing music education solely upon such dualistic and domineering ideas will not position our discipline to contribute to the project of healing the persistent and mistaken thinking at the root of environmental degradation and climate change. I simultaneously fear and hope for a time ahead when both the available resources of time and the primary focus of education will shift rapidly toward the transformation of our culture in the Great Turning. It is for this reason that I am motivated to find ways that music can support these efforts so that musicians and music teachers are prepared to contribute to society in new ways.

In this chapter, I consider how listening, sounding, and music-making can serve as an intentional healing practice that might help us to locate the crisis in our society's mistaken but prevalent perceptions that we are separate from both the natural world – and one another – to open a potential way for healing. In addition to facilitating my own healing, I have engaged in this exploration to seek a way to help my students to gain a greater awareness of their situatedness within the natural world. I endeavored to find ways to help them to become more aware that the climate crisis is not "out there" in the cyclones, heatwaves, floods, fires, melting glaciers, and species extinctions, but in the structures of our societies, our cultural practices, and in our thinking. The following describes my initial journey through the spiral from a musical and sound perspective, and as such reflects only one set of possibilities to engage musically with *The Work that Reconnects*.

Process

In order to complete this self-study, I engaged in a four-step process. First, I re-read the relevant chapter in *The Work that Reconnects* to determine and plan musical means to approach the aims of each cycle. Second, I dedicated one hour of ritual time to carry out the work of each phase. Third, I allotted between thirty and forty-five minutes to reflect and document what occurred in each phase. The process of traveling through the spiral took approximately six and a half hours. After the phases were complete, I wrote a series of reflections that informed this report.

Pre-cycle Reflection

I knew that I would be opening within myself a deep well of emotion in doing this project. However, that is why I felt I must proceed. Macy and Brown (2014) make it clear that those who lead others through the spiral need to attend to their own emotional pain and grief beforehand so that they have the capacity to hold a safe space for others to encounter grief during the process. I have found that many people tend to hold climate-related fear and grief inside waiting for the rare opportunity that they might express it to others who will take them seriously. It is as if many are searching for spaces to "come out of the closet" as concerned citizens.

I discuss below how music listening and engagement, both individually and collectively, might work to provide such support.

Cycle 1: Gratitude

The purpose of Cycle 1 of the spiral is to center in "our love for life on Earth" to stimulate empathy and confidence. I chose to start Cycle 1 as suggested by Macy and Brown (2014), with deep breathing. I decided to sit outside on my patio which faces protected forested wetlands. As I focused inward, gentle breezes invited me to exhale deeply and freely which allowed me to release the business of my preparations. As I became more mindful of my breath, I also became more open to the sounds around me. A pair of chipmunks were chirping their "red alert" call to one another, which made me curious if a predator was in the vicinity – or was my presence the reason for their call? While sitting and checking the forest for a larger animal, a very large bee came for a visit instantly drawing me into a more immediate experience of the present moment. I decided this was a good moment to respond with sound and joined the bee in buzzing sounds to move the nervous instinctual energy from my body. Bzzz. BzzzzZZzzzzzz. Afterward, I realized that I owed the bee gratitude for calling me to the present moment as I had strayed into thinking.

Continuing with the focus upon sound, I alternated between listening and responding to the various sounds around me. Bird calls, chipmunk chirps, insect buzzes, wind rustling through the trees … and then …. the bee returned and this time much more persistently. So much so, that I instinctually bolted out of my chair and danced with it until the bee realized perhaps that my lavender-scented hair product would not yield the nectar it sought. However, I was up from my chair and had a new vantage point. I could see that the butterfly garden was beginning to produce its first flowers, attracting smaller bees and other insects that I noticed were barely audible.

Having centered in my breath, and then having engaged with both sound and silence with my surroundings, it was now time to open my awareness to what I was grateful – the main purpose of Cycle 1. The first and quite overwhelming thing that came to my heart was how grateful I am to live in such a beautiful place. We had chosen carefully a home that would nourish our wellbeing, but the business of setting up house and starting new academic positions had prevented me from receiving the full benefit of our lovely surrounds.

Shortly after this moment of awareness, a commuter train whizzed by. The train on the rail line, just a few miles beyond the protected wetlands, is something I hear many times a day as I am working in my home office. Today, I received the sound openly in gratitude that I am fortunate to live near the only high-speed rail line in the United States, and that I have the option to take a commuter train to Boston for work. This naturally extended to a sense of gratitude that I have for living near such a beautiful city, that I live within an hour of the ocean, and that I live near an organic farm located on the grounds of a bird sanctuary where my partner and I enjoy hiking.

The distant sound of an airplane making its descent into Boston reminded me that I live near an airport that I have flown from many times to visit some of the most exquisite natural spaces as well as many lovely cities, and that I love flying to see the world from a bird's eye view. That traveling has indeed taken me into deeper awareness of how much I love the diverse landscapes of our planet. The chime of my alarm then sounded to remind me to bring my meditation to a close, and I gave myself a moment to make the transition to documentation. I realized that I am grateful for this project to open a space for *being* in my active *doing* life.

Cycle 2: Honoring My Pain for the World

The aim of the second cycle is to acknowledge feelings about the suffering of others and the destruction of the natural world. Entering this phase, I realized that I could no longer deny the pain that I had been struggling to repress for several weeks. As I mentioned, I absolutely love flying, but know keenly how destructive it is on many levels. Just two days before, a friend had sent an article (Irfan, 2019) describing just how large a piece of the polar ice cap a single flight was responsible for destroying. Ugh. All of this came at a time when I was eagerly anticipating my own travel to the UK and Norway for music education conferences, and to Iceland on the journey home to enjoy a few days of holiday. How can I justify these trips, knowing that I am contributing to such an unsustainable and destructive result? In struggling with this conflict, I had carefully planned three purposes for the overall trip to reduce the impact of taking multiple trips and planned to offset the carbon expended from the travel, but I fear – I know – that this is not enough.

The guilt and shame I had tried hard not to feel welled up just as a gentle rain started to fall. I quickly moved indoors, and once settled I decided to breathe into the pain as is recommended by Macy and Brown. As the intensity of the rain shower outdoors increased, so I was able to deepen my awareness of feelings of grief, shame, and sorrow. As I did so, a hymn from the Mennonite hymnal came into my heart:

> Rain, down, rain, down,
> Rain down your love on your people.
> Rain down, rain, down,
> Rain down your love, God of life. (Faith & Life Resources,
> 2005; Hymn 49, Chorus)

Though I was raised in a Protestant Christian faith, I admittedly no longer have faith in a deity, but instead hold a more panentheistic view that here is Intelligent design in the self-organizing universe or in nature itself. My pain and sorrow lead me directly to an awareness of a faith crisis that I am currently grappling as a result of the climate crisis. I wonder if Gaia and the Cosmos are waiting to see if we will come together and collectively choose life … or not.

I went to find the hymnal because I could not recall from memory all of the words. I sang through the verses. Trying to translate the "God language" to fit with my current spiritual understandings (D'Aprano & Shaw, in press), I skipped over the words that conflict with my beliefs and focused upon phrases that resonated … full of God's love is the earth.

Well, I suppose I do believe that. The natural world is teaming with love in the form of vital life force … So why are we killing it??? Why are we killing ourselves?

> … God of creation, we long for your truth;
> you are the water of life that we thirst.
> Grant that your love and your peace touch our hearts:
> all of our hope lies in you. (Faith & Life Resources, 2005; Hymn 49, Verse 3)

… Does it? I absolutely do not have faith in some savior, be it carbon-capture technology or polices like the Paris Accord – my only faith that the human species will survive rests upon our capacity to have a change of heart so profound that we find the courage to radically change our ways of living – The Great Turning.

I believe that we are well into the Great Unraveling of unsustainable systems which are maxing out and beginning the process of breakdown. Because of this, I have intense feelings of dread about what I might witness in my remaining years. I am already grieving as I read almost daily of losses of life both human and other-than-human, losses of vital landscapes, losses of stability and ways of life. Recently, I read that an Australian think tank (Spratt & Dunlop, 2019) projects that the Great Unraveling will peak in the year 2050, the year I will turn 80 years old. When I read such reports, I feel dread and grief, yet I typically stuff them down and dive back into my work. I admittedly struggle to breathe through the pain into a deeper aliveness but acknowledge that this practice holds potential to build re-siliency and hope for new possibilities.

As I reflected further upon this pain, my heart and mind went to battle:

How can you have hope when the carbon count is now peaking as high as 417 ppm (Nace, 2020)?

I must have hope to stay present to life!

How can you have hope when the US government seems hell-bent to expand fossil fuel extraction and erase all sensible environmental protections (Milman, 2020)?

I must trust that there are enough citizens that love the natural beauty of their country and love their own life.

After wrestling with my conflicting thoughts, I was inspired to change the words to the hymn. Because hymns have been traditionally used to reinforce or invoke faith, I wondered if I could use song to reinforce my oft-wavering faith in the future.

> Rain, down, rain down;
> May we love all of the earth;
> Rain, down, rain down:
> Rain, down, a vision for life.

When the chime of my alarm sounded, I looked up and noticed that the rain had stopped and that the sun had started to shine. My heart was still aching, but I felt more grounded and alive.

Cycle 3: Seeing with New Eyes or Hearing with New Ears?

The purpose of the third cycle is to expand awareness of one's relatedness to all aspects of the self-organizing world as well as to past and future generations. As I considered the activities offered in the chapter, I decided to try an adaptation of the Bodhisattvan Check-in or Owning My Life exercise that was outlined in the chapter (Macy & Brown, 2014, p. 156). In the ritual, one is to contemplate the long panoramic journey one has made *as* life on Earth. Macy and Brown suggest that we invoke the memory of all of the beings who have inhabited the past, all the beings who inhabit the present, and all of the beings who will inhabit the future.

I wondered what music might be from the perspective of other-than-human creatures or of the earth. To do this, I considered the soundscape I imagined was indicative of the past. Specifically, I imagined the sonic landscape of the place I was sitting during the time before the colonists arrived to settle New England – a time when the Wampanoag people stewarded the land (New England Historic Geneological Society, 2020). I imagined how different the sound of the wind might be rushing through tall pines with six-feet wide trunks, which were likely three times taller as compared to the current and less robust reforested surroundings. I imagined the sounds of the forest without the hum of traffic from the interstate highway several miles away, without the sound of the high speed and commuter trains, without the sounds of air traffic, without the sounds of lawnmowers and delivery trucks in the neighborhood. I wondered what animal sounds I would have heard that are no longer a part of the soundscape today. I also imagined the ritual music of the indigenous persons who lived here, wondering if I was even remotely close to conjuring their musical traditions.

As I moved to the project of invoking the sounds of all of the beings in the present time, I thought about how technology has come to mediate or disrupt most of the sound in our daily lives. The natural soundscape around my home is a mix of natural and mechanistic sounds, and much of the music we hear today is digitally mixed and mastered, sometimes even dissected, auto-tuned, and reconstructed by software creating a type of beyond-human perfection – a type of cosmetic surgery of sound. In contemporary worship services, ballparks, and performance venues, amplified sound is often so pervasive that I cannot hear the voices of others speaking or singing nearby.

I then considered invoking the sounds of the future; I decided not to project my worst fears such as the sounds of war, storm, and catastrophe. Instead, I opened a space for sonic wellbeing, and wished upon my future self and others an increasingly harmonious and supportive soundscape. Such a soundscape might include a reduction in the human-made sound and a more robust and diverse collection of bird and animal sounds. I also imagined the sounds of more humans enjoying natural surroundings not only in remote places, but also in cities and densely populated areas that had been created to heal, cool, and beautify those spaces. I then thought about how musicians might be called to the work of creating a healthier sonic environment. Will our sensitivities be needful as we orchestrate a balanced ecosystem? Might we be called to sonically assess soundscapes for their relative diversity of other-than-human species (Krause, 2016)?

Going Forth

The purpose of the fourth cycle of the spiral is to ponder inspired actions that are aligned with one's unique situation and gifts. Macy and Brown (2014) suggest that the earlier stages of the cycle work to heighten our awareness, to help us face issues without going into denial or numbing out, to reclaim blocked energy and put it to use, all so that we are ready to embrace our unique role in the Great Turning. But to go forth, we need to prepare for taking the "leap of courage and creativity" that is required of us at this time (p. 192). The authors outline many group activities for this work; however, a set of vows or commitments stood out as something I could work with individually. I reflected upon each of the five vows (p. 213–215) which reflect the aims of *The Work that Reconnects* to consider musical practices I might use to reinforce or strengthen my resolve to uphold each.

I Vow to Myself and to Each of You to Commit Myself Daily to The Healing of Our World and The Welfare of All Beings. As I consider this vow, I acknowledge that I have to some extent been living it in many ways. That said, I realize that almost daily I learn of something that I do that is harmful. It seems to me that this vow demands that I remain open to my own healing, that I learn more about creating healing spaces in education, and that I need to be willing to forgive myself for engaging in hurtful practices out of ignorance or denial. To work with self-forgiveness, the chant "I Will be Gentle with Myself" comes to mind.

> I will be gentle with myself,
> I will love myself,
> I am a child of the universe
> Being born in each moment. (Libana, 1990)

To continue my own healing work, I have found quiet immersion in the natural soundscape to be one of the most healing practices for me. To create healthy and potentially healing spaces within education, I seek to consider structures for music-making that are inclusive and have near equal power dynamics such as free improvisation (Johansen et al., 2020) I need to personally engage musically in order to heal from more oppressive structures and to become more comfortable creating healthy spaces for this type of music-making.

I Vow to Myself and to Each of You to Live on Earth More Lightly and Less Violently in the Food, Products, And Energy I Consume. As with the issue of healing our world, I have been working to change my eating and resource use practices for several years, yet I continue to sometimes engage in actions that I know are unsustainable or hurtful at times due to social pressure or convenience. In order to strengthen my resolve, the chant "Put peace into each other's hands" could help me to stay focused upon how my action or inaction might have a direct impact upon another person, and to reinforce my intention to practice peace.

> Put peace into each other's hands and with loving expectation;
> Be gentle in your words and ways, in touch with God's creation
> (Faith and Life Resources, 2005, Hymn 87, verse 2)

This is particularly important when I am faced with social pressure to conform to unsustainable practices. The more that I can keep in mind that in facing awkward social moments I am actually serving others, the easier it may be to keep my resolve.

It has also occurred to me that as musicians, music teachers, and scholars it is important that we consider carefully how our field utilizes resources. The global pandemic has interrupted air travel, perhaps one of our most unsustainable habits as a profession. Yet, there are many other areas for us to consider modifying such as our tendency to overwork and live in ways unsustainable to good health (Kuebel, 2019) our need to heat and cool the large venues we use for performances, insisting that the natural resources that we use to make instruments and performance spaces are both renewable and recyclable, and demanding that the energy we use from our homes, classrooms, and rehearsal spaces is clean and renewable.

I Vow to Myself and to Each of You to Draw Strength and Guidance from the Living Earth, the Ancestors, the Future Beings and Our Brothers and Sisters of All Species. With this vow, it seems appropriate to set this as an intention and reflect in quiet meditation in the natural soundscape in order to be present to the living earth. Earlier in the cycle when I was contemplating my gratitude, I engaged in listening or attuning to the earth. This practice seems particularly valuable to do in one's primary living place. Understanding one's watershed, climate, and the species of plants and animals that inhabit it all might contribute to the gaining of a deeper knowledge of the messages the earth is conveying in albeit non-verbal ways.

To attune to the messages of the ancestors, we can turn to the vast collection of recordings as well as the indigenous oral traditions that can be traced back in time in most every culture. Although some of these traditions have been eradicated or suppressed by colonial empires (Perea & Solis, 2019), we can certainly benefit from learning the wisdom that is carried forward in the rich story and song carried by those who may be more connected to the earth's wisdom. Connecting to future generations, however, will take both empathy and imagination – both of which can be facilitated by music-making in the form of improvisations, arrangements or remixes, or original composition.

I Vow to Myself and to Each of You to Support You in Your Work for The World, and to Ask for Help When I Need It. To support this vow, a hymn from the Unitarian Universalist hymnal came to mind. "We'll Build a Land" is a hymn of commitment and action.

> We'll build a land building up ancient cities,
> Raising up devastations from old;
> Restoring ruins of generations.
> Oh, we'll build a land of people so bold (Verse 3).
> (Chorus)
> We'll build a land where sisters and brothers,
> anointed by God, may then create peace:
> where justice shall roll down like waters,
> and peace like an ever-flowing stream. (Unitarian Universalist
>   Association, 1993; Hymn 121)

In other verses, the hymn speaks of the need to support one another in the work of mourning, liberation, and reparations; therefore, I find this hymn to be helpful in focusing my mind and heart.

I Vow to Myself and to Each of You to Pursue A Daily Spiritual Practice That Clarifies My Mind, Strengthens My Heart and Supports Me in Observing These Vows. Musical daily spiritual practices might include those that can either be short in duration or longer when time allows. One short hymn that could be sung or recalled silently by memory is "Spirit of Life."

> Spirit of Life, come unto me.
> Sing in my heart all the stirrings of compassion.
> Blow in the wind, rise in the sea;
> Move in the hand, giving life the shape of justice.
> Roots hold me close, wings set me free;
> Spirit of Life, come to me, come to me. (Unitarian Universalist
>   Association, 1993; Hymn 123)

Longer practices might include listening to or playing/singing multiple songs that help to clarify one's mind and heart or could include writing one's own lyrics and music specific to one's inner wisdom.

With this going forth activity, I have drawn upon my own internal music repertoire and experiences, and I suggest that supporting others to do the same would be the most appropriate course. In this way, each person can identify the music that is most meaningful to them to support their commitments to the earth and one another. As a collective activity, sharing such songs with others might work to expand other's repertoire of such music, and might strengthen and amplify the power of this spiritual practice.

Music and Sound Attunement to Heal Our Sense of Separation from the Earth

As I worked through the four cycles to rethink the role of music as a means for fostering attunement to and the eventual perception of integration with the natural world, I found that music was especially helpful in the work of expressing gratitude for the earth, as well as providing a container for the grief and fear I feel when I honor my pain for the world. In adapting Macy and Brown's (2014) focus upon seeing with new eyes, I found that it was possible to also hear with new ears in attunements with the music made by the other-than-human world or the natural soundscape. Songs of commitment and action can help us to strengthen our resolve and clarify our mind and heart upon life-sustaining actions. Therefore, listening to human and other-than-human sources of music/ sound, and active music-making can both serve as intentional healing practices and modes of empowerment as we face the immense challenges of our uncertain future on the earth.

Although I engaged in a self-study to test ways to connect music with *The Work that Reconnects*, I honor that Joanna Macy is known for emphasizing that you cannot do this work alone (Kaza, 2020). My intention was not to stop with self-directed reflection, but to consider more broadly how musicians and music educators might bring forth musical pathways for the work. Drawing upon one's individual and a group's collective musical experiences might afford a means to help individuals to emote the deep emotional expressions that can arise during the process, and to call upon the power of music to sustain the work. I assume that we as musicians, music educators, music therapists, and theologians are passionate about music because we know intimately the power it has to transform, inspire, and heal (Boyce-Tillman, 2000). What then, if we consider that musical integration with the natural soundscape could facilitate the awareness of oneness with nature? I suspect that doing so might allow us to create experiential performances, as well as pedagogical and therapeutic approaches that contribute to the project of healing ourselves and creating a sustainable future for our species.

Bibliography

Boyce-Tillman, J. (2000). *Constructing musical healing: The wounds that heal.* Jessica Kingsley Publishers.

Bradley, D. (2012). Good for what, good for whom? Decolonizing music education philosophies. In W. Bowman & A. L. Frega (Eds.), *The Oxford handbook of philosophy in music education* (pp. 409–433). Oxford University Press.

D'Aprano, M., & Shaw. J. (2021). Inclusive songwriting for wellbeing in the LGBT+ Christian community. In K. S. Hendricks & J. Boyce-Tillman (Eds.), *Living song: Singing, spirituality, and wellbeing* (pp. 127–149). Peter Lang.

Faith and Life Resources. (2005). *Sing the journey hymnal: A worship book – Supplement 1*. Mennonite Publishing Network.

Intergovernmental Panel on Climate Change. (2018). *Global warming of 1.5° C*. <https://www.ipcc.ch/site/assets/uploads/sites/2/2018/07/SR15_SPM_version_stand_alone_LR.pdf>

Irfan, U. (2019, August 7). *This website shows you exactly how guilty you should feel about flying*. Vox. <https://www.vox.com/business-and-finance/2019/8/7/20756833/climate-change-flying-calculator-arctic-ice>

Johansen, G. G., Holdus, K., Larsson, C., & MacGlone, U. (2020). What have we learned about improvisation pedagogy? In G. G. Johansen, K. Holdus, C. Larsson, & U. MacGlone (Eds.), *Expanding the space for improvisation pedagogy in music: A transdisciplinary approach* (pp. 261–272). Routledge.

Kaza, S. (2020). *A wild love for the world: Joanna Macy and the work of our time*. Shambhala.

Krause, B. (2016). *Wild soundscapes: Discovering the voice of the natural world* (Rev. ed.). Yale University Press.

Kuebel, C. (2019). Health and wellness for in-service and future music teachers: Developing a self-care plan. *Music Educators Journal, 105*(4), 52–58. <https://doi.org/10.1177/0027432119846950>

Libana. (1990). *I will be* [Song]. On *Fire within*. Ladyslipper.

Macy, J., & Brown, M. Y. (2014). *Coming back to life: The updated guide to the work that reconnects*. New Society Publishers.

McNiff, S. (1995). *Art-based research*. Jessica Kingsley Publishers.

Milman, O. (2020, November 21). A destructive legacy: Trump bids for final hack at environmental protections. *The Guardian*. <https://www.theguardian.com/us-news/2020/nov/21/trump-environmental-protections-rollback-climate-crisis>

Nace, T. (2020, June 10). *Carbon dioxide levels just hit 417 ppm, highest in human history*. Forbes. <https://www.forbes.com/sites/trevornace/2020/06/10/carbon-dioxide-levels-just-hit-417ppm-highest-in-human-history/?sh=1d03c497229f>

New England Historic Geneological Society. (2020). *Native nations of New England*. <https://www.americanancestors.org/education/learning-resources/read/native-nations-of-new-england>

Perea, J. B., & Solis, G. (2019). Asking the indigeneity question of American music studies. *Journal of the Society for American Music, 13*(4), 401–410. <https://doi.org/10.1017/S1752196319000348>

Smith, T. D. (under review). The trauma of separation: Understanding how music education interrupted my relationship with the other-than-human world.

Spratt, D., & Dunlop, I. (2019). *Existential climate-related security risk: A scenario approach.* Breakthrough – National Centre for Climate Restoration.

Unitarian Universalist Association. (1993). *Singing the living tradition.* The Unitarian Universalist Association.

Notes on Contributors

LAURA BENJAMINS is a Ph.D. Candidate in Music Education at Western University, Canada. Her SSHRC-funded doctoral research focuses on musicians' perceptions of inclusion, participation, and relationality in religious worship contexts. Laura holds degrees in piano performance and music education and has experience as both a private and elementary school music educator. She currently teaches undergraduate music courses at Redeemer University and Western University while also serving as a local church musician. Laura has published several papers in journals such as *Journal of Popular Music Education* and *Canadian Music Educator* and has presented her research at various national and international conferences.

BRUCE ELLIS BENSON is Professorial Fellow at the University of Vienna and Honorary Senior Research Fellow at the University of St. Andrews. He is the author of five books, including *Liturgy as a Way of Life: Embodying the Arts in Christian Worship* (Baker Academic, 2014) and *The Improvisation of Musical Dialogue: A Phenomenology of Music* (Cambridge, 2003). His recent work on improvisation includes "Taking Responsibility for Letting Go: The Improvisation of Responding to the Call," in *Improvisation: On the Competence of Not Being in Control* (Routledge, 2021); "Improvisational Phronesis: The Interplay of Aesthetics and Ethics," in *The Routledge Handbook of the Philosophy of Improvisation in the Arts* (Routledge, 2021); and "Improvisation," in *The Oxford Handbook of Western Music and Philosophy* (Oxford, 2020).

JUNE BOYCE-TILLMAN, Ph.D., MBE read music at Oxford University and is Professor Emerita of Applied Music at the University of Winchester. She has published widely in the area of education and music, often on spirituality/liminality and eudaimonia. Her doctoral research into children's musical development has been translated into five languages and supported the development of improvisatory activities in the classroom.

She has written about and organized events in the area of interfaith dialogue using music currently the international improvising Peace Choir on Zoom. She has held visiting fellowships at Indiana University and the Episcopal Divinity School in Massachusetts, USA. She is an international performer, especially in the work of Hildegard of Bingen. Her large-scale works for cathedrals such as Winchester, Southwark, and Norwich, UK, involve professional musicians, community choirs, people with disabilities, and school children. She is a hymn writer – *A Rainbow to Heaven*. She is the convenor of Music, Spirituality and Wellbeing International (<www.mswinternational.org>). She is series editor of the Music and Spirituality series of Peter Lang, to which she has contributed three single authored books and several co-authored or co-edited books. She is an Extraordinary professor at North-West University, South Africa. She is an ordained Anglican priest and serves All Saints Church in South London.

DAVE CAMLIN, Ph.D., is a musician based in Cumbria, UK, whose practice spans performance, composition, teaching, socially engaged music practice, and research. He is Lecturer in Music Education at the Royal College of Music and Trinity-Laban Conservatoire, and was Head of Higher Education and Research at Sage Gateshead from 2010 to 2019. His research focuses on group singing, music health and wellbeing, musician training and Community Music, as well as pioneering the use of "distributed ethnography" as a method for research into cultural phenomena. He performs in various guises, and leads a number of community music choirs and projects.

AMIRA EHRLICH is a lecturer at Levinsky College of Education, Tel Aviv, and Program Coordinator of the Graduate Studies (M. Ed) in Music Education and a faculty member of Mandel Leadership Institute's Program for Ultraorthodox women in Jerusalem. Amira is a music educator with more than twenty years' experience in the field of music, as a teacher, producer, and researcher. Her published writings explore sociological and cultural aspects of music education. Since 2015, Amira has been a member of the international research team of Global Visions Through Mobilizing Networks: Co-Developing Intercultural Music Teacher Education in Finland, Israel and Nepal research project funded by the Academy of

Finland. Since 2020 Amira has been serving International Society for Music Education Special Interest Group on Spirituality in Music Education.

FAITH HALVERSON-RAMOS, MA, LPC, Mt-BC owns and operates the community mental health music therapy practice in Longmont, Colorado called SoundWell Music Therapy, PLLC that serves people throughout the lifespan. With a love for connecting with music therapists from around the world, Faith has additionally volunteered since 2014 as a member of the planning committee for the Online Conference for Music Therapy, and currently serves as its Executive Director. She has presented both nationally and internationally to diverse health care professionals on topics related to music therapy and mindfulness, music therapy and end-of-life care, and music and gerotranscendence.

As a writer and educator, JUNGMIN GRACE HAN is especially interested in spirituality and its relation to the physical principles in the context of Western classical music performance, eventually their connection to lifelong musical transformation and growth. She recently published her work in *Journal of Somaesthetics* (2019) and is currently working on narrative reflections of a musical pilgrimage intersected with the body-mind connection. She received doctoral degrees in cello performance at University of Michigan in 2015 and in music and music education at Teachers College Columbia University in 2021.

KARIN S. HENDRICKS is Associate Professor of Music and Chair of Music Education at Boston University. She has served as an instrumental music clinician, adjudicator, and workshop presenter throughout the United States and abroad. Dr. Hendricks has served in state, national, and international music education leadership positions, including as national secretary and research committee chair for the American String Teachers Association , and on the Editorial Committee for the *Journal of Research in Music Education*. Her research interests include music psychology, motivation, and social justice in music learning settings, with a particular focus on positive student–teacher relationships. Dr. Hendricks publishes regularly in leading research journals and edited books, and makes a particular effort to present research findings to music teachers in meaningful and approachable ways. She was the 2018 recipient of the American String Teachers Association "Emerging String Researcher" Award. Before moving to the university level, Karin enjoyed a successful public school orchestra career for thirteen years, where she won local, state, and national awards for her teaching. Dr. Hendricks has published six books, including *Compassionate Music Teaching: A Framework for Motivation and Engagement in the 21ˢᵗ Century*.

ANNE T. JONES is an experienced relationship counselor in private practice. She was previously working as a counselor and trainer for Relate. She works with individuals, couples, and families using an integrative approach. She has a background in health care, originally working as a pharmacist in cancer care.

ESTELLE R. JORGENSEN is Professor Emerita of Music (Music Education), Indiana University Jacobs School of Music, USA, and Contributing Faculty Member, Richard W. Riley College of Education and Leadership, Walden University, USA. She is editor of the *Philosophy of Music Education Review* and *Counterpoints: Music and Education* book series at Indiana University Press, and author of *In Search of Music Education, Transforming Music Education, The Art of Teaching Music, Pictures of Music Education, Values and Music Education* (in press, expected 2021) and articles and chapters in leading music education journals and books internationally.

MICHELE KEIM holds diplomas in both Eurythmy and Eurythmy Therapy. Alongside raising a family of five children with her husband, she has worked for twenty years with special-needs children and young adults at the Sheiling Ringwood, a residential Special Educational Needs (SEN) school in Hampshire (UK), where she has taught Eurythmy classes, worked therapeutically with individual students, gave religion lessons, and was centrally involved in the school's festival life. Throughout her career, one of her central concerns was to work from an understanding of each individual – staff and students alike – as a whole human being of body soul and spirit.

Living in Dorset, England, and now approaching retirement, JENNIFER KERSHAW has been fully accredited as a psycho-spiritual counselor and psychotherapist for many years. her deep and lifelong love of both music and the natural world has always been integrated with her work in a seamless way.

FABIAN LOCHNER, Ph.D., is a musician, educator, and independent researcher based in Ringwood (Hampshire, UK). He holds degrees from the Royal Conservatoire of Music of Brussels, the Université Libre de Bruxelles and the University of Notre Dame (Indiana, USA). Fabian has taught and performed widely in the United States and in the UK, often in the context of SEN communities. He directs the popular world music choir, *Voices of the Forest* (voicesoftheforest.co.uk), as well as the Gregorian chant ensemble, *Schola Nova Silvana* (scholanovasilvana.org.uk). Fabian is currently working on a monograph about the music and liturgy of St. Osmund of Salisbury.

MARIA GIULIA MARINI is an epidemiologist and counselor with thirty years in health care. She has a classic humanistic background, with Latin and Ancient Greek, followed by scientific academic studies, chemistry and pharmacology. She is currently Director of Innovation of Health Care of Fondazione ISTUD, acknowledged by the Italian Ministry of Research. She is member of the board of Italian Society of Narrative Medicine, a tenured professor of Narrative Medicine at La Sapienza, and referee for the *World Health Organization for Narrative Method in Public Health*. She is author of *Narrative Medicine: Bridging the Gap Between Evidence-Based Care and Medical Humanities* and *The Languages of Care in Narrative Medicine: Words, Space and Sounds in the Healthcare Ecosystem* (both published by Springer) and has written international publications on narrative medicine in scientific journals. She is currently President of the EUNAMES – European Narrative Medicine Society.

JANELIZE MORELLI is manager of the Musikhane Community Music Engagement Programme at the North-West University's School of Music. She is also a member of the Musical Arts in Southern Africa: Resources and Applications (MASARA) research niche and primary investigator in the Social Cohesion through Community Music Engagement research project. She teaches community music at undergraduate level and serves as supervisor on postgraduate studies in the fields of community music and music education. In particular, Janelize is interested in the ethics of community music, challenges around inclusivity in the practice, and the transformative possibilities afforded by participatory musicking experiences in diverse contexts.

CHRIS ROBERTS is a freelance performer, composer, and community musician. He works with Live Music Now, Music in Hospitals and Care, and Gloucestershire Academy of Music. During his postgraduate studies at the Royal Birmingham Conservatoire, supported by Help Musicians UK, he was awarded the Postgraduate Pedagogy Prize for his wide-ranging work in community music settings. His particular interests lie in the intersection of music and ritual studies and the role of ethnomusicology within music education.

STEPHEN ROBERTS, Ph.D., is an academic theologian, Anglican priest, and amateur musician. He is Tutor in Practical Theology and Mission at the South Wales Baptist College and Honorary Lecturer at Cardiff University. He worked as a parish priest and university chaplain in London before moving into theological education (St. Michael's College, Llandaff) and then academic theology (University of Chichester). Rooted in the interrelated disciplines of practical and public theology, he has particular interests in chaplaincy, interfaith relations, ritual, liturgy, and the relationship between music and theology. He is a proud member of the South Wales community big band, Wonderbrass.

DEBORAH J. SAIDEL, Ph.D., is an interdisciplinary scholar who is based in Richmond, Virginia where she is known for her innovative work in the humanities, designing and teaching classes that draw from the research areas of history, religious studies, musicology, sound studies, anthropology, and women studies. She also works as a freelancing artist specializing in flute performance and lecture recitals regarding women in music while maintaining a private woodwind studio. Dr. Saidel regularly performs at festivals, presents research at conferences, and is an executive board member of the International Alliance of Women in Music, serving as its treasurer.

JILLIAN SCHOFIELD is a psychotherapist and a shamanic practitioner. Her doctoral thesis was an integration of shamanic healing with modern day psychotherapy, based on her experience as a psychotherapist, a shamanic healer, and time spent with shamans in Peru, Ecuador, and Siberia. Jillian has spent many years teaching psychotherapy at the University of Derby. She runs shamanic healing and personal development courses, based on the integrative approach she developed. She also holds weekly shamanic gatherings where people come together to journey and heal.

GARETH DYLAN SMITH is Assistant Professor of Music (Music Education) at Boston University. His research interests include drum kit studies, popular music education, sociology of music education, and punk pedagogies. His first love is to play drums. Recent music releases include progressive smooth jazz tracks with The New Titans, the *Sun Sessions* EP with Stephen Wheel, and the *Ignorant Populists* EP with Build a Fort. Gareth is a founding editor of the *Journal of Popular Music Education*. His recent scholarly publications include *Eudaimonia: Perspectives for Music Learning* (with Marissa Silverman) and an essay titled "Rap, Racism and Punk Pedagogy."

TAWNYA D. SMITH is Assistant Professor of Music (Music Education) at Boston University. She teaches graduate courses in research, curriculum, and arts integration, and undergraduate courses including creating healthy classrooms, and the arts and environmental justice. Tawnya has published articles in the *Journal of Applied Arts and Health, Gender and Education, Music Educators Journal*, and the *International Journal of Music Education*. She has contributed book chapters to *Art as Research*; *Key Issues in Arts Education; Queering Freedom: Music, Identity, and Spirituality*, and the *Oxford Handbook of Musical Performance*. She is co-author of *Performance Anxiety Strategies* and co-editor of *Narratives and Reflections in Music Education: Listening to Voices Seldom Heard*. She is Senior Editor of the *International Journal of Education and the Arts*.

KEITH D. THOMASSON is Senior Chaplain and Spirituality Advisor for Alabare Christian Care and Support in Salisbury, UK. This charity supports adults who are vulnerable due to learning disabilities or homelessness. Keith supports a network of Voluntary Christian Chaplains and the development of spirituality across the charity. He is a pastoral supervisor. Prior to ordination in the Church of England Keith taught music in comprehensive schools in the North West. Keith has been involved in community music as participant and conductor. Currently living near Salisbury, he conducts The New Sarum Singers and sings with the Farrant Singers.

GIORGOS TSIRIS, Ph.D., is senior lecturer in music therapy at Queen Margaret University and arts lead at St. Columba's Hospice Care in Edinburgh, UK. He is the founding editor-in-chief of *Approaches: An Interdisciplinary Journal of Music Therapy* and his work has been published widely to include two books on service evaluation and research ethics, respectively, and a special journal edition on "Exploring the spiritual in music: Interdisciplinary dialogues in music, wellbeing and education" (2019, co-edited with Prof Gary Ansdell).

LIESL VAN DER MERWE is an Associate Professor in the School of Music at the North-West University, South Africa. She is a National Research Foundation (NRF) rated researcher and grant holder of the NRF research project: *Social Cohesion Through Community Music Engagement in South African Higher Music Education*. Her research interests lie in the fields of music and wellbeing, Dalcroze Eurhythmics, spirituality, and lived musical experiences. She supervises postgraduate studies and teaches research methodology, music education, and bassoon. She has published articles in high impact journals. She also performs in chamber music ensembles and is the conductor of the North-West Youth Orchestra.

CATRIEN WENTINK received her DMus degree in piano performance at the North-West University in 2018, where she specialized in ensemble performance. She did her research on Dalcroze Eurhythmics and ensembles. She has also been actively involved in community work at a care facility for the elderly since 2018. As a performer she received the ABRSM performance licentiate (solo piano) and the UNISA performance licentiate (two pianos) with distinction in 2009. She performs regularly as accompanist and chamber musician. She is currently a senior lecturer in Music theory at the School of Music of the North-West University, South Africa.

Index

abandonment 58
abundance 4, 62, 121, 160
abuse 189, 335
accompaniment 92
accuracy 169
   see also instruments
achievement 39, 72, 119, 158
   achieving communitas 321, 327
   artistic achievement 123
   human achievement 191
acoustics 85–88, 90, 91, 96, 104, 142, 145,
     147, 249
   see also archaeoacoustics
active listening 224
activity 137, 171, 192, 193, 207, 210, 211,
     259, 264, 265, 266, 268, 276, 302,
     303, 320, 331–2, 348
   human activity 38
   musical activity 4, 130
   social activity 39
adaptability 274
addiction 111, 119, 121, 124, 241
adolescence 48, 49, 51, 52, 56, 58, 61, 63,
     64, 67, 263, 325
   patho-adolescence 238, 241
adulthood 7, 67–73, 76–9
aesthetics 8, 48, 58, 62, 70, 86, 95, 102,
     134, 136, 144, 146, 171, 177, 205,
     232, 285, 311
   aural aesthetics 86
   relational aesthetics 304, 309
   Western classical aesthetics 62
affirmation 300
age 9, 53, 67–70, 73–74, 76, 78–9, 112,
     122, 124, 132, 136, 174, 256, 259,
     276, 280, 287, 325

digital age 307
Ice Age 86
Middle Ages 190
New Age 196, 278
Paleolithic Age 86
pandemic age 103–7, 308
Stone Age 88
ageing 275, 287, 288, 289, 290
   see also gerotranscendence
agency 8, 9, 84, 95, 97, 227
aim 18, 22, 47, 50, 58, 59, 63, 79, 119,
     141, 186, 189, 190, 209, 256,
     256–7, 258, 265, 324, 325, 328, 338,
     340, 345
album 20, 24–5, 26, 27, 53
ancestors 24, 86, 178, 206, 237, 294,
     301, 346–7
anger 78, 186
   anger management 123
angels 184, 267
animals 90, 92, 186, 265–6, 271, 297–8,
     244, 347
animism 90, 92–3
anthem 104, 107, 109, 159
antiphon 329
anthrophony 337
anthropology 85
anthropomorphizing 137–8
anxiety 186, 194, 200
   performance anxiety 101, 160
apocalypse 108
appreciation 22, 54, 159, 172, 271, 313
   see also re-appreciation
archaeoacoustics 86–8, 90–1
archaeology 87
   see also music archaeology

archetype 100

art 8, 10, 13, 42–3, 50, 52, 112, 117, 119, 124–5, 136–7, 144, 162, 189, 191, 194, 196, 198–9, 211, 220, 221, 230, 258–60, 273, 274, 304, 306, 307
  artistic achievement 123
  ArtsCare 192
  arts education 62
  art therapy 114–5, 202
  cave art 86
  expressive arts 336
  figurative arts 106
  musical arts 97–8
  parietal art 91
  rock art 85, 90–1, 94
  vibroacoustic 250
  Western art music 149

artifacts 88–91, 170, 171

artistry 69, 70–1, 72–3, 250

assembly 261, 266

attachment 105, 276, 281, 287, 296, 297, 298, 307

attunement 5, 7, 34–6, 40–1, 249, 298, 348–9

authenticity 3–15, 29, 47–65, 77, 84, 95, 147, 156, 161, 207, 227, 232, 233, 237–253, 284, 319

autism 10, 255

autonomy 12, 38–9, 95, 277, 281

awareness 5, 6, 11, 75, 84, 97, 109, 173, 177, 220, 228, 230, 231, 275, 282, 336, 337, 340–1, 343, 345, 349
  explicit awareness 63
  feminist awareness 84
  horizontal awareness 40
  intuitive awareness 41
see also self-awareness

Baby Boom generation 276, 279–80

ballad 104

beauty 104, 159, 160, 162, 175, 198, 205, 269, 271, 300, 343

beliefs 12, 51, 69, 79, 90, 109, 119, 170, 172, 175, 223, 227, 240–1, 273, 277, 278, 306, 341
  doctrinal belief 29
  religious beliefs 256–7, 264, 282
  spiritual beliefs 105–6, 118
  see also non-belief

bells 89

bereavement 117

Bible 99, 118

biophony 337

Black 23–5, 41–2, 237, 240, 241, 247, 252

blackbird 317–8

blend 38, 41, 147, 154

blessing 78, 134, 267, 316

body 23, 43, 51, 57, 104, 106–8, 132, 146, 149, 153, 160, 162, 185, 186, 196, 198, 262, 282, 297, 305, 317, 322, 328, 339
  body transcendence 283
  mind, soul, and body 75, 142, 211
  mind-body healing 8, 95
  mind-body unity 97–101

boundaries 23, 175, 227, 231, 265, 295, 308
  boundary object 176–7

Boyce-Tillman's model 142–3, 146

brain 103, 132, 153, 174, 210, 297, 303
  see also singing for the brain

breathing 3, 98, 104, 108–9, 113, 120, 148, 238, 240, 242, 249, 250, 313, 317, 339, 341, 342

Buddhism 20, 30, 200, 246, 272, 278

calm 132–4, 148, 152, 199, 203, 206, 208, 210, 211, 259, 260

Candlemas 268

candles 259, 261, 263, 266–7

capacity 73, 97, 98, 99–100, 175, 212, 257, 284, 293, 300, 306–8, 335, 338, 342

capitalism 11, 308

care 15, 38, 67, 69, 70, 71, 72, 76, 105, 107, 110, 173, 175, 180, 219–235, 244–246, 250

care homes and systems 104, 108, 111–127, 129–140, 171, 189–217, 242, 277, 278, 284, 289, 319–334, 378

carers 9, 107, 109, 191, 211, 225, 226, 244, 246, 262, 276, 300, 306, 310

self-care 161–162

case study *see* methodology

cathedral 201, 354

see also church

caves 86, 88–90, 91, 93, 185

cello *see instruments*

challenge 5, 6, 23, 40, 49, 59, 63, 78, 85, 119, 130, 142, 172–3, 176, 247–8, 281, 294, 315, 349

change 7, 21–22, 41, 43–4, 93, 108, 114, 119, 124, 143, 162, 187, 247, 258, 269, 272, 342, 343

climate change 7, 11, 280, 295, 308, 335–51

cultural changes 280

inner–personal change 175

musical change 175

social change 79, 280, 308, 325–6

chant 27, 267, 314, 345, 346

see also Gregorian chant

chaos 114, 150, 154

chaplain 111, 112, 116, 118, 122, 124

Chiasmus 238

choir 6, 72, 74, 132, 161–2, 191–3, 272, 302, 304

see also community choir

chord 38, 123, 206, 210

childhood 67, 76, 78, 120, 221, 279, 280, 287

children 3, 68, 72, 124, 132, 133, 136, 257, 260, 266, 274, 283, 285, 314, 317

Christ 100, 118

Christian cross 201–2

Christianity 17, 21, 43, 99, 100, 111, 115–6, 118, 132, 201–2, 256, 272, 314, 320, 322, 323, 332, 341

Black Christian theology 24

Christmas 268

see also festival

church 18, 24–5, 115, 116, 133–4, 135, 159, 161, 162, 260, 323, 327

circle 74, 89, 109, 201, 210, 224, 245, 248, 261, 266, 316

class 17, 50, 52–3, 68, 69, 74, 78, 89, 122, 125, 145, 196, 224, 226, 227, 229, 255, 258, 263, 266, 272, 276

classrooms 147, 249, 346

cliffs 89, 91, 194

climate change *see* change

closeness 12, 70, 136

cosmology 86

coding 131

cognition 194

cohesion 154

social cohesion 130, 221–3, 228, 229–31

colonization 20, 167, 240, 248, 337, 343, 347, 350

comfort 75, 109, 280, 318, 330, 346

commentary 27

communication 35, 36, 93, 107, 172, 210, 316, 324

musical communication 299–301

personal communication 121–2, 124

communitas 4, 5, 11, 192, 198, 228–30, 302, 305, 319–33

community 4–5, 6, 7, 11, 12, 41–2, 54, 70, 72–4, 75, 93, 115–7, 117, 122, 129–30, 135, 151, 162, 167, 192, 196, 210, 212, 219–20, 223, 228, 232, 238, 306, 319–20, 321, 325–30, 333, 336

compassion 5, 11, 35, 116, 117, 135, 122, 237–8, 244, 249, 273, 348

compassionate music teaching 4, 14,
126, 237, 246, 252
see also empathy, love, nurture
competition 12, 101, 109, 295
composer 19, 36, 59–60, 61, 104, 153, 159,
226, 324
composition 17, 19, 58–9, 60, 61, 97, 109,
225, 226, 347
concert 21, 22, 53, 57, 59, 104, 146, 161,
313, 314, 319–20, 322–4, 326, 327,
329, 331–3
conductor 329
conflict 22, 169, 177, 202, 247, 341, 343
confidence 123, 125, 158, 178, 270, 336, 339
congregation 133, 159, 162, 278, 324, 327
connection 8, 50, 86, 99, 101, 125, 130,
146, 152, 153, 161, 162, 173, 186,
187, 195, 198, 201, 209, 221, 222,
227–8, 258, 263, 282, 283, 302,
321, 333
authentic connection 4–6, 9–10, 11–
12, 29, 95, 232, 237–8, 242, 243–4,
245, 247–50, 319
human connection 3, 7, 11
social connection 138, 299, 303
virtual connection 3–4, 238–40
consciousness 60, 153, 184, 186, 191, 198,
204, 245, 248, 277, 313
consolation 70, 75–6
construction 47, 52, 55, 142, 143, 146,
149–50, 222, 223, 321–2, 329
consumption 26
contemplation 51, 54, 62, 63, 101, 198,
199, 203, 211, 249, 284
see also meditation
context 8–10, 17, 25, 26, 27, 36, 40, 86, 89,
91, 94, 98, 112, 119, 143, 151, 153,
167–79, 190–212, 221, 222, 238,
240, 46, 250, 257, 271, 274, 277,
278, 321–2, 324, 326, 327
contemporary context 6

cultural context 19, 106
continuum 68, 91
contribution 17, 18, 22, 26, 48, 73, 91, 250,
260, 299, 300, 330
conversation 8–9, 10, 11, 18, 29, 37,
44, 77, 111–25, 132, 141, 144,
146, 147, 162, 171, 192, 241,
330
conversion 43
cooking 121–2
co-operation 22, 300, 301
cosmos 113, 100, 101, 153, 183–5, 198, 201,
266, 268, 242
costumes 262
counselor 9, 157–63, 278
courage 11, 70, 75, 186, 248, 265, 266,
341, 345
COVID-19 3, 6, 8, 11, 77, 103, 108, 157,
191, 212, 237–8, 242, 281
see also pandemic
creativity 29, 61, 62, 71, 97, 111–25, 148,
159, 160, 226, 255, 271, 306,
308, 345
culture 7, 12, 19–20, 21, 23, 25–7, 28, 29,
36, 48, 54–5, 63, 68, 76–8, 79,
85–7, 91, 92, 93, 94–95, 106, 108,
135, 143, 144, 147, 150, 151, 152,
169, 175, 177, 190, 191, 195–6, 198,
212, 221, 223, 272, 275–7, 280, 282,
300, 304, 306, 308, 319, 322, 332,
337–338, 347
cure 193, 194
curiosity 12, 70, 71, 130, 175, 298
curriculum 50, 52, 53, 255, 258, 259, 261,
264, 266, 267, 271, 274
see also pedagogy
cymbal 146–7

darkness 60, 113–4, 120, 123, 242, 265,
266, 268

data 88, 90, 131, 146, 169, 192, 332
death 11, 74–5, 106, 107, 109, 117, 174,
        191, 193, 195, 197, 202, 271, 283,
        313, 317
    see also dying
debt 111
degradation 12
    environmental degradation 335–7
dementia 73, 191, 194, 279
demons 185
depression 130, 134, 135, 190, 192–3,
        200, 211
desert 113
despair 298
development 54, 55, 61, 93, 97, 123, 147,
        167, 200, 228, 230, 258, 273, 275–
        8, 279–80, 283, 284, 307, 353
    developmental needs 257, 300
    human 276, 286
    identity 51, 130
    motivic 322
    phylogenetic 109
    psychological 296
    skill 219
    student 50
    trust 120
dialogue 7, 10, 18, 20, 22, 37, 43, 58, 60,
        84, 167, 179, 220, 224–6, 229, 230,
        248, 299
    musical 22, 29, 36, 44, 225
dignity 70, 269, 271, 277
    see also respect
dimensions 8, 26, 42, 106, 175, 250,
        276, 277, 282, 285–7, 302, 304,
        306, 316
    spiritual 9
disability 136, 257
    learning 115–6, 124
discussion 17, 57, 58, 85, 86, 91, 92, 115,
        117, 137, 145, 146, 172, 189, 195,
        246, 257
    musical 53, 285, 286

disease 132, 186, 190, 192, 194, 237,
        295
dissonance 210, 294
distraction 133, 134, 192, 195, 273
diversity 5, 6–7, 17–25, 29, 86, 91, 177,
        249, 257, 272, 282, 344
divine 9, 36, 97, 100, 114, 270, 273, 314
    see also God
DNA 152
documentation 340
dopamine 103
drama 189, 210, 255, 256, 260, 261, 264,
        269, 274
drone 26, 209
drum 12, 24, 26, 59, 89, 108, 120
    Mud Drums 9, 141–54
    Shamanic drum 10, 183–7
    see also instruments
drum kit 26, 143, 145, 146, 150, 191,
        262, 329
    see also instruments
dying 42, 75–6, 100, 108, 191, 192, 195,
        201, 212, 195

earth 60, 113, 184, 201, 263–5, 268, 269,
        270, 294, 316, 335, 336, 339, 341,
        343, 345–7, 348–9
    see also ecology and nature
ecclesiology 59
    see also church
echo 60, 89–90, 146
ecology 5, 11–12, 13, 154, 155, 168, 170, 173,
        175, 177, 195, 196, 213, 241, 242,
        291, 296, 336, 337
education 9–10, 67–79, 219, 221–2, 223,
        226, 237–250, 256, 258, 265, 271,
        274, 276, 307, 337, 345
    religious education 47–63, 101, 119
    special education 256, 257–8
    see also music education
elderly 129–132, 194, 280

elders 10, 73–4, 75, 77–8
embodiment 8, 56, 95, 99, 101, 141, 154,
    156, 247, 262, 334
embodied knowledge 149
    see also knowledge
emotion 3–5, 6, 8, 24, 60, 61, 95, 109, 119,
    123, 130, 147, 158–9, 162, 174, 185,
    186, 189, 192, 193, 198, 202, 221,
    229, 243, 247, 249, 297, 298, 300,
    302, 304, 315, 321, 338, 349
    see also feeling
empathy 4, 5, 7, 14, 33, 35, 37, 39, 103, 148,
    205, 223, 238, 240, 241, 244, 245,
    246, 249, 265, 287, 306, 308, 336,
    339, 347
employment 72, 78
encounter 10, 22, 23, 26, 29, 56, 73, 112,
    117, 154, 160, 185, 220, 224, 226,
    231, 245, 247, 248, 265, 270, 273
endorphins 103, 299
energy 3, 8, 10, 56, 70, 73, 94, 95, 100,
    108, 109, 174, 183–4, 185–6, 187,
    198, 209, 249, 315, 339, 346
    blocked energy 336, 345
    spiritual energy 54, 92
engagement 58, 120, 125, 143, 167, 168,
    219, 221, 224, 225, 227, 229, 232,
    250, 260, 306, 320, 321, 324, 327,
    328, 332, 339
    active engagement 336
    authentic engagement 207
    musical engagement 4, 223, 231, 335
    mutual engagement 4, 11
entertainment 273
entrainment 5, 208
    musical entrainment 4, 259, 298, 301,
        304, 305, 307
    rhythmic entrainment 4
equity 5, 10, 237
Erikson 67–79
eternity 315
ethics 39, 40, 220, 222

ethnicity 17, 69, 287
ethnomusicology 87
ethos 115–6, 256, 257, 263
eudaimonia 4, 5, 13, 15, 144, 155, 156, 233,
    234, 251, 252
    see also wellbeing
event 85, 89, 92, 93, 97, 107, 122, 142, 146,
    147, 151, 158, 161, 170, 204, 267,
    276, 284, 315, 319, 322, 324–5,
    327, 330
evidence 48, 88, 89, 90, 99, 106, 107, 130,
    160, 191, 194, 195, 303, 336
evocation 24, 147, 321
experience 21–2, 23, 26, 36, 50, 56, 58, 59,
    62, 68, 69, 76–7, 78, 86, 89, 90,
    91, 100, 105, 106, 111, 114–5, 117,
    120, 123, 125, 141, 142, 144, 151–3,
    158, 159, 160, 168, 170, 173, 175,
    176, 184, 192, 196, 201, 202, 205,
    207, 209, 211, 224, 229–30, 246,
    250, 256–8, 260, 265, 271, 274–7,
    279–80, 282–3, 296, 302, 303,
    305, 306, 313–4, 320, 323, 330
    lived experience 6, 9, 87, 95, 129–39,
        243, 281
    musical experience 8, 72, 73, 75, 153,
        198, 219–20, 222, 226–7, 228,
        244, 250, 284, 286, 300, 307, 321–
        2, 325, 328, 332, 348, 349
    sonic experience 83–4, 91–4, 300
    spiritual experience 4–5, 25, 85, 97,
        124, 134, 137, 153, 199, 221, 273
    transcendent experience 281–2,
        284
exploration 7, 28, 51–2, 55–6, 57–8, 143,
    167, 168, 170, 171, 177, 201, 223,
    232, 279, 286, 336, 337
expression 34, 52, 60, 111, 112, 142, 147,
    159, 173, 202, 220, 222, 238
    authentic expression 7, 244, 247,
        248, 257, 259, 301, 321, 328,
        336

emotional expression 158–9, 162, 349
explicit expression 115
implicit expression 116
musical expression 58, 72
spiritual expression 57, 94

facilitation 222
faith 17, 23, 29, 51, 58, 59, 75, 116, 212, 341–3
multifaith 221
family 35, 56, 71–2, 75–8, 111, 116, 161, 162, 174, 195, 196, 210, 212, 296, 306, 318, 326
father 131, 132, 137, 159, 262, 265, 270
fear 21, 98, 246–8, 264, 298, 337, 338, 341, 344, 349
feelings 60, 98, 120, 123, 132, 138, 154, 199, 224, 264, 277, 281, 285, 286, 336, 340–2
festival 258, 264, 268, 314, 319
fieldwork 49, 87, 171, 172, 173, 176
flow 68, 108, 114, 150, 198, 209, 210, 222, 250, 285, 286, 303, 322
forest 26, 262, 270, 339, 344
framework 42, 47, 49, 83, 85, 86, 113, 118, 142, 150, 172, 177, 196, 228, 229, 231, 237, 277, 282, 321
freedom 38, 39, 44, 136, 226–7, 240, 247, 270, 274, 330
friendship 70
fun 148, 150, 257, 270
see also play, humor, and laughter
functionality 94, 148, 205

gaia 341
gender 17, 50, 53, 56–7, 68, 76, 78–9, 86, 122, 267, 276, 306
gender-identity 69

Genesis 113–4, 120
geophony 337
gerotranscendence 10, 67–8, 70, 74–76, 275–87
ghosts 185
globalization 72, 295
goal 36, 37, 50, 54, 62, 69, 84, 152, 209, 219, 230, 307
God 20, 47, 57, 59, 60, 100, 113–4, 120, 132–3, 134, 136–7, 159–60, 190, 220, 262, 265, 269–70, 341–2, 346
government 49, 342
grace 60, 67, 70, 75, 117, 133
gratitude 109, 135, 313, 316, 336, 339–40, 347, 348
grief 3, 11, 107, 159, 161, 338, 341, 342, 349
group 4, 39–40, 49, 53–4, 62, 73, 74, 115, 117, 124, 151–2, 159, 187, 191, 208, 210, 225–6, 255, 260, 285, 299–301, 302, 303–4, 327, 335, 345, 349
spirituality group 118–9
growth 98, 114, 157, 167, 202, 219, 221, 230, 260, 271, 275, 335–7
guardian 27
guide 67, 77, 167, 185, 186, 204, 221, 285, 293
guitar see instruments
habitat 295
happiness 70, 72, 198, 210
harmony 34, 40, 108, 132, 159, 189–90, 195, 208, 209, 303
healing 8, 93, 119, 124, 152, 160, 178, 183–7, 228, 237, 273, 314–6, 335, 337, 345–6, 349
spiritual healing 84
health 6, 51, 74, 103–4, 106, 107, 109–10, 111, 119, 130, 136, 168, 185–6, 190–3, 198, 200, 208, 210–2, 239, 266,

276, 278, 280, 281, 293, 298, 301, 302, 306, 315, 320–1, 333, 346

heart rate 298

Heaven 134, 136–7, 270

Hebrew 113, 114, 190

helpless 138, 243

hierarchy 84, 223, 231, 297, 320, 324

hierophant 95

Hinduism 20
  see also Faiths

history 8, 21, 27, 50, 53, 54, 72, 83–95, 137, 142, 147, 151, 190, 191, 209, 240, 241, 248, 269, 280, 295, 301

holistic 94, 144, 175, 196, 247, 293, 301

Holy Spirit 120, 134, 159

home 3, 10, 70–2, 74–7, 106, 107, 129–39, 146, 157, 171, 173, 189–212, 258, 278, 316, 317, 319, 320, 323–4, 325, 326, 327, 332–3, 340, 341, 344

homelessness 111–25, 191

homeostasis 298

hope 6, 12, 28, 59, 67, 70, 73–5, 109, 112, 122, 124–5, 171, 178, 224, 255, 269, 275, 287, 320, 333, 337, 342

hospice 76, 171, 173–4, 176, 278, 279, 280

hospital 107–9, 131, 191–2, 194–6, 200

hospitality 5, 120, 122, 230, 249
  see also inclusion, welcome

hum 207, 224, 344

humanism 295–6, 306, 308

humanity 8, 12–3, 36, 69, 85, 91, 93, 95, 100, 179, 244, 250, 258, 277, 280, 293–308, 335

human nature 117

human rights 116, 294

humility 7, 34–44, 100

humor 3, 314

husband 115, 131–3, 135

hybridity 20, 25, 28–9, 178

hymn 21, 133, 134, 137, 159, 162, 280, 324, 341–3, 346, 347–8

icon 47, 149, 150, 264, 265

identity 25, 72, 121, 130, 173, 175, 179, 251, 276–8, 280, 282, 304
  cultural identity 27, 195
  Jewish identity 7, 52, 58
  musical identity 7
  religious identity 20, 47, 51

image 57, 88, 89–90, 91, 92, 94, 100, 109, 113, 147, 189, 202, 205, 207, 243, 265, 273, 294, 321

imagination 70, 71, 98, 118, 258, 273, 300

imagining 249, 320

impact 50, 53, 55, 56, 63, 72, 138, 168–7, 192, 194, 195, 204, 231, 277, 279, 287, 307, 341, 346

improvisation 12, 19, 33–44, 53, 61, 150, 151, 175, 209, 210, 224, 226, 303, 321, 329, 330, 346–7

inclusion 4–5, 7, 10, 12, 17, 70, 72, 74–5, 78, 79, 83, 105–6, 116, 219, 238, 249, 255, 256, 258, 272, 274, 314, 345

infant 68, 296–8, 300

infinity 99–100, 101

initiation 100, 270, 320, 325–6, 329, 330

inspiration eight 24, 75, 95, 250, 255, 332

instruction 329

instruments 21, 73, 74, 89, 129, 133, 142, 146–7, 170, 198, 199, 262, 327, 328, 329, 331, 346
  accordion 133, 136
  bells 89
  cello 98
  guitar 59, 120, 133, 154, 208, 209, 314, 329
  keyboard 26, 20, 123, 209
  piano 59, 61, 75, 132, 157, 158, 159, 160, 161, 162, 163, 174, 262
  viola 161

intention 51, 92, 135, 137, 138, 152, 173, 175, 211, 222, 271, 273, 299, 335, 336, 337, 346, 349

interaction four, seven 29, 42, 47, 61, 62,
  130, 135, 136, 192, 195, 200, 225,
  231, 238, 242, 250, 257, 267, 280,
  320, 331, 336
interest 49, 68, 71, 74, 79, 87, 123, 171,
  176, 207, 224, 240, 241, 244,
  245, 270, 277, 294, 295, 301,
  304, 313
intergenerational groups 278, 285, 286
integrated 91, 260, 261, 275–6, 281
internet 212, 237
  see also social media and Zoom
interpretation 27, 87, 90–2, 94, 202, 207,
  245–6, 250
interpersonal 227, 229, 298, 301, 304
intervention 994, 211, 212, 285
interview 25, 38, 59, 60, 61, 131, 161, 168,
  171, 307, 317, 332
intrapersonal 103
inventing 320, 324
invitation 52, 119, 160
Islam 21, 24, 57, 314
  see also Faiths
isolation 6, 77, 78, 280–1, 294, 295,
  320

jamming 145
jazz 7, 37–8, 40–2, 53, 55, 61, 147, 148–50
  jazz-funk 26
  jazz-rock 57, 59, 61
journal writing 157
journey 12, 67–79, 100, 113, 114, 119, 120,
  158, 161, 183–4, 186–7, 192, 201,
  203, 206, 211, 226, 249, 255, 259,
  264, 273, 314, 317, 338, 341, 343
joy 70, 72, 74, 75, 79, 134, 141, 147–8,
  159, 160, 175, 184, 198, 249, 269,
  298, 317
Judaism 7, 21, 47–63, 201, 314
judgment 317

justice 116, 141, 167, 219, 280, 347, 348,
  355

King Arthur 270

lament 21
landscape 91, 92, 248, 302, 331, 337, 340,
  342, 343
language 23, 26, 34, 36, 103–9, 172, 178,
  179, 192, 220, 226, 256, 276, 299,
  300, 305, 328, 337, 341
  metalanguage 104–8
Latinx 27, 107
laughter 270, 271, 304, 317
leader 39, 41, 47, 129, 133, 226–7, 248,
  278, 294, 299, 313
leadership 62, 231, 270, 273, 329, 330
learning 7, 10, 56, 101, 119, 160, 161, 179,
  184, 219, 221–2, 223, 226, 230, 231,
  238, 243, 244, 246–9, 255, 257,
  329, 331, 347
  informal 73
  learning disabilities 115–6, 124
lesson 53, 73, 120, 160, 255–60, 261–74
liberation 7, 202, 347
life 43–4, 67–79, 100, 104, 120, 122, 124,
  132–3, 160–2, 185, 192, 194, 188,
  200, 203, 206, 211, 219, 240, 246,
  247, 258, 264, 269–71, 276–7,
  278, 281–5, 287, 294, 296, 306,
  308, 313, 315–7, 335–49
  Black life 23
  cultural life 86
  life conversation 118, 119
  life-giving 4, 8
  multicultural life 26
  Paleolithic life 85, 92
  pandemic life 6
  religious / spiritual life 115–7, 248

limbic system 297

liminal nine 10, 26, 100, 114, 120, 143,
153–4, 189, 194, 196, 198, 199, 203,
209, 211, 220–1, 222–3, 227–8,
230–2, 319, 320–2, 325–32

listening 18, 35, 37–8, 39, 40, 41, 53, 55,
75, 86, 104, 108, 109, 136, 142,
151, 159, 194–6, 207, 209, 224,
22135, 259, 264, 267, 299, 223,
224, 335–49

literature 19, 28, 130, 168, 194, 196, 219,
220, 221–3, 231, 556, 284

lithophones 89

liturgy 36, 260, 324

lockdown 61, 158

loneliness 12, 74, 320

loss 98, 99, 138, 160, 185–6, 191, 231, 245,
266, 275, 277, 281, 342

love 24, 33–5, 67, 69, 70, 104, 113, 122,
132, 134, 135, 147, 161, 191, 205,
275, 293–312, 314, 316–7, 336,
339, 340–3

lyrics 33–6, 55, 60, 159, 209, 300, 3

marginality 78, 172

materials 142, 146–7, 222, 271, 321–2,
328, 331

maturity 272, 284

meaning 51, 62, 86–7, 91–2, 95, 101, 113,
116–7, 125, 170, 171, 175, 176, 178,
198, 207, 210, 220, 222, 223, 227,
246, 250, 263, 274, 276, 280–1, 282,
297, 300, 302, 304, 323, 326, 331
cultural 143
musical 10, 41, 137, 151, 244, 246

mediator 9, 134–5, 137

medicine 189, 190–1, 196

meditation 11, 148, 189–212, 285, 286, 313,
340, 346
see also contemplation

megaliths 91

melancholy 295

memory 74–5, 150–1, 191, 193, 194, 197,
315, 330, 341, 343, 348

mercy 273

metamorphosis 175

metaphysical 154, 206, 263

methodology 28, 84, 87, 88, 167–181, 188,
191, 305
case study 17, 20, 23, 25, 50, 112, 212

Michaelmas 265–6

micro-narrative 131

mind (mental) 5, 8, 43–4, 70, 73, 74,
75, 95, 97–101, 103, 106, 107,
120, 142, 153, 162, 186, 201, 238,
279, 298, 304, 305, 307, 313, 314,
342, 345–8
mindfulness 10, 189, 199–200, 207–
8, 211, 220
mindset 93, 94, 282, 335

ministry 49, 54, 58, 59

mirror neuron system 299

mistake 38, 44, 98, 243, 337

mood 108, 147, 159, 186, 190, 194, 207,
208–9, 210, 211–2, 259–60, 66,
267, 271, 321
see also emotion

morality 14, 38, 54, 126, 138, 220, 222,
233, 234, 241, 252, 273, 294, 295,
309, 337

mother 108, 109, 115, 132, 133, 158, 162,
205, 262, 269, 271, 296–8, 300

multisensory 260

music archaeology 87
see also archaeology

music education 48–9, 67–79, 145, 219–
235, 237–253, 337, 341
see also education

music-making 12, 37–9, 41, 73, 99, 111,
151, 190, 209, 219, 240, 248, 250,
286, 335, 337, 345–7, 349

musicking 5–6, 9–12, 28, 97, 141, 143, 150,
    152, 169, 196, 219–32, 238, 244,
    299, 306, 307, 322, 325, 327, 332
musicology 8, 84, 85, 87, 95
mutuality 177, 189
mystery 260
mythology 89, 318

narrative 8, 12, 59, 61, 83–5, 87, 95, 108,
    112, 131, 172, 242, 243, 305, 335–6
    see also micro–narratives
national 17, 27, 49, 168, 239
nature 10, 38, 86, 91, 97–100, 107, 109,
    117, 176, 185–6, 191, 202, 203, 231,
    258, 264, 269–70, 295, 300, 302,
    303, 341, 349
near-death experience 313
neoliberalism 293, 295–6, 306, 308
nervousness 28, 319, 330, 339
New Testament 264, 267
    see also Bible
non-belief 17
    see also belief
notation 111
nun 246
nurture 113, 117, 152, 193, 212, 220, 267–8
objectification 176–7
occupation 194, 335
online 59, 72, 103, 168, 209, 306, 307
    see also internet
Orthodox 47, 49, 50, 59, 62
    see also Judaism
Orthodoxy 308
othering 85
other-than-human 138, 185, 342, 343,
    344, 349, 351

painting 88, 90, 92, 119, 124, 130
Paleolithic 83, 85–6, 88–94

pandemic 3–4, 6, 8, 11, 103–9, 59, 162,
    237, 238, 280, 293, 295, 307,
    308, 346
    see also COVID-19
paraclete 20
paradox 6, 159, 167, 169, 200, 285, 294,
    295, 307
paramusical 304
participant 73, 104, 106, 129, 130, 131, 134,
    135, 136–7, 138, 158, 169, 170, 176,
    192, 195, 205, 209, 211, 228, 259,
    299, 300, 302, 305–7, 320, 322,
    323, 327–9, 332
Passover 269
pastoral supervision 113
patriarchy 85
pattern 37, 40, 91, 97, 149, 172, 196, 273
peace 21, 79, 107, 167, 192, 200, 203,
    204, 206, 278, 282, 314, 317, 342,
    346, 347
pedagogy 5, 14, 47, 48, 49, 52, 53, 68, 79,
    98, 101, 223, 235, 246, 249, 251,
    256, 259, 349, 350
Pentecostal pedagogy 5, 249
percussion 89, 262, 327, 329, 332
    see also drum
perfection 35, 344
performing arts 71, 258–9
performance 6, 19, 21–2, 53, 58, 61, 154,
    170, 175, 177, 219, 225, 227, 59, 265
    Three or four 313, 314, 315, 319,
    322–4, 326, 328–30, 331, 332, 344,
    346, 349
    musical performance 36, 54, 93, 97–
    101, 123, 129–39, 248, 293, 321–2
    performance anxiety 160, 248
performing 55, 56, 71, 97–8, 99, 304
personhood 8
phase 174, 210, 341
philosophy 5, 18, 27, 42–3, 43, 75,
    163, 205

physical 3–5, 8, 12, 75, 91–2, 97, 99, 108,
    116, 146, 154, 174
    come on 185, 189, 190, 192, 204, 238–
        40, 61, 281, 283, 284, 301–3
    free 08, 316, 322, 326
    see also metaphysical
piano *see* instruments
piety 241
pilgrimage 100
planet 10, 11, 85, 242, 282, 293–4,
    308, 340
play 10, 28, 37, 38, 39, Forty, 50, 54, 67, 75,
    76, 98, 99, 114, 129, 130, 132–5,
    137, 141–5, 146, 149–50, 158, 159,
    161, 162, 174, 184, 187, 196, 205,
    225, 227, 246, 275, 279, 280, 284,
    298, 315–6, 328, 331, 335
playlist 107, 108–9
pleasure 70, 200, 285, 314
policy 18, 76, 241, 243, 295, 342
pollution 240
posthuman 205
postwar 293, 294, 296, 306
potency 304–5
potential 20, 22, 28, 53, 60, 85, 87, 91, 98,
    112, 120, 122, 146, 168, 169, 172,
    175, 178, 199, 207, 209 212, 230,
    244, 249, 272, 277, 301,
    306–8, 320, 337, 342
power 9, 24, 29, 83, 94–5, 99, 154, 167,
    169, 173, 183, 185–6, 200, 231,
    240, 242, 249, 250, 256, 263, 300,
    304–5, 307, 313, 319, 337, 346,
    348, 349
practice 12, 17, 29, 37, 39, 42, 43, 58, 68,
    69, 71, 79, 88, 95, 118–20, 142,
    150, 159–62, 167–70, 172, 178,
    179, 205, 206–7, 211, 240, 241,
    248, 249, 257, 263, 277, 322,
    333, 346
    compositional practice 19
    meaning–making practice 92

meditative practices 199–200
music therapy practice 9, 284
musical practices 345
performative practice 19
practice of authenticity 246
practice of care 219–32
practice of freedom 247
practice of pastoral supervision
    113
private practice 157, 278, 279
sexual practice 57
Shamanic practice 183, 187
singing-songwriting practices 53
spiritual practice 91, 93–4, 173, 177,
    278, 348
sustainable practices 335–6
praise 115, 135, 271
prayer 60, 245, 264, 316
presence 9, 59, 89, 98, 99, 144, 161, 210,
    222, 250, 252, 273, 278, 339
privilege 39, 52, 78, 79, 122, 237
professionalization 169, 173
process 12, 18, 26, 41, 43, 51, 55, 58, 98–9,
    100, 101, 106, 114, 131, 138, 160,
    161, 172, 173, 176, 205, 207, 211,
    223, 228, 230, 231, 244, 247, 249,
    257, 260, 271, 275–6, 279, 281, 283,
    286–7, 298, 304, 305, 321, 332, 335,
    336, 338, 342, 349
    creative process 23, 123
    GIM process 204
    healing process 183, 185, 186
    human process 86
    microprocesses 169
    musical process 25, 226
    therapeutic process 175
protest 298
Protestant 341
    see also Christianity
psychedelic 280
psychology 160, 171, 278, 279
punk 280

purpose 67–9, 86, 91, 114, 147, 158, 170, 172, 175, 183, 198, 199, 203, 211, 238, 241, 242–3, 246, 248, 276, 280–2, 302, 327, 339, 340, 341, 343, 345

quarantine 3, 6, 106, 158

Rabbi 54, 57, 59, 278
   see also Judaism
race 17, 68, 69, 78, 276, 306
racism 7, 23, 238, 240, 242, 248
   see also White supremacy
realities 6, 40, 43, 53, 77, 78, 93, 153–4, 170, 177, 184, 196, 198, 219, 222, 241, 246, 249, 258, 276, 295–6, 308
re-appreciation 171
   see also appreciation
rebellion 7, 48, 55–6, 57–8
recital 199, 314
recitation 21
recovery 119, 157–63, 192, 293–4, 306–7
regulation 130, 295, 298
rehearsal 145, 346
relational aesthetics 304
religion 10, 17, 19–21, 23, 24, 27–9, 47–8, 51–2, 55–7, 99, 116, 198, 220, 221, 255–7, 258–9, 260, 266, 272–3, 282, 332
religiosity 52, 74
repertoire 47–9, 52–4, 194, 327, 330–2, 348
resilience 162
research 47, 49, 50, 57–8, 60–3, 84, 86–8, 91, 92, 103, 109, 118, 130, 131, 138, 167–8, 169, 175–8, 186, 194, 212, 221, 232, 256, 287, 302, 305, 330, 336
   National Research Foundation 129, 139
   see also methodology

resistance 23, 170, 242, 243, 304, 308
respect 22, 24, 50, 91, 93, 105, 116, 121, 122, 147, 149, 230, 243, 266, 313, 326
rhythm 4, 40, 92, 103–9, 152, 154, 157, 183, 187, 208, 209, 250, 298, 300, 306
riff 123
rock music 48, 52
role model 95
Roman Catholic 78
   see also Christianity

sacred space 97–101, 198
safety 6, 75, 174, 239, 250, 266
saints 184
saxophone 59
scripture 50, 55, 116, 190, 191, 238
   see also Bible
secular 24, 49, 50, 54, 60–1, 62, 129, 167, 173, 227, 280
self-awareness 100, 119, 147, 212
   see also awareness
self-care *see* care
self-reflection 6, 226, 248, 249, 286
self-transcendence 284
semantics 104, 105, 108, 110
shadow 172, 307
shaman 9–10, 93, 94, 95, 96, 183–8, 191, 214, 215, 272, 313, 318
silence 8, 104, 107, 108, 174, 178, 224, 265, 313, 314, 317, 339
singers 21, 23, 31, 35, 55, 59, 62, 191, 302–3
slavery 240, 242, 269, 335
sociability 304
social capital 301
social cohesion 130, 221, 222, 223, 228, 229–30, 231
social justice 116, 141, 167, 219, 280
social media 3
social prescribing 306

social selectivity 276, 279, 282, 283–84, 286

solace 75, 186, 250

solidarity 3, 336

solo 59, 154, 262

song 9, 11, 20, 21, 24, 34, 60, 75–6, 93, 104, 106, 109, 111, 115, 123, 133, 138, 159, 162, 191, 194, 259, 266, 269, 302, 317, 328, 329, 330, 331–2, 343, 347

    sacred songs 129, 130, 132, 136

    songwriting 8, 53, 55, 59, 62, 104, 112, 285, 286, 350

sorcerers 185

sorrow 107, 108, 341

    see also grief, lament

soul 8, 42–3, 51, 59, 75, 103, 111, 119, 142, 150–85, 186, 191, 211, 241, 244, 247, 248, 255–74, 313, 314, 318

sound 19, 22–7, 35, 61, 83, 84, 85, 86–87, 88, 88–89, 90–9, 104, 107, 108, 142, 146–147, 149, 152, 153, 158, 183, 199, 206, 208, 209, 250, 271, 280, 299, 300, 303, 304, 306, 317, 329, 336–338, 339, 340, 343, 344, 346, 348–349

source 21, 60, 72, 75, 100, 111, 159, 172, 256, 264, 349

space 6, 10, 18, 22–23, 51, 58, 61, 69, 75, 85, 88, 91, 93, 95, 109, 112, 114, 118, 119, 120, 122, 135, 142–3, 144, 145, 147, 153, 169, 171, 172, 174–6, 200, 206, 209, 210, 219–32, 243, 245–7, 249, 259, 261, 266, 282, 300, 306, 319–24, 326–7, 331, 338, 340, 344–6

    liminal space 9, 10, 26, 189, 194, 203, 211

    sacred space 97–101, 192, 198

    space of trust 4

spiral 266–7, 270, 335–351

spirits 8, 20, 24, 89, 90, 93, 185, 265, 318

spiritual 5, 17–29, 38, 50, 51–2, 56, 60–1, 70, 74–5, 83–5, 86–7, 89, 91–4, 94–5, 97–100, 106–7, 111–2, 116–9, 125, 142–3, 146–153, 162, 167–79, 196, 198, 201, 211, 220–2, 231–2, 239, 256, 258, 267, 273, 274, 277, 278, 280, 282, 302, 316, 341, 348

    exercise 33–44

    experience 4, 134–5, 137

    healing 8

    shamanic spirituality 184–6

    see also shaman

spontaneity 38

stamina 264

Star of David 7, 55–6

    see also Judaism

stillness 198, 267, 268

    see also peace and silence

storytelling 3, 328

stranger 6, 76, 121, 323, 326

strength 8, 59, 67, 95, 161, 186, 187, 230, 243–4, 246, 264, 265, 268, 269, 299, 315, 324, 336, 345, 346, 348–9

stress 190, 192, 200, 211, 274

suffering 73, 112, 114–5, 192, 250, 336, 340

supremacy notions 238, 239, 248

surgery 344

sustainability 293, 307, 335–6, 341, 346, 349

symphony 33–34

symptoms 192, 194

synagogue 57, 314

    see also Judaism

teacher 49, 50, 52–4, 56, 57, 59, 62, 79, 106, 228, 243–4, 246–8, 259–61, 272, 273, 278, 337, 346

teaching 4, 10, 52–4, 101, 219, 223, 226–7,
230, 237, 243, 246–7, 249, 255–6,
257, 258, 272–4
see also pedagogy
technology 73, 87, 88, 239, 342, 344
television 210
tempo 187, 329
tension 38, 40, 44, 85, 100, 113, 150,
304, 306
see also stress
theory 18, 36, 42, 50, 53, 67–9, 79, 90,
104, 276, 282, 296, 321, 324–5
therapy
art therapy 202
music therapy 9–10, 105, 167–79,
203–5, 275–87, 321
psychotherapy 183, 194, 201
threshold 120, 192, 223, 227, 271
timbre 108, 145, 187
time 4, 6, 26, 33, 41, 70, 71, 72, 74, 83, 85–
6, 88, 95, 100, 108, 119, 120, 123,
144, 153, 172, 175, 185, 1989, 206,
207, 212, 222, 226, 231, 245, 250,
263, 268, 270, 282–3, 306, 307,
335, 338–40, 343–4, 347–8
toleration/tolerance 284
touch 43, 79, 100, 176, 247, 265, 269, 270,
314, 342, 346
touchstone 116–8, 125
tradition 19, 21, 24, 28–9, 50, 57, 59, 60,
61, 71, 73, 77, 83, 95, 98, 136, 151–
4, 184, 248, 343
musical traditions 22–3, 25, 48, 77,
144, 149, 207, 260, 264, 322,
344, 347
musicking traditions 12
religious traditions 17, 20, 27, 51,
201, 272
spiritual traditions 93, 259, 273
trance 93, 183, 186
transcendence 67, 75, 117, 154, 175, 282,
284, 285, 305

see also gerotranscendence
transformation 30, 41, 45, 79, 84, 87, 93,
96, 98, 99, 100, 102, 115, 125, 126,
136, 154, 171, 175, 189, 191, 194,
198, 200, 204, 212, 213, 223, 227,
228, 230, 232, 234, 238, 248, 259,
311, 312, 313, 321, 322, 327, 333, 336,
337, 349
transition 210, 278, 295, 319–20, 323, 324,
325, 327, 330, 340
transpersonal 10, 198, 275–83, 287, 313
trauma 107, 111, 117, 120, 122, 162, 241,
276, 279, 281
Trinity 18
trust 4, 5, 7, 8, 12, 14, 15, 33–45, 120, 121,
122, 131, 175, 178, 190, 195, 225,
226, 230, 238, 242, 249, 250, 301,
302, 307, 314, 326, 329, 331, 343
truth 22, 40, 60, 143, 170, 191, 238, 241,
273, 305, 342

understanding 7, 12, 18–9, 28, 62, 73, 85,
94–5, 97, 101, 112, 114, 116
come at 141, 144, 151–3, 172, 177, 202,
210, 220, 223, 224, 220
to 7, 229, 231–2, 250, 276
five 282, 305, 321, 328, 341, 347
Unitarian Universalist 347–8
United Nations 294
unity 74, 97, 152, 153, 245, 302
artificial unity 169
cultural unity 28
university 71, 83, 129, 132, 144, 157, 278
unpredictability 150
uplift 198, 302, 305

values 12, 62, 67–80, 109, 111, 116, 121–2,
142, 143, 146, 151–2, 167, 170,
172, 178, 222, 227–8, 231, 249,
321–2, 328

verse 123, 159, 245, 259, 263–4, 329, 341, 347
vibration 97, 249
video 3, 123, 239
viola *see* instruments
vision 62, 113, 247, 248, 250, 270
vitality 71, 75, 79, 91, 92, 274, 276, 326, 329, 342
vocalizing 27, 301
voice 18, 19, 22, 23, 25, 26, 29, 33, 35, 41, 44, 72, 133, 169, 174, 209, 219, 299, 317, 332, 344
volume 107, 108, 187, 224
vulnerability 5, 9, 11, 12, 103–5, 111, 116, 122, 124, 125, 161, 196, 207, 208, 210, 215, 226–7, 230, 238, 246–9, 250, 268, 281, 287, 319, 320

walking 92, 122, 266
welcome 95, 111, 190, 227, 250, 262, 272, 299
  see also hospitality, inclusion
wellbeing 5, 7–8, 83–101, 103, 106, 109, 119, 124, 130, 168, 198, 200, 221–2, 223, 229–30, 231, 256, 293, 297, 298, 303, 306, 319–21, 335
  see also health

White supremacy 78, 240–241, 251
  see supremacy
wisdom 67, 69, 70, 73, 84, 91, 101, 203, 276, 347, 348
wonder 12, 54, 174, 175, 243, 258, 315
words 76, 104–6, 107, 123, 159, 160, 176, 240, 242–3, 245, 248, 258, 263–4, 265, 300, 318, 341, 343, 346
work 5, 8, 11–2, 18–23, 26, 27, 41, 49, 52, 53–54, 55–6, 58–9, 70, 72, 76, 88, 90, 108, 112, 118, 119–20, 121, 123, 142, 148, 152, 154, 159, 160, 167, 170, 175, 178, 191, 195, 204, 205, 224, 227, 244, 248, 259, 269, 275, 278, 296, 297, 304, 314, 315, 318, 322, 324, 332, 335–6, 338, 345–6, 347–9
  sacred work 9
  social justice work 116
  workshop 125, 207
worlds 8, 11, 53, 73, 76, 91, 93, 94, 130, 171, 183, 184, 195, 241, 245, 265
worship 57, 159, 162, 196, 259, 344
writing 9, 60, 68, 69, 83, 84–5, 86, 106, 118, 119, 123, 141, 157, 238, 246, 275, 306, 325, 345
  see also songwriting

Zoom video technology 145, 162

Music and Spirituality

Edited by
JUNE BOYCE-TILLMAN

Music and Spirituality explores the relationships between spirituality and music in a variety of traditions and contexts including those in which human beings have performed music with spiritual intention or effect. It will address the plurality of modern society in the areas of musical style and philosophical and religious beliefs, and give respect to different positions regarding the place of music both in worship and in the wider society. It will include historical, anthropological, musicological, ethnomusicological, theological and philosophical dimensions and encourage multi-disciplinary and cross-disciplinary contributions.

It looks for well-researched studies with new and open approaches to spirituality and music and will encourage interesting innovative case-studies. Books within the series are subject to peer review and will include single and co-authored monographs as well as edited collections including conference proceedings. It will consider the use of musical material in either written or recorded form as part of submissions.

The Series Editor

The Rev. Professor June Boyce-Tillman MBE is Professor of Applied Music at the University of Winchester, where she runs the Centre for the Arts as Wellbeing and the Taverner centre for Music and Spirituality. She has wide experience in education, spirituality and music and has published widely in these areas. She is an Extraordinary Professor at North West University, South Africa. She is a self-supporting ordained Anglican Priest and received an MBE for her contribution to music and education.

Proposal submissions should be sent to oxford@peterlang.com

Vol. 1   June Boyce-Tillman
          In Tune With Heaven Or Not: Women in Christian
          Liturgical Music. 2014. ISBN 978-3-0343-1777-1

Vol. 2   June Boyce-Tillman
          Experiencing Music – Restoring the Spiritual: Music as
          Wellbeing. 2016. ISBN 978-3-0343-1952-2

Vol. 3   Sarah Morgan and June Boyce-Tillman
          A River Rather Than a Road: The Community Choir as
          Spiritual Experience. 2016. ISBN 978-3-0343-2265-2

Vol. 4   Nancy L. Graham
          They Bear Acquaintance: African American Spirituals
          and the Camp Meetings. 2016. ISBN 978-3-0343-2211-9

Vol. 5   June Boyce-Tillman (ed.)
          Spirituality and Music Education: Perspectives from
          Three Continents. 2017. ISBN 978-1-78707-416-3

Vol. 6   June Boyce-Tillman
          Freedom Song: Faith, Abuse, Music and Spirituality: A
          Lived Experience of Celebration. 2018.
          ISBN 978-1-78874-219-1

Vol. 7   Karin S. Hendricks and June Boyce-Tillman (eds)
          Queering Freedom: Music, Identity, and Spirituality
          (Anthology from North America, UK and South Africa.)
          2018. ISBN 978-1-78874-508-6

Vol. 8   Lynn Whidden and Paul Shore Environment Matters:
          Why Song Sounds
          The Way It Does. 2019. ISBN 978-1-78874-493-5

Vol. 9   June Boyce-Tillman
          Enlivening Faith: Music, Spirituality and
          Christian Theology. 2019. ISBN 978-1-78874-620-5

Vol. 10   Solveig McIntosh Rivers of Sacred Sound:
          Chant. 2019. ISBN 978-1-78874-439-3

Vol. 11   June Boyce-Tillman and Anne-Marie Forbes
          Heart's Ease: Spirituality in the Music of John Tavener.
          2020. ISBN 978-1-78874-748-6

Vol. 12   Olugbenga Olusola Elijah Taiwo
          The Return Beat - Interfacing with our Interface. 2021.
          ISBN 978-1-78707-939-7

Vol. 13   Karin S. Hendricks and June Boyce-Tillman (eds)
          Authentic Connection: Music, Spirituality, and
          Wellbeing. 2021.
          ISBN 978-1-80079-159-6

A rich collection of reflections based on sound research and representing a commendably diverse range of experiences and viewpoints make this volume a significant contribution to the growing literature on music and spirituality with its own distinctive voice and timbre. I recommend it to with an interest in this important area, whether as practitioners, students or observers.

Ian Bradley
Emeritus Professor of Cultural and Spiritual History, University of St Andrews, UK

Printed by
CPI books GmbH, Leck